In the Hour of Chaos

CALIFORNIA SERIES IN HIP HOP STUDIES

H. Samy Alim and Jeff Chang, Series Editors

1. *Women Rapping Revolution: Hip Hop and Community Building in Detroit,* by Rebekah Farrugia and Kellie D. Hay
2. *Rebel Speak: A Justice Movement Mixtape,* by Bryonn Rolly Bain
3. *Freedom Moves: Hip Hop Knowledges, Pedagogies, and Futures,* edited by H. Samy Alim, Jeff Chang, and Casey Philip Wong
4. *Nairobi Hip Hop Flow: Diasporic Blackness and Embodied Performance in the Underground,* by RaShelle R. Peck
5. *Values That Pay: Complicity, Sincerity, and Hip Hop in Contemporary Moroccan Life,* by Kendra Salois
6. *In the Hour of Chaos: Art and Activism with Public Enemy's Chuck D,* edited by Chuck D

In the Hour of Chaos

ART AND ACTIVISM WITH PUBLIC ENEMY'S CHUCK D

Edited by Chuck D

UNIVERSITY OF CALIFORNIA PRESS

University of California Press
Oakland, California

Library of Congress Cataloging-in-Publication Data

Names: Chuck D, 1960- editor | Alim, H. Samy editor | Lamontagne, Samuel editor | Shawel, Tabia editor
Title: In the hour of chaos : art and activism with Public Enemy's Chuck D / edited by Chuck D ; with H. Samy Alim, Samuel Lamontagne, and Tabia Shawel.
Other titles: California series in hip hop studies 6.
Description: Oakland, California : University of California Press, [2026] | Series: California series in hip hop studies ; 6 | Includes bibliographical references and index.
Identifiers: LCCN 2025027950 (print) | LCCN 2025027951 (ebook) | ISBN 9780520427389 cloth | ISBN 9780520427396 paperback | ISBN 9780520427402 ebook
Subjects: LCSH: Rap (Music)—History and criticism | Rap (Music)—Social aspects—History | Hip-hop—History | Hip-hop—Social aspects
Classification: LCC ML3531 .I57 2026 (print) | LCC ML3531 (ebook) | DDC 782.421649—dc23/eng/20250905
LC record available at https://lccn.loc.gov/2025027950
LC ebook record available at https://lccn.loc.gov/2025027951

Manufactured in the United States of America

GPSR Authorized Representative: Easy Access System Europe, Mustamäe tee 50, 10621 Tallinn, Estonia, gpsr.requests@easproject.com

35 34 33 32 31 30 29 28 27 26
10 9 8 7 6 5 4 3

You could either be a caretaker of the culture, or an undertaker of the culture.

Chuck D

Inaugural Artist-in-Residence and National Advisory Board Member, UCLA Hip Hop Initiative

Contents

Illustration inserts are placed after page 148.

Preface ix

Introduction: Living in the Hour of Chaos 1

Chuck D

1. Fear of a Black Planet: Black Geography, (Im)migration, and Sound 9

Chuck D, H. Samy Alim, and Robin D. G. Kelley

2. Welcome to the Terrordome: History, Context, and the (R)evolution of Hip Hop 46

Chuck D and Jeff Chang

3. Don't Believe the Hype: Technology, Media, and the Importance of Community 77

Chuck D and Davey D

4. Gotta Give the Peeps What They Need: Hip Hop and Funk 107

Chuck D and Scot Brown

5. Revolutionary Generation: Women, Gender, and Sexuality in Hip Hop 135

Chuck D and Cheryl L. Keyes

6. World Tour Sessions: Global Hip Hop Culture 163

Chuck D, Samuel Lamontagne, Mikko Kapanen, Amkelwa Mbekeni, and H. Samy Alim

7. Prophets of Rage: Hip Hop and the Futures of Black Radicalism 195

Chuck D and Gaye Theresa Johnson

8. Black Steel in the Hour of Chaos: Hip Hop, Justice, and the Prison Industrial Complex 223

Chuck D, Bryonn Bain, and Maya Jupiter

9. Harder Than You Think: The Poetics of Hip Hop 255

Chuck D and Adam Bradley

10. Show 'Em Whatcha Got: Hip Hop and the Visual Arts 278

Chuck D and Joan Morgan

Bibliography 297

Index 305

Praise for Chuck D 319

Preface

The UCLA Hip Hop Initiative (HHI) at the Ralph J. Bunche Center for African American Studies was established in 2020, building upon decades of hip hop scholarship at UCLA. HHI explores and strengthens the relationships between the hip hop arts, activism, and academy through rigorous scholarship and meaningful community engagement.

In the spring of 2022, HHI hosted Public Enemy's Chuck D as our inaugural artist-in-residence, and National Advisory Board member. This book is unique in that it captures Chuck D—or "Professor Chuck," as we affectionately referred to him on campus—at his professorial best, engaging UCLA's brightest students, leading hip hop studies scholars, and some of the nation's most insightful writers and thinkers on hip hop culture. Chuck D's brilliance is on full display as he lays out a blueprint for hip hop studies in the academy while he lectures, laughs, and learns alongside the UCLA academic community and broader Los Angeles community.

In *In the Hour of Chaos: Hip Hop Art and Activism with Public Enemy's Chuck D*, Professor Chuck "shows and proves" the transformative power of a culture that rocked—and continues to rock—the globe. No other book captures this academic journey, at this critical juncture in our history, as we consider fifty years of hip hop history and chart paths forward with one of its most important and most globally recognized voices. In the process, we catch glimpses of how we might reimagine not only hip hop studies, but higher education itself—what it looks like, sounds like, feels like, and to whom it is held accountable.

HHI has also hosted critically acclaimed artists like Detroit writer and filmmaker dream hampton, Oakland hip hop artist and filmmaker Boots Riley, Jamaican-born and Bronx-bred hip hop feminist writer Joan Morgan, Los Angeles legend Medusa, and Cape Town hip hop trailblazer Emile YX?, among others. We have learned from and worked alongside each of them to co-theorize hip hop and to co-produce knowledge about the culture. In that vein, we launched, in partnership with the University of California Press, the world's first book series dedicated to hip hop studies, of which this book is a part.

All creative projects are the result of collective effort. Shout out to LeKeisha Hughes, UC Press associate editor, for her tireless work on this manuscript and the entire hip hop studies book series. We are incredibly fortunate to be working with a brilliant editor who not only listens and encourages but also forces us (gently) to make the difficult decisions that we are too often reluctant to make ourselves. We have benefitted tremendously from our continued engagement over the years. Thank you, in short, for making this possible. We also had a stellar production team on board, all helping in their own way to push this book over the finish line: Nora Becker, Francisco Reinking, and Richard Feit, among others. Special thanks to Casey Wong for all that you do, always, to make sure our collective work is at its best.

Shout out to all of the communities that make this work possible, including: The crew at Soul Kitchen Music (Kevin Abrantes, Lorrie Boula, and to Dominique Ridenhour), the Hip Hop Studies Working Group within the broader UCLA Hip Hop Initiative, the entire family at the Ralph J. Bunche Center for African American Studies, the School of Education, the Department of Anthropology, the Discourse Lab and Culture, Power, Social Change interest groups, the broader community of Los Angeles, and of course, our global hip hop family. We all shared a collective sense of how historic Chuck D's residency and course were. We have produced this book, and the companion documentary film by the same name (which premiered at the Grammy Museum in downtown Los

Angeles on August 24, 2024) as attempts to preserve this experience and disseminate the knowledge as broadly as possible. Chuck, of course, wouldn't have it any other way!

Last but not least, to Chuck. The opportunity to learn at the feet of one of hip hop's giants, the art form's most consistent and searing political voice and one of its foremost artistic innovators, was for us, *invaluable*. It's impossible to overstate that point. One of the most important lessons that we learned from you was that you're either a caretaker of the culture or an undertaker of the culture. You have inspired all of us at HHI to make sure that we do our part to be good caretakers of the culture that has meant so much to so many of us. Chuck, *you* have meant so much to so many of us. Your strength in the face of extreme challenges, your unwavering commitment to justice, your pedagogical brilliance—and some important characteristics that need to be mentioned: your sense of humor, your humility, and your generosity, the way you give so much of yourself to all of those who come into contact with you. None of that was missed by our students, their parents (some of whom you met), or any of us on campus.

As you say in this book, artists must support the community, yes, but the community must also support artists. Whenever we discuss "the state of hip hop," we should also be discussing our responsibility in supporting culture and the arts. As you have lifted up hip hop culture for four decades, it's our turn now to lift you up. On behalf of everyone at the UCLA Hip Hop Initiative and the Ralph J. Bunche Center for African American Studies, we thank you, from the bottom of our hearts, for your invaluable contributions to hip hop, to rap music, and to all of our lives. Much love.

H. Samy Alim, UCLA Hip Hop Initiative (HHI) Faculty Director
Samuel Lamontagne, HHI Co-Lead
Tabia Shawel, HHI Co-Lead
November 21, 2025
Los Angeles, California

Introduction

LIVING IN THE HOUR OF CHAOS

Chuck D

On March 11, 2020, the night before the COVID-19 pandemic shut our world down, I was part of a panel with Rakim and Talib Kweli at the California African American Museum in Los Angeles, hosted by UCLA's Ralph J. Bunche Center for African American Studies and the UCLA Hip Hop Initiative. We were celebrating Rakim's contributions to hip hop. I've always said he was hip hop's Miles Davis, our Louis Armstrong. That night, I remember breaking down the significance of Rakim's lyricism and how his unique style of poetics *changed the game*. I wanted the audience to really grasp the levels of hip hop MCing and verbal artistry, and it occurred to me how under-explored and underappreciated our talents are. I also pointed out that the intricate details of our history often go undocumented. I said something like, "But y'all don't know this, because universities don't got classes on this, and if they do, they don't go that deep!"

Immediately after that panel, I was approached by linguistic anthropologist and UCLA Hip Hop Initiative faculty director H. Samy Alim, who asked me, "Do *you* wanna teach that class at UCLA?" To make a long story short, we connected with the Bunche Center team, Tabia Shawel, Kelly Lytle Hernandez, and Gaye Theresa Johnson (who was instrumental), and two years later, post-pandemic, a class was born—a ten-week course in the

Department of Anthropology at UCLA with an impressive roster of undergraduate, masters, and PhD students, teaching assistants (Samuel Lamontagne and Tabia Shawel), visiting scholars and professors, and a hell of a research team. Out of that class comes the book you're holding in your hands right now, *In the Hour of Chaos: Hip Hop Art and Activism with Public Enemy's Chuck D*, as well as the companion film by the same name. Both the film and the book lead us toward a new way of doing hip hop studies in the academy, with the culture creators themselves.

This book salutes hip hop studies scholarship, and I also hope that it reinvigorates it. It takes a lot to create serious works of scholarship, yet scholars are often ignored, disrespected, and undervalued. But scholars read and comprehend thoroughly. They don't just read what they like or what they want to read; their job is to read the whole field and to sometimes cross into reading other fields. Dr. John Henrik Clarke, the highly regarded pan-Africanist historian, read comprehensively until he was blind, and there are so many other scholars who are just as dedicated. The seasoned ones toss around ideas in their heads for decades. The scholars I engage in this book have done this with Hip Hop. Thinking through the past, present, and future of Hip Hop, as we do in this book, requires academic discourse, thought, and dialogue. But as I told Samy, I wanted to make sure that the knowledge that UCLA students were getting in this class wouldn't just stay locked up in the hallowed halls of the academy but would get to the people, including the communities that love, create, and participate in hip hop. They call this kind of work "public scholarship," but we often go right past the word "public" and straight to "scholarship"—but "public" is about *the people*. And you don't have hip hop without the people.

So while scholars are incredibly important—as I say throughout this book—hip hop doesn't need the academy. If anything, hip hop is on loan to the academy, and scholars must work to make their important research and writings accessible to the people, and more than that, to involve the people *directly* in their ideas, theories, and documentation of the culture. That's what the UCLA Hip Hop Initiative and the University of California Press hip hop studies book series have done. They bring together leading scholars with artists, journalists, and the community, all in the same "room," to build knowledge about this culture that we love. As I told the

UCLA students many times throughout my residency, if you love something, it behooves you to at least know *why* you love it, to do the knowledge and investigate the roots of this culture, where it comes from, the Black geographies, histories, movements, and peoples that gave birth to this culture, and the political circumstances surrounding those communities. Don't just say you're "for the culture." Do the work. Study. Build with others. Reach back to those before you. Listen. Support the culture with your actions. That's how you love the culture.

My entire career has been for the love of hip hop culture and Black people worldwide and all people in the struggle. As I say in this book, hip hop is deeply connected to Black people's history. It's just the name given to the next iteration of Black creativity for survival. I know what I was living and studying in the 70s and 80s—the movements, the arts, the culture—and I just happened to be able to come out at this specific historical moment in time where hip hop and rap music were my springboard to the future. Hip hop was an extension of all of the artistry and music and culture that I was fortunate enough to have my family bestow onto me.

Later, I was introduced to speaking at colleges and universities in the late 1980s by a sister named Lisa Williamson a.k.a. Sister Souljah, who contributed her efforts, strength, and mind and became a powerful voice in the record industry. At that time, we felt that hip hop and rap music could infiltrate into society, under the radar so to speak, and spark a revolution. In a way, this book builds on my twenty-year period of lectures and conversations in front of hundreds of prisons, colleges, and universities between 1991 and 2012 and updates it to the current times. I released my first book, *Fight the Power: Rap, Race, and Reality*, in 1997, and two years later, I added "technology" to it, which was important because at that time, the turn of the century, everything was about to change. We had seen technology lead the music into places that we could never have expected. That's why I testified in Congress with politicians and senators to fight for internet filesharing. The underlying mission was to not have our freedoms violated or limited in the upcoming digital age. So I have spoken everywhere from prisons to universities to Congress and beyond out of a deep love for the culture and a deep commitment to justice.

In the Hour of Chaos was being recorded, produced, and arranged during hip hop's forty-ninth year, 2022. Then it was edited, revised, and reread thoroughly during a very busy, action-packed 2023, as we geared up to celebrate hip hop's big fifty-year milestone. During those extremely packed ten weeks of my UCLA residency, I was also involved in the PBS documentary series *Fight the Power: How Hip Hop Changed the World*, produced by Lorrie Boula. That four-part series cleared up a lot of myths because it shows artists speaking with scholars, historians, and others who were there in New York, Los Angeles, and other influential sites of hip hop culture. While we were filming this, it was also business as usual for me doing everything I do in the rap music and hip hop realm. I still did my weekly radio show, *And You Don't Stop!*, on my app radio network called RapStation. At the same time in March, I built the first cultural app called Bring the Noise, which was an answer to how hip hop was going to snatch back some of the narrative that technology, industry, and government had taken from us. It was also in this period that I was appointed to be a chairperson for the Hip Hop Alliance, the first hip hop union, in partnership with SAG-AFTRA in the United States, along with Kurtis Blow, KRS-One, MC Lyte, and other folks who work hard to advocate for the labor concerns of hip hop and R & B artists. This all happened during hip hop's fiftieth. And the biggest question we had was what lies ahead in hip hop's fifty-first year and the culture's continued evolution.

In the Hour of Chaos is not an autobiography. It's not a manifesto. It's a deep investigation into hip hop and rap music as I engage with some of the world's leading scholars and thinkers on hip hop as the UCLA Hip Hop Initiative's inaugural artist-in-residence. This is an effort to preserve the legacy of hip hop culture and rap music, to tell the story ourselves before corporations and technology distort and twist it into something we can't even recognize—and then sell it back to us! As I told the students, I've been a fan of hip hop since 1976, and I'm still a fan to this day. I know it was hip hop that brought the students in the door, but I also hoped that by the end of our ten weeks together, what they learned in this class—and what you will read in this book—would be something that would help them GPS their way through the next decade. The goal of this class was that everyone would leave better and more well-equipped than they were when they came in the door.

In this book, we begin with Black geography and migration to go deep into exploring the history, context, evolution, and revolution of hip hop.

We delve into the relationships between technology, media, and the importance of building and sustaining community; hip hop feminism and the importance of women to hip hop culture, music, and scholarship; the relationship between hip hop, funk, the blues, and other Black musical forms, as well as Black poetic and literary forms; hip hop theater and the visual arts; art, politics, and the futures of Black radicalism; freedom and the abolition of the prison industrial complex; and the globalization of the culture across Australia, Africa, the Middle East, Latin America, and throughout Europe, among other themes. The content is heavy. *In the Hour of Chaos* is a serious examination of the culture and the music, and I don't think it could have happened anywhere else.

This book comes in the hour of chaos when so many of "the masses" are being turned into "them asses" by being taught to listen with their eyes. As I told the class, we are all being turned into "screenagers," regardless of our age, and losing the important arts of listening, deep reading, and critical thinking. All of the information we receive, even sound, is coming at us through a screen and at a million miles an hour. Reading this book is not scrolling on your phone. We also know that change is constant. The Earth moves underneath us. It doesn't stop. It keeps spinning. We live in a time when so many humans are connected to the internet by gadgets and have the opportunity to voice their concerns on social media, but we miss so many details of what make us who we are in the first place, what makes us human. I'm no exception.

Today, everybody has the tool or the gadget, but net literacy is suspect. Some people know how to read through the misinformation, while others just believe everything that's coming at them. When I coined "Don't Believe the Hype" in 1988, it was really an extension of what I studied as a student at Adelphi University, reading the innovative theories of Noam Chomsky and others about the subliminal seduction of the media, the selling of items through advertising, marketing, promotion, and so on. "Don't Believe the Hype" simply told folks to stop and question this blizzard of data and lightning-fast information coming at them and to not just believe it. With this book, I froze time so we can pause and take stock of the importance of this culture and music. What we are doing in this book is engaging in a thorough examination of society, the current climate—the past, present, and future—and coming up with an understanding of what our current position should be when it comes to a range of critical questions and issues regarding hip hop. This is my place in the music, and these are some detailed thoughts in the context of this current time, in this particular hour of chaos.

I want to conclude with a final word about living in the hour of chaos. My nearly four-decade career as a professional has been in truth and honesty for the culture. I don't think I remember a time that we, as Black people, were *not* in an hour of chaos. But the culture, the art, the music, and the people are what I've always been about. That's what's always gotten us through the chaos. It's beyond politics, though we can deal with politics along the way. Hip hop, in that early period, was part of a Black music lineage that made us feel good collectively. In this course, we really tried to tap into that spirit, because I think *to feel* is the essence of human beings. Give me cultures that end governments. Governments are the cancer of civilization. I'm not here to teach anyone about how to make a better government, but I will tell you this: Culture is what brings human beings together. In culture, and in the arts, we look for our similarities. Through culture, when it's actually rich so that we communicate with one another, we overcome our differences. Beware when the government says it is in control of culture.

Hip hop, globally, has functioned to counteract the oppressive works of governments. Ever since the 1980s, I have considered myself an ambassador for hip hop, travelling to 116 countries around the world. My mission was not only to assure that hip hop would at least be taken as seriously as all other genres of music, but more importantly, to make the country and the world look at Black people as equal human beings, fighting the powers that be for equal rights. That was my goal in the music. And we connected with artists all over the world who were fighting against oppressive governments, whether it was South Africans bringing down the racist apartheid regime or Palestinians fighting the illegal Israeli occupation.

I am not a politician by any means. I am an artist. In my first album, *Yo! Bum Rush the Show*, in 1987, the underlying subtitle was, "The government's responsible. The government's responsible. The government's responsible." My first records were talking about a revolution of the mind. We were never about bombs, bullets, or bloodshed. We knew that technology was going to create the future battlegrounds, and it began with the music. And what music is more evident of a technological takeover than hip hop and rap music? In 1990, I said, "Welcome to the Terrordome," a decade before the turn of the century and the millennium, two years after "Don't Believe the Hype" and nine years before *There's a Poison Goin On*. The inspiration for "Fight the Power" was sparked from the Isley Brothers. Every title that Public Enemy has used in its songs and albums has a meaning like a tree line on a husk. Our music has always put culture first.

I am a culturalist. I believe in the power of culture and the arts to not only bring people together but also to bring about political change. Music means so much to those on the margins, to those treated as "less than" or as "second-class citizens," to those people displaced from their homelands, to those locked up behind the wall, to all those who suffer some form of oppression. My music has always come with a message. That's what Public Enemy has always been about, and that was my mission in 2024 as a US global music ambassador—to bring the music, and the message, to as many people as humanly possible.

My ambassadorship was single-focused: How do we make this culture and music in its fifty-first year hold industry, technology, and government accountable and responsible? How does music galvanize peace, love, understanding, knowledge, and wisdom to counter the bullets, bombs, and bloodshed that we've seen from governments hell-bent on war? And in this new technological/AI bot farm/deep-fake era, how do we recognize that it isn't even necessarily land that's being bombed. What if what's being bombed is our minds? We know that governments and conquerors are trying to buy up every available square inch of land here on Earth and beyond, but what if our minds are the most valuable real estate of this millennium? These are the kinds of questions that artists, beyond hip hop, are grappling with, and these are some of the difficult questions we deal with in this book.

I am also an optimist. To the brilliant UCLA student body of this class, I don't believe things can go back to "the way they were," as the song goes. I believe they go *forward*. What comes out of the ashes like a phoenix becomes new art, new music, new technologies, and new ways of understanding the world. In this super convergence of technology, government, and industry, making sense of the chaos will be even more difficult.

Nothing remains the same. The players change. The goalposts move. Movements shift. The board flips. But it's up to *you* to make a way forward. That's what hip hop has always done. And that's what this generation must do. You are living in the chaos of extreme social divisions, the ever-present threat of fascism, and heightened levels of uncertainty. But you gotta step up and rise to the challenge, like generations before you have always done.

Thank you for your commitment. Thank you for every moment. We've shared a lot of beautiful moments during our time together. My hope is that what we talked about in each one of those ten weeks helped change the way you think about hip hop, about yourselves and each other, and about your world. Every second, every dynamic moment, will last a lifetime. You are now equipped to dispel all the myths. You can now look at yourself and say, "I am the art, I am the culture, and I am able to take it forward. *We* are able to take it forward."

1 Fear of a Black Planet

BLACK GEOGRAPHY, (IM)MIGRATION, AND SOUND

Chuck D, H. Samy Alim, and Robin D. G. Kelley

H. SAMY ALIM: Welcome to the UCLA Hip Hop Initiative (HHI) and to a course that will change the way you think about hip hop culture—and, hopefully, the way you think, more generally. My name is H. Samy Alim, faculty director of HHI, along with assistant director of the Ralph J. Bunche Center for African American Studies Tabia Shawel and ethnomusicology doctoral student Samuel Lamontagne, who both have worked tirelessly with me as co-leads to launch this initiative. We have two incredibly special guests with us tonight, the great historian Robin D. G. Kelley and the one, the only, Chuck D of Public Enemy.

With decades of wisdom and insight, Chuck D and Kelley will shed light on the origins of hip hop culture as rooted deeply and undeniably within Black musical and oral traditions (as Chuck D notes, "Fight the Power" has roots in the Isley Brothers, for example).[1] We are all familiar with how Chuck D, along with Kelley, use personal narratives as springboards to discuss the urgent social, economic, and political issues of the current moment. Today, we begin with those personal narratives as we explode traditional definitions of musical genres by talking about the interconnectedness of Black musical, cultural, and linguistic production over the centuries and the complex urban geographies and Black flows of migration and immigration that shape Black music and hip hop. Now, let's bring on "Professor Chuck!" [*Applause.*]

Chuck D, the musician, writer, rapper, producer, graphic artist, and political activist rose to prominence through his groundbreaking, mic-shattering, politically conscious hip hop recordings and performances. Chuck D assembled DJ Terminator X, Professor Griff, and Flavor Flav, along with Hank Shocklee and Bill Stephney, into one of the most prominent and powerful hip hop groups of all time, Public Enemy, who was inducted into the Rock and Roll Hall of Fame in 2013. From *Yo! Bum Rush the Show* to *It Takes a Nation of Millions to Hold Us Back* to *Fear of a Black Planet*, Chuck's booming voice urged us not to believe the hype and to always fight the power. He's done remarkable things both inside and outside the industry and serves as an inspiration to so many of us. Please welcome HHI's inaugural artist-in-residence, Mr. Chuck D. [*Applause.*]

CHUCK D: I'm very happy that we can experience each other at this crossroads. I've been part of the genre since 1976 as a fan, and I'm still a fan to this day. The conversation that we're going to have in this room over the next ten weeks will hopefully be something that will continue through your bloodstream and the mind frame of your life. And as it becomes part of you, the whole goal that we had talked about—myself, Samy, Sam, Tabia—is that you would hopefully leave here better and more equipped than how you came in. This is gonna be heavy. This will be something that will be an examination that I don't think will happen anywhere else on this planet. We've come to this point where we've seen the books being written, but where's the directory for all the books that are out there? Where's the information for all the films that are out there? Everybody is kind of like saying what hip hop is and what it ain't, from so many different vantage points. We're not even going to say what's false, what's true, what's a myth, and what's not. But we *will* examine these things. And we'll have a lot of fun doing it. And I'm here to tell you; I'll put it to you right here: you're not going to get this anywhere else on the planet in 2022 or 2023. It may happen in 2029, but hopefully without the corporations, because if the academics and the designers and the architects of this culture don't take over some of these things that we love, big business has now become the narrative and the dictating force of what the art and the culture is, who the people are. You know you don't want to purchase your existence; you want to be able to have it be a part of you. Those are some of the fun aspects that we're going to be touching on.

H. SAMY ALIM: Now, we're going to lay the groundwork for this course by asking a very basic but fundamental question: What is hip hop culture? When was the last time you heard somebody ask that question? But as we consider fifty years of hip hop cultural history, we're going to make sure we're asking those fundamental questions again at this moment in time as we go back and try to understand the history and the culture a little bit deeper. This is not going to be the oft-heard definition: "Hip hop culture is four elements with an additional element of knowledge." And I know Chuck and Robin are laughing because we've been through that for decades. This is not going to be "postindustrial, urban, ghetto, New York," etc. We have readings on that, and we're going to have entire weeks on that. That's important. This is going to be about laying the groundwork of what hip hop means, particularly from the perspective of artists themselves. Y'all ready?

The title of this presentation is "What Is Hip Hop Culture? The Activism and the Aesthetics, the Politics, and the Poetics." And as you go through these next three hours, right, you're writing down the evolution of your understanding of hip hop culture as it changes from minute one until the end of our time together. You're going to do that every single week.

Sister Sonia Sanchez, a brilliant poet of the Black Arts movement, attended the funeral of the late, great historian James G. Spady with us in February of 2020, right before the pandemic.[2] She told us that hip hop was both the beauty of the music and the message. And this was a simple statement, but it was deep, right? She was saying that hip hop was both saying what needed to be said and saying it in a style that was unforgettable. So when Imani Perry wrote *Prophets of the Hood* in 2004, which I think is one of the most profound pieces of hip hop scholarship to date, she focused on the politics and poetics of hip hop, but she didn't do it as if the art of hip hop were separate from the politics of hip hop.[3] She said the art, the poetics, and the aesthetics are themselves political. And so we're thinking about both politics and poetics, activism and aesthetics.

I'm going to tell you a story now that captures a beautiful night to me. The night was historic, with Chuck D, Rakim, and Talib Kweli. We had this huge conversation at the California African American Museum in Los Angeles. March 11, 2020. And on the morning of March 12, the entire thing shut *DOWN*—the entire city of Los Angeles and the country would enter the pandemic shutdown phase! So this was actually the last public event that we all gathered to do. And maybe it's not coincidental that Chuck is here with us on our first public event in this time.

Speaking in front of an audience of approximately five hundred people, Chuck D explained how hip hop, as a continuation of Black freedom culture, or in his words, the next iteration of "Black creativity for survival," has always imagined new futures, even within the most brutal of contexts. I have been thinking about that statement since it was uttered two years ago because of the concise and profound nature of the phrase "Black creativity for survival." "The Black culture had to speak loud," Chuck continued, "because we had to be in code because we just couldn't say 'Slavemaster, put your fucking whip away!' We had all kinds of code in our music, and our music was everything emitted from us. We spoke it even when we didn't speak it. We hummed it to say so many things when we didn't want to have to say it in words."

This story continues, with Rakim cosigning, and Talib Kweli explaining, "Because it's folk language." So you all are taking notes on what hip hop culture is from the artists' perspective, right? "Because it's folk language. Hip hop was speaking in a language that everybody could relate to. It's like Dr. King called a riot 'the language of the unheard.' Chuck D talked about 'a riot going on' just like Sly and the Family Stone did. And so when you talk about the language of the unheard, what you're talking about is hip hop music." Then Kweli historicized hip hop even further, rooting it in African traditions. "You're talking about something that goes back before us, before The Last Poets and Gil Scott-Heron, before the Negro spirituals and gospel songs that slaves sang to get them through the day. You're talking about things that go way back, all the way before the African griot tradition, banging on a drum and telling our story."[4]

The story continues now with not just banging on the drum and telling the story but *how* you tell that story—the aesthetics. Chuck explains:

> Look, a lot of times emcees make a mistake to try to look for the perfect beat. That's why Bambaataa and them wasn't looking for the perfect beat. The beat is the emcee and Rakim was significant. He's our Miles Davis. I mean, I'm really serious. He made the beat go to him. Ra had the audacity. The beat walked and followed him. And it opened me because I did my first album,

> *Yo! Bum Rush the Show*, and I was on another beat trying to catch up with the beat and nailing the beat. But when I heard Ra on those two records, I was like, "Yo, this is a whole new way to . . ." Rakim is like Louis Armstrong to jazz phrasing. He changed the phrasing of hip hop and we went from there. When they came out with "I Know You Got Soul," it made you want to quit, cry, or lock yourself up in the lab and try to get that shit back. And you love the competition because it raised your bar. The bar was raised as you had to come with the bars and Ra changed it overnight. So 1986 was a significant year where not only am I changing the phrasing, but the words were magnificent, like, "Oh my God, it's poetry, but it's, yo, man, this dude is a problem!"

So, you're getting a sense of the history, right, as it ties into both banging on the drum and telling our story. It's both what you say and how you tell the story, the politics and the poetics, the activism and the aesthetics.

Talib continued, emphasizing the literary, lyrical, imaginative and metaphysical:

> If you listen to people like Alice Coltrane, they talk about astro-traveling and going to visit the planets and the moons and the stars. But you don't have to leave the ground. You're still grounded right here on Earth. But your mind is that powerful that you can leave your body and really go visit the stars and Rakim took us up there to the stars. And at that time when Chuck D and Public Enemy and Eric B and Rakim was out, crack addiction was very prominent in our neighborhoods. And what Chuck D did with "Night of the Living Baseheads," I feel like Rakim and Eric B did with "Microphone Fiends," because that record wasn't about drug addiction. But for me, in an era where crack was so prevalent, it was good to hear a record that was like, "I'm fienin' for this microphone, feed me hip hop and I start trembling." That's how I felt. It felt like we were fienin' for that in an era where crack was taking over for us to be like now we fien for these rhymes, and these beats was very important for the culture.[5]

Okay, so you're getting a sense from the artists themselves of the deeper significance of hip hop culture in many ways. From that story, I want to touch on two pieces of scholarship. One is Tricia Rose's *Black Noise* in 1994, one of the earliest scholarly texts on hip hop culture, an incredibly important book for anyone studying hip hop. Rose's definition of rap music is, "Rap music brings together a tangle of some of the most complex social, cultural, political issues in contemporary American society, a black cultural expression that prioritizes black voices from the margins of urban America, articulating both the pleasures and the problems."[6] She has this amazing chapter where she writes about "Shooting in the Ghetto: Locating Rap Music and Video Production." It's not the headline that you might be thinking about in your head, given how hip hop is stereotyped in the media. It's more about filming in the ghetto and describing hip hop as primarily about *identity* and *location*.

Why this is important is because rappers' emphasis on neighborhoods has "brought the ghetto back into the public consciousness."[7] So "the ghetto" could just be a term that people throw around. It could be an adjective that people say inappropriately—"Oh, that's so ghetto." But what hip hop was doing at this time, according to Tricia Rose, was shining a light on those who would be otherwise forgotten and cast aside, swept under the rug, displaced, etc. It was shining the light on Black communities and making sure that they were brought back into public consciousness, and all the sociopolitical and economic issues that came with that also were brought into public consciousness and not forgotten.

I want to offer some concrete examples of what that means. We're going to play a segment of this classic Tupac Shakur interview:

> If I know that in this hotel room they have food every day. And I'm knocking on the door every day to eat, and they open the door, let me see the party, let me see, like, they throwing salami all over, I mean just like, *throwin* food around, but they are telling me there is no food in here. You know what I'm saying? Every day I'll stand outside trying to sing my way in, you know what I'm sayin? "We are hungry, please let us in." After about a week, that song is going to change to, "We hungry, we need some food." After two-three weeks, it's like you know, "Give me that food or we breakin down the door!" After a year, you just like, you know what I'm sayin, "I'm pickin the lock comin through the door blastin!" You know what I'm saying, it's like you *hungry*. You've reached a level. You don't want to ask anymore. We *asked* ten years ago. We was *askin* with the Panthers, with the civil rights movement. . . . Those people that was asking are all dead or in jail. So now what do you think we're gonna do? *Ask?!*
>
> [And they say] that we shouldn't be angry, that my raps that I'm rappin to my community shouldn't be filled with rage, or that they shouldn't be filled with the same atrocities that they gave to me. And in the media they don't talk about it, so my raps have to talk about it. . . . So it's like, all that society is doing is leeching off the ghetto. They use the ghetto for their pain, for their

> sorrow, for their culture, for their music, for their happiness, for their movies to talk about "boys in the hood," you know what I'm sayin? I don't want to be fifty years old at a BET We Shall Overcome Achievement Award, you know what I'm sayin? Not me. I want when they see me, they know that every day when I'm breathing, it's for us to go further. Every time I speak, I want the truth to come out. Every time I speak, I want to shiver. I don't want it to be like they know what I'm going to say because it's polite. They know what I'm gonna say even if I get in trouble. Ain't that what we're supposed to do? I'm not saying I'm going to rule the world or I'm going to change the world, but I guarantee that I will spark the brain that *will* change the world. That's our job, is to spark somebody else watching us. We might not be the ones, but let's not be selfish, and because we're not going to change the world let's not talk about how we should change it. I don't know how to change it, but I know if I keep talkin about how dirty it is out here, *somebody* gonna clean it up.
>
> And this world is such a—and when I say "this world," I don't mean it in an ideal sense. I mean it in an every day, every little thing you do. It's such a "gimme gimme gimme! Everybody back off!" Everybody like learnt that from school. Big business. You wanna be successful? You wanna be like Trump? Gimme gimme gimme, push, push, push, snap, snap, snap, crush, crush, crush! How's all this going to help Black kids, Mexican kids, Korean kids, whatever? But it needs to be real. And it need to be before we all die, and we say, "We made a mistake, we really should have helped these folks." It's gon be too late. It's too much money here. I mean, nobody should be hitting the lottery here for thirty-six million and we got people starving in the streets. That's not idealistic, that's just real. . . . There's no way! There's no way these people own planes and there's people who don't have houses, apartments, shacks, draws, pants! I know you rich. I know you got $40 billion, but can you just keep it to one house?! You only need one house. If you only got two kids, can we just keep it to two rooms? I mean, why you got fifty-two rooms when you know it's somebody with no rooms?! It just don't make sense to me. It don't.[8]

I feel like we need a minute to digest all of that. What Tupac gave us was his own version of Robinson's "racial capitalism," his own version of Rose's "voices from the margins," and telling it in the way that only *he* could tell it. If more academics could tell a narrative *like that*, maybe some of that knowledge would actually be transferred [*laughter*].[9]

I want to keep it going with another example from San Quinn out of San Francisco. I'm keepin it West Coast today. And if you look at hip hop, from Tricia Rose's example and from James G. Spady's work, as the fundamental matrix of self-expression for generations of Black people, not only do artists bring the ghetto back into America's public consciousness but hip hop is "a powerful conglomeration of voices from the margins of American society speaking on the terms of that position," on what it means to occupy that position.[10] I want to play a music video for you, which is, "Look What I've Done for Them," by San Quinn. San Quinn, JT the Bigga Figga—for years, when I was up in the Bay, I was hanging out especially with JT. And this is some of the music that really captures this idea of "voices from the margins." [*Plays music video.*]

As you can see in this music video, there's a notepad. And what's being scribbled literally *in the margins* of the notepad are people that he has lost in the community. Black people that have been lost, the phrase "rest in peace," over and over again. Hip hop clearly in this video becomes a way to remember the otherwise forgotten. When you take that one person, that one Black life, and think about this moment and this Movement for Black Lives that we're in right now, who remembers a Black life? Who keeps it alive? Who archives the presence of not just one life, but an entire community?

Let's take the Fillmore District in San Francisco, which was a predominantly Black community and is now being gentrified. A lot of my time in San Francisco was spent on the corner of Third and Revere with JT the Bigga Figga. We'd go to the mosque. We'd go out with *The Final Call* and all of that. That was what we were doing every single week. The reason why this is important for me to communicate is because hip hop, where it's *lived*, people are not just righting wrongs but they're literally writing for their lives. Like Chuck said, it's the next iteration of "Black creativity for survival." What you have in this video is a perfect example of how Black people refuse to be forgotten, and in this kind of way, San Quinn is fighting for Black lives in ways that document them forever. In fact, we're here in this course right now at UCLA talking about this production and what it means, right, talking about hip hop, not as four or five elements, but as this kind of *deeper meaning*. This is why people produce hip hop music, in part, to provoke thought.

I say this because during this time there was a three week period in Bayview-Hunters Point, in that neighborhood, where twenty-one Black lives were lost. Young Black men, especially. I witnessed the kind of havoc that that creates in a community. I witnessed people going to church and having town forums and people literally losing their minds as they explain the pain and what's going on for their children. You have this art coming as a response to all of that and embedded within that context, and at the same time, trying to transform that context.

Remember we're talking about the activism and the aesthetics, the politics and the poetics. Imani Perry writes about hip hop artists as "prophets of the hood." Like Rose, Perry argues that what unifies hip hop throughout the world is the fact that it speaks from all up inside the belly of the beast. But at the same time, she kind of steps aside from purely historical or sociological explanations and decides that to understand hip hop culture, we need to focus on it as an art form, that sometimes when we do all the sociological work, all the political work, all the historical work, we neglect that hip hop is an *art form*. And all the artistry and the genius that goes into the production of hip hop culture, we sort of put it aside in favor of what it's saying politically, what it's doing sociologically. That's important. But in order to understand hip hop culture, according to Imani Perry, you have to understand it as an art form. And any serious engagement with any art form, including hip hop, requires one to enter a world of "complexity and contradiction."[11] That means you're viewing hip hop culture the same way you would view a literary production, the same way you would view any form of musical production. You're doing all this deep thinking and analytical work around the meanings, the symbolism, the layers of intertextuality and connections. She brought all of that depth to our collective analysis of hip hop culture. Why? She said, "To miss the point that hip hop is an art form," right, "first and foremost is to radically misread the culture and to limit the literary imagination."[12]

So you have all of these important sociohistorical and sociological elements that are embedded within an art form that, at least in some of my writing on the language of hip hop culture, is also transforming American poetics, rooting itself in African American traditions to do something new every single time and every single generation. You don't hear the same styles. It's flexed anew, right. The politics change as the context changes. The poetics change. And the politics and the poetics, the activism and the aesthetics, continue to inform each other with each generation of artists.

These are all very important points that Tricia Rose and Imani Perry are making. Like Rose taught us early on, I always teach my students to be both celebratory *and* critical of hip hop, at least if you love the culture. In this last little bit, I want to focus on some of the things that we need to unlearn. Because we've learned a lot from hip hop culture, but there are some things we need to unlearn, according to Shaheen Ariefdien of Prophets of Da City (PoC), a foundational hip hop group in South Africa, the ones that performed for Nelson Mandela's inauguration and really set the scene for hip hop culture. You could think of them in relation to what Chuck D and Public Enemy are here to the States; that's what PoC is to South Africa. That photo is of him and Emile YX? of Black Noise. They are two of the foundational pioneers in South African hip hop. Shaheen says, "Hip hop was a way to say 'I am somebody.' It acted as some kind of medicine. It was about reconnecting to Africa." I could say a lot about what it means that hip hop to Africans was about reconnecting to Africa, right. There's layers of depth there that relate to the ravages of European colonialism and white settler colonialism in South Africa. But Shaheen continues, "It was also about ghettocentrism, thinking about the ghetto as a repository of energy, livelihood, community, and not just as racial spatial presence that symbolized abandonment and containment. It was also about hypermasculinity, which was really a sign of powerlessness, and it reified heteronormativity. And I think it's important to mention that it was a lot of things we needed to unlearn as well. As I mentioned earlier, medicine often has some serious side effects."

Why this is important is because often, at least in my work, I privilege the perspective of artists themselves. I always have from the beginning. That's training from James G. Spady. Rest in peace, again. He always urged us to privilege the perspective of the artists, because the artists are themselves cultural theorists and masters of their craft. So not just artists in terms of they can lay it down, right, or they can create something that we can vibe to, but cultural theorists who are theorizing music and art as they're producing it. So, in terms of what's happening with hip hop as it continues to evolve, you start to see some of the critiques that were levied at hip hop culture decades ago—"hip hop is too this, hip hop is too that"—are now being raised from inside the culture itself as it continues to expand and evolve, not just globally but to other communities. A new set of folks are picking up the microphone and spinning the records and doing what they do with hip hop culture.

What we see now are new articulations of Black, queer, disabled futures coming from *within* hip hop culture. I'm not talking about the decades-old critiques from the outside. You have people who are hip hop heads from the inside, transforming hip hop from that position. So, of course, you've got Joan Morgan, Brittney Cooper, Treva Lindsey, Kaila Story. These are legends in the game as well, particularly Joan Morgan, and her coining of hip hop feminism from the book *When Chickenheads Come Home to Roost*.[13] Hip hop feminists and queer folks provide new language for articulating a politics of pleasure that lovingly critiques hip hop, sexism and misogyny and reductive views of Black women's bodies as no more than sites of intersecting impressions of racism, sexism and classism, as well as both hip hop's and Black feminist theory's lack of engagement with Black queer identities. So, they're taking on the culture of hip hop and the establishment of academic thought at the same time. I think it matters where the critique comes from. The critique coming from outside the culture is often a scapegoating critique that blames hip hop for every single thing that's wrong with society. The critique that's coming from within the culture already understands that that's some racist, classist bullshit, right, and works with folks within the culture because they are part of the culture too. They seek to transform it from the inside out. That is like what Black feminists call transformative love or transformational love and what Joan really refers to as "a loving critique."

Another example of this internal critique is the Krip-Hop movement, and I gotta give a shout out to Leroy F. Moore, who is right there in the front row, one of the cofounders of the Krip-Hop movement, in the house, and is now a first-year doctoral student in anthropology.[14] But he already was the expert before he came. And Stephanie Keeney Parks, who is also here, also in anthropology, getting her doctorate. Represent, and much love. We have people who are legends in the movement, right, also critiquing the movement in a loving way to bring it to where it needs to be in order that it's justice for all in the movement, not justice for some. This is about the project of justice for all. So they are not just critiquing the ableism of hip hop culture, but also the whiteness and racism of the disability rights movement, and also the ableism within the Black communities to which they belong. As Leroy asked in his chapter in the book

Freedom Moves, "When can Black disabled folks come home?" That's why it's important to have that transformation of love from within the culture.

Three more artists to cap this off. And we're talking about defining and redefining hip hop. I was in Cape Town, South Africa, in 2014. First time I interviewed Mos Def was in 1999 in San Francisco. Bookended it with this fifteen years later in Cape Town in South Africa, where he said one of the most beautiful things about hip hop, which took the meaning of hip hop to the personal, psychological level, that kind of depth of meaning. He said,

> And hip hop is a huge hero for me. I love it. I love its vitality. I love the fact that it speaks to young people the way it spoke to me and recognized my talent and recognized that I was beautiful and recognized that I was lonely. It recognized my despair and it told me, "Don't cry, don't despair. I understand you. I got something for you to do with your energy. I got something for you to do with that hopefulness in you. I got something for you to do with the anger inside of you. With the sadness inside of you. I got a way for you to turn that around."

That's not a definition of hip hop that you'll hear in a textbook, right? But it *does* provide another layer of meaning.

Lyla June and hip hop artists from the Dream Warriors are next. Here, Lyla June is talking about her understanding of hip hop: "Sharing wisdom, sharing our way of living and helping people just exist on this earth while at the same time giving them joy and beauty and connection to their heart and their heartbeat. And I think what we see as Dream Warriors, among many other things, is our youth are safe. Our youth love themselves." She's speaking from a community where sometimes folks are decimated, oppressed communities where you start losing your siblings and your brothers and sisters all around you. She continues, "Our youth feel empowered and our youth have the older sisters and brothers they need not just to survive, but truly thrive and be the people they were born to be, whatever that is, whatever they choose that to be."

Lastly, we hear from A-lan Holt. Black queer, feminist, playwright, poet, hip hop writer, etc. How does she define hip hop? "I write impossible worlds into existence because visioning is a collective act, one that invites new ways of being in relationship, one that acts as a useful tool toward collective liberation." Those are three perspectives from three very different hip hop artists.

What is hip hop culture as we consider fifty years of hip hop cultural history and thirty years of hip hop scholarship? Hip hop continues to be one of the most profound and transformative artistic, literary, linguistic, cultural and political movements of the late twentieth and early twenty-first centuries. Over the past half-century, hip hop culture has become a global lingua franca from the South Bronx to South Africa. An innovative, transformative arts movement rooted in Black expressive culture and Black freedom culture that is constantly evolving in rich, creative ways that highlight style, pleasure, and joy, yes, but also a collective politics of healing and growth that helps oppressed communities imagine alternative futures, expand the project of justice for all, and ultimately make freedom moves. This is coming from everything we've been hearing from inside of the culture.

But I want to end with a quote from our guest Robin Kelley himself. Because there's so much going on with culture, not just hip hop, but culture is also commodified. It exists within a world. Chuck reminded us of the capitalist forces, corporations, decision makers, power holders, wealth holders, and the racial and economic politics in a world of racial capitalism. This context is the context within which culture is created and exists. As Robin says, "But the fact remains that hip hop's corporate face is one that promotes raw capitalist values, violence and extreme materialism. There is no simple way to characterize what is at once a global social movement and a multibillion dollar industry. The vinyl ain't final simply because it ain't finished."[15] On that note, I think we have some food for thought on "what is hip hop culture." Thank you. [*Applause.*]

ROBIN G. KELLEY: Before we start this conversation, I just have to say that we've known each other for a little while, but I've never said it publicly in terms of being a fan. Samy mentioned Tricia Rose. Tricia Rose and I became friends in 1987, and we both were doctoral students. We bonded around Public Enemy because *Yo! Bum Rush the Show* just came out in '87. I didn't know she was writing her dissertation on hip hop, which became *Black Noise*, but we were hanging out hard and all we talked about was Public Enemy. You have to understand how important it is for me to be here with you, to have this conversation, because we're basically the same age. I'm about eighteen months younger than you [*laughter*], but still, we're basically the same generation. I want to begin with a personal question, if you don't mind. Can you take us back to Roosevelt, Long Island?

CHUCK D: One-square-mile town, which is called the hamlet on Long Island, and they are actually four counties. Two of them are called boroughs because New York City is broken into five counties which is boroughs in New York. Queens and Kings, and y'all know Kings as being Brooklyn, then Nassau and Suffolk counties. The whole island is a hundred and eighteen miles long and about twenty-three miles wide. I think y'all might have heard of the Hamptons or something like that. The island's sort of the head of a fish, which is sort of Queens, and gills, and so the south of the fish is where Roosevelt is.

KELLEY: Right in Hempstead, not too far, because Hempstead historically . . .

CHUCK D: It's called the Blackbelt. So north to south of Long Island you have Hempstead, Uniondale, Roosevelt, and Freeport and that little area where white flight led to Black folks moving in and it made one town and led to another town. And it was, I guess, cut off by force.[16]

KELLEY: Right, blockbusting and redlining, all that stuff. When did you discover hip hop and what was it to you?

CHUCK D: Growing up in the sixties, I had young hip parents. So there's a record player in there and a TV, and it's records in there. I grew up in a Motown, Stax, Atlantic household. I was born in the 1960s, so it was 45s and albums to go on. Whether it be Stevie Wonder, James Brown, Aretha Franklin or Miriam Makeba or Nina Simone. There were like aunts and uncles in the crib, so these artists were played all the time, especially when I wanted to go outside and I had to do house chores. And people would always be like, "Oh man, Black people on Long Island, y'all musta been middle class." My people, it just happened to be my mother and my father combined, we were able to move in the area and have a house instead of rent an apartment back where our relatives were. We were lucky to actually get out into this town.

But yeah, in that house it was Motown, Stax, and Atlantic, my father was a part of Columbia Jazz Club. Not that I didn't love jazz. I loved sports, and that's where the affinity was. But I guess I was a casual listener, and I was a big fan of AM radio. You could get a million songs with a transistor radio! I grew up kinda casually listening to music. I was a sports fan, but music was just organically in the house, automatic. And you felt like Aretha Franklin was your aunt, because somebody could play these records in the house, *loud*. And it was nothing in there that you could not hear, even if you couldn't understand it. Music was already a part of it. It wasn't that much different from the person across the street or people you go to school with. It was that commonality. We all kinda listened to the one radio station on AM. And we listened to anything that was cross cultural, and pop radio. Because New York is not a big place as far as how it's spread out geographically. It's concentrated, especially when you get into New York City. It's what you call a vertical city. So you have a small amount of space surrounded by water.

What I'm saying, in short, is everybody's gettin the same information! If somebody gets it in the Bronx, you got cousins that got it to you the next week anyway, especially if you moved out here from one of the boroughs. Hip hop started to form as this thing that you heard cousins and people doing in the city or on the short ride to the city. In Roosevelt in 1976, '75, you know, I was sixteen, seventeen years old. I wanted to go to this event, because girls are there. I started getting interested in girls two years before. See, it wasn't like today, when you interested in a girl at five years old [*laughter*]. Back then, it was a clear, you know, "I'm about sports. I'ma play ball." And once upon a time, they had this event on Long Island at nighttime called Higher Ground, which was borrowed from Stevie Wonder's song. The reason why basketball is so important in Roosevelt is because that is where Julius Erving a.k.a. "Dr. J" is from. He's actually Jordan before Jordan, LeBron before LeBron. He comes from that town. So everybody's like a ball player, or they know sports. And music, they got bands, and bands are cool, but bands were like so far distant because it was a lack of access to equipment. So we go to this event called Higher Ground in the wintertime, and you walk up there, but half of the gym is basketball, a whole bunch of people and two refs waiting for the next game. You could be there waiting all night until they closed the door. And the other half was this thing called a DJ. Girls were on the other side of the gym, dressed. The DJ was playing a song that we heard on the radio. So, I mean, I'm next to these sweaty-back brothers. Man, it look like I ain't gonna get a chance to play anyway. You have no choice but to focus on the other side of the gym.

And I heard this record, and it was by this group called War. They had this song called "Galaxy." We heard it on the radio. It had a short little intro and it went right into the song. I'm looking across at this DJ, and this record starts, but I don't hear no words. It felt like the words ain't came in. The DJ was going from one side to the other side. So I'm thinkin in my country mind, "That record must be this big. He's got a big record, and I don't hear the words. What record do he got?!" [*Laughter.*] Then I got more and more curious, and that was the beginning of me looking at hip hop, and it was the technical aspect. Because he was cutting in the words, and I was like, "Oh, he's got two turntables?" I always thought that you got two turntables, because if one break down you got this other one. So it was mind-blowing, the technical aspect, and my brother and sister was into it. Then the guy would get on the mic with the instrumental and sometimes say a small rhyme or two, like Muhammad Ali. We knew the person that rhymed the most on TV grabbin the mic was Muhammad Ali. Matter of fact, he was the only Black man *on* main TV! You didn't see a lot of Black people on TV back then, and he would rhyme. It was like, "Wow, this guy's doin the same thing!" From that point on, I was curious because the electronics aspect made me go "Damn!," and I asked people how they were mixing. When they first said they made a mixer in an electronics class, I was like, "You're making a cake mixer? What's a mixer?" [*Laughter.*] So this is 1976, '77. That struck me.

We started getting tapes, and then all of a sudden, it wasn't so much the music and the records; it was the *application* of the music and the records and the voice. I was like, "Whoa, this is rappin!" The whole culture was hip hop, because it wasn't just rap music. I'll give you a quick definition. Rap music is not a music. It's never been a music. But it's always *used* music. The great Lord Jamar from Brand Nubian says, "Hip hop didn't invent anything, but it *reinvented everything*." Rap music is—and you can write this down. I don't care where you go in the world, you're not gonna find a definition any clearer than this. It's not a music. It's vocals on top of music. It's a hybrid. Rap is the vocals.

Now, music is why you can't detach rap music from history or the music that's already been described. Look, I'm a sports fan. If you go into any sport situation, you only can speak within the context of what that sport is. You got to follow the context that it was formed from, and it's the same thing with music. That's why I feel like hip hop cannot detach itself from history. It can't detach itself from Black people. It can't detach itself from musics.

We might not have been in there defining the music terms before, but when they said something was country western music or Appalachian music, they were only describing the music. They never called the *vocal* anything. Saying that rap will disappear, like I heard in 1978, 1979, when the first record came out, is as stupid as saying, "I wonder when these singing records gonna stop." So, a lot of the definition or the undefined things in the music are already there. But they also have to be backed up with logic. Logic gotta back up everything.

I had those basics when I was seventeen and eighteen. I was an architecture student, and I went to Adelphi University to become a renderer. I had a scholarship to go to New York Tech, but I didn't want to go into the architectural field. It's a field where you had to be perfect. It's like doing somebody's hair. In the hood, you know, a barber's gotta be perfect, or there will be problems, you heard [*laughter*]? Same thing with architecture. You cannot make a mistake. On the twelfth stair, if you design it wrong and the engineer follows through, someone gonna keep bustin they head!

KELLEY: You gonna get sued too [*laughter*]!

CHUCK D: I didn't wanna be bothered with it. So I went in wanting to be a renderer, which is before computers, looking at a blueprint foreshadowing what it's gonna look like. But I went into Adelphi with that in mind and saying, "OK, OK, I'ma do this." Communication was my minor, because I wanted to become a sportscaster. But the first hip hop records happened in '79. I got kicked out in 1979 for hangin out on campus too much. What got me back in? Well, shit, I could now hone my talent level to a skill and start graphic departments for hip hop labels. So that's what pushed me through school.

KELLEY: But when you were in school, though, didn't you cohost a radio show?

CHUCK D: I cohosted a radio show later in my tenure as a student because I also was part of Spectrum, which was mobile DJs in Long Island

and became a member in '79 at the same time that I got kicked out and found my way back in, when I realized that DJs and rap groups weren't graphically at the level of rock bands. Long Island, New York, was laden with an unbelievable period of rock bands. Kiss comes from that area. I was always looking at DJs, and I was like, "Wow, why DJs can't have a dope logo like the Rolling Stones, and how come MCs can't have proper photography?" It was somebody bootlegging a 112 camera and thinkin that's gonna do. I never bragged about my music career in public. I wasn't as humble in arts. I looked at Basquiat and said, "I can get that kid." I was that type of dude. I would look at three quarters of the graffiti on the train and say, "It's garbage, it's garbage." I'd be that type of cat. And I would show them, I said, "I'll put some graffiti on here that'll be based on maybe hieroglyphics, and make you stare at it for a long time." The bottom line of art is not just taking whatever is in you and getting it out through your creation. That was my training. Now, how do you turn your talent, which we all had coming in, into a skill? How does it work for you?

Being in the radio station, one thing led to another, at Adelphi University in 1983, 1984, and we were doing the greatest hip hop radio shows ever. Here we are in *college*, so how the hell you gonna call this just adolescent kids' music? Or something that ain't gonna last long? We tried to do syndicated radio in 1984, when people were like, "Syndicated radio on rap?" Because we would listen to Casey Kasem. He's still around on SiriusXM, posthumously. We wanted to be professionals, and we were influenced by people like Mr. Magic, who had the first hip hop radio show, and Lady B, who had the second hip hop radio show in Philadelphia in the wee hours on the weekend. Before, they only used to play hip hop and rap music when it became records. Its first twelve years, only on the weekend. So this brought up a lot of angst for me and my cohosts at WBAU college radio station. This is a music that people were thirsting for. People wanted to hear more of it, and they wanted to hear it played the right way. There's a right way, because we were DJs. It's a right way to play a record, and it's a million wrong ways to play a record. And the reason is, you can't take hip hop away from dance culture because dance culture is DJs, and back in the day, if you're on the floor dancing by yourself, you might ask somebody on the floor, "May I have this dance?" Or better yet, back in '79, you'd nod your head like "Mmmmmm. . . ." I mean, really, it *does* matter if the DJ is good, just killin it, or if the DJ is wack. If the DJ is wack, it's like, "I don't wanna dance no more." That's the deal breaker.

We come from a dance culture, so that was very important to us to be able to understand what we can bring to the radio, the right way to play these records. We happened to play and break guys like Run D.M.C.—two young, scared kids coming up to our radio station. We played the record—"Two years ago, a friend of mine asked me to say some MC rhymes." I used to play that record, that's how far I go back. So that's my background, and not just me, but the team, everybody. We used to sit up at the radio station til five in the morning, after the show was over at one and have high discussions on rap and hip hop music the same way that jazz heads would talk about jazz.

That's why I say it's *impossible* to detach the music and put it in an isolated bubble all on its own. But corporations will do that, because what they want to do is parcel generations. If they could get a hold of a generation and put it in a bubble and sell that generation, they'll do it. And that gets dangerous when corporations start to dictate and define the culture.

KELLEY: I want to pull out one thing that you said or at least intimated. It has to do with *geography*. You're in Long Island, the edge of Queens. There's a kind of—I don't wanna call it a fetish, but this idea that everyone's in the South Bronx. It's one of these common mythologies. But in New York, as you said, it's a pretty small place, relatively speaking. But you also got your boroughs. And there's hip hop happening in Staten Island, in Long Island, etc. What was your sense of the geography? In other words, when you heard that DJ, you weren't thinking, "Oh, this comes from the South Bronx." You're thinking, "This is right here, where I am now."

CHUCK D: Yeah, because Long Island, during "white flight" and the era of Blacks moving into this hamlet, one-square-mile town, everybody came from a different part of New York anyway.[17] Queens, Brooklyn, you had a lot of clashes in the early seventies, late sixties, where people came from Queens like my family did. Brooklyn, Manhattan, and the Bronx, not Staten Island or Shaolin.[18] Staten Island was to itself, all the mobsters were there. But a lot of talent comes from Staten Island as well. My parents are from Harlem, so everything else in New York was country. Everything outside of Harlem for Black folks is "suburbs," "country." Bronx,

Brooklyn—there was no reason for somebody from Brooklyn to go to the Bronx at all. It's its own little planet. Therefore it's like immigration.

That's another important point. You cannot separate *immigration* and the *in-migration of Black people* from the culture. Because the migration of Black people really shapes the music in New York City. It doesn't take place if you don't have the most elaborate transit system in the world where you can go a hundred square miles at one particular time for a quarter, a dime, a nickel. But there was no cultural reason for somebody in Brooklyn to go to the Bronx at all unless they had family. I mean, my family in the Bronx, you had not a lot in Brooklyn, Queens, and also Manhattan. I hated to go there. "But we gonna go to Aunt Emma's house in the Bronx." "Ahhh man, here we going again." I wanted to stay on Long Island with trees. I didn't want to go there. I didn't want to go to the Bronx and see one of my uncles and people shooting up in the early 1970s. I mean, puttin the thing in they arm, that's what made me say no to drugs.

Saying no to drugs to a kid does not mean that you make it a public announcement [like Nancy Reagan]. It means they got to see something that makes them say, "Uh-uh. I don't wanna be that." That's what we tried to do later on in "Night of the Living Baseheads." We wanted to make crack look *nasty*. And we succeeded using culture like Samy said. You make a kid go, "Uhuh, uh-uh, eww, naw, damn!" You can plant a seed.

But yeah, you cannot take away the power of the New York City transit system for making somebody go from Brooklyn to Manhattan or from the Bronx to Manhattan. If they had to go from Brooklyn to the Bronx to check out Grandmaster Flash, cats was getting on that train and getting up there. Long Island, you gotta take a bus to the train. But that train was significant. The first album we did, *Yo! Bum Rush the Show*, the "A" side was the "E" side, meaning for the E train. And the "F" side was the "B" side, meaning that in order to travel to the spots in the city, Long Island, you take the bus or get a ride to Queens, catch the E or the F train into the city. The train was very significant because they were not expensive. They were under the ground. They were the warmest place for many people. People got shelter there in the coldest of days and could get from point A to B in long distances for the cost of a small fee or jump over the turnstile. There were no cameras then.

KELLEY: Exactly! When I was a kid, the train was a nickel. And you still jumped the turnstile [*laughter*]. I grew up on 157th between Broadway and Amsterdam and never went to the Bronx. There was no reason to go there.

CHUCK D: Yeah, so this detachment of Harlem from hip hop is *crazy*. The reason that the Bronx built a scene is because it was left out of the scene that Harlem had. They had their own thing happening. Really, a lot of this started because youth culture ain't in the clubs. If you're fourteen years old, you gonna go to the *park*, because you can't go to the club. There's a lot that is lost in the mythology. Because when you talk to an old head about blues and they tell you how they ended up in Chicago looking for a job, you go, "Oh, we goin up the river?" Congo Square in New Orleans. Then you got the next town, Memphis up the river. What's the next town from Memphis—up north? St. Louis. From that point on, you go to Omaha or you go up, obviously, into Chicago. But *Black geography* and *Black migration* has long been an afterthought. So if you don't even have that in your frame, you can't even begin to talk about the music.[19]

KELLEY: Right, and there's Caribbean migration too.

CHUCK D: Caribbean folks come up into New York City and in the Northeast. Also in Miami, a little bit in New Orleans. The seventies. Where does disco come from? Disco came from Philadelphia. Earl Young's four-on-the-floor beat, you know, Caribbean influence, calypso influence. It was a lot of that in Brooklyn. Faster music. The soca music. The technique of the MC on top of the DJ comes from toasters in Jamaica playing dub-plates. What's a dubplate? It's an instrumental that they put the vocal on top of with the microphone. That's the process of overdubbing. That's a Caribbean contribution. The use of two turntables has its own historical context of when it was brought up to New York. What makes Kool Herc not go to Brooklyn but go to the Bronx, when we know all that Caribbean people, West Indian people, are in Brooklyn, they not up in the Bronx? Another place which was a Black, *Black* city, because of a whole bunch of restraints—didn't have a lot of Caribbean mix—is Newark. You gotta put Newark up there if we're gonna go to the New York City area. Because there's Newark, Manhattan, Brooklyn, Bronx, and those are the major areas. Queens gets a little bit more, cause my grandparents moved out there in 1955. They were like, "We're moving out to Queens." My mom moved out there. That was a big migrating move.

But what made Kool Herc go to the Bronx instead of Brooklyn? Because when Black folks move, you usually moving to a spot where somebody already is at who's gonna hook you up. I asked my great grandmother, born in 1892. I asked her, like, "Yo, what made you move to New York from Rockingham, North Carolina?" She said, "Jobs." Her sister worked in the hospital in lower Manhattan; she had a job. The building they lived in was a fantastic, incredible building that the landlords knew that the Black influx was coming in in the twenties. And they chopped one apartment into like two or three apartments. So she said, "I have a place for you to stay. I got an apartment. I work downtown." She migrated, as did a host of relatives from North Carolina, chased outta there by Jim Crow with no opportunity. And come up to New York in 1937, '38, '40, the years of swing and the Savoy Ballroom and all these things that happened right before World War II. Music is following. Music is up in New York, but there's music where they come from, and everybody is bringing *everything*. That's how the music takes up a whole bunch of different sounds that wasn't there before—*the migrations of Black people and sound.*

KELLEY: Speaking of music that wasn't there before, you have this relatively long history of Black music, but then Public Enemy comes later. And you can disagree with me, but as far as I'm concerned, when Public Enemy came out, there was nothing like it. I mean, nothing like it, not even close.

CHUCK D: Which also can get you a whole lot of nothing, too, because it's so crazy that there won't be no place for it! And there was a great chance that there would be no Public Enemy if it wasn't for the eccentric Rick Rubin, who asked me to be part of the Def Jam situation. He asked me for two years. I was like, "I don't want to make records. I want to go into syndicated radio. I believe that this music can be played and done right." This was our dream in 1984. So when I signed to Def Jam in 1986, it wasn't an accomplishment. That signing picture was a surrender, as we call it, the great surrender. I was already twenty-six years old in 1986; LL Cool J's seventeen years old. I'm like, "It's a young person's music." And Bill Adler at Def Jam says, "No, I disagree, because I feel that you guys can at least bring something to the table that takes all of your well-roundedness about music."

I mean, I used to categorize rooms full of records and come up with a Dewey system for how the DJ gotta carry twenty-five crates. I first worked with Spectrum. The first thing on my mind when I joined was like, "Why are we taking twenty-five crates? That's insanity." You were doing more loading than anything. So I said, "I'm gonna list every single record in these two rooms"—there was two rooms of records. One thing you learn is never to put them in alphabetical order. Why? Because there's always gonna be more M's than X's. Somebody says, "I got my record collection, and I got it in alphabetical order." See that person twenty years later, they say, "Man, I had to rearrange all these records." So the only way to do this without computers is to number each of them, put in the title, and keep them in books, instead of thumbing through all these records. I mean, you can't find the record going through the spines. You're looking at them, and it's like microscopic, like, "Oh, there you go, the Righteous Brothers." Pull it out, happens to be the wrong record. So you go through the book like, "Oh, here Righteous Brothers 1362, that's in room B." And then you go, and it's gonna be a small section. Those are the things I brought. I said, "Shit's gotta be backed up by logic because we can't be moving twenty-five crates of records." Logic backs everything and is really a brilliant thing, because it saves you time. It saves you backache. It saves you, "Ok man, we finish the gig at 4 a.m., now with all these damn crates we get in the crib at 6, gotta work at 8." What the hell? So logic brings you into the practicalities. A lot of this music is based off of practicality too.

KELLEY: Yeah, that's true. But I'm really curious about the aesthetic. How did you come up with those rhymes? I know that you started writing in the seventies.

CHUCK D: I was an art student for the first twenty years of my life. I always won the art contests and didn't care about poetry contests. I mean, it would be almost like it was unfair. At school all the way up to whatever grade—"Oh, we got an art and poetry contest." Well, he's taking the art contest. I had never written a poem. I didn't write a poem until I was twenty years old. I liked the music. I liked what it was saying. But I only got on the microphone at college. I started college before the first rap record was out. But as you know, people in the city at that particular time, everybody thought they could rhyme.

KELLEY: And they still do!

CHUCK D: The thing about it, when you have an event and the DJ has an open mic and a lot of people are gettin in line, and you tryna get your dance on, right? And the DJ's acting up, and the rhymer don't know how to rhyme, then you not getting no dancing. So I tell my boys, I said, “Listen, I'ma get on the mic to sit all these wack-ass people down,” and I did it. My guys were like, “Yeah, right.” So I got on the mic, and nobody wanted to get on the mic. That's when me and Hank Shocklee first hooked up because I was turning the party out. I turned the party out so much one time that I heard words behind me. The party was rockin. “Good Times.” I heard words behind me, so I just lip-synced. That record was “Rapper's Delight.”[20]

But I turned around and said, “Whoa, they finally did it!” It was a rap record. That was the first official rap record. I was like, “Wow! This is a thing!” Because before, I thought it was inconceivable when somebody said, “There's gonna be a hip hop/rap record.” I'm like, “How you gonna put rap on a record? This is a three-, four-hour event. That record would have to be like four to five hours!” And when it was done I was like, “Oh wow, they shortened it.” The first rap record, ironically, was sixteen minutes. But in hindsight, when you look back, it's a long time. But really seriously, it's not how *long* that sixteen minutes is; it's how they truncated that sixteen minutes from a three-hour event!

That was the big bang theory, from that point in August of 1979. Well, it was first “King Tim III,” by the Fatback Band in March 1979 on Spring Records. Even when you want to talk about rappin on top of records, we gotta look at Pigmeat Markham in Chicago on Chess Records. In 1968, Pigmeat Markham, a comedian, is doing a flow on top of a funky beat in the Chess studios; it was produced by Gene Barge. Anybody heard of the great singer Minnie Riperton? Minnie Riperton is on that record “Here Comes the Judge.” She's the one that says, “Well, I'll take two cans of beer, please.” So I tell people Minnie Riperton is on a rap record in 1968. It's debatable, but when you listen to the song, well dang, that sounds like rapping to me, on top of the music with the rhythm and flow that we are used to applying in rap and hip hop. But if we wanna say the first rap record to be released in the middle of what we view as hip hop and rap music, people tip their hat to “Rappers Delight” because it took a song that we were familiar with and had somebody spit over it. It's two songs we were familiar with in 1979, but we'll just keep it to “Good Times” and not get long-winded on the other song used.

But when we put music in the rhymes, I come from a think tank of cats talking like that for six years before we made records. You take me in a room like this and we're talking until six in the morning, every night about rap music and hip hop. People were wondering if it would be a fad or if that was gonna last. I knew it when I signed to Rick Rubin. I said "Shit, I ain't gonna let nothin stop me!" But I only brought to the table this one quality of talent that I don't think anybody ever been better than me at all. It has nothing to do with words or with what Public Enemy meant; it's only the fact that I claim to be the loudest MC ever [*laughter*]. Ice Cube, LL, everybody said "Yeah, yeah," so I ain't lying. It definitely ain't my fault, though. It's DNA, because my father was the type of person if he yelled across the street tellin you to come in the crib, you could *not* say you did not hear him. That was the only thing I had going for me. All these other parts we made work with equipment and made work with maybe doing the right thing or the wrong thing, a whole bunch of characters. The problem with Public Enemy is it comes from within a square mile of Roosevelt and are themselves—Flavor Flav is the craziest fuckin person in the world! He's the world's oldest teenager. So take eight to ten people talking about this all the time. You knew what nobody else was doing, so you would do what nobody else does! We like what everbody's doin, but we know what they *not* doin. It's easy to do what somebody's not doing if you know how to do it.

KELLEY: Yeah, *if* you know how to do it. Because I think about the lyrics, the language, the rhyme schemes, even from the first record. There's some politics there that wasn't really articulated in the same way too. I'm not saying that no one was thinking politically, but you expressed a particular kind of politics. In light of Samy's framework for us today—the activism and aesthetics, the politics and poetics—Public Enemy was really really unusual.

CHUCK D: We had to *listen*. We don't listen today. People now are listening with their eyes, which also leads you to being tricked. All of a sudden, the closer you get, you think you see what you see, but it ain't really what you see. Right now, everybody is listening with their eyes a little too much. What you had back then is that your only antenna to the world was listening. You couldn't see a lot of Black people, or Black men, in areas other than sports, and they didn't give them the mic for long. So you had to go to some books. What's it about? So you're in a circle that might spread that information, spread that love. If you were in a crew of ten to twelve people, and you got somebody who didn't read what you read, but they *know* what you read because their antennas was up and they was listening. Listening is a last century trait. We don't know when it's gonna return. Seeing is everything now. Today people are *screenagers*. Whether you're ten years old or sixty years old, you're a screenager, meaning everything that you receive and get is coming through the screen. Even the *sound* is coming through the screen. This has already been planned and orchestrated, and even in the last two years. I'm not even being a conspiracy theorist, not in the slightest bit. It's like they said, "If we can get everybody to be still for a minute, the only connection between them and the rest of the world is through what? A screen." Not only what you hear, but also what you see. Welcome to this gigantic, recording, monitoring game. So hip hop was always about what you heard and what you spit and what you *experience*.

For example, I'm not a kid in 1985, so me and my friend would go to the city. What was the chance of us catching a taxicab? Not that high. So that sticks with you. The first thing you gonna tell somebody is, "I can't catch a cab." That's as strange as telling somebody how you got your last name. "Oh, that's a different last name." And you go into the process of telling them about Black last names in the United States of America. "I had no idea that wasn't your name." Same thing with taxicabs. Hip hop had the ability to lay a little bit on you and keep it movin. I mean, "Don't Believe the Hype" was me figuring out how I could hip folks to Noam Chomsky. I was twenty-seven years old. I knew who Noam Chomsky was. But I'm not going to say, "Noam Chomsky," you know what I mean? You have to look for the information *through* this information.

But you should be able to say things like Samy said earlier about the brilliance of artists that's doing it now. So, we're at a crossroads right now where academia could at least seize back the balance that a culture and genre needs away from a company that's gonna try to dictate it according to its bottom line. Friends of mine, 300 Entertainment, they sold to Warner Brothers for about $500 million, right? Because they see value in anything that comes through that would be able to speak to millions. And, "It's not just a Black thing and there's a lot of white kids who are involved with it," and it does make a difference from a business perspective. The core of cultural balance comes from knowing that it is related to the DNA of our people, for the future of our existence or communication survival.

You cannot detach that. Once you take geography and history away from a people, you got a carcass. You got a taxidermist of culture coming after that. A whole bunch of stuffed-ass people that got the look but they ain't got no insights. So, it needs a balance. Everything has a time and place. I just think that everything needs some sort of management where it thrives in its soil of time and place.

That's how we were able to introduce Public Enemy in a less populated field. We were the first album or rap act that came from nowhere. Before, you wasn't getting an album unless you was a hot single on the block. We had a situation in Def Jam where we were gonna be the first album-oriented group, like the rock groups, that would take a while to catch on. But also we knew that when I signed with Rick Rubin, I signed with what? A multinational corporation, meaning that I'm not just dealing with the United States of America. Public Enemy thrived because our first base was London. Not New York, not Philadelphia. London, UK, is what started us. That's where our most popular album began at. Then we became big in the United States the following year. But we also became big because of our peers and our allies. We promoted Run D.M.C. If it wasn't for Jam Master Jay and Ad-Rock and MCA, the Beastie Boys dragging me into it, it wouldn't have been possible. So that's how that happened.

KELLEY: I want to talk about the visual. You have this visual sense. You're an illustrator, I would say an artist, and Public Enemy emerges really at the beginning of video culture. You go from the old, very simple videos to these elaborate ones, whether it's "Black Steel in the Hour of Chaos" or "Night of the Living Baseheads." These were essentially short films.

CHUCK D: It wasn't being played on any radio stations whatsoever in the US that second year that Public Enemy came out. I did the first prison show at Rikers and therefore was banned for the rest of my career. "No Johnny Cash for you." I said, "He's the man in black, I'm the Black in man, what's up?" Though I got banned, we had a positive day. But they considered it propaganda, contraband, or whatever they want to say. It's like, "No, you are infiltrating their minds." "Well, we're not going to start a prison riot." But we are going to be able to have a riot going inside their thought. And also not waste time fighting some situation that don't want you anyway. So we let the music speak for itself. I mean, "Fight the Power" was voted the number one most influential rap record ever. But you gotta be humble and say, "That isn't because of us." It was number one because of *Do the Right Thing*. Spike Lee takes it into the world of Hollywood. Therefore, you're able to see "Fight the Power" in that activity, through the movie, and through the video that Spike Lee directed. But also more importantly, because 2020 to 2021 were big years for "Fight the Power," when everybody protested and spoke truth to power in terms of what was happening in Minneapolis and other places with police brutality. People were saying, "Well, Chuck, you should do 'Fight the Power.'" But I didn't want to get in the way of young energy, because it's the number one violation when you have old heads get in the middle of young energy. I said, "I could be here for advice."

But with all due respect, the original "Fight the Power" that me and you, Robin, grew up with spoke volumes to us. So when I decided to write "Fight the Power," it was only to know that in the 1980s, the Isley Brothers was about "In Between the Sheets," but it's like *this* is the Isley Brothers too. You might not hear the music, but the words, "You got to fight the powers that be." That's the Isley Brothers! So when somebody brings up "fight the power, fight the power," I tip my hat to the Isleys because that's the first record I ever heard with a curse word. You heard it on AM radio 1975. I'm fifteen years old, and I hear all that "beep" go down, I'm like "Whoa, what did they say?" Cursing wasn't like that until ten years later. But cursing at one particular time, in the seventies, was a real violation. The N-word, you better not! And you better not be white saying the N-word because it was gonna be going down. We grow up in the time of—Dr. King was killed in 1968, that gravity was around for what?

KELLEY: That was for like a decade.

CHUCK D: Yeah, like for a decade. Questlove just won an Oscar for *Summer of Soul*, which was about a music festival that took place just one year later.

KELLEY: Yeah, summer of '69.

CHUCK D: Where it's just a lot of uncertainty. That concert right there, you feel that concert. This is taking place in Harlem, in Mount Morris Park. Like, "Look, man, we don't even know what the 1970s gonna look like. But let's try to get it together." That's why some things are more than what you hear and what you see. Some things back in the last century, there was an element of feeling, on good things. Back then, it was like we had at least a little bit of a window and lineage to feel good collectively. So maybe at the end of this class, ten weeks, we at least know that there's a seed in the *feel*. Because I think "to feel" is the essence of human beings. Give me cultures that end governments. Governments are the cancer of civilization. Now I'm not here to tell y'all how to make a better government. But I will tell you this: culture is what brings human beings together for our similarities and put all our differences to the damn side. Culture, when it's actually rich so that we communicate with one another, differences are slapped to the side. Beware when the government says it is in control of culture. Right now, the uncertainty that we feel through a screen, we kind of like don't know what's going on—or maybe we *do*. And from the last two years of everything being paralyzed during this pandemic, even the music, it's difficult to go to the music to try and give us clarity. People are asking for it to come back. I don't believe things come back. I believe they go *forward*. What comes out of the ashes like a phoenix becomes new art and new technology and new ways of doing things.

KELLEY: Okay, let's take some questions.

QUESTION 1: I really appreciate that you mentioned the idea that America means all of the Americas. You bring up "USAers." In Spanish we say *Estadounidenses*. There was a new song by Residente and Ibeyi called "This Is Not America." It has a lot of really powerful imagery, including showing Victor Jara being murdered during the coup d'état in Chile.[21] Are there conversations now among your peers on what could possibly happen as an effect of this major culture shift that we're seeing from white people responding negatively to Black and Indigenous people fighting for pan-Africanism and Indigenous solutions?

CHUCK D: You need people with brains. Brains are connected to the heart. You need that. You have artists who are artists, who are just going to be artists. But who's actually turning on the lights to that room of artistry? Who actually put together a situation where artists are led to know that they can do art that could be beneficial to the people? Don't think James Brown said, "I'm Black and I'm Proud" because all of a sudden he felt that there was an urge in his head to say it. Stokely Carmichael, a.k.a. Kwame Ture, said he was on James Brown's ass every day! And James turned it around. Artists are gonna be artists. And sometimes you don't want an artist at the steering wheel of society. I think we need more administrators. I think we need more academics, more book writers, more film makers, more people in government, local government. We don't need people who have the biggest voice to tell the people not to vote in their local area. So I feel, "Sit the fuck down for a minute, dog. You ain't the one that's supposed to speak on that." You do what you do and let this person who's trying to figure out how to feed kids in this county, let them get the biggest mic.

QUESTION 2: You said that hip hop comes from the city and urban blight, but what about groups like the O'Jays that talked about partying and dancing? I don't see enough of hip hop going back to that era before then.

CHUCK D: A lot of hip hop came out of Philadelphia International Records with Leon Huff and Kenny Gamble and Thom Bell. Everybody should watch the *Unsung* documentary—you gonna learn more about Black music! They don't make many mistakes. Returning to Philadelphia International Records, Leon Huff and Kenny Gamble, they are in Philadelphia, songwriters. They actually have a record company that was able to get major distribution in the 1970s to become that 1970s version of what Motown was in the sixties. One thing about Leon Huff and Kenny Gamble coming out of Philadelphia and Camden, New Jersey, is that they realized that they had a responsibility to the music and the communities that the music came out of and that there should be a message in the music. And sure enough, Leon Huff and Kenny Gamble, back in the 1970s, laid out a platform that rap music came up out of, knowing that they had a social obligation as much as they wanted to party and drink and do whatever that people still do to this day. But they said there's gonna be at least one or two records for the neighborhood, that we want to try and pull ourselves out of what was actually up on us. So it was always a message in the music because Black music always looked out; it was love music, up to a certain point. Meaning that I got your back. I love you.

So a lot of those older heads in the sixties and seventies, they looked at some of the rap music twenty years later and said, "Okay, we don't understand where the hate came from." But there are social and economic reasons for that. . . . It was like what Tupac was talking about in the clip we heard earlier. After a while, I keep knocking at the door, I'm knocking nice, singing along, but at the end, I'ma come in with my gat and we gonna be pointin at people. And that was hip hop in 1996, where we lost two significant rappers [Tupac and Biggie]. Now it's to the point, if you look at music today, you got to watch the flow of what's happening when it comes down to business. We lost Nipsey Hussle how long ago?[22] Where did we lose him? Not far from his crib, right? We lost Young Dolph?[23] Where did we lose him? Right around his crib. There's a series of young Black rapper deaths as well as now old Black rapper deaths—from two different conditions. Old Black rappers die from what? Health. Young Black rappers die from what? Murder. And it's also what? Overdose. These are the people's problems.

With Leon Huff and Kenny Gamble—it's not just the O'Jays songs—they had a song by the Philadelphia International All Stars called "Clean up the Ghetto." It made me clean up my room. It just hit me, man. I didn't want to keep a sloppy room after that song. You never know when you're being touched emotionally by something.

QUESTION 3: A lot of people linked the phenomenon of Motown with public school education and the arts. I was wondering if you can point to any other cultural, political, social, economic changes that influence music, for example, defunding arts education, when playing an instrument, learning how to read music, became a *privilege*.

CHUCK D: You can't detach hip hop from the rest of music. I think that this whole rush to "Let's get this high-level hip hop understanding in a college setting" isn't enough. I think music and arts culture has to be taught from grade *zero*. I mean, as a Black person, right, I'ma break it down like this. If you didn't give me anything else, I could study the music from the last 150 years because it's documented. That's why they call it a record. It's recorded, right? We know when the first recording is: Thomas Edison, "Mary Had a Little Lamb," 1877, right? So it's all documented. Give me records to go from 1900 to 2000 and I'm gonna learn everything in there. Now you can break down just the recordings and the science inside the recordings and break it down into courses of whatever, especially just history or point of view, and spread that over twelve years. And you gonna have people that when they finally get to the college level be like, "Okay, I got it."

I'm just saying that you got to teach people about people. My advantage is when I went to school, I knew everything about white society and they didn't know anything about me. I came out my school, and I was killing it, like, "I know everything about you. You know nothing about me." The things that come across the screen about each other instead of face to face—and we don't even kinda know our own as much as we did. So I think knowledge like this will help bring people together.

QUESTION 4: Given the rise of screens/screenagers, there are still people becoming a lot more politically minded, across the world all over; it's a global movement. What new directions do you see hip hop headed in?

CHUCK D: In the United States of America, if you keep it to the three thousand mile, forty-eight continental box, you will therefore be limiting your knowledge. What we need is probably something that brings you day-to-day knowledge, wisdom, understanding, and information about the great things going on in this music. Protesters have been protesting to try to get people to understand and finally they got our attention because they burned a building. I think we need people that properly curate, and we need a million curators. Podcasters are stepping in the right direction because people say, "Well, I have podcasts, and I wanna talk to so and so and so and so," but also you gotta be able to dig instead of just thinking that information is just gonna wash up on your shore about somebody doing something great and hip hop or rap music going outside of that culture or audience in society and making changes. I think discovery has got to be worked on in a society.

Also common sense. If the community doesn't take care of the arts, the arts will never be able to take care of the community. The community has to support the arts and the artists. They spend a lot of money in school systems. When you look at school budgets, grade school, high school, you look at the budgets and the salaries and what they're spending and what the youth and kids are getting in their curriculum. They need updates, but then that's a political fight. Matter of fact, if you go into some school systems and you talk about changing that budget number or spending that budget over here, you're probably looking to be tarred and feathered. You're messing with people's money when you talking about making changes. You better be ready to fight.

QUESTION 5: I don't see a division between academia and rap, because they're both always producing knowledge. Do you see any rappers today that are not even necessarily carrying the torch from the old heads but just doing the work that needs to be done given our current social and political circumstances?

KELLEY: Can I just address a couple of things as well? One, on the question of defunding. I just want to remind us that defunding of the arts is uneven. It's differential. If you are Black or Brown or poor, chances are your public school will be defunded differently, because there's lots of schools that have huge budgets for the arts. Also, the neoliberal turn has elevated STEM above everything else. Florida is a good example. High School graduates entering state colleges are eligible for bigger scholarships if they choose majors in STEM rather than liberal arts.[24] So like Chuck was saying, it's a political question, and it's a political question worth fighting for.

This goes back to your question about the production of knowledge. I mean, this is a very special class and a very special space. But UCLA, like most universities, also produces knowledge for war, dispossession, and violence. Not all knowledge is for good. In fact, universities have their hands dirty as well in terms of producing knowledge that many artists are trying to resist. I think it is important to remember that because we have fights, all of us as faculty and students, have fights with the university about what kind of knowledge we are producing. They're getting money from the Department of Defense, what do you think they're gonna do with that money? So these are things that we always have to keep in mind. This class is a very special space for that reason.

QUESTION 6: You spoke on the need for academics to write about hip hop culture and the need for more academics. Do you think there is a need for removing academics, and intellectuals more generally, from state control and state government?

KELLEY: You're asking how do we separate academia from state control and state funding? Well, there's state-sanctioned and there's private money. There's a lot more private money, to be honest. So what you're asking is, How are we able to produce without being compromised by funders? Ford, Rockefeller, and other big corporate funders have some progressive program officers who often support projects that Henry Ford himself would be really pissed off about. On the other hand, the Department of Defense is actually interested in defense, and that's their funding priority. For example, we have an anthropologist here at UCLA who got money to create predictive policing software.[25] Now that's jacked up. It will mainly affect Black and Brown communities. I'm sure that a lot of us do get some funding someplace, including the state. When we get paid from UCLA, that's state funds. In some ways, we have a right to state funds. We should demand state funds to do this. I'm just suggesting that maybe it's not a matter of freeing ourselves from that funding as much as being ethical about what funding we take and what we do with the funding we do take, and more importantly, making demands so we have complete autonomy over the funding that we have. And this is not just for academics. It's for social movements, which also often depend on outside funding.

QUESTION 7: I want to start by saying I'm a Staten Island native. I'm representing for Shaolin. Richmond County. You have talked about the state of hip hop and its impact in Black communities and how rappers are dying or being taken into the prison system. Their lyrics are being used against them literally in the court system. How can this music take a different direction yet stay true to the culture and represent what they are going through right now?

CHUCK D: The community has to support the arts so that the arts can support the community. When it comes down to rap music, if you go back to what they used to call gangsta rap thirty years ago or whatever, it was real casualties too. So you gotta have the community somehow figure out how to nurture this culture. Every community gotta figure out how they reward the energy that's in that area. If you don't reward youth energy, how are youth gonna feel good about being there in the first place? They have no ownership. It's like, "We're just here, we're captives in here." So that is a conversation that I think educators need to figure out, how to deal with explaining the arts. Don't have these other places out here have the final say-so on the arts and culture because they got all kinds of ways to get a young person's attention.

NOTES

1. "Fight the Power" by Public Enemy was released by Motown Records in 1989. Later in this chapter, Chuck D credits the Isley Brothers' song, "Fight the Power, Pts 1 & 2," Epic Records, 1975, as the inspiration for Public Enemy's, "Fight the Power," and the line, "Fight the powers that be!" See Chuck D and Ernie Isley's conversation in Phil Harrell's *Morning Edition* piece on NPR, https://

www.npr.org/2018/12/07/673845242/fight-thepower-american-anthem-public-enemy-isley-brothers.

2. Poets like Sonia Sanchez and Amiri Baraka, among many other Black writers, artists, and thinkers in the 1960s and 1970s, constituted the Black Arts Movement (BAM) and worked to radically transform understandings of Blackness, Black music, and Black literary production. See H. Samy Alim, *Roc the Mic Right: The Language of Hip Hop Culture* (Routledge, 2006). James G. Spady was lead author of the first trilogy of books about hip hop with *Nation Conscious Rap* (1991), *Twisted Tales in the Hip Hop Streets of Philly* (1995), and *Street Conscious Rap* (1999), ultimately adding a fourth volume with *The Global Cipha: Hip Hop Culture and Consciousness* (2006). See James G. Spady's obituary penned by Samir Meghelli on March 2, 2020, for the *Philadelphia Tribune* at https://www.phillytrib.com/obituaries/james-g-spady-75writer-and-historian/article_4e576aa6-815b-5376-bc86-6cde6b556ad6.html.

3. See Imani Perry, *Prophets of the Hood: Politics and Poetics in Hip Hop* (Duke University Press, 2004).

4. Early hip hop was profoundly shaped by groups such as The Last Poets—Jalaluddin Mansur Nuriddin, Umar Bin Hassan, and Abiodun Oyewole—and poet-performers like Gil Scott-Heron. See Kevin Fitzgerald's *Freestyle: The Art of Rhyme* (2000), https://www.youtube.com/watch?v = lcow3pz3L80.

5. See Rakim, Chuck D, and Talib Kweli, "Sweat the Technique: The Politics and Poetics of Hip Hop," in *Freedom Moves: Hip Hop Knowledges, Pedagogies, and Futures*, ed. H. Samy Alim, Jeff Chang, and Casey Philip Wong (University of California Press, 2023), 29–52. See also Rakim, *Sweat the Technique: Revelations on Creativity from the Lyrical Genius* (Amistad, 2019, with Bakari Kitwana).

6. See Tricia Rose, *Black Noise: Rap Music and Black Culture in Contemporary America* (Wesleyan University Press, 1994). Quoted text is on page 3.

7. Ibid., 11.

8. This interview with hip hop icon Tupac Shakur can be heard at https://www.youtube.com/watch?v=GLZoNhUFmc&list=RDQMo4vWBoNiMtA&start_radio=1; and https://www.youtube.com/watch?v = I0XMJMphPT4.

9. Robin D. G. Kelley writes that Cedric Robinson, the scholar most associated with the term "racial capitalism" (see Cedric Robinson, *Black Marxism: The Making of a Black Radical Tradition* [University of North Carolina Press, 1983]), first encountered the term as it was used by European intellectuals to describe South Africa's apartheid economics. See chapter 8 for more on racial capitalism.

10. Rose, *Black Noise*, 19.

11. Perry, *Prophets of the Hood*, 1–2.

12. Ibid., 3.

13. See Joan Morgan, *When Chickenheads Come Home to Roost: A Hip Hop Feminist Breaks It Down* (Simon & Schuster, 1999).

14. See Leroy Moore and Stephanie Keeney Parks, "When Can Black Disabled Folks Come Home?," in *Freedom Moves: Hip Hop Knowledges, Pedagogies, and Futures*, ed. H. Samy Alim, Jeff Chong, and Casey Philip Wong (University of California Press, 2023), 376–95.

15. See Robin D. G. Kelley, foreword to *The Vinyl Ain't Final: Hip Hop and the Globalization of Black Popular Culture*, ed. Dipannita Basu and Sidney Lemelle (Pluto Press, 2006), xi–xvii.

16. See Lynda R. Day, *Making a Way to Freedom: A History of African Americans on Long Island* (Empire State Books, 1997). For how racial segregation and white flight continued to impact Chuck D's hometown of Roosevelt, see Michael Powell, "Separate and Unequal in Roosevelt, Long Island," *Washington Post*, April 20, 2002.

17. See Thomas Sugrue, *The Origins of the Urban Crisis: Race and Inequality in Post-War Detroit* (Princeton University Press, 2014); and Kevin M. Kruse, *White Flight: The Making of Modern Conservatism* (Princeton University Press, 2005).

18. Shaolin is a nickname for Staten Island that was popularized by the Wu Tang Clan.

19. See *African American Music: An Introduction*, 2nd ed., ed. Mellonee V. Burnim and Portia Maultsby (Routledge, 2015); and Eileen Southern, *The Music of Black Americans: A History*, 3rd ed. (W. W. Norton, 1997).

20. "Rapper's Delight" (1979) by The Sugarhill Gang is considered the first hip hop record to gain mainstream success. It was preceded by the Fatback Band's "King Tim III" in March 1979 on Spring Records and other recordings that included rap, like Pigmeat Markham's "Here Comes the Judge," on Chess Records in 1968. As Ernest Hardy has noted, there are many other recordings that precede the modern rap era but that feature rapping, such as "Noah" by the Jubalaires in 1946.

21. Victor Jara was a popular Chilean folk singer who became an international symbol of resistance. General Pinochet overthrew Chile's democratically elected president Salvador Allende on September 11, 1973, and Jara was brutally murdered the day after. Nine ex-soldiers have been arrested for his murder. See "Victor Jara Killing, Nine Ex-soldiers Arrested," BBC, July 4, 2018, https://www.bbc.com/news/world-latinamerica-44709924.

22. Nipsey Hussle was a hip hop artist from the Crenshaw neighborhood of Los Angeles known for his entrepreneurship and his commitment to community. In 2019, Hussle was gunned down outside his clothing store, Marathon Clothing.

23. Young Dolph was an artist from Memphis and founder of the Paper Route Empire record label. His album *Rich Slave* (2020) was a reference to the contradictory condition of being Black and wealthy in the United States. He was murdered one year later in Memphis.

24. Divya Kumar, "Florida Law Offering 'BOGO' Tuition for STEM Majors Raises Faculty Concerns," *Tampa Bay Times*, July 5, 2021, https://www

.tampabay.com/news/education/2021/07/05/florida-law-offering-bogotuition-for-stem-majors-raises-faculty-concerns/.

25. UCLA professor of anthropology P. Jeffrey Brantingham's work with the Los Angeles Police Department on predictive policing analytics has been the subject of considerable controversy regarding how technology can perpetuate racial discrimination. See "LAPD Ended Predictive Policing Programs amid Public Outcry. A New Effort Shares Many of Their Flaws," *The Guardian*, November 8, 2021, https://www.theguardian.com/us-news/2021/nov/07/lapd-predictive-policing-surveillance-reform.

2 Welcome to the Terrordome

HISTORY, CONTEXT, AND THE (R)EVOLUTION OF HIP HOP

Chuck D and Jeff Chang

CHUCK D: This week, we're going to talk about the evolution of hip hop artistry by examining hip hop history, context, and politics. There is no better book to start from than *Can't Stop Won't Stop: A History of the Hip-Hop Generation*, the title of which is drawn from the vernacular of hip hop artists in the late 1970s.[1] As a matter of fact, it was a key bridge before the break of Grandmaster Flash and the Furious Five's 1979 record "Superrappin'" coming out of the Bronx. Before the break, they say, "Can't, won't, don't stop, rockin to the rhythm."

The book is all about history and relevancy, myths and mythology. We have a lot of it in this culture and in hip hop and rap music. Maybe we have fallen victim to the people who write the books and do the films, as they control the narrative. That's been a problem. When the story is told about whatever you say that you love, at least you want it to be held close to the facts. If there's going to be any comprehensive film about hip hop to come out in this century, that cuts it from A to Z, it'd have to be based off of Jeff's book. What struck me about the book is I thought I was looking in a mirror. When Jeff was telling these stories, a lot of it was explaining the reasons why things happened. It made me almost think, "Damn, yeah, that's what happened." To me, there is something behind the reason why things happened in the first place. Art comes from the aftereffect of some event.

When you talk about hip hop and rap music, if you don't talk about the migration and the in-migration and also the internationality of human beings and people in the US when it comes to Black music, you can't even begin to tell the story. If you study the "blues," that term for that music, it starts from a combination of people in one area and slavery in a big port area, at the bottom of the Lower 48, called Congo Square in New Orleans.[2] Back when many of y'all were probably six years old or even younger, Hurricane Katrina happened in Louisiana and Mississippi. Big shock effect on the US; when they looked on television, they were like, "Damn, I didn't know so many Black people lived down there." New Orleans was ultimately the largest slave market in the US that Black people were brought into, in the Gulf of Mexico, and up the Mississippi River.

The reason why all of this matters is if you take geography and history away from a person, you're damn near attaching slavery to their state of existence. In the US, the first thing they tried to do is strip the sense of community and history from us because that's what was keeping the art, and us, alive. They tried to destroy your background. "That language you spoke wherever you was did not matter. That shit y'all talking in Africa, y'all talking a whole bunch of different stuff, and we're going to throw you in the same area of Mississippi to sell your asses." New Orleans was this area where all these different languages came together with Black human beings who were ready to be sold up the river. "Maybe you don't know my language, but you know if I could make a beat, and you can hum, we can hum and sing and moan together." Out of that magic of Congo Square, that magic of communicating with each other, that music then goes up the river.

What's the next major city up the Mississippi River? Memphis—home of Stax Records, and where Young Dolph just lost his life. It's also the same city where Dr. Martin Luther King lost his life. Memphis, Tennessee, across from a state called Arkansas. Mud Island in between. That area was known for the blues as well. City of the blues, Memphis. That is also the distribution center of the US. Why? It's right in the middle with the biggest river, the Mississippi. If you go north, south, ship those big ships and barges up just like Mark Twain's stories. Go east to west. Especially when the Eisenhower Interstate System came into play.[3] Memphis was that middle city. That's why one of the big distributors of shipping is located in Memphis, Tennessee. Before Jeff Bezos and Amazon, that was the hub.

Before that, the hub was Cincinnati. The beginning of the South, North, East, and West, when that country was kind of leaning just to the east, that was the major hub. It got rivers running through it. You can send ships, going up and down the road system and all that. Distribution is very important. When you distribute products, you also distribute people. You also distribute the culture and the music that go along with it. Up the Mississippi, you got what? Another city of the blues, St. Louis, Missouri. They still got a hockey team called the St. Louis Blues. And farther up, you got Chicago, at the end of the river and farther east, which is the home of the electric blues and a place where Black folks followed the river to find work. That's the story of the blues, with respect to the river and the migration of people.

Jeff covers this story of hip hop and the migration and in-migration and the internationality of people coming into the port of New York. Taking the story from toasts and rhythms and technical equipment. Last week, we joked about the two turntables, and I told you how country I was, thinking that if one was broken, they'll use the other. In Jamaica they'd make sure that it is "can't stop, won't stop." You got a party going on in Kingston, you want to keep it moving. No dead air. There might be a problem if the music stops. Keep it poppin, let it go on and on to the break of dawn. Keep people happy to stay captured on an island where their rights and everything else is taken away. The rhythms. The beginnings of Island culture where they took the majority of the people and worked them as slaves to serve the minority of people.

What made people out of the Caribbean go to New York in the first damn place? Well, what made people in the South go to the North? Opportunities, work, get away from Jim Crow, even if he changes his name to different languages. Hip hop starts that same way in the Northeast, the migration of people coming from Georgia, South Carolina, North Carolina, Virginia, Florida. And usually, they head north to get away from Jim Crow through the Eisenhower Interstate System. It's called the I-95 that takes you from Atlanta and also the I-75 that takes you from

Virginia, takes you straight up to Cleveland and Detroit. The Motown movement was basically a process of people getting up out of the South to go up there and get a job in car plants and industrial factories, whether it's war equipment or refrigerators. To go from Georgia, or picking cotton in Alabama, to take your ass to a job up in Detroit, Cleveland, Cincinnati, or even damn near on the edges of Lexington, Kentucky. "Go north people, get up out of that South." Same thing happened in the Caribbean, in places like Jamaica, getting up out of there in the forties and fifties. "Now you all are free. You are independent in the sixties." And these places like, "We ain't really independent with the white hand holding the gun to the president's head. We're kind of a colony still with a name that says we're independent. We'll look for a better opportunity than the islands. We'll open up a little bit to migrate to the US to opportunities in the plants and opportunities in the industrial situations."

The music's fire follows this route, and hip hop growing up in New York from the Caribbean, it was a very key point to have Kool Herc. Even though I was the first person to put Herc in a recording studio on Terminator X's album in 1994, I never asked him, "What made your people move to the Bronx instead of Brooklyn?" In New York, people from the Caribbean would go to Brooklyn. I mean, Puerto Ricans would go to the Bronx because of chain migration. If there's a body of people that have already come from one place to another place, they seem to settle in Brooklyn for a lot of logistical reasons. How come there's not a large Caribbean contingent, especially in the seventies, in the Bronx? I will ask Jeff that question. That's a question we probably both have to ask Kool Herc, because his family went to the Bronx. This is why in the beginning of hip hop in the Bronx, the technique of playing a record on two turntables came out of that. Playing that reggae shit ain't gonna work up in the Bronx. But if you actually have the two turntables and you play some James Brown then you got Black faces and Puerto Rican faces saying, "Yeah, I feel you on that one. But I don't know about that Bob Marley shit. Play one of those and keep it moving."

In terms of language, instead of a person saying, "One two, man," in their Caribbean vernacular, it's like, "One two, one two. I'm from the Bronx, what's up!" There's a difference in vernacular, a difference in dialect. It will determine whether you will get on a microphone and say anything! Because if you're talking in a language that people don't understand, with a tone and in an accent that people aren't feeling or don't know back then, "Shut that microphone off. Nobody understands what you're saying." You're heard in Brooklyn, but you ain't heard in the Bronx. That's a big question I'm going to ask.

This migration comes from the Caribbean, but at the same time, this technique of two turntables and a microphone starts to be prevalent in the Bronx and also the Mecca of Black New York City up to the sixties. Sixty years of Black folks going to New York from the South, the first place they went to is where? Harlem. This is at the top of an island, of a city that's made of islands and peninsulas. Most of New York is water. Geography is very important. One of the most criminal things you can do on the planet Earth is strip your knowledge and understanding of it and throw a GPS at your ass and make sure you trust that screen. Knowing geography will save you. No matter where you at, know where you at, and respect the people who are in that place and start asking them questions about the place. Know where you living. Because when you start to open up the conversation of geography and history, it makes you understand what culture is about and makes you even overstand what the music that you dig comes from.

I said last week, music is sight, story, sound, and style. As human beings, music is something that we feel. At least knowing where it comes from and the reasons for it can help us understand the art form and develop a road-map going into 2030, 2040, and maybe 2050, if they don't bomb this shit up. Young energy is going to determine the strength of culture taking us into the future. It's important for young energy to absorb the beauty of culture, how it ties us together to our human spirit and not society's differences. It doesn't matter what the fuck you look like. Those are constructs. So when you talk about hip hop, it behooves you to at least define what you love. When you leave this class, you should be able to come up with at least a few reasons why you love hip hop and know why or where it comes from.

Returning to hip hop and its flows and migrations, it also goes from the New York metropolitan area to places like Philadelphia, Pennsylvania, Washington, DC, with the fragment called go-go, then farther out into the West Coast.[4] Once it came to the West, it never came back. It planted itself in this area of Los Angeles, California, which is also the home of Hollywood. How the hell are you going to plant in LA, in Hollywood, which is the controller of imagery across the goddamn planet? How do you think hip hop ain't going to be influenced by that when it's transmitted off to the rest of the world? That's the bomb that we set next to the spook that sat by the goddamn door. Hip hop in Los Angeles next to Hollyweird. "Burn Hollywood, Burn." Hip hop humbly landed in Los Angeles with a sea of politics happening around it in New York.

That's what Jeff deals with in his book. He explains the importance of geography and history and context. Hip hop landed into a political situation that influenced what the music was going to say and where it was going to go. Then, of course, it goes to places like Texas, Louisiana, same place as Congo Square. Before Lil Wayne, it was Master P with his own Black-owned record company, No Limit Records. Before Master P, it was Luke Skyywalker (Uncle Luke) out of Florida. [And J Prince with Rap-A-Lot Records out of Houston.] Why was Luke Skyywalker in Louisiana, in Lake Charles, and all of that? Because nobody in the major record companies out of Los Angeles and New York saw that area as being fertile. New York and Los Angeles deal with New York and Los Angeles, and they didn't think hip hop was going to succeed there in the first place. "Who the hell gives a fuck about the swamp of Texas and Louisiana? Backwater people. They ain't got no money."

Luke Skyywalker, a.k.a Luther Campbell, sets up a company, and he takes over the whole bottom of the US, from Florida, the Panhandle. Let's get geographic. He's in Miami-Dade County, and the rest of Florida, which might not be here because of climate conditions in the next twenty years. Then you got the west coast of Florida, Tampa, then you got the Panhandle. Then you got what? Alabama, the city of Mobile, right across New Orleans, straight over through the bottom of Louisiana, that little Panhandle has Mississippi on top of it. And you got New Orleans, and you're back in Texas. Then you got that whole area off of Galveston up in H-town, and you got the rest of Texas, which is a whole nation in itself. That's the whole bottom that Luke Skyywalker was selling records to. The industry was paying them no attention. Luther Campbell sells some records not just because he threw sex in it, he threw dollars into those records.[5] Then they said, "There's some fertility in the record sales down there. We want that."

Then you had Master P. He advertised every month in *The Source* hip hop magazine with about a thousand records each month that he's releasing. How is he going to do that? How is he going to do Silkk the Shocker and all these other artists? Well, they still ignored that. Until one day they said, "We want that market. That market's got a lot of record sales." They went to Master P and said, "We'll make you an offer you can't refuse." Master P's like, "Go screw yourself. I ain't Luke. I got more territory than Luke ever had." So what did they do? They did what corporations do. "We're going to finance your competitor." Master P had a takeoff on the Masterdon Committee, which is a group out of New York City, with a great instrumentalist named Pumpkin, made hip hop records out of Harlem for Enjoy Records and Profile Records up in New York. Master P actually did a remake fourteen years later of their 1983 song "Funkbox Party," with his song "Make Em Say Uhh." He had his No Limit Army, making videos with it. They went and said, "Alright Master P, we'll take Juvenile, another artist in the area, and put our money behind this thing called Cash Money Records. We're going to finance your competitor."

In a three-year period, from 1997 to the end of 1999, Master P went from being on top of the world, dominating the territory, to looking at a competitor that was well financed from corporations in Los Angeles and New York. So when it comes down to the narration of the culture, you at least got to adhere to the beginning of the revolutionary spirit that was made in the first place. Because once we start getting into the evolution, you start getting into a whole bunch of side effects that will fuck it up. You got to know that history too. But few people could write this book. The young adult edition was also done with another great hip hop historian, David "Davey D" Cook.

Politics shift everything when you talk about this music. Like I said last week, in 1975, I'm getting involved in hip hop, how can I at least not have politics somewhere around me? It wasn't a bad buzz word; it was a part of my existence. Ten years before, in 1965, I'm five years old, I'm getting my polio shot. I would ask questions. "Now, what do civil rights mean? Oh, now we're civilians now, right? We got the right to be civil. We got to ask for it or do we fight for it?" You have people around you like my parents, explaining what the Civil Rights Bill means.[6] We know we don't need it, but obviously it's something that this country better have for us. They got to put it in writing, because when they don't put shit in writing any bullshit can happen. Sometimes watch it when they put it in writing too.

Today I was on KBLA with H. Samy Alim, talking to Tavis Smiley, who has seriously been a portal and a technological force and an outlet for culture, politics, and people to be able to get their word out. The thing that influenced me in hip hop was radio itself, and today I was on a radio station, and it made me feel exactly like the beginning of my days of listening to WLIB radio in New York City, which would break down all the happenings of New York City in order for me to say, "Well, damn, I wanna say something about *something*. I don't gotta be overly political, but I can't just be talking about the same old shit a sixteen-year-old is saying at twenty-six." So it's the type of songs that we made because it meant something to do a song saying, "Yeah, you making this money, but you can't pay your rent." So how could that song be irrelevant as opposed to something that you pretending all goddamn day? "Oh, yeah, we gettin this money." After a while, most people ain't got money listening to somebody who talk about how much money they got. That shit is robotics to me. They're making your ass into a puppet.

Right now, you don't want corporations to have the final say. We have people who put in the work, and they put in face-to-face, eye-to-eye, body-to-body, soul-to-soul work to be able to get a story and to make it honestly as a foundation. I'm proud to say when I read this book—and I've read a lot of books on hip hop—this book spoke from a different vantage point, other than just the facts. It hinted at the reasons behind the facts and broke down the context surrounding hip hop and rap music and where it came from, as well as the reasons why it seems to keep moving forward. We have people's trust alongside it, not just being fanatics of it, but joyously having people feel that they could participate in it. And that's what the corporation angle won't want from you. They don't give a damn if you participate in the narrative; they just want you to be a *consumer* of it. But the music always strongly says, "Come on, let's get down together and have a good time. Speak your piece, your word is as good as mine. Get this party going."

Without further ado, I'd like to bring in Jeff Chang to sit with me. I'ma jump right into this. Why did Kool Herc's family move to the Bronx?

JEFF CHANG: His family had been there for generations in Jamaica. Jamaicans get their independence from Great Britain in 1962. They become part of the Commonwealth. Actually, there's a debate now that coincided with the visit of the royals last year about why Jamaica is still even part of this Commonwealth, right?[7] But when Britain decided that they were going to get out of the empire business, they basically just said, as France and others did, "It's up to you all. You do your thing." So immediately, investments go down. Jobs start drying up. And these original colonizer countries start encouraging folks from the colony to come and become cheap labor in their country. In Britain, they're called the Windrush generation.[8] You literally see in the years following independence a whole bunch of Jamaican folks moving to Britain. I could diverge into Bob Marley. Bob Marley was one of those folks actually who moved to the US, to Delaware for a brief period in the mid-sixties looking for work. Kool Herc's mom was a similar type of person. She was looking for work. She was a nurse. I think she just was able to find a job at the Bronx Hospital. So you had a group of Jamaican immigrant folks who were working alongside Puerto Rican and Black nurses at that hospital. Later on, what you have is folks moving into Brooklyn because, of course, you get Flatbush. They move into Queens, you have Jamaica, Queens.

CHUCK D: When Herc comes to the US in '68, '69, I remember growing up in Long Island, in Nassau. Queens is next door. Brooklyn's next door. We started having Jamaican students in our classroom around '73, '74, who had just moved in. But they were from Brooklyn, or Queens, and on the Southside of New York City. So that makes sense, job proximity. It's the same reason my great-grandmother moved. I asked her a question: "What made you move to New York from Rockingham, North Carolina, in 1937?" She said her sister got a job, and she said another opening was coming up, and there was a place for her to stay up in Harlem. Because that's a big deal from the Bronx where there is a sparse Caribbean population and then Brooklyn where you can go to a lot of different enclaves that make you feel like you never left Montego Bay.

CHANG: Yeah, exactly. Then the other push factor is that you have all kinds of political violence happening in Jamaica. This actually takes hold in the 1970s. This is the backdrop for Bob Marley and his rise. It's interesting because Bob Marley and DJ Kool Herc and Bruce Lee in 1973, it's the beginning of this new global culture. Bob Marley's *Catch a Fire* album comes out in April of '73.[9] You have Herc's party jumping off in August of

1973, and then you have Bruce's movie *Enter the Dragon* opening like a month after he passes away on July 20, 1973, which is literally eight days after that first hip hop party in the Bronx.[10] So 1973 creates the culture that we all live in now. You talk about the importance of culture and the importance of what culture holds. Bruce is upper middle class, Kool Herc was middle class in Jamaica. Bob Marley, you know, dirt poor. But these are folks who are from marginalized communities who break the whole thing open. So we're now living in this world where folks of color can be represented. And of course, you were huge in that as well.

I remember one of the things that you used to say that was just mind-boggling for all was that hip hop was the Black CNN. It's weird to be able to look back on it now because everybody's connected on social media. Everybody is able to access what's happening all the way around the world instantly. We could just pull out our phones and be like, "What kind of dance are they doing in Indonesia?" But back then, it felt like you were pointing out something that was brand-new, that there were no places for young Black folks, urban Black folks, even Black suburban folks, because Black suburban folks are mostly living different from white suburban folks, to be able to tell their stories.

CHUCK D: Because usually, if you say you're the Black CNN, that's saying that the real CNN is not telling your stories. There will be no Black news on CNN unless we have a catastrophe. They say, "Our analytics say that people don't give a fuck about that. So why would we have a positive Black story?" Ted Turner wants numbers. So that's why I called hip hop and rap music the Black CNN, because it automatically by default connected everybody to a vibe. Motown could have been a Black CNN if there were such adherents to it in the sixties. And you know, Berry Gordy called it "the sound of young America." With hip hop, I just said, "Okay, it's not the sound of young America. This is the Black CNN, and young America will follow."

When I was growing up in the sixties, a very important element of Black households was not only the monthly *Ebony* magazine but also *Ebony*'s weekly magazine, *Jet*. If you look at the structure of *Jet* magazine to connect the Black communities, enclaves, Black belts, Black pockets, states from New York to Nebraska, to California, to Arizona, *Jet*'s editorial staff was so thorough in the fifties and sixties that it was like the Black CNN. *Jet* saw that they could be everything to the Black community without any white intervention, with no white filter on Black America. But more important than the photography, it was the amount of news content.

In the 1970s, when I was in my teens, the news had been sliced into half. More pictures, more images. *Jet* centerfold, the Top 20. This is where people got their music, from the *Jet* Top 20 albums and singles. That was like a bible for the Black community. Later, when the Black community started to become more integrated into American society, began the dilution of the content of *Jet* magazine. If you look at the *Jet* magazine Top 20 singles in 1969 and look at it in 1983, you got like two different worlds. There's more style than substance. Back in '69, it was more substance than style. And back in '59, it was really a lot of editorial content, and I think they might have got a little bit out of the *Chicago Defender*. The *Chicago Defender* was the Black newspaper that went to all the Black communities in the South, East, North, and West. So everything rolled through that, culture, photography, etc. It was like the national Black newspaper, and Chicago was the base. John Johnson starts *Ebony* in 1945 as a magazine for Black people looking at *Life* magazine saying, "We can have our own." And in the fifties, I think, was when they introduced *Jet*. It was a tremendous week-to-week update on where you were in the US and the world and who you were. So when Ghana or Jamaica go independent, it's covered in *Jet* magazine. I think there's an *Ebony* and *Jet* museum exhibition in Berlin.[11]

CHANG: I think this is a beautiful thing that you're pointing that out. This is the pre–social media, pre-internet era. But now, there is the opposite problem, which is there's so much media out there. How do you actually get the information that you really need in order to be able to come together to make change?

CHUCK D: Today, everybody has the tool, but net literacy is suspect. Some people know how to read through the misinformation, while others just believe everything that's coming at them. Like I said when I did, "Don't Believe the Hype," it wasn't necessary to say, "Don't believe misinformation." Be like Noam Chomsky and "challenge information." Information today, as opposed to in the eighties, is like a thousand Bruce Lee kicks coming at you. On the one hand, it's so much coming at the average mind that I think minds today are equipped to handle data coming at them better than we were. But on the other, the barrage is not decreasing by any means, and the level of what a mind can handle is being tested. But like you said, when it comes down to the music, we had something that made me say, "Okay, this is a time period that this is the Black CNN." I knew it was a time period because nothing lasts forever. I knew that was a window of time where we could say, "We can grow from this connectivity. Now everybody's connected."

But turning back to your book, what's the difference between the two editions?

CHANG: The first one is twice as long. There's two chapters on you rather than just one in the YA edition. So if you want to find out more about Chuck, you can read the original edition. But the YA edition was an opportunity to take the narrative and add another generation to it. The first book ends in 2001. The second goes from 1968 all the way to 2021. So we start with Black Power and we end with Black Lives Matter. If I were to rewrite the original book, that's how I think we would have done it anyway, because it's just a way of being able to represent the entire arc of a fifty-year process, fifty, sixty-five years.

CHUCK D: What happens in the next five to ten years?

CHANG: I don't know. If I'm still around, maybe we can come back at it, or maybe we're in the metaverse of that time and it's not even a book form anymore.

CHUCK D: It'll be mind paper. Before, we used to look at culture as something that would unlock you and set you free. But also, it's a two-way street, sometimes it can lock you up.

CHANG: The chapter that you assigned to the class illustrates hip hop being on two tracks. This is a period in the nineties where everything is really blowing up. I think it's interesting because you've got that song "No" on your album *The Autobiography of Mistachuck*, which is literally talking about hip hop becoming this global commodity. And on the other hand, you have these individual communities, these scenes that are launching all of these acts in the South, in the Bay Area, and across the country. Your song illustrates this breaking point for hip hop, where it moves from being this form that's accountable to the community, because now the sales are beyond the Black community. You were talking about Luke Skyywalker, when he went gold and platinum on his first records, it was all Black audiences, but no one knew anything about it.

CHUCK D: And no one knew anything about where this record was coming from. Therefore, you take the corporate structures—they have no idea what Lake Charles is. And really, the truth in this country is most people in the US don't know enough about the United States of America. Can't name the fifty states, can't name the cities within these states. But now in these times, no one could ever have anticipated a pandemic where you couldn't leave your crib. So we're in a different place, and the question is how much can hip hop speak to what's about to happen in the next two years like it used to. I'm not a fan of, "Let's go back to how it used to be." No. But in this case, people need a cultural GPS to tell them, "Damn, I want my senses to be up. How am I going to be looked upon and treated here? If I feel like I'm being degraded, for my gender, or my background, the way I look, the way I feel, and the culture is actually disrespecting me, like where do I log on to?"

CHANG: I feel like this is a question for you all: Can hip hop help us move into the future? There's always been that struggle between hip hop as a commodity culture and hip hop as a community culture. One of the things that I don't think that us older folks would be able to talk about is the community piece. We play a different role in the community at our age. We're truth tellers. We're folks who get to point out like, "Oh, watch out for that; that's going to be an obstacle." But it's up to you all to be able to create the movements that will build communities that will take us where we got to go. So, I just avoided your question, but hopefully I did it skillfully [*laughter*].

CHUCK D: That's one of the biggest differences. It might have been a song or a movie, but I knew when I checked out this song or that movie, it felt like a pot of greens. It felt good, you know? I don't know how much of the good feeling can actually be injected into hip hop in the next five years. I think you put a seed in that book, yes hip hop was hip hop, but we definitely tried to get out from under that foot that was stepping on our necks. Hip hop gave us a lot of relief and escapism, and it gave us some answers. Because young energy needs answers. I think young energy has seen that most of the last thirty-five years, adults fucked it up. We left a wack-ass world for them to go forward and live in.

CHANG: One of the things that's always been interesting to me about hip hop is it takes a certain amount of hope on the part of the folks who are creating it, as well as the folks who are in the position now, like we are, to teach it and pass it on. In between there is a huge gap that we're fighting for, like people's minds, hearts, and spirits about this. I agree with you that young energy is what's going to make it happen. But I'm interested in the fact that this culture that we live in is so disposable. It's so "I need mine." It's about individuality. I come from a culture where you're not allowed to say shit until you get to be the age of seventy, you know what I mean? Elders are the folks who are holding it down, and they'll tell you when you should start preparing to become an elder. Like, "Okay, you've been showing up. We see that there's something in you. You're prepared to be a carrier, a stakeholder, somebody who's bearing the culture for the next seven generations." Because that's how they think. So it's interesting because for those of us who are hopeful within hip hop, we've always worked with the young folks. Because we're putting our faith and trust that young folks will be able to move it forward. But at the same time, that stuff can go wild because there's this other culture out there that's leading folks in a different direction. And that's the dominant culture.

I'm wondering if you could talk a little bit more about that. What did artists need to do at that time? I mean, fundamentally, like you said, two turntables, if there was a break in the music, shit could jump off, like that was real. I'm wondering if you could talk a little bit about the artists' responsibility. What was the importance of rockin a party at that particular time, and how has it changed now?

CHUCK D: The responsibility was, "Just be dope." If your ass was wack and wasted people's time. . . . I'm from a time that if you're wasting somebody's time and money, you got a problem leaving here. In the seventies, you had problems leaving if you was wack! Grandmaster Flash would say, "If DJs wasn't correct, they might get shot at." You're wasting people's time and money, and they ain't got no money. Let's go back to West Memphis, Arkansas, 1947. Howlin' Wolf's just getting ready to hit up Chicago. People are drinking corn liquor. They're working in the yards of West Memphis, across the bridge, dirt poor. They're going to the little juke joint club that's taking like fifty cent each person, while so and so in there is going to be playing piano or the guitar. Entertainment better be poppin! Because if it ain't, they're mad you got their money, and at the same time they gotta go to work the next fucking day.

In the beginning of hip hop, the acts were so good, you didn't even want a drink. If I wanted to check out Melle Mel, I didn't want to be drunk or high. I wanted to get this hip hop at a hundred percent unfiltered dopeness. That's why they called it "dope," because it replaced dope. All you had to do in the Bronx is go back five years and see cats shooting up heroin in their arms. Nobody wanted that life. You had old head Vietnam patriots with purple hearts, and they shooting up and they had to wean the Vietnam vets off the drugs and the Agent Orange that they were exposed to in Vietnam as soldiers. Because you're up there in Southeast Asia, and like Muhammad Ali said, you're fighting an enemy that they say is your enemy, but you're looking at people like people. But they say, "Your ass better go there."

That's why I wrote "Black Steel in the Hour of Chaos." 1967, I'm at my grandparents' house, my uncle is there, just got out of high school. "Boom, boom, boom!" Knocks on the door. Military, Marines. Officers say, "John Robinson?" He goes to the door, gives him a letter, goes to his car, goes around the block to also drop off letters to other newly fresh-faced high school graduates in June of 1967. John opens up the letter, reads it. I'm seven years old, so it ain't like I'm four. He reads it, drops the letter on the table, goes in the back stone faced. Come to find out he got drafted by the United States Marines. You are to report to camp in June next week en route to Southeast Asia, Vietnam, to fight. These things that we addressed were real things in our life. We addressed and we confronted them. There was a rhyme and reason for a lot of those particular things.

In the seventies, people seriously did not want their time wasted, because they didn't feel like they owned their time. Today, what do you feel belongs to you? I would say that now you have to watch out for the real estate of your mind. Because the conquerors and governments, they've already conquered every tangible inch of the planet anyway. That's why all that superficial talk comes up with like, "Oh yeah, well, maybe we'll oxidize Mars and maybe we'll figure out if we can create something that makes Venus habitable. And we got the James Webb telescope showing that another galaxy that possibly if we can travel past the speed of light . . ." All this ridiculous fucking shit, right? Whereas on Earth, they said they sold every single inch, and you got modern-day czars, like eighty-year-old Biden talking to a seventy-year-old Putin about what you can't do as far as taking territory when there's only still one Earth. So a young person, twenty-one years old, looks at an eighty-year-old president talking to the seventy-year-old wannabe Hitler guy and thinks, "What the fuck is going on? Do I own my time?" Now people wondering, "What's the real estate ownership of my mind?"

I don't care if you dig me or not, but I want you to leave this room with your own mind, because it's hard to make up your mind if somebody already got it under their control. This is why we say that artificial intelligence will be governing in every mindset in the next four to five years in ways that we can't see right now. So when they talk about World War III, it could already be in its beginning stages, and it ain't got nothing to do with weapons and bombing. Weapons and bombing is last century. The bombing could be inside your mind. When you think I'm thinking for my free self, these are my thoughts. And you start looking, like, "Wow, this ain't my thought, and I'm trapped mentally inside this physical body. I can't get out of it. Whoa. Mind control is happening." This is what the art form fought against. At least that's what I thought I fought against in making hip hop music to actually be subversive and go underneath the battle zone.

CHANG: Going back to the Bronx in 1973 and what they're jamming to, you were saying, Kool Herc puts on Bob Marley or he puts on a reggae tune or rocksteady tune. People are like, "What the fuck is this?" They don't want to dance to it. But you put on Jimmy Castor, you put on James Brown, and everybody fills the floor. So there's two things going on. One is the beats per minute. If you're a DJ, rocksteady is at eighty bpm, and if you wanted to amp it up, you could go double time and you could just be jumping around like it was a rock song. But when you really want to get dancing, you want to be up in that 115–125 range. When you did "Bring the Noise," it was like 109 to 114. So that's what they want to dance to in the Bronx. The Bronx is faster than Jamaica. It's the type of thing where people want to move. It's cold, they want to stay warm. You got to keep moving.

I grew up in Hawai'i, and the music there is folk music. It is country music. The generation before me was folk music. It was slack-key guitar *ki ho'alu*, and that kind of stuff. For me, listening to funk music or listening to the eighties stuff, when it goes to electro, I'm like, "Where do these beats even come from?" Just listening to the music was an education. Because if you're thinking about what's happening in that moment, in the music, you've got James Brown going to Africa. You got Jimmy Castor meeting the *salsero* musicians. You got folks on the West Coast like Santana, who are mixing up Chicano rock with soul beats. You got folks in the Bronx doing Boogaloo, which is basically a mix of R&B and Latin rhythms done in a four/four. You got basically the sound of all of these rhythms from across West Africa that have been distributed across all of the fucking so-called New World by slavery, coming back together in the break. Even if you go to Trap now, it's the same type of vibe. You got all of the Afro-Caribbean, Afro-Latin tinge on the music. It's got a swing to it, and it's in the clave a lot of times.

CHUCK D: And in the sixties and seventies, Santana might have had a player inside his band that introduced another vibe.

CHANG: Exactly, percussionist, *timbalero*.

CHUCK D: I think what today's music and tomorrow's music can offer to take it to the next zone is a reintroduction to musical collaborations. Because we've seen everything reduced to solo acts. I think that's cool to a certain point, but where does it grow from there? The only thing it could grow into is collaboration. When you have one solo producer and one solo artist, what they don't do as much is they don't go into third gear. And third gear is introducing a sonic to that sampling of sound that takes it to a totally different place. I think that's on the horizon musically for hip hop, and that's what we haven't seen out of music makers, since technology has made it easy for one person to lock it down in the laptop or in the lab.

CHANG: If you look at it like the way that we work now, our jobs, you're sitting there in front of a computer, and under COVID, you're not even in the same place with anybody anymore. So you're tethered to all these folks all around the world, and you're isolated. Actually, hip hop, when it moved from the turntables to the production stuff, you guys were all still in the same room when you were making the music. You guys were still doing analog, but you were experimenting as a group.

CHUCK D: We came from that basic understanding that even if you're not in the same room, your head is in so many similar places. So you could pick up a segment, and then at the end of the day, it's going to be evaluated by four or five people. That's the important thing. I was half-confused by the Grammys because I said, "Well, what makes these people different from an independent artist that delivers their music on SoundCloud?" What keeps the independent person that might make music in this room from being part of the academy? Is it numbers? Is it if they're dope? And what about this artist that's been doing it in their community of three or four people? Does that count? What made Picasso different from another artist on his block? Was it the quantity, the quality, the style? In this academic context, you hope that these questions are seeds that sprout into a forum about how we receive and engage ourselves in the arts, because we need to have this type of activity to consider it being part of an arts program of the next fifty years.

CHANG: It comes back down to what you were talking about earlier, which is community and the artist's relationship to the community, and then for artists to be in community with each other, and out of that the learning that happens. Returning to this point about the music, I'm hearing all of this stuff in the music and that actually opens up all of these things for me to learn. "Where does this rhythm come from? What is it a part of? What are these lyrics about?" The music is leading me into all these different directions to actually be able to really understand Black freedom cultures, and that's leading me into the Black Freedom movement.

In this moment, young people have access to stuff past, present, future, global, much more than we ever did. We had to go out and search for African music. Now, Afro-pop becomes a thing right away. All the variations. South African *amapiano*, stuff that's coming out of Ghana and Nigeria. And everybody is using this template that comes from Black freedom culture, from Black music—or we should just say Black music in America. That's the way people produce stuff, the way people hear the music now, that's the way people want it to move. That's the ideal. So in that music is the seeds of something that's really liberating all around the world. As opposed to the old style, which was like a Black artist makes a song and then they have to give it to a white artist to cover it so that they can actually sell it. That's a revolutionary change that's happened like before our lifetimes. And you've been leading in that revolution to be able to take it around the world so folks can actually see how all of these things relate, and then everybody can be able to tell their story. But the question is, What are the stories that are going to get lifted up by us? What are the sounds? What are the things that bring us together? Are we going to start seeing things in a global kind of a way, as opposed to seeing it just in terms of a "USA, USA, USA" type of thing?

CHUCK D: What do you think about the US's bias on culture and music in hip hop? I've been to 116 countries, thanks to hip hop. If this was the Olympics, where would the US rank? From 1998 on, I'm not sure if the US would be getting the gold or even the silver. But then again, if you want to hold on to the US's arrogance, of course, you'd do the same Trump pep rally thing saying that everybody else is wack and we're the greatest. Sam is from the second largest hip hop nation in the world. But if you don't know a French rap song, does that mean that they're wack or that you're wack? Are their mouths wack, or are your ears wack? Because you can't connect because you don't know what they're saying, then you *definitely* ain't trying to hear an MC that's spitting three languages on one song. Well, I know MCs that spit two languages and braid them in the same bar. And they can flip and turn bars and juggle bars. When does this country acknowledge this brilliance as competition?

It would be great if we were more globally minded in the US, but like I said, I can't even transfer the feeling of that realm of hip hop between 1976 and 1981, where it was better than any drug. Of course, because of the areas that it was in, the music grew out of drug-laden territories. New York City at that time, where hip hop evolved, you're at the beginning of the cocaine wars. After they had the "undesirables" coming out of Vietnam, and people rejected, "No, I'm not going to shoot heroin up in my veins. No, that's some Vietnam shit." They reintroduced weed in the city streets. Then for some reason, weed disappeared from every area in the New York metropolitan area, and it was the introduction of cocaine from 1975, '76 and '77. There was an initial rejection of cocaine on the streets. Cats wanted weed. Old heads associated cocaine with *Superfly*, and they associated heroin to Vietnam vets.

That was the first doorways opening up to cocaine in the New York City area in '76, '77, '78. Now, these discussions of the area that people like Frank Lucas, Nicky Barnes, had something to do with people finding out later on. But I'm saying that the drug culture and the music culture was head to head with each other. And the hip hop culture that came out of that was rebellious to the disco culture in some ways. The entertainment had to be perfect to keep people distracted from drama. That's where I remember you could cut hip hop with a knife for how dope it was. I don't know if there was going to be another time where something is going to be so infectious that that's all I want.

CHANG: You don't think it's just you getting older?

CHUCK D: Of course. I'm old as hell [*laughter*].

CHANG: The thing that I love about what you just broke down is music is the most social art form of all art forms. Music is something that you actually enjoy best when you play it for somebody else and that person is reacting to it in real time and space with you. If you're in a crowded room and everybody is jumping to a particular song, that song is automatically going to sound better than if you heard it in a room alone. Music is community building. And what you're talking about with the phone use is that our media has changed so that it's isolating us.

CHUCK D: We're bringing the essence of something that can't easily be explained, but it is felt. This is a large part of what the culture is. A lot of it is to be *felt*. How do you explain a feeling? How do you process a feeling that has also tried to be commodified into a product? Sometimes you can't put the feeling into a bottle. They damn sure are going to try, and they're going to try to sell to y'all first.

H. SAMY ALIM: In listening to the conversation, two or three things struck me. One is, Chuck, the chilling effect of thinking about the mind as the real estate of the next century, that comment will stay with me. I hope it stays with folks, especially since we know the big tech companies are already trying to embed AI into every facet of university life. Two is thinking about, Jeff, when you said that the hip hop heads that are the most hopeful are those that work with youth. I want to connect those two points in order to think about pedagogies and futures. In many ways, Jeff, when me, you, and Casey worked on *Freedom Moves: Hip Hop Knowledges, Pedagogies, and Futures*, we began working with East Palo Alto Mural Music and Arts Project (MMAP) and Sonya Clark-Herrera and others.[12] So, there's a generation of folks who have embedded themselves at the community organizing level who come between those who you write about in *Can't Stop Won't Stop* and the young people who are seated here. They're hip hop. They're not the artists producing it right now, but they're hip hop on this level, and they're working in the community organizing space.

I think of MMAP in East Palo Alto, and I think of Kuumba Lynx in Chicago, Black, Latinx, and Indigenous women, leading these organizations.[13] They put on these projects where the youth involved in hip hop culture get to investigate their own communities, police departments, their mayors. And they have major victories like reparations in terms of hip hop education, in terms of investigating policing, etc. I think of Jasiri X in Pittsburgh, and 1Hood.[14] That project there is raising the critical literacy of youth and is also from someone of that generation. This hip hop organizing is happening in every major city in the US.

I also think of a lot of the work that goes on overseas and where hip hop's future is multilingual. It's a whole movement that's not bound by national borders. I think of Susi Álvarez Mariño and La Llama Rap Colectivo in El Raval in Barcelona, same thing.[15] She's like "the twin sister" of Sonya Clark-Herrera in East Palo Alto. They formed these youth organizations, and now entire generations of youth are coming through these organizations. That's their entryway into hip hop culture. It's not just the music that they're hearing. They're in the organization and they're feeling the community vibe that you're talking about in a very real way.

The last example I will give, of course, is Heal the Hood in South Africa with Emile YX? and a whole crew out there in Cape Town.[16] They have played the role of not just the artists that are setting it off in Cape Town historically, but they're playing that mediator role through community organizations in helping raise the next generation of hip hop heads and artists. So, I'm thinking about what you're saying about the mind being that real estate, Chuck, and also how hope comes from working with youth, Jeff, and trying to find a way that we can counteract that occupation of our minds. That's how hip hop will bring us into the future.

CHANG: To relate to Samy's point, and again you all know the greatness of Chuck D, but you still don't really know the greatness of Chuck D. One of the things that Chuck would do is he'd go to different cities, and he would meet with folks like the community organizations there, the artists, the organizers, and sit with them in an exchange of ideas. Chuck would share his wisdom and knowledge. In that way, you would see all these things sprouting. Afrika Bambaataa used to do this, too, wherever he went in Europe and Japan. So Chuck and Public Enemy were carrying on the

Zulu Nation tradition. Out of that, all of these revolutionary groups got started all around the world, in Africa, Brazil . . .

CHUCK D: When you went into a place, you wanted to show them that they could do it, too, if not better. But that's just how human beings operate anyway. You want to encourage them. That's why the arts were always great. "Wow, I'm a fan of that. Could you play that again?" If you have somebody that could show you how to play that thing that you were fascinated with, I think that's a brilliant beginning into self-discovery. I think the beautiful thing about young energy is if you get young energy to find something that they can discover to take on themselves, to be able to participate in, with proper teaching and without the teaching being too loaded up, I think you got a person who's gonna do it forever.

QUESTION 1: What are your thoughts on the commercialization of hip hop?

CHUCK D: I believe that you need teachers and curators in any industry that claims that it's going to commodify arts and culture. I think we need more people like everybody in this room, more students, more Samys, more Jeffs. People that mediate. If it's big business, then what's the distribution of the big business then? If it's a part of capitalism, then where is that capital being shared, without the usual complaint of "Oh that's socialism, they're sharing all that music"? The problem I think that the industry has had is being a closed industry which hasn't embraced all of the machinery's parts in order for this to be prosperous all the way across the board. If it remains a closed industry, then that's just somebody selling you a product saying, "Only thing you're good for is spending your money."

The Coachella music festival is a very clear example. You're going to come to see all these acts in exchange for your money. You are just going to be a fan. You're an audience, and that's it. They're not asking you if you aspire to be an artist yourself or the work you put in your artistry. The industry is like, "Oh, we try to sell you this product for three times the amount that we sold it to people ten years ago." That's the crime. But the only reason you up in here is because you was able to afford that ticket.

The Travis Scott debacle was just so crazy.[17] It's not so much "Oh yeah Travis has Satanism going on." No. There's gotta be somebody that put him in that building. There's gotta be somebody that owns that building, who's accountable. You don't leave it up to the artist to be controlling the crowd like that. That building better control every single life that comes in there. Their number one objective is safety. Travis doesn't own no building. He'll come in and do his act. When his act goes a little bit crazy, that's when the building should cut the sound. I'm telling you how buildings acted back in the day. Number one, the sound. It's the first thing they cut out. Then the mayor probably step up like, "Ladies and gentlemen we had to cut this concert." That's called crowd control.

And that ticket price is basically Live Nation trying to get their money back for the last four years. My oldest daughter is right here [*pointing to his daughter*]. Late nineties, take her and her friends to a concert. Seven acts on it. The only ones that could throw a big hip hop conglomerate concert was radio stations because the promoters got priced out. So the radio stations would have the only ability to pay for the acts because they're part of the corporate big wheel and they get into the new buildings. Therefore, the tickets would be like $100 tickets. I'm giving you 2004 prices. So I drive them. They're seventeen. They see the show. I pick them up in my 1994 Montero. They all get in the truck. I say, "How was the concert?" And they all like, "It was alright." I'm like, "Y'all paid $100, and y'all only getting a 'alright'?" Number one thing going on with young audiences is they just happy to be out anywhere without you. The problem is, when Live Nation charges you three times as much as ten years ago, that shit ain't no damn inflation. That shit is robbing you.

How much is Coachella? Three hundred dollars for three days. This is Live Nation getting their money back. They can't get it back without a new generation coming who can't wait to get into the world and be together. It's not the music's fault. I would like the industry, building administrations and authorities to do a better job in taking care of young people who are going inside those huge places. Back in the days in hip hop, there was concern on how you left, because if you left the concert like, "Yo, that shit was dope!," they knew you were coming back. And they knew they had to take care of that building because if one hip hop incident went down, they weren't getting that building again. That thing that happened with Travis Scott, you best believe it had a resonating effect over hip hop artists or those type of artists. But mainstream white artists are going to be able to get in there. Everybody's going to be able to get in, except the hip hop thing.

ALIM: Part of what Chuck's also talking about is the "gentrification of hip hop culture." You know what it means when Brown and Black communities are gentrified. Think about what it means when culture is gentrified. The question you're asking is, What happens when culture gets commodified? That's the root question. We live inside the belly of a capitalist beast. It's inevitable that culture will be commodified. You got scholars like Robin D. G. Kelley, Gaye Theresa Johnson, and others who have been exploring that question for decades.[18] That's the complexity of what you're asking.

The other part of the complexity has to do with a conversation that I had with dream hampton just the other day. There was a big conference in the UK. It was dream, Tricia Rose, KRS-One. And dream said she's still dealing with something that Tricia Rose said on that stage, which is, "Hip hop has become the cultural arm of capitalism." Just think about that phrase for a second. Not that all of hip hop is the cultural arm of capitalism, but we used to speak about hip hop culture in real terms as the cultural arm of the freedom movement, the same way the Black Arts movement was the cultural arm of the Black Power movement. So when you think about the cultural arm of a movement, do you think of Dr. Dre and the Superbowl Halftime show with respect to what that meant for Kaepernick and those who supported his critique of the NFL? Y'all forgot about Kaepernick already.[19] But when you think about that dynamic, the question still remains: What do you do if hip hop is perceived as the cultural arm of capitalism? That's a whole different kind of question.

I'll tell you a perspective that comes from my engagement in South Africa. I spend a lot of time with that community of artists, some of the dopest, most creative people you will ever find on the hip hop planet. Talk about rapping in three languages, Chuck, try like seven or eight. The creativity is through the roof! I'm saying this to say that I have debates with them all day and all night. Because people want to look at US hip hop culture and be like, "Oh yeah, yeah, yeah they not talking about nothing." I said, the difference is you can't hardly make a dime off of hip hop in Cape Town. But what happens when culture gets commodified? Who's pushing the buttons? Is it payola on the station or in the concert arena? What does the culture look like when you can't make a dime versus when you can make a few million dollars off of it? All of a sudden, culture starts to shift as it becomes a commodity that can then be bought and sold for incredible amounts of money. So that's the depth of that question that I think you're asking, and it's one to grapple with every single week of this course: What happens when culture is commodified?

QUESTION 2: In the Arab world, after the Arab Spring, there was a lot of hip hop coming out.[20] Soon after, rap music there entirely changed. Do you think there are governmental or institutional forces against rap?

CHANG: Just to recount, there were a lot of youth uprisings that led to the Arab Spring, and hip hop played a really crucial role in that. Of course, with the backlash that shuts down a lot of these revolutionary movements, hip hop culture changes. So the question had to do with governmental institutions, corporate institutions. What I say is, there's a big case study in both versions of the book that gets into something specific to Los Angeles. Right after the LA uprisings in 1992, what you see is the far right actively targeting hip hop and trying to get rap artists off of their labels.[21] Chuck was one of the targets of all of this. Ice-T, of course, one of his best friends, was the person who absorbed the brunt of it. But literally, you have this political far right movement that's affiliated with the police. You got some of this in that movie *Straight Outta Compton*. The NRA, Charlton Heston, all of these folks coming together and trying to shut this stuff down.

This is, in part, what Chuck is talking about, about the danger of culture to institutions and to governance. The thing about it is that the cultural resistance is not going to go away. I'm sure the folks that were there in the Arab Spring who put out this music, they're not gone. Some of them may have been made martyrs actually, but they're not gone. So that's the opportunity always for culture to be able to represent community. But this is something that you should really answer, Chuck, as somebody who was at the front line.

CHUCK D: They wait for things to be culturally relevant to a new generation and then age it out. They can age out a struggle by shortening generations. If you're twenty-two, they make another generation at nineteen, and you will have nothing relatable with nineteen-year-olds, and nobody twenty-six years old is relating to you. Where really, it's the same generation, but they chopped the generations up to dissipate the movements. There's a natural order of younger people rebelling against something older. But is it natural that you rebel against somebody three years older? But you could throw more things in the middle of the mix and create a larger divide if you refer to them as different generations. And once you've got generations divided, you can do anything with it. I think you have to stay relevant to the cause of any movement instead of thinking that it has age categories.

QUESTION 3: Hip hop artists across all generations have often been dehumanized. That prevents us from taking seriously the issues that hip hop artists are bringing up, especially in today's time, unless they're like Kendrick Lamar or J. Cole. But someone like Pop Smoke, they don't understand what he's talking about. How do we begin to see the humanity in these artists, particularly those that are seen as gangbangers rather than intellectual thinkers and critics of their society?

CHANG: I think it's partly an individual process. Part of it is how we're seeing and hearing these artists and how we're interpreting these artists and what they mean to us. Any good artist, as Chuck would tell you, is somebody who you can't just easily stereotype. They're going to be complicated. They're going to be contradictory. They're going to be somebody who has a lot of different sides to them. It's so important for artists to feel like they're being seen for the stuff that we want to uphold in them. Case in point number one is Tupac Shakur. I think that that's part of the hard lesson that a lot of us learned, particularly those of us who had followed Tupac's career from the early nineties when he was a dancer for Digital Underground, all the way on up. Tupac is coming up during this period where suddenly, all this money is coming into hip hop. He gets out there, and he feels like he's getting rewarded for controversy, for stirring up shit with other folks. He's a very complicated individual. He's a guy who writes a song called "Dear Mama," and he's somebody who's convicted of sexual assault.

CHUCK D: We participated in putting Tupac on and helping him in his first film, *Juice*, 1991. His role in there is on some psycho tip, but he's showing his acting chops, real street b-boy film, one of the first of its kind in the nineties. The next movie, John Singleton puts Tupac in a positive role in *Poetic Justice* where he's trying to keep his head straight. And what Tupac saw, as far as the critical analysis and accolades, is that in *Juice*, he was lauded as this second coming hip hop's version of James Dean. With *Poetic Justice*, it was, "Tupac fell off." That was the consensus.

Tupac's next movie was what? *Above the Rim*. Aggressive. He's acting his ass off, so he could act any role. But he had seen everybody put him up on this pedestal for certain roles. And when he tried to do the right thing, they lowered him. That also means that this Black male hip hop stereotype started permeating across the American mainstream. The next movie, he was like, "Yo, I'm a thug, and it's going to go down!" That fascination didn't necessarily come from just the Black audience. It came from a US audience like, "Wow, hip hop, that's how they be. Don't touch it, and don't get close to it. But I still want to buy into it because it's exciting."

Pac saw this difference, even in his music. "Brenda's Got a Baby" moving into "Dear Mama," which is to me the most courageous song that you ever could make. It was a song about Black women and Black mothers. Those songs were harder to make than thug shoot-'em-up songs. Anybody can make those. They wouldn't make a song about their mother. That's hard to do. He did it and pulled it off.

One time, Ice-T and I were waiting for Pac to come over and be part of this America's Most Wanted tour in Europe. The tour was Ice-T, Public Enemy, and we brought Tupac along. Ice-T and me are waiting, and all of a sudden, we find out that Pac got shot up. He survives, goes to jail. But as far as the bullshit of street cred—what the fuck is street cred?—in 1995, his street cred persona went through the roof! He kept playing into that because then Suge gets him out of jail. They don't want no *Poetic Justice* Pac. You gotta move these joints. And Pac was a whole bunch of personalities. So right there, that arm of capitalism put him in a chokehold, saying, "Yeah you're going to be this character."

With everybody, you always need somebody to come along and say, "Yo, yo, yo, you're slipping, slow down." Couple of times, I would run into Pac, he wouldn't even look me in the eye. He'd look at my kneecaps. But he was also, "Yo, I'll turn it around, but I'm going to get the large audience first, and I'm going to flip it." And I'm like, "Yeah, but time ain't on everybody's side. You're bringing goon headache to the party, and you're not a goon headache dude."

But one thing Pac was, is a muthafuckin hell of an actor. This is right at the turn when you can look at something and emulate it. Back then, actors couldn't really do that in the 1970s because you couldn't go to the videotape or your phone. You had to basically act off of paper and then go into acting mode or be in the middle of some theater. Pac had that background where he could go off of paper and come up with a persona. Pac had the experience so he could act like anybody. This was new in the nineties where he could do this in a street way, like "I'm going to be that dude for real." Today you see a lot of that cause cats can damn near emulate five or six different personas, but Pac was able to do that in a time where it was not even seen. He moved every circle that he was in and captivated his circle. He was a real dude, but he could throw on that extra spice that throw a mode on to get you like leaned in on it.

The problem is, when you lean in and throw that mode on, what are you going to attract? You are going to attract real goons to a real goon party. And real goons are going to be like, "All I do is street shit, and all I do is shoot shit up." That's what Pac got caught up with, some real muthafuckas. You got real cats like, "You know what, my life expectancy, I don't even know." Cats would tell him, "You're in music and movies. Be over there." Pac was a loyalist too. He would show that "I'm down and I'm a real dude. I'm gonna be down for you." But as your parents might tell you, your OGs, "Be careful with the crowd you run with. Choose your friends wisely. Choose your surroundings wisely. You don't know everybody. Make sure you got some distance before you break somebody in your cipher." Basic shit. Not to say he didn't have it. He knew it, but that was his dance.

You know, Pop Smoke—all these cats, though, Nipsey—they didn't shoot themselves. It wasn't a suicide. They got shot by somebody. So this is a problem when somebody actually feels that they gonna get somebody. These were assassinations. And when the authorities look the other way, it's a problem. This is why when Eric Adams in New York City says, "I'm going to put a hold on drill rappers because they're using code with each other." We need to get in the middle of this shit and try to guide it. I'm not saying it's the same shit that's connected to Sacramento. But in Sacramento, you got cats who code with each other, and how they coded each other out and what beef they might have had that ended up being a public problem. You got to catch the code. A lot of the music now is cats coding each other. "I'm coding it deep in the bars on the second verse. Nobody knows what the fuck I'm talking about, but dawg, you know what I'm talking about, and you know who I'm talking to." So it's different from the police chief thirty-five years ago. This police chief knows what drill is. He knows who's doing what.

He might not know their names, but he says, "I know what is happening. I'm fifty-five years old. I'm from Brooklyn. I'm not stupid." You got to be on top of culture, like, "This is what they're trying to say with this music."

But what if we thought about ways to respond other than punishment? Can we give a great opportunity for this person to maybe teach something? Can there be a summer job for people that just want to spit and rap and dance? I'm pretty sure the city or the county could pay for some part of the arts. My point is you can employ a lot of people out of crazy shit but it takes a community to change things and turn things around. And that's why we're embedded in the culture. Can the community protect and assist the culture? Whenever the community doesn't get involved with at least helping the culture have a platform and a voice then you can't expect the culture to protect the community.

NOTES

1. See Jeff Chang, *Can't Stop Won't Stop: A History of the Hip-Hop Generation* (St. Martin's, 2005); and the young adult edition, coauthored with David "Davey D" Cook (St. Martin's, 2021).

2. See Freddi Williams Evans, *Congo Square: African Roots in New Orleans* (University of Louisiana Press, 2011).

3. Eisenhower's sweeping infrastructure legislation resulted in the displacement of many Black communities. See Chang, *Can't Stop Won't Stop* for how builders of the Cross Bronx Expressway, for example, bulldozed through Black communities in the Bronx.

4. See Kip Lornell and Charles C. Stephenson Jr., *The Beat: Go-Go's Fusion of Funk and Hip Hop* (University of Michigan Press, 2001).

5. On the literary and cultural significance of the legal cases involving 2 Live Crew, see Houston Baker, *Black Studies, Rap, and the Academy* (University of Chicago Press, 1993).

6. See Clayborne Carson, *Civil Rights Chronicle: The African-American Struggle for Freedom* (Publications International, 2003).

7. On Jamaica's referendum for independence from the British monarchy, see Emiliano Rodriguez Mega, "Charles Is Jamaica's Head of State," *New York Times*, May 6, 2023, https://www.nytimes.com/2023/05/06/world/americas/jamaica-monarchyreferendum.html.

8. See the oral history by Colin Grant, *Homecoming: Voices of the Windrush Generation* (Vintage, 2020).

9. For more on the cultural impact of Bruce Lee, see Jeff Chang, *Water Mirror Echo: Bruce Lee and the Making of Asian America* (HarperCollins, 2025).

10. See Chang and Cook, *Can't Stop Won't Stop*, 15–18.

11. In 2019, Theater Gates in Berlin hosted an exhibit titled *The Black Image Corporation*, featuring images from the Johnson Publishing Company archive, the entity that owned *Ebony* and *Jet* magazines. See https://www.theastergates.com /exhibitions/the-black-image-corporation.

12. Mural Music and Arts Project (MMAP), founded by Sonya Clark-Herrera, is a nonprofit organization in East Palo Alto, California. See Sonya Clark-Herrera with Measha Ferguson Smith, hodari blue aka Adorie Howard, Reagan Ross, and Casey Philip Wong, "Ripples of Hope and Healing: Sustaining Community by Creating a Social Justice Arts Ecosystem," in *Freedom Moves: Hip Hop Knowledges, Pedagogies, and Futures*, ed. H. Samy Alim, Jeff Chang, and Casey Philip Wong (University of California Press, 2023), 193–212.

13. Kuumba Lynx is a youth-based arts program located in Chicago. See Jucinda Bullie, Jacquanda Salter-Villegas, and Leyda "Lady Sol" Garcia, "'Protection from Police Who Hinder Respiratory Airways': Hip Hop Theatre and Activism with Kuumba Lynx in Chicago," in *Freedom Moves*, 180–92.

14. Jasiri X is involved with 1Hood Media, an organization committed to social justice via the arts. See Jasiri X, "1Hood: Hip Hop Art, Activism, and Media Creation in Pittsburgh," in *Freedom Moves*, 159–79.

15. For more on the work of Susi Álvarez Mariño, see La Llama Rap Colectivo with H. Samy Alim, "'Luchando Derechos' in Neoliberal Spain: Hip Hop Visions beyond Racism, Xenophobia, Islamophobia, and the Gentrification of El Raval, Barcelona," in *Freedom Moves*, 131–56.

16. Heal the Hood, founded by Emile YX?, is a community organization based in Cape Town, South Africa. Read more about their important work: H. Samy Alim, Quentin Williams, Adam Haupt, and Emile Jansen, "'Kom Khoi San, kry trug jou land': Disrupting White Settler Colonial Logics of Language, Race, and Land with Afrikaaps," *Journal of Linguistic Anthropology* 31, no. 2 (2021): 194–217.

17. In 2021, ten people were crushed to death by crowds at Travis Scott's performance at his Astroworld Festival in Houston. See Leah Willingham and Ken Miller, "10 People Died at the Astroworld Music Festival Two Years Ago. Will Anyone Be Held Accountable?" Associated Press, July 29, 2023, on the search for accountability: https://apnews.com/article/travis-scott-astroworld-music-festival-deathsceded7d0ea08d71b5ce32d4b8218a3fe

18. See Robin D.G. Kelley, *Yo Mama's Disfunktional! Fighting the Culture Wars in Urban America* (Beacon Press, 1998); and Gaye Theresa Johnson, *Spaces of Conflict, Sounds of Solidarity: Music, Race, and Spatial Entitlement in Los Angeles* (University of California Press, 2013).

19. Colin Kaepernick made headlines in 2016 when he refused to stand for the national anthem because of the rampant police murders of Black people in the US. See Kurt Streeter, "Kneeling, Fiercely Debated by the N.F.L, Resonates in Protests," *New York Times*, June 5, 2020, https://www.nytimes.com/2020/06/05/sports/football/georgefloyd-kaepernick-kneeling-nfl-protests.html.

20. See Rayya El Zein, "From 'Hip Hop Revolutionaries' to 'Terrorist-Thugs': 'Blackwashing' between the Arab Spring and the War on Terror," *Lateral: Journal of the Cultural Studies Association* 5, no. 1 (Spring 2016).

21. This conversation between Jeff Chang and Chuck D occurred just prior to the thirtieth anniversary of the LA uprisings, which occurred on April 29, 1992, after the acquittal of LAPD officers for their grotesque, video-taped beating of Rodney King, an unarmed Black man. See the *Los Angeles Times* series "The L.A. Riots, 30 Years Later," *Los Angeles Times*, April 28, 2022, https://www.latimes.com/california/story/2022-04-27/full-coverage-30-years-since-the-1992-la-riots.

3 Don't Believe the Hype

TECHNOLOGY, MEDIA, AND THE IMPORTANCE OF COMMUNITY

Chuck D and Davey D

CHUCK D: Our conversation this week is with a gentleman who back in the days of the telephone, before they had cameras, we used to get on the phone and chop it up for hours at a time. I'd just be a sponge and try to absorb everything that he was saying. He also would be somebody who would give futuristic advice on where the music should go from a technical standpoint and also from an aesthetic standpoint. This is a guy that came from the Bronx. I don't know if he was born in the Bronx, but he definitely had Bronx written all over his forehead [*laughter*]. I took instructions from this great man and then we befriended each other.

Earlier [chapter 1], Robin D. G. Kelley asked me some questions about my beginnings. The first record that I did as a member of Public Enemy was called *Yo! Bum Rush the Show*, and the meaning of that title is, if you can't get in the door and you're on the outside, then you posse up as a collective and you get in that door! If you could get a toe into a place that doesn't want you on the inside, then once that door is open, BOOM! You and about a thousand other people are inside. I learned that experience from being on the other side of being a concert party promoter, head of security, trying to keep people on the outside from sneaking in. We were very familiar with bum-rushing the door from the outside, and also from the inside, trying to get in places that we weren't wanted.

Hip hop wasn't the favorite music of that particular time. It was the underclass. I was one of those parking-lot dudes. It was poppin inside the club, but I was happy to be in the parking lot, and we had a bigger party in the parking lot than they had inside the club because we did not wear shoes. Only guys in the Bronx, they wore playboys, uptowns. We're from Long Island. My first pair of what I called shoes was leather Puma Clydes. They were the official b-boy shoe of the late seventies. Walt "Clyde" Frazier is a Hall of Fame basketball player. *Yo! Bum Rush the Show* signified those beginnings.

It Takes a Nation of Millions to Hold Us Back and going into that period of '88 and '89, that was a nationalist record. Collectively, us finding ourselves working, fighting for hip hop, for our people, for Blackness, making sure we connected in the US as a force to be reckoned with and not be stomped upon. It's a very aggressive record. It was punkish in many ways. It had to stand out amongst the beginning of the golden era of hip hop. When I say the golden era of hip hop, it was a singles medium, meaning an A side and a B side. When we did *It Takes a Nation of Millions*, it was our second album, but it also signified the beginning of albums being packageable, meaning that they could now package a hip hop album as being the item coming from a rap artist, as opposed to albums evolving out of singles. Many of us think that that was just a natural evolution. It was evolutionary to big business that it happened because the technical tools that we had in the early eighties—turntables, microphones, speakers—they were pretty rudimentary. You couldn't carry your speakers and your turntables on your back, although people in the Bronx tried to do that.

We also need to consider the technical aspects of rap music at that time: boomboxes, cassette players, how people recorded off the radio, how they made their own little mixtapes, how the cassette culture was able to permeate inside the record business at the particular time and give it some legs that they didn't see coming. Let's go back to 1978 and 1979, when disco was king and many of your parents had on Swedish knits and bell-bottoms and high platform shoes. Both parents! And maybe some Afros or long hair. Disco was big, but once again, disco was a twelve-by-twelve-inch marketplace where people took their big twelve-by-twelve-inch vinyl records and put them on record players. In 1978/79, the people that ran the seven major record companies—it was seven majors at the particular time—were music people, and they were creative people.[1] Loved the music, partied to the music, promoted the music. They were really music heads. But as great as music people are, especially if you mix it with a little bit of partying and too much drugs and drinking, they might run a big business into the ground. And that's what happened.

By 1979, there was questions, of course, about the law of diminishing returns in the music business. Did it explode? Did it get oversaturated? Is disco dead? Is there rebellion from the rock of the late sixties and the early seventies, and the mid-seventies? You know, everything's a copycat industry when you're talking about arts. Long story short, the creative people ran the music business into the ground. They would be like, "We're going to have a promotional party at Studio 54 with our one act who is going to perform. We're going to get a fifty-foot line of cocaine and invite all the radio DJs to the party in the back rooms."

What would come out of those parties is that the record DJs would convene and go back to their radio hamlets and different parts of the country and play records like "Ring My Bell" [1979] by Anita Ward five hundred million times. They would make hit records because that was also using the process of programming. But at that particular time, radio was a thing where if you wanted to get something moving, throw a million ads on TV, and play a song on the radio a million times, and you're going to have a hit. Disco exploded until the time where people were like, "It's a lot. I need a change." But the music people had the entire record business into the red, ran it into the ground.

So who comes to save the day? In 1979, I know I was rockin "Ain't No Stopping Us Now," by McFadden & Whitehead. Philadelphia International Records, started by Gamble and Huff and Thom Bell in Philadelphia had a subsidiary through CBS Records, which later became Sony. That wasn't enough. Disco started out with Gamble and Huff making records for the O'Jays with their four-on-the-floor Earl Young beat on the drums. In the beginning, disco was soulful. By 1979, Ethel Merman and everybody was making disco records because they said it was a beat that you could easily sing to. That's an entire other story. Anyway, the people that came to save the day of the seven major record companies were the lawyers and the accountants. Because the accountants were like, "Yo, I know this might be a hit, but we're fifteen million in the red. We gotta do something." They're going to go to the stockholders. The stockholders are going to say, "Well, we replaced this person with this person and then that person, we still had the same problem. You gotta figure it out."

Then what happened in 1979 and 1980 is the lawyers, then the accountants, assumed the position of music people who kind of threw the record business into the ditches, and they came with solutions to try to save the recording business. They realized that "Hey, something's not working here. We're sending these records to the stores and they're coming back as returns." If I send you a hundred records on consignment, you only pay a small amount. Let's say I sent you more records than your space can hold and you only sold two records. You gotta move things out so you can have more space. You gotta return those records to that record company, even though they've been paid for on a discount. Well, what happened is that they needed space in record stores, because the most important part of retail is space. If you can't build a bigger place, then you got to build within. And records are about this big, twelve by twelve inches. It was like, "Listen, man, we can't have all these records stacked up when we need to bring in new stuff to keep our doors open. So we gotta send these wack-ass records out of here." Companies were like, "Listen, we can't take them back."

They had to figure something out. They couldn't keep making vinyl, which at that particular time and even today is an expensive process. Even if you got all the plants in the world, it's a process to take the material and press it up with heat and machines. Then you got packaging. Well, anyway, those numbers got skewed all over the place, and they realized that making this item doesn't mean that they're going to be making a profit, and they will continue to lose money by the millions. "We don't care how much you like Earth, Wind & Fire or Meat Loaf. Stores ain't going to increase their space." So the lawyers and accountants figured something out. "We gotta come up with a new configuration." Matter of fact, they came up with three configurations. One configuration came up in 1964, which was the eight-track. But your configuration ain't no good without the player. If you got a piece that needs to get played, it ain't gonna get played unless you have the hardware for you to play it on. My first car was a '68 Chevelle. I had an eight-track player, but I also liked cassettes, so I had that cassette adapter in my eight-track. It was so wack sounding. But you got what you got and you dug what you dug.

So the other thing that came up in 1965 was the cassette that was just a smaller version of the reel-to-reel tapes. And the record company said, "We got some cassettes that we put out." But there was a lack of cassette players. It wasn't until Panasonic and the Japanese companies started integrating radios with cassette players, which was the beginning of boomboxes! Because cassette players were separate from the radio. And before that, you had the transistor radio. They figured a way they could put all three into one. They even tried for a time to put a turntable on it, but that was going a little bit too far. Even though I do know cats from New York, they used to ride a five-speed Schwinn Stingray backward, holding a record player and a box on it! I was like, "This is more miraculous than Einstein!"

Then 1980/81 comes along, that's the beginning of R&B, and that's Reagan and Bush. All of a sudden, the record companies figure out, "We gotta change this configuration, and we need to make our money back." Scientists got together with laser technology in Europe, a company called Philips, which was also affiliated with Polygram, one of the seven majors at the time. They came up with the invention of the laser disc. It was the beginning of the CDs. Many of you all, when you were infants, you would see your parents' CDs, and they were shiny. But with this particular invention, the record company said, "We are going to come up with something that's going to save our asses."

They first tried it out on classical music because that's the "pure" music, right? Then they got involved with making CDs for big acts, rock and rollers. The beginning of a manufacturing endeavor is expensive, but once they figure it out, they can make it really cheap. Number one, because it's small. So when they first came out with the CDs in the middle of the 1980s and people like Michael Jackson and Prince coming from their record companies, CBS and Warner, respectively, they said, "Retail, we got a new item that you can sell, and it's going to be smaller than the twelve-inch big records." They said, "We're not going to change our racks for you to come up with a configuration. Our stores will remain the same. What do you got?" Record companies said, "You ain't got to change the racks. We got this thing called the CD, which you can sell for four times as much as you selling the albums."

When they first released the CD, they would put them in this thing called the long box. The long box is actually half of what a twelve inch is. "So we'll give you five Prince albums that you can sell for eighteen dollars as opposed to the vinyl that you gotta find space for, which you sell for only seven dollars, and it's on you what your retail price is going to be. We just have a suggested retail price of eighteen dollars." They made the deal with the record companies. But then you need a CD player. So some of the major companies started becoming the manufacturers. So in the beginning, you would have the CD, and you had some companies owning the CD player. Record stores weren't mad. They could take eight CDs, put them in the same racks to stick up like albums, and make four times as much. All of a sudden, there was a money boom in the retail area, and the record companies were making money now too. They didn't get around to rap music until the late eighties and the early nineties. Another thing that fell in their lap is the boomboxes allowed for the major record companies to say, "We couldn't sell a lot of these Julio Iglesias cassettes, but we can move this cassette to this hip hop market." And that was the beginning of the major labels looking at hip hop as being a viable album selling marketplace.

Major record labels come in wanting to make money. They don't want to make four dollars for two songs. They ain't in *that* business. They sell albums. When people go to the store, they gotta buy at the suggested retail price. They want eight dollars, seven dollars an album, meaning, we got to deliver twelve songs. Again, that's the beginning of hip hop's golden era right there when it gets into the album-oriented artist marketplace. That means that if you got Bruce Springsteen over here, this is selling in the same river that the Beastie Boys are going to be selling on CBS Records, which later on became Sony. That merger happened because Sony was making the hardware for the software to be played on. If you own the hardware and the software, then you got a one-stop shop. "We're selling players, and we sell whatever is played on it." End of the day, we got the hardware moving.

Hence the Sony Walkman was the first portable cassette player, which means that you had to get headphones. You could play a cassette in there. You could be on the train and not interrupt nobody's space. Everybody started to form their own little sonic bubbles. "My music is my music, and my music don't bleed into your music." Before music used to bleed into each other, even if you had a little radio. For the first time, music became *personal.* Hip hop was the last fight because some people would boast around and carry their boomboxes, like, "This is my music and *everybody's* going to hear it," to the point where, "Yo, can you turn that down?" And then, that could lead to problems. People's cars, car culture, cassette player, speakers booming, bam! "Radio ain't gonna play hip hop. My car's playing hip hop, and it's the loudest on the block. I'm doing the programming yo, for real!"

Cassettes exploded. Independent companies moved on it, but the major record companies moved right behind them with more muscle. Later on, CDs became more commonplace, easier to manufacture. By 1990/1991, major record companies would sign many rap artists. They went from seven, down to six, down to five major record companies. Today there's three. They got into CDs, and then CD manufacturing became easier. Then came the rap departments on top of the Black departments to say, "We have CDs and rap artists making albums," and so on.

My first CD in 1990 was *Fear of a Black Planet.* It was the first CD that came through rap music on Sony. That was the year after *It Takes a Nation of Millions to Hold Us Back,* which was heavily sold as a cassette. It was moved somewhat as a twelve-inch record, but those were the configurations that it had. It didn't actually become a CD until way later in the 1990s. *Fear of a Black Planet* was that first CD. Actually, all the plants were on alert that the CD was going to be this new thing in the 1990s. Nineteen eighty-nine was a turbulent year for me, career-wise, and also personally. But it was a good year. That's the year that "Fight the Power" came out. But also, Public Enemy was in the crux of controversy. Every year was some kind of controversy. That was the result of making some music that dared to go out and say what it had to say. Quite punkish, like the Clash, if you would like to say.

But the biggest thing about *Fear of a Black Planet* is that it dealt with the planet. It was our international record. By 1990, I had already toured and performed it in as many as forty-five countries, not only just going there but absorbing every place that I went to. *Fear of a Black Planet,* on the heels of what I dealt with in 1988/1989, was to look at rap music and hip hop as not just being juvenile, adolescent music, as some journalists were saying. But me at thirty years old, what the hell kind of music was I going to make anyway? I wasn't going to make a high school record. The biggest thing about hip hop is to be yourself. That's the most genuine thing you could do. Don't try to pretend to be anything else. I come from Long Island. I ain't gonna pretend I'm from somewhere else. And I ain't gonna pretend I'm anything else other than thirty years old. Although Flavor Flav was the oldest teenager on Earth and still is [*laughter*].

Fear of a Black Planet in its essence is a dissertation. I worked with the ideas of political scientists and theorists and professors like Dr. Frances Cress Welsing's *The Isis Papers: The Keys to the Colors* and "The Cress Theory of Color-Confrontation and Racism," basically saying that we're all from one seed.[2] And saying that there is a color-confrontation issue in the US and abroad due to the simple fact that those with darker skin seem to be viewed as the scourge of society and taking this as something that we should look into. So *Fear of a Black Planet* is the fear of genetic annihilation. The way that you actually defeat the fear is with love. So it got into that, and I spent all of the summer of 1989 putting together this dissertation into bars and music. I traded back and forth quite often with this brother sitting right in front of me, Davey D, who will probably tell you more about it. There are sounds and voices inside the *Fear of a Black Planet* that came directly from this man right here who was the mass collector of tapes. We had a saying that Afrika Bambaataa was the master of records, and I used to say Davey D is the master of tapes. He would lend me a tape from his radio shows in the Bay Area.

DAVEY D: And it wound up on the album!

CHUCK D: It was a really tripped out thing. Because we began to talk, and when I came out to California back in the eighties, the place I felt aligned with was Oakland, where I had a lot of friends in the Bay Area. I was just enamored of Oakland. Number one, growing up, to me, Oakland meant the Black Panther Party because I was in the Panther lunch program in Harlem and my relatives, my grandmothers, where I stayed, were part of the program.[3] Of course, we looked to Oakland, California, as being the source, because the Panthers were superheroes to us. Before Wakanda.

Now, many of y'all saw *Black Panther* the movie, but understand this. Y'all were swimming in the mind of Stan Lee. Stan Lee wrote Wakanda Black Panther for comic books in the sixties.[4] This is why it's a tripped-out fact when people start saying, "That's old." Yeah, that's old, but why does everything old end up being movies today and y'all thinking it's new? Everything that Marvel did. Yes, they did some enhancements to bring it up to the future, but the original core of these stories is from the past. How many times are they gonna regrow Batman? And then Spider-Man? Evolution says that Black Panther is going to be next. They were going to find something that fit the Black Lives Matter or the #MeToo movement.[5]

But to me, the *real* Black Panthers were heroes to us kids. I ended up meeting most of these heroes. I was also encouraged by my parents to know that they were heroes. Stokely Carmichael (a.k.a. Kwame Ture), Angela Davis, Elaine Brown, Bobby Seale, Eldridge Cleaver, people who we would read their words in *Jet* magazine. They were real people. Somebody told me one of the ploys of COINTELPRO [the counterintelligence program] in the United States of America led by J. Edgar Hoover, FBI, CIA, and all that was to be able to get the Black movement after the assassination of Dr. Martin Luther King to start to praise and salute fictional heroes.[6] Movie heroes, not real muthafuckas. We were looking at real people. And yes, I read Marvel Comics, too, but there are *real* Black Panthers. For years when all the turbulence is going on, the media would keep news on the low and submerged, so that you wouldn't know what was going on.

In 1989, when Public Enemy played at the Kaiser Convention Center up in Oakland, we stopped the show because Huey Newton was in the front row standing on the sideline. We brought him onstage. I was like, "You're Huey Newton for real?" He came to see me play at a concert. As we say, we're the Black Panthers of rap, but I'm seeing real Black Panthers. Michael Tabor. I mean, whoa! Huey Newton would call me every once in a while in the middle of the night, just to chop it up, not long, twenty to twenty-five minutes or so. He gave me some advice, asked some questions. I asked him some questions. It was real funny because at that particular time, my phone was going dead for about two years, every night between 11:00 p.m. and 1:00 a.m. I knew my phone was tapped. I made a song about it called "Louder than a Bomb." I don't have no secrets at all, because

I'm louder than a bomb, so . . . what? You're accusing me of something? I'm already saying it as loud as I can. I ain't pushing no drugs, nothing like that, so you're going to hear me coming with the deepest contraband, which is called the truth, as far as I see it.

So my trips up to the Bay Area were real trips, seeing real people, and Davey happened to be one of those. In the middle of 1989, we had "Fight the Power" coming through as a part of Spike Lee's *Do the Right Thing*. We were deep in the controversy, and I was telling people I already finished *Fear of a Black Planet* in July of 1989. It was a damn lie! [*Laughter.*] But the concept of where I wanted to go was there, and Dave kept feeding me these tapes from his radio show, and everybody who I considered a hero and some coming to the radio station and actually doing the interviews. As I traveled through 1989 on Greyhound, my crew was taking the tour bus. I just couldn't be with them. It was a lot of tension with the crew. So I would take a Greyhound from city to city and write the album *Fear of a Black Planet*. I got my headphones, my little box, and my tapes. Real truth.

Fear of a Black Planet was a dissertation of those scholars and theories I talked about. Hence the song titles—"Contract on the World Love Jam," "Brothers Gonna Work It Out," "911 Is a Joke"—which talked about services in the Black community being sketchy. "Incident at 66.6 FM," which talked about media manipulation on radio stations. "Welcome to the Terrordome," which meant that we were going into the 1990s, and for Black folks, we were going into the last decade before the turn of the century. It could be a turbulent decade. If we stick together, we'll come out of it in good shape to deal with the twenty-first century. If we don't stick together, it's fucking doom. That's what "Welcome to the Terrordome" was about. "Meet the G that Killed Me," "Pollywanacraka" dealt with race relations and people being able to get together and questions solidarity across social lines. "Anti-Nigger Machine" is about the police. "Burn Hollywood Burn," all the way up to right now, I don't know what the hell Hollywood is doing. "Power to the People," "Who Stole the Soul?" The question who stole the soul is the same question as who stole the people! You know damn well they're going to steal your soul. It's even more prevalent right now. Who is stealing your soul? I said before that minds are the real estate of the millennium. They ran out of any land that they could go out and buy and take over, so where's that real estate of the future? It's already inside you. Instead of people losing their minds, people are giving their minds away.

"Fear of a Black Planet," we see that every step of the way. It's paranoia. I don't know you, so therefore, I fear everything you stand for. "Revolutionary Generation," what's the future of women in this world? It's ridiculous to say, but I mean, do men have to run every goddamn thing? "B Side Wins Again," "War at 33 ⅓," which is the rotation of the record, but also thirty-three and a third as you get into numerology and telling you the importance of that. "Final Count of the Collision between Us and the Damned," that's the musical interlude that comes right before "Fight the Power." So I decided to title these tracks and also make some kind of calico blanket out of the sonic tapestry. At the end of it all is a question: How do you defeat the fear of a Black planet? It is with love. You gotta fight for love. You gotta fight hate with love. And you got to fight your ass off!

So in 1990, I'm writing a record for a thirty-year-old. I wasn't trying to make a record for a twelve year old. If we could get enough people to look at the creativity of hip hop the same way they look at classic rock and other musics from the past, hip hop is genius. I'm not saying *I* was. I come from a collective collision of many, many forces and contributions. People look down on rap, but when they look into hip hop, they see it's deeper than they can swim in. You got to challenge information. That is what "Don't Believe the Hype" was about, a challenge to information. You have to be literate, deeper than just falling victim to what the title tells you. We want to salute intellectualism and disrespect anti-intellectualism. You need smart people wherever the fuck you want to go. You don't need a dumb motherfucker trying to find your way out of a fucking problem. I'm telling you where we're going to unwind by week ten. It's going to be like, hip hop and rap, okay that's what got you through the door. But when you leave here, it's going to be how to really seriously GPS your way through the rest of this decade.

With *Fear of a Black Planet*, when me and Dave had exchanges back in the eighties, in the nineties, we saw there was going to be a lot of wildness going into the next century. We also saw human beings being hatched and formed into that wildness. We said, "Yup, they're just going to be different." They got different obstacles that have already been planned for them. Maybe you couldn't see it in 2010, but 2030 will slap you up a different way coming from a different area you never ever imagined. This is what *Fear of a Black Planet* is about. To this day, people don't know that it's a dissertation from scholars and scientists broken down into a rap album. It ain't *The Chronic* y'all, for real. No shade, but it ain't, and if it's shade, then it is. So I would just like to bring Dave to sit next to me so we can chop it up. Ladies and gentlemen, no further ado, the great Davey D Cook.

DAVEY D: Everywhere you go and every discipline that you embark upon there is going to be a process where the information, or the protocols that govern the discipline, are going to be passed down to you. When I worked in the tech industry, they make *sure* you know the history. When you're at Apple, they're like, "This company is a trillion-dollar company started by Steve Wozniak and Steve Jobs." Even at San Francisco State, they go, "You're in this class at this school and these were the landmark moments of it." This speaks to Chuck's point about rearranging what should be a natural thing. I think all societies, communities, and nations have always had elders who passed on information to younger generations. We called them griots, *djelis*.[7] It's only recently when it comes to our culture in hip hop and Black people in general, there are powerful forces that want us to believe that our information "don't count."

So we get into a cycle of reinventing the wheel over and over again, and that prevents us from gathering traction. We talk about generational wealth. I like to talk about generational *knowledge* that we build upon. Even in the middle of those attempts to distract us, bore us, and move us in another direction, it's important that you stay the course, because institutions always remember, and they're counting on people to always be forgetful. They rely on us to forget, both important information and the vital connections from the past to the present, along with essential interactions that we're supposed to carry with us.

I'm talking about the importance of community, the importance of us building with one another. I'll say one other thing that is often forgotten. When I first came to Cal [UC Berkeley], during our orientation the administrators said, "Look to the left and look to the right. The person to the left and the person to the right is most likely not going to graduate with you." In retrospect, I came to understand that was a shortsighted scare tactic. The hope was to scare us into staying focused, otherwise we were gonna get kicked out of school. It didn't work. Today I tell my students to look to the left and look to the right. I then tell them to take the name, number, and email addresses of the people on either side of them. I tell them to do this because these are going to be the people that you build community with. The person to the left and to the right are the folks that will one day help you get through the door. That's how it's always been. There were people that were to my left and to my right that I certainly helped get from point A to point B and then later in life, they became lawyers and doctors and radio programmers, etc. and then were able to help me. These are the people that you can pick up the phone and go, "Hey, I need a little help with something." It's like, "We went to school together. What do you need?" You know, "You have an illness? Come to my clinic. I'll take care of you."

The responsibility that we all have to each other—and this is related to hip hop as well—is we have the responsibility to know each other in our community and everybody has a responsibility to bring their A-game to the table. That means no shortcuts. That means all of us are operating on a high level at all times, not so much to impress one another but just because we're a community. Community means depending upon those who come before us to kick down doors and those who come after us to be able to hold those doors open for the next group.

The relationship that me and Chuck D have is that Chuck was like a superhero. He was Public Enemy. That's a really big deal. His group was the most covered group in music at that time in the late eighties, early nineties. They were on the magazine covers. They were on the radio. They were on TV. And Chuck, with his generosity, he came to places and helped bring attention and shine a light on us "little guys." He was one to say, "I'll come do your college radio show. I'll come talk to your class. I'll put your name on the back of the album." And with that came a lot of dap. Chuck D put my name on the back of several Public Enemy albums. The attention that generated and the doors it opened was incredible. People would come up to me and say, "Yo, your name is on the back of the Public Enemy album! Your work must be important."

What I came to realize over the years is that not everyone would do what Chuck D did. In fact, many would go in the opposite direction. Some people, when they get that sort of recognition, they sit back and they go, "I made it on my own." People like Chuck D realized that once they go through that door, it was their job to help others. On the flip side, it was folks like me who benefitted to make sure we were not an embarrassment to Chuck who basically cosigned us. For many of us, we came up in the era of crack, so family was broken up, and we ran into the embarrassment of, like, "Is that your moms out there fiending? Is that your pops out there all strung out?" That was the trauma that many people went through. The substitution came when you got put on. You couldn't sit there and just fall back. You had to put your A-game on.

I want you all to carry that attitude, because it's a hip hop attitude that's almost been erased from the conversation. When you were in a crew, you couldn't be the one in the crew that was fucking up. I'll give you an example: Summer Jam 1995. I was there when it happened. The Notorious B. I. G. brought DJ Kap onstage. There's a whole backstory to it. Biggie was kind of nervous. He had some crazy beef with E-40. E-40 was there. Biggie realized that the Bay was, you know, the Bay [*laughter*]. So he was there, and he wanted to turn the house out. People were shouting in the audience, "Tupac, Tupac, Tupac!" There was all this craziness. So Kap got on, and Biggie was like, "I'm gonna turn this out." But his DJ kept messing up. I remember he picked up a water bottle and threw it at him, like, "Stop fucking up my sound," because at the end of the day, people don't remember the DJ, they remember Biggie. So I say emphatically before we get into this: We all have a responsibility to each other in the communities that we form. All of us have to be on point. If you're sitting in the back half-steppin, it's going to reflect bad not just on you but on the community that you are a part of. I want us to keep that in mind.

This mindset is germane to hip hop. We used to call it "show and prove." You had to show and prove and understand that people are watching, and you would always be challenged. But the show-and-prove mentality really comes from the standpoint, historically-speaking, that many people outside our community held the belief that "Black people ain't about nothing." They thought we were inferior. Our collective counter to that was to adapt the mindset best personified by Jay-Z when he said in his song "I will not lose." I, for one, will not lose in situations where I am doubted. I'm going to rise to the occasion. "I will not lose." We got to say that over and over again, because institutions are counting on us to lose.

This is very important at the moment of time that we're in, because where I'm sitting, as Chuck was saying, there's a lot of people that see you all as demographics and not as human beings. You are demographics to be conquered. Data to be mined. Hip hop was about creativity, not being a consummate consumer. Our challenge now is to motivate and to remind people of that history from where it came. The corporations that control this culture or an aspect of the culture have made hip hop become a shell of itself. They help make it a culture that's focused on "stuntin." It's about throwing money at the TV. It's about dissing one another on a song. It's about materialism and hyper-capitalism and not being a challenge to those very institutions that fostered the negative economic, social, and political conditions which led to hip hop music and culture emerging in the beginning.

To Chuck D's point about *Fear of a Black Planet*, there are two funny stories about this album, which Chuck may or may not remember. One, we drove around the Village, which is in Manhattan, for two and a half hours, while this fool looked for a Boris Karloff record. We went everywhere, driving around, going to record stores. He got this Boris Karloff record, which at the time you just couldn't sample, you had to play the record, press a button, wait twenty seconds, play it back. Not good? Do the process again. So that's another two hours, and you got a laugh from that song because when you heard the album, it was buried in a wall of sound. We spent like four hours looking for a Boris Karloff record that is just part of a musical collage. That's one thing.

But when we came back from the shopping and you all did the sampling, we stepped outside and you weren't there. You were inside. But we got pulled over by the police. They pulled guns on us that day and accused us of threatening somebody, which we didn't have nothing to do with. There was a white dude across the street. He got into a tiff with a sister. The sister got a boyfriend. Boyfriend took care of the matter. The white dude ran off. Next thing we know, we had these cops pull up on us and draw guns. They weren't trying to hear us when we told them we were Public Enemy and in the studio recording. Finally, people came out of the Green Street Studios and were like, "These people are with Public Enemy." Your crew came out and actually was getting ready to have a fistfight with the cops. This was the night that you all did "911 Is a Joke." So it had special meaning for me.

CHUCK D: I remember. The whole *Fear of a Black Planet* is a collage that doesn't have one original musician note in it, for every second. This is the last album I really produced, because it burned me out. I just did directing after that. But yeah, because I couldn't get away with just getting that Vincent Price laugh [that was used on Michael Jackson's "Thriller"]. So I had to find Boris Karloff. This is how scientific we got. What you said brings us right back to the point. You did not want to—forget being wack to the rest of the world—you didn't want to be wack to your crew. Hip hop as a community is knowing that I could do what you can't do, you can do what I can't do. Together, we get this done, and it's us against the world, as a community. We were doing that record *as* we were figuring it out. We weren't like, "We're going to do this and this is going to be what it is til the rest of time." No, no, no. What you do have is the trust that you can work with somebody that has your trust that you can take this job to the next phase.

DAVEY D: Everybody on that project was on their A-game. I bring this up because we're made to believe two things about hip hop. One, that it is an individual endeavor. Because we see E-40, but we don't see his family. We see Too $hort, but we don't see Too $hort's crew. We see Chuck, but Chuck is the tip of an organization called Public Enemy, a larger organization of people that was made in community that held you accountable, the Nation of Islam among them.[8] Learning how to operate as a unit and a crew, you need to think about how you will solve conflicts, how you all share the wealth, even though somebody may be the front person. How you make sure people are taken care of, how you make sure that you don't bring your baggage into the space that then contaminates things. All that is a challenge that almost every crew had to face. Most importantly is the apprenticeship within the crew. You know, "each one, teach one," that's a real important concept as well.[9]

The second thing I want to bring up is hip hop and technology. Hip hop is never considered for its technological prowess, and hip hop people are never considered technological geniuses, when in many ways we are. Let me give you an example of what I'm talking about. Going back to the Apple example, Steve Wozniak and Steve Jobs came up with this way to figure out how to make long-distance phone calls and not pay for it. They made these blue boxes which basically say, "You can make the calls for free." They were cast as innovative, as curious. They found a way to beat the system, and we celebrated that. It's the ultimate rags-to-riches story. You went from basically being two people who committed what you could say is wire fraud—you did a criminal act—to having a trillion-dollar company. In many ways, it's the story of America, when you think about it, whether it's enslaving people, colonizing people, exploiting people, all of that. But when Ray-Ray comes to my house and go, "Yo! That cable, I can figure out how to flip that so you don't have to pay for it," he's going to jail. Nobody's saying, "Hey, Ray, how did you figure out how to get through all the security protocols that AT&T had so that your neighborhood can get free cable?" How do we nurture that ingenuity and cultivate it?

The prowess that hip hop exhibits is often framed as criminal activity. You got the graffiti artists, for example.[10] There were no cell phones back in the seventies when we were coming up or even in the eighties. You had dogs, you had electric third rails, you had police that were like, "At all costs, we're going to stop them." You had folks that were fifteen years old that were going into train yards in the dark of night, who didn't have formal artistic training. Yet they figured out how to take a spray can that they stole because you couldn't buy it at the time, and make the line be *real* thin, and then would do all kinds of crazy gradient colors and then scale it up so it's on the full side of a train car—in speed time and it's dark! How did you do that? Even today as I'm driving down the 580 in Oakland, I'm like, "How did you, in the middle of this crowded freeway, get up and paint your name on there?"

CHUCK D: You could also explain how they would go into a light pole and take the electricity to power an outdoor event.

DAVEY D: All this is considered vandalism, against the law, versus, like, "Let me see how these people were able to create something and take it to the next level." I use the graff example because one of the things that we start to see is a cat figured out how to put their name on the top of this building, and then people disapprove, like, "I can't believe they put their name on the top of that building." Six months later, a big corporation is going, "Many people can see that name. Let's put an advertisement on the top of that building." The guy who did the tower up on top of the train, now you have entire ad companies that charge you hundreds of thousands of dollars, like, “We can take a train and we can put the *Black Panther* movie, and we can wrap it.” Those people are then paraded out—“Here’s Mr. Jones. He’s a genius for coming up with a new way to do advertising.” Ray-Ray, on the other hand, if he gets caught, will probably do jail time for vandalism versus having his talents cultivated. Hip hop comes from that tradition, and I always want to make sure that we recognize it. The ability to rearrange people’s negative perceptions to make them say, “I never thought about that.” Our ability to constantly evaluate and be able to pivot and improvise, that’s a hip hop thing. It’s counter to what the institutions that we constantly have to engage with want to do because they’re like, “We own your name. We own all these different things.” At the end of the day, you wind up creating but not owning. Breaking down the whole mechanics of the industry, like, artists be on the radio all the time but be broke. Because the record label gets 90 percent, the artists get 10 percent, but that’s after they spend everything.

Then you start looking at things differently. So we clearly understood that you had artists that were talking about pimping that were getting pimped. Our job was to change that around. Those are things that we had to learn as a crew. We had to learn from other people who made mistakes in the past and passed the information on to us so that we could benefit from that. And then we pass the game along to other people so that they don’t make the same mistake.

So when you see Nipsey Hussle and others who were able to go further, it was because they learned those lessons from people who had run into brick walls in the past. These were people who were like, “Okay they played us. This is what we need to do.” It used to be, “Just do a record.” Then some people said, “My name is out there. I’ll do the record. I’m going to do a movie. I’m going to use that brand to make a clothing line,” etc. The first person I saw do that was somebody who, when he did it, they were laughing at him. In fact, they called him a sellout. That was MC Hammer. He was like, “I used to be a hustler from High Street in Oakland,” and he broke the whole thing down. He would tell me, “I’ma put on these genie pants and dance. It’s a stage prop. It means I don’t have to do nightclubs for $500 a pop. I can perform at a stadium for $100,000 a pop. And anybody who wants to laugh at the genie pants, I can see them after the concert and let them know I’m from High Street. But in the meantime, these genie pants are what's going to allow us to do these stadium shows and do a cartoon, have a clothing line, and do other things that enable us to open doors." He went on to explain how he and his brother Louis opened up their own stores. That's how TROOP clothing stores started.

These are lessons that we had to learn through hip hop because it wasn't taught in school. We didn't have family members that clearly understood. Some people had uncles and aunts that maybe dipped in that, but we didn't fully understand. We didn't go to Haas Business School or Wesleyan. The record companies were trying to catch up afterward. It was like, "Let's do a new contract." I remember the first time I saw that contract.

CHUCK D: You mean the "360 contract"?[11]

DAVEY D: Yes. If you do a movie or you open up a grocery store, the record company would get a piece of the pie. That's the 360 deal. The argument was because they helped promote you, they should get a percentage of everything you create.

CHUCK D: You gotta always know it's going to be a battle. Because even if you think three steps ahead, your adversary is taking five steps ahead, especially if they're a collective and you're not. The problem with being solo versus a collective, you're going up against a machinery. That's why I might have been a little bit long-winded on the technology point. When I was explaining how the golden era started from a technological perspective, it was because that's the beginning of where we are media instead of just a recording artist. *Fear of a Black Planet*, once they said, "You're a major corporation album artist. That means you're a multinational media magnet conglomerate and you need to start thinking that way." So us running into each other was really the beginning of the hijacking of media. But yet, still knowing that you don't start waving the victory flag at all, it's a battle and the whole key is that you're standing on the shoulders of giants.

DAVEY D: That just sparked two things. The biggest lesson that I learned was when our radio station consolidated and we became Clear Channel.[12] So "The Beat" was part of us. Our rivals, which was WILD 94.9FM, we're all in the same building. Prior to the merger, I came down to LA for an event, and I'm at this house, and I see the rival program directors from all over at the same party, hanging out, joking, and sharing war stories. It was eye opening. On one hand, they're telling us [the talent],

"You're the Black station, that's the Latin station. You all got to be going head to head." I'm at this picnic, and they're sitting back there cracking jokes and literally having tea and crumpets and the whole nine. It was then I realized, as an institution, they were all locked in together. But the people who are on the front line, mostly Black and Brown, were going at each other, when the people in the back were all friends. So that's one thing that we learned about how business operates.

A second thing we learned is this. Some people talk about "We got killers." Well, you better have killers of another sort. So you're the creative person. But who's your lawyer? Who's the person with the business acumen? You've seen LeBron James do that with his crew. He pulled them up. He said, "Your job is this, your job is that. We're gonna control the destiny for all the things that we do." But prior to that, we were learning and seeing that there were other people within hip hop that understood primarily because they came out of a culture where some of them were hustlers on the block where you had to have people play different roles. "I'm going to grind behind the scenes. Don't ever mention my name. Somebody else is going to be on the corner." It is an operation with multiple people. You had to bring that to the table in this industry in a different way.

Let me show you one group of people that took that hustle to the next level. E-40, good friend of mine. When he was doing the documentary *E-40: Charlie Hustle: The Blueprint of a Self-Made Millionaire*, we were down in LA. They had all the trimmings, all the Hollywood stuff, free food, weed, women. None of that was interesting to me. But his brother D-Shot, who's a big guy, and Mugzy, they were sweatin the camera man, like, "Yo, man, what kind of camera is that? What kind of lens is that? How do you work that?" And it's like, "Yo, 40, are they trying to rob the cameraman?" And 40 was like, "No, we paid $50,000 to do this video. We're not paying $50,000 again. Their job is to soak up game." Their job for the weekend was to shadow him and soak up his expertise. Some people would be like, "Oh, that's unfair. He worked hard." But institutions come to our communities all the time and be like, "What's the newest slang? How do you all dress?" Taking pictures. They'll trademark it that evening and make billions off it. And they don't have to go into the community where those expressions came about through a lot of blood, sweat, and heartache. You feel what I'm saying? So E-40's attitude was like, "I paid you fifty G's. My brothers are going to follow you around and learn how to do this."

I go to his house. He had a studio in the house, and he's teaching his son, Droop-E, how to use the studio. It was all about making sure the unit, the family, the click were able to operate in what is oftentimes a predatory industry. Later on, you see him investing in beverages and all these different ventures because they understand you have to diversify. But again, it's not a one-person operation. It's a crew. It's the people that were to the left and the people that were to the right. On their A-game. "If you mess up, we're not eating." But as somebody who's running the crew, then I also have to change the dynamic. I can't be the exploitative institution that we've seen people ultimately get burned out from and run away from. I've got to be like, if this sister's in the crew, "You're part owner of all this." Cooperative economics. These are things that I'm seeing a lot of artists have done, having learned those lessons. And they're doing it in a way that I'm actually pretty proud of because they're not necessarily bragging about it. They're just quietly doing it behind the scenes.

CHUCK D: At the same time, it is hopefully gravitating to a level where they realize that the blood flow is the art itself, and that's intangible. When something is just taken, used, and thrown to the side looking for the next thing, that's not hip hop. That's not what it is meant to be. That's consumption. Hip hop is this thing that's innate. It's organic. It's energy. It can last forever when you recognize its essence of sparking the creativity and the productivity as a collective. Today's topic was that it's also media. How can hip hop as an energy be protected in the next ten years? It's one thing to be a fan of it and a consumer. It's another thing to say, "I want to be a *participant* in it."

DAVEY D: One thing I would say is, what are you creating? Every step of the way, in hip hop, I've seen creativity. Transformative creativity. We might have started with Grandmaster Flash figuring out how Kool Herc was playing these breakbeats and being like, "Let me use technological prowess to come up with the clock theory so that we can keep those breakbeats on time. Let me figure out how I can take things and then switch it up so I can actually hear the records or queue them ahead of time so that I can keep this clean feed." But one thing that comes to mind is this thing called intentionality. Intentionality is related to being creative, meaning, "I'm going to give this definition. We're going to have purpose and we're going to move this forward."

Oftentimes, when you have that creativity, they don't put it in the same box. Let me give you an example. Paradise Gray, who was with the group X Clan and the organization Blackwatch, explained this to me. He noted that one of the things that we know about the golden era of hip hop is that people started talking about Afrocentricity. They started wearing the medallions. They started talking about knowledge of self. Some of that was organic, but a lot of that was like, "We're going to have these clandestine meetings at the Latin Quarter." Paradise was the one who ran the LQ at the time. We didn't know about all this til years later when he revealed that there had been a series of clandestine meetings. He said they had a series of secret meetings with artists and community members in which people concluded, "Look, this is going to be the protocol for now on. When you do a video, put at the end of your video some heroes and sheroes that people can look up to." Look at the KRS-One videos. Look at MC Lyte. Look at the videos that came out at that time. Queen Latifah is the most subversive because her and Fab 5 Freddy said, "We're going to do an anti-apartheid video while we're singing 'Ladies First' and get that on MTV." But that didn't happen by accident. It was like, "Okay, you put Malcolm X in there, you're going to put Haile Selassie in there." It was intentional to say, "Okay, we have a stance against apartheid" or "Anybody who goes onstage at the Latin Quarter can't wear their gold chains." And they're like, "Who's you?" This is where community comes in. "Who's me? Well, I'm the son of Sonny Carson in the December 12th movement, which is a militant organization, and I'm a former Black Spade."[13] So you have a crew that's like, "Nobody is getting on this stage that we control without wearing an African medallion, because we don't want to support the degradation and death that's being levied on our folks in South Africa where the gold is being mined." There was intentionality there.

We can fast forward. Let's go to the Bay Area where I'm at. People sat around and said, "You know, nobody's playing the Bay. We're not getting national attention." So Mistah F. A. B. and a bunch of people said, "We're going to call ourselves the new Bay." The OGs like Richie Rich and E-40 and others were like, "The new Bay? We're still around. Y'all can't call yourself the new Bay." So they had to have a meeting. They were like, "We're not going to have the new Bay, but we're going to have this thing called the hyphy movement. We're going to have a set of protocols to collectively bring attention to the region." At the same time that was going on, the crunk movement was happening in Atlanta, at the same time the screw movement was happening in Houston. When you talk to these people, it was like, "We all knew that we wanted to define ourselves regionally, so we started to do certain things." The same thing in LA with Nipsey Hussle and that movement, YG and them. They were all coming up at the same time. They didn't necessarily have names for it. They didn't necessarily see where it's going to be ten years from now but they knew that regionally they weren't being heard and they needed to have some firepower. People came together and figured out how to structure their activity collectively.

People are doing their own documentaries. There are about five documentaries in the Bay right now with people who said, "We'll tell our own story." You can see the first documentary *Boogaloo: The Greatest Story Never Told—Identity Theft*.[14] You can see how people are looking at the whole hijacking of the dance called the boogaloo. That's what people are doing. Again, it ain't one individual. It's a bunch of people that are taking matters into our own hands like, "We're going to define our community. We're going to uplift our community, and we're going to make sure our community benefits from this." People take that seriously, and they have pride in that. That's what, ultimately, we want to see continue.

These are the things that I think we should be thinking about because at the end of the day, we're talking about self-determination. We're talking about owning the things that we create and ending the pimp game that's been levied on our communities for generations. I'll give you one person who's in the audience who is part of that innovation. My man, Leroy Moore. Stand up, brother. Here's somebody that brought into the fold the notion of krip-hop, people who are disabled in hip hop. The attitude he has is, "I'm not going to lose." I'm not losing. Family ain't losing. The block ain't losing. The community's not losing. We're going to win. That's the message. That's hip hop to its very core.

QUESTION 1: You just mentioned boogaloo. How do you feel about cultural appropriation?

DAVEY D: I think that's a difficult thing to pin down, because on one hand, historically, there are a lot of expressions that we do that everybody's picked up on and some things that we don't even know they picked up on. Then there's other things that we have rejected and don't even know like the jitterbug and the Lindy Hop, which my grandma was a part of. People are like, "That's not us," because they haven't done the history to understand. I also believe that we're also products of our environment as well.

I think the root of the problem that we're dealing with is that folks are very intentional about being anti-Black, and that's where the rub comes in. Upholding anti-Blackness as you're doing our dances? I mean, the irony is you're dancing to the music, but you don't like us.

A lot of things that we've traditionally done, especially as Black people, have always been an ingredient that other people would extract so *they* could get paid. "Oh, that jazz music, it's devil's music. It's crazy. Don't do it." And yet today, you have Kenny G, Benny Goodman, the kings of jazz, and "This is an American art form." People are now getting paid off of things that they once crapped on. Same thing with rock and roll. So be proud of the things that they called dirt and understand that there's value in it. Everybody in this room got value. The things that you create, the conversation you have is valuable.

CHUCK D: You cannot say that you love what comes out of us more than the people itself. You should dig human beings. You can't go off and say, "I love rap. I love hip hop." How about this classification of people—Black people—who have basically been looked at as being worthless? Do you love them?

DAVEY D: The other thing is that hip hop is a continuation of expressions that we've always done, so we want to be mindful of that. The biggest appropriation is by the corporations. I'm not concerned about individuals. The corporations are very clear; that institution is what we should be battling. Or when calamities happen, why are David Banner and Young Jeezy raising money for Katrina and maybe not all those record companies that made money off the culture of New Orleans? That should be the question you're asking. "Y'all made billions of dollars. What are you all doing for the recovery efforts?"

Because as you make the typical cultural appropriation argument, then you have a group of people that's like, "Well, you know, I'm from the Caribbean, and we created that shit out of Jamaica, and y'all are culturally appropriating us." Now you start having ridiculous arguments that make no sense. When we put out the book with Jeff Chang, somebody called me up like, "Y'all are gonna continue this myth about Caribbean folks and Jamaicans, Kool Herc and all this other stuff?" We had to shut that down with a quickness. But that's the train of thought. "Where's this coming from?" Like, "Oh you're doing this dance, so you're appropriating the culture out of LA and you're living in New York." No, let's look at where the real pimping is going on. We are constantly creating and expressing ourselves, because that's part of what we've always done as people, all of us, as people of the drum. Maybe just different rhythms. We all have oral traditions, whether you're Indigenous, whether you're from Mexico. I mean, all around the world. This thing called hip hop, it could just be a New York thing. But then you have to explain that at the same time hip hop was jumping off in New York, go-go was jumping off in DC. Same time that hip hop was jumping off in New York, house music was jumping off in Chicago. Same time that was happening, funk and funk bands were prevalent all throughout the Bay with a dance culture. You have to take a step back and go, "Okay, these were people trying to make a way out of no way." They were all looking at the same thing but picking up different angles of it. In other words, we all may be subjected to the same sort of challenges, oppressive conditions, but we have these different responses. In New York, we just called it hip hop. But it's all music-based, drum-based, movement based, etc. As Funkadelic sang, "One Nation under a Groove," just different languages and different flavors. I enjoy seeing the regionalism. I enjoy seeing the different ways in which people express themselves.

Hip hop at its core is open source. It's open for anybody to take aspects of it and infuse their own cultural aesthetic to it. When I was in Lebanon, they used to try to sound like New York, but now, "We don't need to do that. We're going to add our cultural aesthetic." Now you have something that's unique to them, and that's a way in which we should always be making music. We put our own flavor to it, remix it, spit it out for the next generation and next people, and we can see those regional takes on the music and culture. I think that's a beautiful thing.

QUESTION 2: I was introduced to this culture through the community. Are grassroots movements and hip hop movements being co-opted and bought by these huge corporations?

DAVEY D: One of the things that we should keep in mind is that not everybody who did hip hop back in the days was trying to be grassroots. That's a myth that we just need to clarify. There were cats that was around my way, that was like, "I'm trying to get paid, period." There were hustlers, gangsters, folks flossing. I bring that up because that's our community. We can't discount those folks. There's always been rough and rugged people in the community that had a different ideology and could be just as ruthless and just as exploitive. The question is, What's our relationship with those folks? Because in many ways, they're just as underground as some of the people that come out of movement spaces. Some of them were cats that financed this thing called hip hop. Too $hort made his money selling his tapes to dope boys. There were cats in the community that was like, "I got you. How much money do you need?" Some of them were just as capitalistic as anybody else. At the same time, they were our neighbors, they were uncles, they were aunties, and they were part of the community. The question is, If they came from dirt, and I was part of something that wasn't dirt, how do we elevate *together* so that you don't have to do the dirt anymore?

CHUCK D: In terms of education, if there's a school system that's teaching you "two plus two equals four," the culture, too, at its form where it could be teachable, cannot be held outside educational systems. Why? If it's an "outsider thing" or it's a "you can't teach this culture because it comes out of the community," it still has to be appropriated somewhat into a teaching system inside. It could go a bunch of different ways, but it could still be taught like you teach jazz or you teach blues in some kind of school setting. To keep it as an outside thing and not having it plugged into the community to me does a disservice to the culture.

QUESTION 3: I want to come back to our discussion of hip hop as the cultural arm of capitalism. There were a lot of Black nationalist, Africanist, politicized conversations inside hip hop, but now we're not seeing that in a lot of mainstream hip hop. Do you think we can reorient hip hop in a direction that is Afrocentrist or Afro-futurist?

DAVEY D: When did you feel that hip hop was doing the things that you are advocating it should be doing? When did you feel that it was really political in the mainstream? What was your experience with that?

STUDENT: Kendrick Lamar sometimes, but it's hit or miss.

DAVEY D: So let's walk through this for a minute. Kendrick does something political. Why is it a hit or miss? Where is it stopping? How is that political vibe continued after Kendrick releases his political missive?

STUDENT: Right after Black Lives Matter started really getting traction.

DAVEY D: Would you consider BLM part of hip hop or an evolution of the type of activism that somebody like Chuck had to shoulder because there was no social media? It was him with the big microphone, KRS-One with a big microphone. A few artists with a big microphone. Now, a lot of people got big microphones. Do you feel that those activities that have shown up now are connected to hip hop, or do you feel that there is a schism there?

To me, I think it's more active than it's ever been before. The counter is, I'm not going to let you have that activism on mainstream radio. But if I was to take a poll with my class, not one person mentioned radio as a source of information. Record labels want to come and look at the polls I do, which I don't let them do. Get your own class! [*Laughter.*] Hip hop doesn't always have to just be somebody with a microphone or somebody dancing and singing. The fifth element of hip hop, which came out of those meetings of the mind, was knowledge. The knowledge was to kick in toward activism. At those meetings of the mind, there were movements like Blackwatch, Sonny Carson, December 12th movement, Nation of Islam. There were those active elements where people were getting their feet wet. They had an excuse in 1987, '88, and '89 to be like, "What do I do now?," because they were just coming of age, and it was the crack era. We're thirty years past that. So now, we actually have some blueprints that we can follow. Arguably, we've seen people come to the streets en masse more than we've ever seen in the history of this country. The challenge as hip hop folks is, how are we engaging those folks to take it to the next level? And what does that next level look like?

One example would be Harry Belafonte meeting with people and quietly telling folks, "Look, when I was your age, we made our money and then we funded the movement. I did the 'Day-O (Banana Boat Song).' People loved it, took the money, and then we were able to do the summer of '64."[15] I'll say this from what I know. Quite a few people have been funding some of these things that's going on and that's what they're supposed to do. They're not supposed to be like, "Yo, I did this song. I'm gonna raise this money. Let me take a bow as the artist." Because you know what the counter would be: "Oh, Chuck is raising money for BLM. Maybe we shouldn't give him that endorsement deal." Instead, it's, "Let me do that endorsement deal. And then, what do you need? $100,000? Do what you need to do. Don't put my name in it." David Banner after Katrina started to do Heal the Hood, and one of the things that Dave talked to me about was he didn't know what to do with this money, because he came off a tour. Nelly had to step in, and he had a foundation, so he could take the money there. But what I didn't know at the time is that Young Jeezy gave him $250,000. He talked about it on our show, and Young Jeezy was pissed, like "Yo, don't tell people I did that. My brand is the 'snowman.' I don't need people to know that." Master P, he paid for the Million Youth March.

At this point in time, those who are going to organize should be very intentional about their relationship with people in the creative community. Again, the model for that would be Harry Belafonte, but there's also a book that talks about what King did. Dr. King was very intentional and had strategies on how he engaged artists because he knew that they had big microphones. Look up *King Maker: Applying Dr. Martin Luther King Jr.'s Leadership Lessons in Working with Athletes and Entertainers* by Marcus Goodloe.[16] That's a good book to read. He used to work with Snoop and all these guys. He was a preacher up at Allen Temple. He breaks down that King had a strategy to engage folks. Our generation now needs to have a strategy.

NOTES

1. See Keith Negus, "The Business of Rap: Between the Street and the Executive Suite," in *That's the Joint! The Hip Hop Studies Reader*, ed. Murray Forman and Mark Anthony Neal (Routledge, 2004).

2. In *The Isis Papers: The Keys to the Colors* (C. W., 2004; originally published in 1991), Frances Cress Welsing discusses theories on white supremacy. It was widely distributed among those seeking "knowledge of self" in the hip hop community in the 1980s–90s. See also Frances Cress Welsing, "The Cress Theory of Color-Confrontation and Racism," *Black Scholar* 5, no. 8 (1974): 32–40.

Published online April 14, 2015, https://www.tandfonline.com/doi/abs/10.1080/00064246.1974.11431416.

3. See Joshua Bloom and Waldo E. Martin, *Black against Empire: The History and Politics of the Black Panther Party* (University of California Press, 2016).

4. Stan Lee's Black Panther was the first Black Marvel superhero (1966). The comic book hero was later portrayed by the late Chadwick Boseman in the 2018 blockbuster film *Black Panther*, directed by Ryan Coogler.

5. In 2013, Alicia Garcia, Opal Tometi, and Patrisse Cullors founded Black Lives Matter (BLM) after the 2012 murder of an unarmed, seventeen-year-old Black youth named Trayvon Martin by vigilante George Zimmerman in Sanford, Florida, and Zimmerman's subsequent acquittal. See Patrice Cullors and asha bandele, *When They Call You a Terrorist: A Black Lives Matter Memoir* (St. Martin's, 2018). See Nadia Khomami, "#MeToo: How a Hashtag Became a Rallying Cry against Sexual Harassment," *The Guardian*, October 20, 2017, https://www.theguardian.com/world/2017/oct/20/women-worldwide-use-hashtag-metooagainst-sexual-harassment.

6. See Nelson Blackstock, *Cointelpro: The FBI's Secret War on Political Freedom* (Pathfinder, 1988). See also "Hip Hop Journalist Davey D on Police Surveillance of Rappers, the National Hip Hop Convention and the 2004 Election," *Democracy Now*, April 19, 2004, https://www.democracynow.org/2004/4/19/hip_hop_journalist_davey_d_on.

7. See Halifu Osumare, *The Africanist Aesthetic in Global Hip-Hop: Power Moves* (Palgrave, 2008); and Catherine Appert, *In Hip Hop Time: Music, Memory, and Social Change in Urban Senegal* (Oxford University Press, 2012).

8. To understand the NOI's profound impact on hip hop, see interviews in James G. Spady, *Nation Conscious Rap: The Hip Hop Vision* (Black History Museum Press, 1991); and Mattias Gardell, *In the Name of Elijah Muhammad: Louis Farrakhan and the Nation of Islam* (Duke University Press, 1996). Louis Farrakhan's Hip Hop Summits have been documented in interviews in James G. Spady, H. Samy Alim, and Samir Meghelli, *The Global Cipha: Hip Hop Culture and Consciousness* (Black History Museum, 2006); and James G. Spady, H. Samy Alim, and Charles G. Lee, *Street Conscious Rap Consciousness* (Black History Museum, 1999). See also extensive coverage in David "Davey D" Cook, "The Nation of Islam Hip Hop Peace Summit," *Davey D's Hip Hop Corner*, April 11, 1997, https://www.daveyd.com/peacesummit.html.

9. "Each one, teach one" is a Black American proverb that emphasizes the importance of knowledge transmission through community-centered practices. See Alim, Chang, and Wong, *Freedom Moves: Hip Hop Knowledges, Pedagogies, and Futures* (University of California Press, 2023).

10. See Chang and Cook, *Can't Stop Won't Stop*, 40–44; and *Style Wars* (1983), directed by Tony Silver and produced by Henry Chalfant, https://www.stylewars.com/.

11. See Wendy Day, "Warning: Hip Hop Artists Need to Know about Today's 360 Record Deals," *Davey D's Hip Hop Corner*, February 5, 2010, https://hiphopandpolitics.wordpress.com/tag/music-industry-politics-360-deals/.

12. Clear Channel Communications is a mass media conglomerate that had a negative impact on Black music after a "wave of consolidation swept the radio industry after Congress passed the 1996 Telecommunications Act, which removed station-ownership caps" (Jeff Chang, "Urban Radio Rage: How Clear Channel Wrecked KMEL," *Davey D's Hip Hop Corner,* https://www.daveyd.com/articleradiosucks.html). See also Jeff Perlstein, "Clear Channel: The Media Mammoth that Stole the Airwaves," *Davey D's Hip Hop Corner,* https://www.daveyd.com/articlesclearchannelbyjeffpearlstein.html.

13. Sonny Carson was a Black human rights activist and a cofounder of the December 12th movement. His son is Lumumba Carson, better known as hip hop artist Professor X, founder of the X Clan. See Mal'kiy 17 Allah, "Sonny 'Abubadika' Carson and the HipHop Generation," *New York Amsterdam News*, June 6, 2024, https://amsterdamnews.com/news/2024/06/06/sonny-abubadika-carson-and-the-hip-hopgeneration/. See Chang, *Can't Stop Won't Stop*; and David "Davey D" Cook, "A Day in the Bronx: Remembering the Black Spades & Their Connection to Hip Hop," *Davey D' Hip Hop Corner*, January 28, 2013, https://hiphopandpolitics.com/2013/01/28/a-day-in-the-bronx-remembering-the-blackspades-their-connection-to-hip-hop/.

14. *Boogaloo: The Greatest Story Never Told* is an independent film that highlights the story of highly influential music and dance genre sometimes known as "pop-locking." Watch the first episode, "Identity Theft," at https://vimeo.com/641776729.

15. See Harry Belafonte with Michael Shnayerson, *My Song: A Memoir of Art, Race, and Defiance* (Vintage, 2012).

16. See Marcus Goodloe, *King Maker: Applying Dr. Martin Luther King Jr.'s Leadership Lessons in Working with Athletes and Entertainers* (Dream Life Loud, 2015).

4 Gotta Give the Peeps What They Need

HIP HOP AND FUNK

Chuck D and Scot Brown

CHUCK D: Tonight, we're going to talk about the land of the funk.[1] Everybody toyed around with funk. Afrika Bambaataa and the Soul Sonic Force on "Planet Rock"—"Can y'all get funky?"—and sped up electro funk. We know that California followed through on so much electro funk, which is still underrated as a genre. From the World Class Wreckin' Cru, Egyptian Lover, and all those cats, that music moved the dance floors. The Bar-Kays, with "Freakshow on the Dancefloor," were so influential. We're going to talk about Midnight Star, those funk bands. We're going to talk about how that funk not only incubated in LA but also just exploded out of LA.

We're going to talk about the importance of Ohio.[2] People in Dayton just walk funky. I mean, I had a label with Sony, and I have a hit record from a group in Dayton called Bonnie N Clyde when they had "Homey Don't Play Dat." They're from Dayton, Ohio. Two women. They actually recorded their vocals in the same spot where the group Sun recorded. Ohio had, like, seven cities on *tilt*. Cincinnati, which is King Records, James Brown. The birth of funk with Bootsy Collins playing with James Brown's band. A lot of cats coming through and recording at King Records, bringing the blues and country sounds into one city. So you got Cincinnati, Dayton, and you go a little bit farther up, Columbus, the state capital. At the top, you got Cleveland, Toledo, Youngstown, the Lions area, the Canton area where the National Football League started. Ohio has bred a lot of the music, even before the funk.

The Isley Brothers are from Cincinnati. They are, to me, the most powerful group. If you say the Beatles, the Isley Brothers gotta be right there. As far as Black groups, the Isley Brothers gotta be number one. People come to me, "Hey, Chuck, fight the power!" But understand that the first, "Fight the Power," was by the Isley Brothers, 1975. So I quickly dip off that credit and roll it right to the Isleys, who are still here to this day in the form of Ronald and his brother Ernie, who is one of the greatest guitarists of all time. Jimi Hendrix stayed at their crib. So Ernie Isley is in high school, comes home and sees Jimi Hendrix in the room just playing the guitar. It *had* to rub off.

In terms of recorded music, we don't have to go far to get to the beginning of recorded sound. What's the first recording ever? Thomas Edison. What's the first number one song on the charts? "Mary Had a Little Lamb." The point is you ain't gotta go past 1876 to look for another cut. We know when it comes down to live music and instruments, though, that's been going on since the beginning of time. And when musicians were being recorded live, it was usually the loudest instrument that would be the most pronounced, and the star would be the loudest muthafucka in the damn place! An example is Buddy Bolden playing the horn in New Orleans because he knew how to bring the power. A lot of that early music coming after Congo Square was horn driven. If you had four or five musicians blowing, they had to stand over on the other side of a building in order for anybody else to get heard.

What's the next loudest instrument in the room other than the voices? Piano. A lot of those early recordings that you hear are horns with a little bit of piano. You have vocalists that came along, and they were funky. Louis Armstrong was the first. He was almost the first MC, because Louis Armstrong changed the trajectory of vocals. Before recorded music, they would have that operatic Enrico Caruso sound. Louis Armstrong had vocals that almost sounded like his horn blasts and scat rapping. It's like Jay-Z's scatting, you know? Louis Armstrong changed the trajectory of phrasing and vocals, and also, he was able to do it with power too. He could be heard with loud instruments being placed next to microphones. He also could be heard in a room.

Then the microphones got louder in the club gathering, but you also had to learn how to project as a vocalist. The microphones made the projection less, and electronics brought the voice out more. You had a guy like Bing Crosby who learned how to use the microphone with his solo voice, but he used it for radio, and it was live in front of a crowd. He used the projection of electronics to bring that voice over the instrumentation. Bands were thick. Players were trying to play with each other and play against each other. Eventually, the electronics came into play around World War II to make the guitar loud.

You already knew that you had to keep the drummer way in the back. One drummer. In Africa, you got eight drummers playing at the same time. It's about everybody drumming on the same beat and that power you can't match. In the US, it was one drummer doing what eight drummers could do. The drum is a *loud* instrument. But guitars with amplification become the loudest instrument in the room. And then the blues. Plantations in those areas, cats is playing their guitar after a hard day of work because they're playing to themselves. The licks and the riffs were organic. But when they was able to record these licks, you had maybe somebody who felt funky. The guitar was the dominant instrument in the thirties, forties, and fifties, and then we hit the 1960s, and we start to talk about drums coming up a little bit more. With rock and roll or rhythm and blues, the bass player was always tucked to the back kind of quiet, like, "Yo, don't disrupt the groove. Just keep your bass line. Don't step out." So the guitars would come out. They got like a twenty-five-, thirty-year history of being the out-front person.

Then James Brown recorded in Cincinnati, Ohio. He was known to tell everybody to "lay out." Y'all know what laying out is? Laying out is everybody stop except for the drummer. I want these beats to be *kickin.* When James Brown had just the beats, he would have the vocal go over the beat; they're the loudest two in the room, and everybody else gotta lay low. The bassline is also what James Brown was kicking the lyrics over. This is the beginning of something that rappers could look at and say, "Yo, that beat is funky. That bassline's funky," and their vocal is doing what Louis Armstrong did thirty, forty years ago.

I mean, don't get it twisted. A lot of stuff comes out of gospel too. Thomas Dorsey, the creator of a lot of gospel tunes, really the father of gospel music as we know it, was a blues dude. And like any lyric writer, he flipped lyrics. He flipped blues lyrics into gospel, threw a little God up in there, and all of a sudden you had gospel music. If it's got some gospel arrangement to it, that's going to come up out of the blues. If you look deeper, blues and jazz is going to come up with some beginnings out of Congo Square. The New Orleans bordello ain't far from the altar. Matter of fact, the church got a bordello jukebox in it! [*Laughter.*]

We're going to talk about the *funk*. We're going to talk to Dr. Brown about what's before James Brown that actually might lead and bleed into the world of funk. We're gonna go back and learn even more about that lineage. Out of James Brown, you got Bootsy, who plays with James Brown. Then Bootsy hooks up with George Clinton, godfather of funk. George Clinton comes out of being in a New Jersey doo wop band, runs into making those hits, trying to be like Motown and being damn good at it with a hit record called "I Wanna Testify" in 1967 with the Parliaments. But also, he gets transformed with maybe a little LSD here and also hanging out with rock bands in the sixties, in the Summer of Love when cats is getting freaky with it. Out of that, you got Sly and the Family Stone. It comes out of that whole freakiness, San Francisco, Bay Area. Not only we're gonna get freaky with it, we're gonna get funky with it. Not only we're gonna get Black with it, we're gonna get multicultural, multinational with it. We're gonna have women leading the gamut. We're gonna come at you with this funk and drill you with it.

Yo, for real! Out of that comes a funky bass player that says, "I got influenced by Bootsy," and that's Mr. Larry Graham, who also was able to get some mic time with Sly, who basically said, "Okay, I'm a bandleader. I'll let you do your thing." It was kind of what George Clinton did. And James Brown was like, "I'ma let you all do your thing musically, but vocally, I'ma hold on to this microphone."

All of a sudden, funk got to a point where it was a new language. I always thought that funk was something you can't really put your finger on. Sometimes we can't put our nose to funk, other than, "Damn, you're funky." Sometimes the preacher got funk. They talk *funky*. Sometime funky is a look like, "Hunh!" How are you going to explain that sound, "Hunh"? Black folks especially know what that is, though. If somebody gives you that "Hmm!," you're in trouble. And it's no way to put that in text, except it's like, "Here you go with that mess again." "Hunh" says all of that in one motion. You got to not just look at it or hear it, you feel it. Not everybody knew exactly what funk was. Because if you used the word "funk" in the sixties, that was like calling somebody Black in the early sixties. You couldn't call nobody Black. "Who you calling Black? I'm a Negro." "Black" was a curse word that ended up being a beautiful word by the end of the sixties—"Black is beautiful." In the beginning of the sixties, on my birth certificate, it says: "Race: Negro."[3]

But at the end of the sixties, you had groups, whether they were the Funk Brothers on Motown or Grand Funk Railroad, which was a rock group. The thing about those rock groups in the sixties and seventies, they was funky. When hip hop DJs, like Run D. M. C. would tell you when Aerosmith took a break out and they were able to come out with "Walk This Way" in 1975, that beat was stompin! Matter of fact, if you take the guitars out, a lot of those rock groups from 1965 to 1975, you got the greatest beats of all time. It's just that they wanted to play the guitar as the loudest instrument in the room. We're going to come up with riffs. We're going to do like Jimi Hendrix.

On my way up in here today, not only am I listening to Sam Cooke, but I'm also listening to Led Zeppelin, "Stairway to Heaven." The drummer on there is John Bonham, and the beats are coming at you like, "Wow, wow, wow!" You cannot tell me that it ain't funky. Jimmy Page is funky on the guitar. John Bonham is ridiculous on them drums. He beat them drums with trees.

Then beginning at the end of the seventies, you got what? Disco. But you got Earl Young from Philadelphia International Records, who was a funky drummer on a different beat count. Earl Young made those disco movement beats happen. People might not compare them to the same type of funky beats, but there was a lot of funk, not just in the bass or the kick drum but in the high hat and orchestration of all these other elements, tom drums and rolls.

You got to understand, funk is not just a one-two. Sometimes that funk is gonna make your head go like this [*makes a circular motion*]. See, the difference in the fifties, people swang. When they listen, it's almost like church. Back in the day, when they're up there, they're swinging their head like this. Now, they might be on one and three sometimes, on a swing. But on a funk, you're on a two and four, like this. So sometimes, if a song is swinging and funky, the head is going around like this. That will put you in a trance. Disco was not wack, not the beginning of it. The tail end of it was, because well, "Once money starts talking, God walks out the room." It became a big business like slavery. Any time you have businessmen dictate what your music should be, that's the beginning of a four-letter word, with W starting over there, and K over there, and AC in the middle. WACK. [*Laughter.*]

Funk was never dead, leading all the way up in the eighties, which were my first years in college. We were known as the DJs in New York that played funk records. George Clinton once told me, "Man, every time we came to New York, they wasn't looking at the funk like that." Because, as we discussed previously, New York is a different migration melting pot [see chapter 2]. You had all kinds of Caribbean influences in there, Southern influences. When you talk about funk straight from the South, uncut, migration would take you to Ohio from Alabama, looking for that job in the car plant up in Detroit. Atlanta, go up I-75. I-75 takes you from as low down at the bottom of the state all the way to Detroit. I-65 takes you from Alabama all the way to the top. I-55 takes you to Chicago from the South along the Mississippi. It's the Eisenhower Interstate System that I mentioned before. Well, follow the funk.

The funk is thick in the middle of the US, and not so thick in New York. But we played funk records. We played Lakeside. We played the Isley Brothers when they were one of the key funk groups. People forget—the Isley Brothers in the seventies were funk. Talk about Zapp. First time I heard "More Bounce to the Ounce," I was at the club, and I couldn't get in. The only thing I heard was the walls wobbling, and I'm like, "What the fuck is that?!" I wanted to get in and hear this song so bad. One of my boys came outside and said, "Yo, bro, they played this record, man. You had to hear it." I said, "I did hear it. I just heard the bass and the walls shaking!" He said, "Yo, dawg, it's *ridiculous*." I said, "Who made it?" "I heard Bootsy made it." Later on, I saw the DJ that played it, and he was like, "Yeah, Bootsy is on it, and Roger Troutman." I didn't know who he was. I didn't know who Zapp was. But I said, "Well, the spirit of it is funk." Bootsy. Right on Warner Brothers, right down the street.

The funk goes further in the eighties. George Clinton was considered over and done with after all the business colludes tried to move him out. George Clinton was probably the smartest entrepreneur ever in the Black record music era, because he said, "The first time I put out a record, I felt I got the jerk job. So now I got in the record industry and with the seven record major labels." At the time George Clinton put about fifteen groups on those record labels, and he was in the middle of every single group with a different name, Dr. Funkenstein, Bootsy's Rubber Band, Parliament and Funkadelic. He went around the lawsuits. They tried to sue him and said, "You can't use this name." So he went to record companies with another name and started other bands. That was the last time that was done. Well, not the last time. There's a smart brother by the name of the RZA. He hooked up with Steve Rifkind and did the same thing with rappers, with the whole Wu Empire. They said, "You know what, we're gonna sign Wu-Tang to this, but we're gonna take all the rappers and sign them to individual label deals." The record companies said, "We gotta stop that one because one thing we don't need is a smart Black man or a bunch of smart Black people." So, the lawyers step in.

Now, I'd like to introduce you to another smart Black man, Dr. Scot Brown.

SCOT BROWN: Let me start with a confession here. It took me a while to warm up to hip hop because I'm from Rochester, New York. I'm from upstate, one hour away from Buffalo, New York, where Rick James was from. I met Prince in 1980 when he was an opening act for Rick. As a musician, I played bass. When I heard "Rapper's Delight," I couldn't wrap my head around the idea of somebody making money by talking on Chic's music. It was cognitive dissonance. Now before that, I'd heard the Fatback Band when they came to town. This brother named King Tim III, he came out and he rhymed, but he was more like a special guest. But when "Rapper's Delight," came out. . . . I recently saw a documentary where a lot of people in the budding hip hop community, they felt the same way I did for different reasons. How did you feel when you first heard rap in recorded form, given that you were somebody who also was socialized by all these other music styles?

CHUCK D: I was told early on in 1979 that a famed DJ was gonna come out with a record. I was like, "How are you gonna make a rap record?" Then when "King Tim III" came out, it was kind of like a crack in the glass. Then when "Rapper's Delight" came out, the hottest record of that particular summer was "Good Times," by Chic. Records traveled slower back then, so when "Good Times" was the hot record, in the middle of the country, like Kentucky, they were still getting off to "Le Freak," because records lasted all damn year. When I heard rap on record, I didn't think it was wack, because I'm from Long Island, so I knew the New York City bias. They had their guys coming from Bronx, Brooklyn, and Manhattan, who were the preeminent cats doing it. The Sugarhill Gang was the first to do it. So the Grandmaster Cazes, the Grandmaster Flashes, the Melle Mels, the Furious Fives was like, "We should have been doing that!" Yeah, but you didn't think of it first. You couldn't get to a studio. It was inconceivable. I was euphoric. I was like, "Yo, I get it now, and I want to hear more rap records."

You're from Rochester, Scot. And Buffalo is the birthplace of the hottest DJs—Frankie Crocker, Gary Byrd. Buffalo is the hotbed of radio. The best radio stations in the world for Black music was all in Buffalo. They're so hot that New York says, "Come on down here!" Matter of fact, Gary Byrd makes a record with Stevie Wonder. I mean, early on. And he makes a record in 1970, "Every Brother Ain't a Brother," where he's doing his DJ talk over a beat. But it was Gil Scott-Heron–like. So all these things were bubbling, and when I finally heard "Rapper's Delight," a lightbulb went on, but not just for me, for the whole New York City metropolitan area.

BROWN: You were being shaped by another era, the groups that we were listening to—the Ohio Players; Earth, Wind & Fire; Cameo, who were also the New York City Players before they became Cameo—all the groups of this big-band funk period. A big part of funk is live performance. I've always felt like the geography of New York is a little hostile, especially in the denser areas, to live performance. There's no garage for a garage band, for example.

CHUCK D: People on top of each other, and somebody's making noise underneath you, you're like, "Turn that down!" Long Island, we're more like Rochester. We played different types of records. Because I'm a little older, born in 1960, we also had influences from Detroit and Memphis. Soul music. My mom listened to Motown, Stax, Atlantic. And then it's jazz and the jazz clubs from Columbia Jazz Club. They would always drop records. So you're getting all those Yusef Lateef, Charles Mingus, and Miles Davis records. My father liked sports, but my mom, if she told you to do a chore and you messed with that record player, you got problems! Then you had Black Panther–type records in there and Hugh Masekela,

Miriam Makeba, and the standards of Harry Belafonte and Nina Simone. My mom filled out the playlist that way.

BROWN: Were there places where you were going to see live bands when you were growing up?

CHUCK D: Well, Long Island is like Rochester, so it's rural, as far as New York goes. The bands would be at the park jam. You had the older bands that played inside places that young people couldn't get in, cafés, bars. The DJ element came out at a funny time because amplifiers and speakers were somehow finding a way with this two-turntable thing out of Jamaica. But they would still use band amps with the two turntables. I remember one time, the Ohio Players came out to Freeport, Long Island. And there was one knock against bands that led people to the DJs. You know what it was? They didn't sound like the record. Ohio Players came out and played "Skin Tight," and it sounded sped up. The record was slower, so when you heard that on the radio, you were already in that groove. So you don't want to hear that record ten beats per minute faster. And bands don't have pitch down like DJs do. Bands are not going to pace themselves down unless you have an orchestrator. That's why DJs came in, because the bands couldn't make the quick adjustment in front of a large crowd.

BROWN: I'm glad you mentioned the Ohio Players. There's something that funk starts to experiment with before rap became the style. I call it pre-rap rhyming on record. Play "Black Cat," by the Ohio Players. The leader of the Ohio Players, Satch [Clarence Satchell], was super cool. He's pre–hip hop rhyming. There was a lot of that happening in funk, where it wasn't the rhythm that hip hop put with rhyme, but there's this idea of rhyming on top of it.

CHUCK D: That's the same style as the Watts Prophets, the Last Poets, and Lightnin' Rod [Jalal Mansur Nuriddin], who became a character. Isaac Hayes had a rap, it was "Good Love 6-9-9-6-9," in 1975, where he actually did a rhyme that many of the hip hop DJs started playing. But really, if you want to talk about the closest thing to what became rap a couple years earlier, it was "Here Comes the Judge," by Pigmeat Markham in 1968. Maurice White on drums, done in Chicago at Chess Records' studio. I happen to know the producer, Gene Barge. Minnie Riperton is on that record, because she was a vocalist in the group Rotary Connection. When you hear "Here Comes the Judge," you got funky drums beating, and the dude's rhyming in the way that we know rhyming in rap music. So even though Gil Scott-Heron, the Watts Prophets, the Last Poets had their style, the one that comes closest is Pigmeat Markham. The beat's so simple, and the lyrics, "Hear ye, hear ye, the court of swing / It's just about ready to do that thing / I don't want no tears, I don't want no lies / Above all, I don't want no alibis." He was a comedian, so it was like a funny parody. But when you hear that record, it's like, "That had to be the first rap record as we know it" [see chapter 1].

BROWN: I was always interested in this connection between funk and hip hop. Even though we have a hard time pinning funk down, we do have some properties that we assign to it. Does hip hop actually have some specific properties that need to be there?

CHUCK D: Hip hop is the creativity of a people, and it goes beyond the music. I think hip hop is the term of creativity coming out of the hood, originally. We were always creative people. So hip hop is just for that era of time. Now, what is a definite is rap music. Just like with "Rapper's Delight," that overdub process is what rap music has always been. It is the vocal on top of the music. So the music could be whatever it gotta be. There's no such thing as a hip hop beat. If I go, "Boom, boom, bap, bap, bap, bap, boom," and someone says, "Oh, yeah, that's a hip hop beat," that's only leading into ignorance and not knowing the history.

BROWN: Yeah, because you can find that drum line in another genre.

CHUCK D: I'm standing on shoulders of giants, and I talk to people who say, "You can't be audacious enough to start the conversation at hip hop when we did it before you." I had to look at musicians and say, "Yeah, what we do is try to honor that magic that you did."

BROWN: That was a part of Public Enemy's intervention that was very appealing to me in the eighties. It was a conscious attempt to make the connection while so many others had tried to divide us. When I heard, for instance, the way that you referenced Black Power and funk, sonically, it let us know that this was more continuity than a break.

CHUCK D: "Bring the Noise" is not talking about anything that you can hear. Back in the eighties, seventies, and sixties, you ain't have to say a word. You brought the noise just with your skin. Black man walks in the room, and here we go again! Our skin was loud as hell in the sixties. Especially if you wore it proudly, your skin was loud. If you matched your mind and your mouth to it, then you was even noisier. "Tone that Blackness down." That's an element of hip hop and funk. Hip hop is more than music; our skin is more than a color.

BROWN: I hear a lot of people talk about the nineties as this golden age of hip hop.[4] The argument that's been presented to me is that that's when rapping matures, in terms of distinctive styles, and a lot of vernacular places get into the soundscape that hadn't necessarily been heard in the first decade or so of it. The reason why I resist that idea is because there was a period in the eighties, in 1989, when you have the movie *Do the Right Thing*. There are no Blacks making films on that level. Spike Lee's already made two or three, and the film starts off with a song by Public Enemy. It looked like the revolution was going to happen. It felt like things were really about to jump off. I remember going to a study group. We were getting into an intergenerational engagement with it.

So as you asked on *Fear of a Black Planet*, "Who Stole the Soul?" I have to ask that question because there's been a lot of conspiracy theories. But all I know is 1989 felt like a certain kind of consciousness was lining up. It was actually cool for a moment to be politically conscious.[5] The top ten records. Like when I talk to students, they say, "Well, Dr. Brown, you know, it's underground." Yeah, but we didn't have to go under the ground at one point. These were the number-one records. So something happens along the way within a short amount of time where that rebelliousness gets redirected. Some groups that I thought were political, I listen to the other songs on their album, and the people they talking about taking out is other Black folks. How do you read that gap from the late eighties to the early nineties where things really shift, in terms of the top records?

CHUCK D: Well, when Public Enemy came to the forefront, we demanded to be ourselves, and we demanded to be respected. We could be on an international record company and go around the world and say, "We are Black." Ain't no need to hide that. Other acts that came after us went to the next level, like X Clan was like, "We're a Black group, and we will come up in those offices and kill all you white people. If y'all joke us around, we will kill you." After a while, the industry was like, "Listen, we got these militant Black groups, and we got a problem with that." Even on the West Coast a little bit later, they made deals with a whole lot of cats who were affiliated. When the record company execs were going home to

Malibu from their offices, they didn't want these people to knock on the door from South Central or Watts. At one point in time, Malibu and Watts seemed like a thousand miles away. Barry White used to say, the first time he went to Hollywood, he had to catch a bus. His mom packed lunch and said, "I'll see you later, baby," like he was going on a two week trip when he was going from South Central to Hollywood. Those roads narrowed in the nineties. "I will see you from Watts to Malibu at the beach, at your house with your family, if you don't give me this record deal."

Companies were like, "I'd rather have these Negroes fighting each other than looking at me as being the devil and the enemy." That's the truth even if you don't wanna hear it. I'm not saying it as part of a conspiracy theory, because remember in LA at that particular time, all the way up to the police beating Rodney King, you had serious conflicts of gangs, drugs, money [see chapter 2]. The thing that really blew the gangs out was the young generations coming in knowing they could get new money. As I said, when money comes in, God walks out the room. Companies were like, "Forget all that 'fight the power' shit, and what's going on in Zimbabwe," like Stetsasonic did a song on Africa in 1985. Eventually, the next generations that came in, the deals became a little fatter. The representation was like, "You know what, the Black lawyer in your mom's basement, it's not gonna work. Use this lawyer over here." I'm not saying the music wasn't authentic, but they steered it into an area of authenticity that could also be deemed counterproductive. I have always said that negativity has always been a cash cow in the corporations of the United States of America to get Black-on-Black hate. It's always been a moneymaker since the minute that a Black person stepped off a boat. I don't care what you say you are. And the next person was like, "Yo, man, I'm not trying to get whipped like that."

So this division starts, and those things accelerate. In the nineties, a lot of white kids was buying that gangsta stuff for credibility.[6] They're like, "I don't know a Black person. I ain't ever seen a Black person. So I guess that's what Black people are like." This is before social media. They lived through the records. They got their Black Power through the records. They also got their Black relationships through the records. They couldn't communicate like in the 2000s where, "Oh, I got an Instagram friend, and they're Black, but I don't know one in real life." So the music really was a social connection as well. And all the corporations knew it. They called it the golden era because you could throw anything out there and it would come back in a profit margin.

BROWN: What I hear you saying is about the relationship between corporations and music. The period that we discussed earlier with the Black bands was the era of "the Black division" in the record label. The period I research, I look at what I call big band funk, which corresponded with a period in which record labels had Black divisions. I interviewed a very prominent executive who says, and also my mentor who recently passed, James Mtume, told me, "Look, the end of the Black division having power was when Michael Jackson's 'Thriller' came." And certain executives had points, and they said, "This is the end of that."

CHUCK D: None of the Black divisions at that particular time wanted a rap song either, because if it failed, they were out of a job. So the white execs took it on or they took on label deals. That's why I partnered with them.

BROWN: That's a very keen observation I've never heard before. People have asked, What is it about rap that the Black executives missed? But the margin for error was too slim to go jumping into something new. Also, a lot of the Black execs were from out here. You had Larkin Arnold.

CHUCK D: They saved the music business after the music makers had executive positions and they got frivolous and the lawyers took over. Arnold was one of the great lawyers.

BROWN: One of the great lawyers who could negotiate deals. Something about hip hop seems to have reintroduced also the boutique label, the small label. The Black division is in the big companies, like Capitol Records, Casablanca Records. Parliament-Funkadelic, all these funk groups were signed to big labels. I remember when "Rapper's Delight" came out, it didn't look like a real record to me. I mean, it looked like somebody typed it on here.

CHUCK D: The first "Rapper's Delight" records were actually on Cotillion Records. Joe Robinson brought Cotillion over to Atlantic later on, because he was already tied with Morris Levy. Sylvia Robinson, his wife, did "Pillow Talk" [1973].[7] So in that period of time, they were really kind of like all in that combo. And matter of fact, Joe Robinson bought all the Chess catalog. I think that was some underhanded deal because GRT [General

Recorded Tape] bought Chess Records. They didn't know what to do with it; they were kinda getting rid of the assets.

I think Morris Levy and Joe and Sylvia Robinson bought all the Chess. Muddy Waters. Howlin' Wolf. All the Chicago blues, all that Chicago soul. They bought it for like cents on the dollar. Marshall Chess told me he was at Sugar Hill in Jersey.

BROWN: We're talking about the Sugar Hill label. Sylvia Robinson is a very important Black woman in the history of hip hop because she was the label owner. She was a soul artist too. And her husband was a union organizer who also had mob ties.

CHUCK D: Nobody was messin with Joe Robinson. In the nineties, as I said, you had real music guys who were intimidated by real street cats getting into the music business. But back in the day, you had mob running guys running the music. So, there was no street cats going at the mob running business, but later on, it became corporate.

BROWN: Now, this isn't always the most exciting part about music, but it is important as far as understanding that the sounds that we hear are not necessarily coming from a meritocracy. They're not the best sounds; they're the sounds that lots of forces that you don't encounter select.

CHUCK D: In my career, we couldn't get on the radio. People might say they don't listen to the radio, but when the radio's on, it is listened to. And I wonder if my music was played on the radio and played this much. . . . I'm in the Rock and Roll Hall of Fame, for whatever that's worth. Jay-Z, for example, take the amount of time he's been played on the radio because he started at a different time, he's in that evolutionary period of pop music. Big business leads to bigger business. If you're trying to get in, you're trying to get the listening audience. This is why back in the nineties it was hip hop, but it wasn't pop music. Today, in the last fifteen to twenty years, hip hop is pop music, not the sounds but how it is treated. There's a business machinery around the artists and the songs, meaning the bigger the business is, the more hands there are in it too. Because if I want a piece of you and I can make it bigger, then I'm going to make it bigger and get my bigger piece. That's common knowledge; that's street sense. If I'm a lawyer of yours, and I get 5 percent, we're going to drive your value up because I want my 5 percent to get fat.

BROWN: The music business makes it a maze to figure out how to get paid. They still consider people geniuses if they figure out how to get paid.

CHUCK D: The first jazz musicians rejected records. Why? Freddie Keppard said, "I don't want nobody taking my riffs." He said, "When I'm live, you can't get my riffs, because I will catch you onstage and cut you. But if they make a record, you could practice my riffs and cut me back." He said, "I'm not making a fucking record, man." So the "first" jazz guy becomes Paul Whiteman and he becomes, "The King of Jazz," because he said, "I'll make records." Paul Whiteman makes records in 1917 and makes a public statement that jazz music does not come from Black people.[8]

BROWN: Would you agree that the music business itself has some levels of corruption that other businesses don't have? We're still talking about contracts in the 1990s from the greatest artists. In the 1990s, Prince was running around with "slave" written on his face.[9] Recently, Kanye West released his whole contract to the public. It just seems like we are still talking about the hyper-exploitation of people that do so much to bring so much joy to the world.

CHUCK D: I've been on both sides of the business. In all fair retrospect, you could keep your music to yourself, or you can get it out there. This is the beauty of SoundCloud. People say, "Wow, I need to get my music out there." I say, "You're already out there. You're on YouTube and SoundCloud. Why don't you just say you need money?" Maybe we need to go to venture capitalists, and figure out how they come in. You make a business deal with them, because when you go to a place that owns the mechanism, you got to understand you're taking the dip, and not in the pool. You're taking a dip in a bay full of sharks.

This is why I got involved with MP3 technology in 1999. Prince got involved with it, too, when he wrote "slave" on his face because he said, "I don't want record labels to tell me I'm making too much music." Because Prince's beef was what? "I want to release four albums a year, just like y'all did in 1966." And the machine says, "You're choking our machine. We can't do that no more." That's when the first beef happened. Not because Prince couldn't deliver, but the opposite, like, "Y'all can't handle what my audience wants. Y'all not moving at my speed."

When the internet came along and the big fights with the Recording Industry Association of America (RIAA), Prince wanted to get involved with the internet, but there was no way to financially pay him then. That's why Prince didn't make a deal quickly with Apple. He's like, "I'm not going to make a deal with them just because the music business gave the music business away to Steve Jobs." Back in the 1990s, Apple was the comeback company. The big companies back then were IBM and Microsoft. They owned the majority of the marketplace as far as the hardware. Apple was what, 5 percent of the marketplace? So when they were approached by the RIAA, they said, "Look, if the thing gets out of hand, they're only 5 percent, so it can't hurt us." The music was given away to Apple Music. What did Apple excel with? Not the hardware, but the software, iTunes. That's what took them down. It was iTunes accepted everything, put it in order, and was off to the races and never looked back from there.

BROWN: Returning to your music, Public Enemy's appeal to me was the production team, the Bomb Squad. You all made the music sound like a band, actually. Even when you listen to "Don't Believe the Hype," just even Flavor Flav's voice. You can hear soul in that from the first time you hear it all the way through.

CHUCK D: Because we didn't trust drum machines. We didn't program the drum machine as much as we played with it. The Bomb Squad is Hank Shocklee, record digger, DJ, my mentor in that. Keith Shocklee, his younger brother, my first DJ partner as I'm an MC. Eric "Vietnam" Sadler is our band dude. We had the same facilities at 510 South Franklin, where we had the DJ studio upstairs, and Eric had a band rehearsal studio. All the bands came through Eric's studio and rehearsed. When we became a team, we had the friction of, "Keep that in tune. No, don't make it in tune. Pull this back. No, it's got to be right." So the conflict made a dance with it, and that was the combination.

One time, I was hanging out with MC J. B. from J. J. Fad, and she took me by Dr. Dre's studio, and his engineer was called "The Biker." He recorded in Torrance, and he was just finishing up the D. O. C.'s album. I looked in there and I saw how Dr. Dre was doing it, Dre and the engineer. See, you can't separate the producer from the engineer of the studio who knows the board. I was so surprised that Dre was recording everything, and they cut it down to a half-inch or quarter-inch tape. I'm like, "How are you going to get that sound on a quarter-inch tape?" They found ways to EQ filter and boost it. I was just stunned by that because it was still coming out like that, but it was a lot of aftereffects that made it come out stronger. The combination of Dre knowing what sounds and records to bring to the table, but also The Biker, because he looked like a motorcycle hippie, but he was the engineer of that studio in Torrance.

Everybody had their techniques on how to make a sample breathe like a band. Because the bands abandoned the 1960s and 1970s sound by trying to go shiny like Earth, Wind & Fire. If you got Earth, Wind & Fire recording on eighty-six tracks, but I mean, they were scientists in masters of knowing what every knob was. Then the Black departments were getting heat from the record labels saying, "Well, you're not coming up with these numbers. We gotta get rid of Midnight Star or Atlantic Starr. One of these stars got to go." Then they were like, "Well, we got the contract. We're tired of looking at all these Black people in the room at once. We got to get the soloists." That's what happened to hip hop and rap. It went from a group thing into solo because solo you can only deal with one head instead of five or six.

BROWN: The same thing that happened with funk also happened with hip hop.

CHUCK D: With the same people from two different generations.

BROWN: That's another continuity that I haven't ever thought about that I'd like to consider here. Given all these things that we've covered and where we are now, I want to ask the question that was asked on a recent Public Enemy album: "How do you sell soul to a soulless people who have sold their soul?"

CHUCK D: I answered that in 2000. You can't sell that. You got to give it away. You give soul back to them. They already made it to where people feel soulless, so you gotta buy your soul back. You gotta buy your history. You gotta purchase so much of yourself back to finally have a soul. If you ain't got a soul you wouldn't recognize soul if you got ran over with it. Your soul is actually your connection with your people, your neighborhood, your family, your friends. People that you feel innately.

Black people never made a big deal out of how somebody looks. If you looking at somebody white, like "Okay he's white, but I don't look at him as white, he's just cool. And if he ain't cool, I'll bust him in his head." So that's how in this society, in this construct, it's a big deal. "Oh, you got a Black friend? Oh woow!" Now we get to a point where, "Okay, ain't such a big deal now." Now it's a soul-to-soul thing. How do we connect as human beings? Your friendships really have to be more about "You feel me, I feel you. We got friendship. We got kinship. We're cool, and nobody's coming in the middle of this." I think what happened with musicians is that the musicians, artists, and rappers, we started to believe in the separation. And the time that we do connect, we connect through these apparatuses, like, "Now you got a fan base because you've got followers." Back in the day, you're in a venue, and you're getting down, and they came to see you. Or like you said, you went to see Rick James when Prince was opening up. You came to see Rick James.

BROWN: But *Prince* got my attention.

CHUCK D: Prince was trying to say, "I know I'm here on Rick James's ticket, but I'm going to leave with some people too." You had to earn it. If Prince was wack, he wasn't leaving with nobody. You had to go on somebody else's ticket and not "take their fans," but you had to say, "Well, you know this is me." When I opened for LL Cool J, I got fifteen minutes, LL got an hour. Then we traveled together in Europe, just us and LL. We had to say, "He's the king. We have to bust our asses every night in order to get a little bit of something." So artists and human beings, the intermediaries are dividing us and keeping us from bringing this back into a neighborhood type of thing, the way we used to do it. Do I think that time is ever coming back? I think there are signs when you start seeing collabs. I think collabs are a great thing. I did a song with Mavis Staples. I think OG hip hop should also line up with OG funk and soul too. This is why I think that the funk musicians won't be forsaken and forgotten if they realize that the future is everybody's. You already see it because Ice Cube, Snoop Dogg, and Kendrick Lamar, they all line up.

BROWN: We've heard some great philosophy, some business strategy, some great music history. But let's not forget that we're dealing with Chuck D, also the artist, the innovator. If you listen to Migos or any of the contemporary artists, they sometimes use something called "the triplet flow."[10] Chuck D was doing that before we had a word for it. In "Bring the Noise," for example, go to about one minute and five seconds in, right when that second verse hits, and just listen to Chuck D's early triplet flow. That's another dimension of the great artist that we've gotten a chance to talk with. Let's open it up to questions.

QUESTION 1: My generation thinks of Bruno Mars when we hear "funk," but where is funk music now?

SAMUEL LAMONTAGNE: I'd like to add something here. Scot, I remember your conversation with Bootsy Collins at the Fowler Museum back in 2018.[11] You asked him about the late 2010s being a funk renaissance moment, and you asked him specifically about Bruno Mars and how new artists were using funk. I remember Bootsy validating Bruno by saying he was "the Michael Jackson of funk." It was an amazing conversation.

In terms of the continuity between funk and rap even in the present, there's Leon Sylvers III, from the group the Sylvers, who went solo and became a legendary funk producer who has been extensively sampled in hip hop. He worked for SOLAR Records in LA, which was the label founded by Dick Griffey and Don Cornelius and originally was Soul Train Records.[12] Leon produced for groups such as Lakeside, Shalamar, Midnight Star, and so many more funk bands in the 1970s, and later on even for 1990s hip hop and R&B groups like Blackstreet and Guy. He has talked about loving new rap artists using auto-tune, Travis Scott in particular, and artists like Kendrick Lamar in general. He recognizes that continuity, even as some of OGs are frowning upon younger hip hop generations.

Also, Dâm-Funk, he's very important in LA, a real catalyst for the modern funk scene, with artists like XL Middleton, Zackey Force Funk, or Moniquea, who have been puttin it down since the late 2000s. They're all influenced by the OGs, from George Clinton, Bootsy Collins, to Zapp, Rick James, and Prince, but really by way of the LA rap culture from Dre, DJ Battlecat, DJ Quik, and Kokane. And to go really back to the originators of LA hip hop, people like Egyptian Lover and Uncle Jamm's Army [a play on the funkadelic album *Uncle Jam Wants You*], they were all funk heads. Folks like Thundercat, the Internet, Matt Martians, and Tyler, the Creator, all have roots in LA hip hop. Then you got other artists like Dom Kennedy, Larry June, YG, Nipsey Hussle, Jay Worthy, and producers like Cardo, who modernized the G-funk sound too.

BROWN: That helps us answer the question about funk, about where it is. To add to that, I always look at what songs become anthems, meaning that they can pass through generations, and everybody knows what to do. When you have a family reunion, what songs do people fall into? Even beyond the electric slide, Frankie Beverly and Maze "Before I Let Go," that's a must-play at a reunion. Cameo's "Candy" has people acting a certain kind of way. I think as we go, we can ask about what hip hop songs can get into that pantheon. Part of what Chuck was saying about soul is also tied to questions like: How do we congregate? How do we get together? How do we celebrate and affirm aspects of the life cycle? What is the soundtrack to that? That's where I think funk has had a pretty good run and probably not gonna go anywhere any time soon.

CHUCK D: Y'all go to the club, right? I can tell you back in the day, that jam comes on, "More Bounce to the Ounce," *everybody's* dancing. Hip hop comes out of a dance culture. Later on, it became a car culture thing where you ain't gonna get out there and dance but you're in the car. But we got out of the car, danced in the parking lot and in the club too. If you go into a club now, what's your vibe?

AUDIENCE COMMENT 1: Well, if you go to a club in New York, if you put on any drill song, there's a dance they're doing. Everybody's doing it. I'm from New York, so when I'm out here in LA, that's how I identify the New Yorkers in the club or at the party, because certain songs by Pop Smoke or Bobby Shmurda will come on, and they're doing the woo.[13] That's how you *know* they're from New York. They don't dance like that in LA, in my experience.

CHUCK D: Like ten years ago, it was the beginning of drill circles. My oldest daughter, Dominique, I went in there and picked her up. I was like, "You gotta come back home." She was still in high school. So I went in there, it's like a large circle, and they were popping in and popping back and popping in. Is that in the middle of a club today? Could we branch out to the point where the whole country is dancing in the same way, or is it just going to be in one pocket and that's it? Back in the day, we watched *Soul Train*, and then everybody was locked in, and before that, *American Bandstand* with the twist. Everybody saw this one dance. But now, you got like eighty million different channels on YouTube, and everybody's over here and over there.

BROWN: I think that's an interesting point, but I think also we're dealing with something deeper than just the music and the music culture. It is the way people are socializing. We're much more in an individualized space. The worst punishment my mother or father could tell me is, "You gotta stay in the house." Staying in the house was hell as far as I can conceive it, because I wanted to be outside playing touch football. I wanted to be doing something outside. If you want to punish a child now, you say, "You gotta go outside," right? Because they'd rather be *in* the house.

Here's the thing that's so different, though. Our audience for dance was where we were. Right now, your audience is global. So do you hold your phone up? It's much more of a performance. So there's something communal that's going on for another generation about making the individual experience go somewhere else.

AUDIENCE COMMENT 2: It also depends on what kind of club you're in, because I haven't been to a club since the pandemic. I go to gay clubs. And you were talking about people not dancing? Is that a thing now? I will tell you this, there are some gay anthems where the entire club, we're all lip-syncing, and we're all doing it together. It's not a specific dance, but we're all performing as if we are that artist.

CHUCK D: Do record companies recognize that demographic, saying, "We need to promote this artist because everybody digs them like that?"

AUDIENCE COMMENT 3: Yeah, absolutely. I feel like especially recently, it's definitely a demographic factor that record companies profit from. Like you have queer icons that aren't even gay, like Britney Spears. Lady Gaga is a queer icon. Lil Nas X, he's doing huge things for the community.

CHUCK D: Yeah, Lil Nas X once they found out that there's a pipeline between him and Elton John.

QUESTION 2: In 1990/91, you toured with Sisters of Mercy. I remember that Andrew Eldritch, their front man, said that America wasn't ready for white kids and Black kids in the same audience; they're too afraid of it. The Latinx community saw a bridge because very few people would recognize that we could associate ourselves with this music from the hood, from the barrio. Today you have a group like Prayers doing what's called cholo goth, but you guys were touring with a goth group back then, but it didn't work out. Was America not ready socially, or was the timing wrong because of the record companies not putting enough into the marketing strategy?

CHUCK D: You have revolution and you have evolution. Actually, that tour with Sisters of Mercy happened before the Anthrax tour. We toured with Sisters of Mercy in June and July of 1991, and then that fall, we did the release of "Bring the Noise" with Anthrax. That furthered the discussion of "You got rap and you got rock, but really you got thrash and hardcore rap." They were like, "Oh my God, they're going to tear down the venue.

They're going to spark race riots." The Sisters of Mercy was a great introduction. We played Radio City. It was a breakthrough. When you're doing things for the first time, it ain't never gonna be pretty. Then it's the copycat industry. When it works, then other people are going to copy it. And you want people to copy. You should want better for your other artists, even better than for yourself. Because you are standing on the shoulders of giants, so that others can stand on your shoulders. It all comes back around. This is like one big circle. If you're good enough, you'll work with the same people over and over again. As a matter of fact, a guy that we gave a job to on the Sisters of Mercy tour later on became the Foo Fighters road manager. So it's a full circle.

From the Public Enemy and Anthrax collaboration, the rap-metal thing came out of it. Music is competitive. You have a competitive edge in you, but you really hope that your competition rises up, because when they rise up, you rise up. There's a saying by people in the music business, "Be careful of the feet that you step on because one day it might be attached to the ass you'll have to kiss." So it's a humbling type of circle. But that was the thing, I was grateful. I saw Andrew on tour a couple of years ago, and we talked about that time and we had a pioneering spirit. There's no such thing as failure when you're trying new things.

H. SAMY ALIM: We were talking about migrations and the movements of music and how it changes as it goes through different cities. There is a dominant historical narrative, but in my mind, it's not as simple. The narrative that's told is, "You have West Coast and East Coast vibin to different forms of music." On the West Coast, the artists really pick up the funk to a whole 'nother degree. East Coast artists revived the funk, too, but not to the same degree, or you had more jazz. Is that a narrative that's historically accurate? Because a lot of folks at least when I was growing up in high school got introduced to funk through *The Chronic*, Dr. Dre and Snoop. People didn't even know it was funk, but they discovered it was funk through rap music.

BROWN: I think yes and no. The yes part is that the era of West Coast hip hop, there's a lot more interpolation. There's a lot more musicians actually playing it as sampling fees became too high. To try to do what Public Enemy did in the nineties would have cost you a lot more. So, some of that is invention by necessity. I wouldn't say that they are more attached to funk, but that it's a different style of funk. So they're tighter with Ohio funk. Roger Troutman is really important, even though EPMD had sampled "More Bounce to the Ounce." But "California Love," what that did for Roger was really reintroducing him to a whole 'nother generation. Also, George Clinton and P-Funk. That's a transcendent artist. I mean P-Funk, we don't have a word to figure out what that actually is, it is so big. Then also even some soul stuff, the way they would interpolate it and sometimes with very little alteration. "Nuthin' but a 'G' Thang" by Dr. Dre, if you listen to Leon Haywood, "I Wanna Do Something Freaky to You" [1975], it's almost like he barely put anything in there but played the record.

CHUCK D: "I Wanna Do Something Freaky to You" wasn't getting much radio play. If they had their publishing rights, Dre seriously took care of that family for life. That's a good thing.

BROWN: It's a way that the West Coast, especially Dre and others, like DJ Quik, are such good curators in terms of digging in the crates and finding something.

CHUCK D: A lot of my homies out here, their uncles, and their moms and dads, they had the backyard parties. Also the Latino families, they had the backyard parties, and those songs were in those crates. So those crates were different from New York crates. We also have to talk about the Watts Rebellion. When the radio stations, Magnificent Montague, them cats were playing funk, soul, Johnnie Taylor. When Stax really had their muscle in Southern California.

BROWN: And they did the Wattstax concert in 1972.

CHUCK D: We used a lot of that for *It Takes a Nation of Millions to Hold Us Back*, I mean, "Don't Believe the Hype."

BROWN: Which I didn't know until I saw the film *Wattstax* and heard "Brothers and sisters!"

CHUCK D: Right at the LA Coliseum. Before we used that record, we didn't use a lot of the Wattstax concert in the grooves, all of it are the interstitials. Rufus Thomas talking, Jesse Jackson opening up, all that concert footage, we kind of went in there. The good thing is I was invited back by Stax and became like a Stax family member. Because I brought a lot of that to the forefront and acknowledged that and also said that that was a beautiful event at the Los Angeles Coliseum. They filled it with a hundred thousand people, and it was a dollar a person. Basically, it was bringing the community together for a concert for the people. This is seven years after the 1965 Watts Rebellion. Everybody came to the table. This was a statement around the world that they felt was necessary in this area.

BROWN: Soul is actually the other end of that. There's a period from the late sixties through the early seventies where Parks and Recreation and politicians understood that if you had these big concert events, you could let off some of the steam.

CHUCK D: Especially after Dr. Martin Luther King's assassination, April 4, 1968. This country with the resignation of Lyndon Johnson, I'm eight years old at the time. I remember, because I was like, "What's going on? Lyndon Johnson is not going to be president no more. So, what choices do we have, teacher?" We had George Wallace, who was then like an Alabama Confederate cracker at that time, who flipped later on like, "Okay, I got paralyzed, got shot. I'm a new man. I've changed." That was crazy. Hubert Humphrey, who was vice president under Lyndon Johnson. And then it was Richard Nixon, who was already the vice president of Eisenhower twelve years before. But he lost to Kennedy, who just got killed five years ago. You grow up in the sixties like, "Okay, the president is getting killed. We just lost Dr. Martin Luther King Jr., Malcolm X. My uncles are in Vietnam." You're eight years old like, "Yo, this place is crazy right?"

Dr. King gets murdered and Nixon comes in, and we as kids, this is 1969, you automatically have a different mindset. The government at this particular time says, "We gotta figure out what calms this movement down." The Panthers are rising up. You had the Panther assassinations in 1969 of Fred Hampton and Mark Clark, and that is when you had a concert taking place in New York. Big applause to Questlove for winning an Academy Award for *Summer of Soul*.[14] Quest makes a statement that at this particular time people were apart, and this concert in New York pulled people together in that region because that region was hot.

BROWN: That was going on everywhere. In my hometown was a Highland Bowl music festival. So all these places had them, but that documentary is a great window into the phenomenon. But also Wattstax is more so at the tail end of that. As you get later on into the seventies, there's less money spent on those types of big gatherings. But that's sort of the heart of it. And that's what Wattstax is. A lot of it gets on wax, the speeches, and the things that are stated.

CHUCK D: That's where the sensibility came from, because *It Takes a Nation of Millions* felt like it was from another time. It was sixteen years later. We sampled from them. "Fight the Power" also felt like it was from another time because the title and the sensibility was from fourteen years earlier. It was 1975 when the first "Fight the Power" was made. I felt, "Can we convey that same message in a rap song?" But *It Takes a Nation* was sixteen years after Wattstax. Wattstax in Los Angeles, California, in 1972, resonated around the world, and they didn't want that feeling to get bigger.

BROWN: To get back to Samy's question, I think there's something distinctive in these areas about how the funk manifests itself, because I think it's more about where these leanings are. Some of it is connected to the migration patterns. I have a lot of students where their folks are from Arkansas, Louisiana, and Texas. There's a lot going on with that. But I also wanted to ask about this whole question of songs that become hits. There are some artists that believe that what makes a hit is kind of arbitrary, that very few people know what a hit is. Then other people say, "From the moment I made this, I knew I had something." Have you ever felt that way?

CHUCK D: Hell yeah, one song out of all the albums I ever did—and it wasn't "Fight the Power." It was "Rebel without a Pause." I knew when we made that record, I could have died the next day and that record was going to live. Only one time it happened, that was like, "Oh, somebody else made that one." It seemed to have made itself. And then, sure enough, that was our first record.

You craft songs. In the session, I'm usually a person where I like to perfect, with a lot of takes. But some of them was like, "Boom!" Like, "Black Steel in the Hour of Chaos" and "He Got Game" was like that. That surprised me. Our biggest record next to "Fight the Power" is "Harder than You Think." It was made in 2007, and it became the theme for the Paraplegic Olympics in London in 2012. It's an international record, so it's the biggest record we have. It's a different audience, a younger audience. It's based on exposure, too, because they put it on TV and in movies. You even hear it on commercials on ESPN today, but you probably don't know it's us.

We mentioned Coachella a couple weeks ago. The acts might not be bigger or better than the past, meaning five years or ten years ago. But what is bigger at Coachella is the infrastructure, the management, the agents and the production and technology is out of this world. I've been on like 117 tours in 116 countries, 5,000 shows, stadiums and all that. I can't even begin to tell you how my brain is blown out. I didn't even go to the night-time shows. They built gigantic geode domes. I just think they're phenomenal. When you see the artists of today with the screens, it's unbelievable. The sonics are loud. The 808, you can hear it all over the whole thing. So it's just the magnitude of the technology. When the artist steps up there today, I don't think you could fail because the screens are just amazing to me. I don't know when y'all go to a big concert, I know you go with your phone, but are you looking at the screen more than you looking at the stage?

I think, like Scot said, if the phone is a new way that people experience live concerts, then that's gotta be it, right? My visual art to me is paint, marker to paper, but you know what? That's only half of it, because my best experience with the art is taking the iPhone photo of it. Back in the day, you do your art and put it away. Now, I do my art, take the picture, frame it, filter maybe, boom, Twitter, Instagram, booooom! I produce something, so I want you all to enjoy it. So the gallery is now our galaxy.

BROWN: Even in concerts and the club, there's something inclusive about the technology in the blurring of the distinction between audience and performer.

CHUCK D: For the first time, I experienced that the stage has been leveled, where the artist and the audience are damn near becoming one synonymous participant. You can't get rid of that enthusiasm at all, especially sixteen, seventeen, eighteen-year-olds, because they're happy to get away from their parents. That enthusiasm ain't got nothing to do with the act. Their enthusiasm is their friends that they're rolling with. It's like "Yo! We here!" I mean, that's what these companies are trying to figure out. How do we take that enthusiasm, before they can sell them a record, right? I think the devices make them the star. I think the bigger it gets, the more people in the audience become like stars and the people on the stage become less of a star. I know it sounds crazy, but it's like the audience now has come up and the stage has kind of come down. That means that stars can easily be replaced. It ain't gonna be "Oh yeah, you will be big for twenty years." Not if I could get up there, too, and do the same thing and be big.

I think you got incredible talent out there. I think nurturing these talents is lacking and also understanding what's going on now. There's not a class out there like this. But hopefully, it could get into explanation and not just be academic but also be like, "Oh, wow. Okay, that makes sense." We don't get that from radio stations no more. We don't get that from television stations no more. We don't get the explanation of why something's dope. That's what we're doing here, as we think about funk and hip hop and how Black music evolves over time.

NOTES

1. See Ricky Vincent, *Funk: The Music, the People, and the Rhythm of the One* (St. Martin's, 1996), and Tony Bolden, *Groove Theory: The Blues Foundation of Funk* (University of Mississippi Press, 2020).

2. See Scot Brown, "A Land of Funk: Dayton, Ohio," in *The Funk Era and Beyond: New Perspectives on Black Popular Culture*, ed. Tony Bolden (Springer, 2008), 73–88. See also Scot Brown, *Tales from the Land of Funk: Dayton, Ohio and African American Funk Bands in the 1970s* (forthcoming).

3. See Geneva Smitherman, *Black Talk: Words and Phrases from the Hood to the Amen Corner*, revised ed. (Houghton Mifflin, 2000), for the meanings of "funk" and other expressions that capture the inventive qualities of Black lexicon, including evolving terms of racial self-reference like "Black," "Negro," and so on.

4. See Nelson George, *Hip Hop America* (Viking, 1998).

5. See writings in James G. Spady, *Nation Conscious Rap: The Hip Hop Vision* (Black History Museum Press, 1991).

6. See Bakari Kitwana, *Why White Kids Love Hip Hop: Wankstas, Wiggers, and Wannabes, and the New Reality of Race in America* (Basic Civitas, 2005).

7. For an in-depth interview with Sylvia Robinson about her decision to record rap music, see James G. Spady, H. Samy Alim, and Charles G. Lee, *Street Conscious Rap* (Black History Museum, 1999).

8. See Maureen Anderson, "The White Reception of Jazz in America," *African American Review* 38, no. 1 (2004): 135–45.

9. The legendary artist Prince wrote "slave" on his cheek to symbolize the exploitative nature of record contracts and his desire to be released from Warner Music. See Andreana Clay, "Prince," *Biography* 41, no. 1 (2018), featuring articles by Clay, Greg Tate, Steven Thrasher, and Scott Poulson-Bryant.

10. See Den Duinker, "Good Things Come in Threes: Triplet Flow in Recent Hip-Hop Music," *Popular Music* 38, no. 3 (2019): 423–56. DOI: https://doi.org/10.1017/S026114301900028X.

11. Watch the January 30, 2018, conversation between Scot Brown and Bootsy Collins at UCLA at https://www.youtube.com/watch?v=ozK364S4vNU. See also

Scot Brown's March 20, 2018, conversation with Bootsy Collins, "Funkology," at Indiana University published in *Liner Notes: Archives of African American Music and Culture* 22 (2017–18).

12. See Scot Brown, "SOLAR: The History of the Sounds of Los Angeles Records," in *Black Los Angeles*, ed. Darnell Hunt and Ana-Cristina Ramon (New York University Press, 2010).

13. The woo is a dance from New York that was popularized by drill rapper Pop Smoke, who also released a song by the same title prior to his untimely death in 2020.

14. *Summer of Soul* (2021), by Ahmir "Questlove" Thompson of The Roots, is an enthralling documentary on the 1969 Harlem Cultural Festival in Mount Morris Park (now Marcus Garvey Park) featuring legendary musicians like Nina Simone, Stevie Wonder, Gladys Knight & the Pips, Sly and the Family Stone, and more. It was Questlove's filmmaking debut and earned him an Oscar.

5 Revolutionary Generation

WOMEN, GENDER, AND SEXUALITY IN HIP HOP

Chuck D and Cheryl L. Keyes

CHUCK D: We're going to talk about the subject of women in hip hop, which includes sexism and gender politics. We will consider the position and politics of women in the world, not just in hip hop. One thing that's always puzzled me is, "Where do we start from?" Like James Brown's record, many men still think "it's a man's world." Even when we look at governments, if we view women as equal human beings, why are males usually the heads of governments? Same thing with corporations, businesses, religion, and other domains across society. We need to balance this out.

When we talk about women in hip hop, we can ask, "Why is it out of balance?" Hip hop would not have the "hop" to it, and especially wouldn't have the "hip" to it, if women weren't involved in its making, its manifesting. It should be a no-brainer that when we talk about all the giants in hip hop that we shouldn't have to say, "She's the best *female* MC" or "She's a femcee" or "She's in the top five women in hip hop." As we move forward and educate folks, we want to ask questions like, How come sometimes when we talk about the greatest, a woman ain't in the top five or top ten, when we know there are many talented women MCs?

Let's run it down before we begin tonight. You want to talk about somebody who can spit and flow, I always thought MC Lyte could spit and sound harder than any dude. Why wouldn't she be in the top ten? Why is this considered an anomaly? In this particular discussion today, I think we're going to have a dialogue that starts from my questions, then we're going to grow from there. We will check the facts as far as hip hop and rap music is concerned.

The first industry recording by rappers on a record was founded by a woman by the name of Sylvia Robinson, who was married to Joe Robinson. Sylvia Robinson was an R&B star in the fifties as part of a duo called Mickey and Sylvia. Her husband, Joe, was part of the music industry. As we mentioned previously [see chapter 4], he was arm in arm with gangsters, but he didn't get overrun to the point where he couldn't do what he wanted to do in the music business. You couldn't overrun Joe, because he was too connected.

Sylvia definitely wasn't taking no crap either. She was a person that was the musical point, while Joe was the business point. She knew the business, but she also knew how to put things together in terms of music production. She knew how to go into the studio and actually make records down to the mastering. She knew all the business insides to make not only a record but the business of the record. Sylvia Robinson was so much a part of this, she had the wherewithal to say, "I'm going to put out this first rap record, and I'm going to put a group together just the way they put groups together in the 1950s and the 1960s. They don't even necessarily have to know each other. All I want is to be able to make this record."

She put together the Sugarhill Gang and the record that we know now as "Rapper's Delight." Sylvia Robinson found the guys, produced the record, and not too long after, she had the idea that started it all with the Sugarhill Gang. She went down to South Carolina and founded the first women group, called the Sequence, who recorded on Sugar Hill Records in December 1979. All women. One of them was named Angie Brown Stone, a.k.a. Angie B. Some of y'all might have heard of Angie Stone as a R&B singer in the group Vertical Hold. Before that, she had a rap career with the Sequence in 1979 with "Funk You Up." Not only did Sylvia take, once again, an out-of-state group—because the Sugarhill Gang were all from Jersey—but she goes to Columbia, South Carolina, and picks the second group out of state, all women, because Sugarhill Gang was touring down there.

At that same time in 1979, a lady does a radio show at an AM radio station in Philadelphia known for its talk but also known for playing soul records throughout the city, WHAT 1340 AM. She goes by the name of Lady B, and she made a record, "To the Beat Y'all," in November 1979. Lady B is significant because she becomes the longest running broadcaster to this day of hip hop and rap music. Lady B is the queen of hip hop and rap music. She broke my records thirty-six years ago. She's been breaking records for forty years. She also significantly makes one of the first female solo rap records, "To the Beat Y'all," which is a vernacular used in hip hop since its beginning.[1]

From there, the branch goes into many other contributors. Pebblee Poo, who was also a vocalist with the Masterdon Committee. "Funkbox Party" [1982] was probably her most significant run of bars, where she spits the bars on the second half of that record. Twenty years later, Master P uses it in his song because it struck him as a Louisianan. Then, of course, you have Queen Latifah, MC Lyte in the late eighties. Queen Latifah takes a step forward and says she's going to basically anoint herself as the queen and empower women to say, "We don't have to rap what dudes rap. I can come from my own point of view." That's very significant. Because up to that point in the mid-eighties, it was always about guys finding a woman to rap with them and ride along the same point of view, or even if they do say something different, they say something different within the context of what dudes feel. Queen Latifah was like, "This is what I'm thinking, from my point of view, and I'm going to step to the plate. I'm from Jersey. I'm a former high school basketball star." If it comes down to head to head, shoulder to shoulder, rhyme for rhyme, bar to bar, Latifah wasn't afraid of nobody. Now she's on TV shows and movies. She's been doing that for almost thirty years as well. But at the beginning, Queen Latifah was known as somebody that could take it to the stage and go head to head.

So this started to grow and form new combinations. If you're gonna have guy groups, out of that, Salt-N-Pepa comes in. They made an answer record to Doug E. Fresh and Slick Rick's "The Show." They were originally called the Showstoppers, and they happened to be a by-product of Hurby "Luv Bug" Azor, a great producer in the 1980s. They spawned a lot of combinations, and matter of fact, it wasn't rare for women in hip hop to have groups in the eighties. Like we talked about in previous sessions, the further the industry went forward, there was this intention on destroying groups so you can only negotiate, or "negrotiate," with one person at a time. Executives felt that the industry was being infiltrated with this new nationalist point of view that was saying, "Own self, be self"—own what you do, own your word and your mind.

"Hip hop" might have been that coinage that we've talked about before, but it came out of the spirit of great poets, great writers, Zora Neale Hurston, Nikki Giovanni, and Sonia Sanchez. Today, you still have people like Toni Blackman that carry that same flow and form. We went through a period of Yo-Yo and understanding that Ice Cube could bring along somebody with a woman's point of view to balance out his dude's point of view, and also kinda giving him license to ill a little bit on the male point of view. But also, he says it got to be a Yo-Yo that puts me in my place and tells me that I'm full of ishhh.

MC Sha-Rock and Roxanne Shante are on Sirius XM Radio. Sha-Rock was the one with the Funky 4 + 1. She's the first woman to actually appear on national TV doing a rap song, and that was "That's the Joint" [1980]. They also was on when Debbie Harry from the group Blondie put rap lyrics in "Rapture" [1980] and really blasted the pop doors open to say that this style is coming from the Bronx and it's real, because "Flash is fast and Flash is cool and Fab 5 Freddy told me so." We can bring it all the way into the nineties and the early 2000s from Foxy Brown and Lil' Kim, all the way up to Nicki Minaj and Megan Thee Stallion. You have people like Nikki D, Yo-Yo, Monie Love, who's from London.

Here's the most hidden fact about women in hip hop. Women in hip hop around the rest of the world, outside of the US, make up 30 percent of rap music. This is nothing new. They don't go about saying "Oh, let's talk about women in hip hop," who make 30 percent of all hip hop around the planet. You talk about hip hop collectives. The Wee Papa Girl Rappers is a group. She Rockers also founded by Professor Griff in the middle of the eighties from London. All the way up to the solo stars like Amy True and Kae Tempest. All the other countries in the world blazing with great MCs, but most importantly, from women's points of view or how they each might look at the world. One of the great rap groups from Cape Town, South Africa, is Godessa.[2]

H. SAMY ALIM: There's another MC in Cape Town named Eavesdrop. The first time I heard her, I almost fell out of my chair. She was kicking it so hard and in many different styles. She goes from the real hard street flow to the sentimental, to the historical. As an MC, she's just pure fire. You got Blaq Pearl, Dope Saint Jude, Andy Mkosi, Natasha Tafari, YOMA, all bringing the heat. Godessa has been doing it for decades, and so the torch keeps being passed on there.

CHUCK D: E. J. von Lyrik who now lives in the Netherlands.

ALIM: That's right, her and Bernadette Amansure and Shameema Williams created Godessa. They're all incredibly talented artists with a social justice mission.

CHUCK D: Internationally, in order to set hip hop free as far as this limitation on women, we have to continue to explore instead of exploit. That's the key. Without further ado, we can explore more of this with the one and only Dr. Cheryl L. Keyes.

CHERYL L. KEYES: Thank you, Professor Chuck D, you brought me back down memory lane. Sometimes when you have been in the trenches, as I have as a pioneering scholar of hip hop, you look up and you finally see things begin to come together. I really pride myself with the knowledge that I know and continue to try to learn from artists from the community, from the streets. Growing up in Louisiana, middle class, I always was attracted to the energy from the streets, beginning with the blues. That is the soul, in my opinion, of Black folks, sort of playing on Amiri Baraka's book [*Blues People*] and as signified in my book's title, *Rap Music and Street Consciousness*.[3] Hip hop is street consciousness.

The street is not all about the negativity that we see being expressed in the media and as a part of a narrative trying to demonize Black people. It is where the soul is. You want to know where people are, you want to know what's going on, you're either gonna go to the juke joints—which, again, that's a Southern thing, a place where many of the down-home Black folks congregate, let their hair down—or you gonna be in church. It's interesting that you can continue to have these kinds of polarities. Street over here, which I love, then you have "the chuuch," as they call it, which I also dabbled in as a music director and learned how to handle that Hammond B-3 organ back in the day.

You brought me back down memory lane when thinking about women in hip hop too. I knew that there was a space in my work that needed to really address what it's like to be a woman in hip hop. Now, I'm not an MC.

In studying something that I do not perform, at least I'm out of the culture, and it may give me a sense of objectivity. I always remember that one of my professors said, "Well, why don't you study a genre like jazz or gospel?" It just wasn't it for me. I kept on with hip hop.

You mentioned the Sequence, just to return to them and tie in my roots as a Black Southerner who basically went to an all-Black-everything in Baton Rouge, Louisiana. I do remember when I heard "We're gonna funk you right on up, we gonna funk you right on up." I said, "Well, that reminds me of all the Black cheers," because I went where they really had Black cheerleaders doing cheers. Just hearing that recalled my days of watching, and I was kind of shy about trying to be a cheerleader, but I was in the marching band. Just hearing it, I told myself, "You got to study this." Because this was, as you said, 1979, and how did it get from the South all the way to the North? So that was one of the songs that I do see coming out of a Black cheerleading tradition. When you mentioned some of my work, even though I continue to write, I had to go back and give props to the Mercedes Ladies.[4] Now that's your neck of the woods with people like Debbie D.

CHUCK D: Sheri-Sher, Lisa Lee of Soulsonic Force, Debbie D.

KEYES: I was reading about them, but finally Davey D had a program where he interviewed a few of them. So I was able to hear Sheri-Sher talking about the fact that the Mercedes Ladies was one of the pioneering crews. They just happened to be women, but there were pioneering crews. Now, it is from my understanding, Professor D, that they were a collective that also had DJs in it as well, not just femcees.

CHUCK D: That was also a term that they were able to give up in Canada, from the pioneering queen of hip hop and rap, Michie Mee up in Toronto. Big up to Michie Mee up there.

KEYES: So it was Michie Mee that pushed or introduced the term "femcees"?

CHUCK D: Well, from Canada. But I'm going to ask you a question: When it comes down to what women say from a woman's perspective in the world of hip hop, when does it get too encroached upon by maleness to where it kind of corrupts it? Especially as we go further on, when you see Megan Thee Stallion, who might say something that's highly charged from her inner soul, and it's the sexuality on the outside as well. For a long period of time, it was men that would be like, "Nah, nobody tryna hear that," or "Nah, you should do it this way." That's no longer the case.

KEYES: For me to answer that, it's somewhat complex, because I have a chapter that I felt I needed to write because I always like to show continuity, that it's not all that new.[5] But then there's something else happening that does provide that space for women in hip hop to express themselves in the most uninhibited way, physically. I'm talking about this Texas gal, Megan Thee Stallion. But what's interesting, though, is the fact that we've had those blues women. I always think about the fact that at one point, people thought that the early blues—let's say the Son Houses and the Muddy Waters—was really a male thing. Of course, we had women singing rhythm and blues. But what's fascinating is that I see these connections with the women blues singers. They didn't hold back in terms of expressing their sexuality, what they wanted. The fact that some of them also loved other women, it didn't matter. I think even in community, at least the streets, the juke joints, they say, "Oh yeah, we knew Bessie Smith was going out with so and so, with Ma Rainey." It wasn't a big deal in the Black community, primarily. This is not to say that the Black working class was promiscuous—no, by no means. But that's why I love the streets. It's always about honesty. When you start dealing with the church thing is when you start moving over there into the Victorian thing, with what you're not supposed to do, trying to hold back. But these women from the blues all the way to what we see now, in my opinion, with the Megans, with the Nickis, and with the Cardi Bs and all of them, they're just extensions of these women.

Through the years, I've noticed that many critics and scholars often associate rap music with urban male culture. We know that women have been involved in the history of this music since its early years, and we need more work that explores Black women's contributions to and role in shaping rap music. One of the things I began to work on early on was the creation of four categories of women artists. During the golden age of hip hop, Black women artists adopted a range of performance personae and their lyrics reflected various subject positions. In my conversations and interviews with women, who were also cultural leaders of hip hop, we learned that during this period, Black women rappers most frequently projected one of four stage or performance personae: queen mother, fly girl, sista with attitude, and lesbian.[6] Of course, these aren't discrete categories. They blur together as women rappers negotiate image, social values, political ideologies, and the expectations of the music industry.

I still hold to these four categories that came out of the many conversations with women artists in hip hop. Even now I'm looking at Black women, because you now see this as primarily driven by Black women in their culture and the sensibilities of being a Black woman. And you mentioned practically all of them beginning in the eighties. I remember Queen Latifah's—and I was just singing it around the house—"Princess of the Posse."

CHUCK D: But also, Queen Latifah would be like, "Who you calling a 'bitch'? I'll punch you dead in the eye." A dude had to step back on that, like, "Okay."

KEYES: Yeah, on "U.N.I.T.Y." From my conversations with the community, the artists and just Black women in general—and I'm part of that community—I came up with these four categories. Because you had Queen Kenya with Bambaataa's crew, but Queen Latifah was the one. She said she doesn't want to call herself "MC Latifah." And then you had the Muslim influence in there. But she was the one who, in my opinion, gave a kind of significance to being a Black queen. She's the queen. Then after that, you start seeing other women who came in that direction as well, like Lauryn Hill. But you also have others like MC Trouble.

CHUCK D: Who passed away in the 1990s, a Motown artist from LA. You also had Nonchalant. She confronted head on what she didn't like. She came along in the waves of MCs with the same spirit as Sister Souljah.

KEYES: I had Sister Souljah in the queen category, because of kicking knowledge about Africanity, Blackness, and political consciousness. All of these categories represent the complexities and the differences among Black women in contemporary culture. So we got the queens. Then another category was the Fly Girls like the Yo-Yos, and you mentioned Salt-N-Pepa. You could also be a queen. I love what you said about what Ice Cube said. Why she's called Yo-Yo—Yolanda Whittaker. When I think about it, "Funk You Up," by the Sequence, they were really fly. But these girls who came after them took it to another level.

CHUCK D: Also, Sweet Tee.

KEYES: TLC.

CHUCK D: Also Figures of Speech, Ava DuVernay's group.[7] Around 1989/1990, you had an explosion of women MCs trying to seriously get heard in the middle of Los Angeles and the record industry. L'Trimm out of Miami. The first group Jermaine Dupri produced, a trio of women—Silk Tymes Leather, out of Atlanta. I put some of those ladies on tour. J. J. Fad, those are my buddies right there, with their record "Supersonic." If it wasn't for J. J. Fad, Ruthless Records doesn't blast off, which doesn't give N. W. A. their platform.

KEYES: So the Fly Girls, they also talked about being sexually responsible, that's where I was going, with TLC, pinning condoms to their clothes. And Salt-N-Pepa with "Let's Talk about Sex" to "Let's Talk about AIDS." So you start seeing, "Even though we fly, we still had to be sexually responsible." What I love about Queen Latifah is that she's a queen mother, came out with a full figure. But in the fly girl category, you also had Missy Elliott.

CHUCK D: Where would you place Lady of Rage? I always thought she was fly too, but that's just personal taste.

KEYES: I have her in my next category, sistas with attitude. Leading that would be Roxanne Shanté. I also have MC Lyte in there, because these women were the ones who won't take no mess. That's what Shanté did with U.T.F.O., making fun of them.[8]

CHUCK D: "Roxanne, Roxanne" in 1984 and then later on, Roxanne Shanté, "Have a Nice Day," and other songs. She would actually just cut you up.

KEYES: That sounds like a Millie Jackson vibe.

CHUCK D: Yes, the Millie Jackson of rap, no question. Unapologetically sassy.

KEYES: That's why you had MC Lyte when she said, "What you say to me is paper thin," on "Paper Thin" [1988]. I interviewed MC Lyte in Irvine. In the interview, I found out how she really worked on her voice, the breathing.

CHUCK D: Her voice is so distinguishable. It's one of those either you got it or you don't. She has it. She's going to be who she is where you can hear it a mile away. I think with a lot of MCs, a lot of their vocal range is the same. The thing that separates them is the topics and their flow in their bars. So they're able to do a lot of different things. People like Bahamadia, she's where?

KEYES: I have Bahamadia with the queens because she's political. As well as Rapsody.

CHUCK D: Rapsody from North Carolina, big ups to 9th Wonder. Also, a crew I helped put together called Crew Grrl Order in 2007, but the industry was so anti-women at that point, they totally wasn't going to take no all women crew. They made a record called "First Lady," where they celebrated Michelle Obama. But the opposition in the music industry, and also the opposition to rap music in the government, when the president and the first lady just got in there, it was almost like, "We can't be associated with that because they're going to attack us." The conservatives attacked Michelle Obama just for having a short affiliation with Common. They tried to rip her, like, "Oh, you got this gangsta rapper in here." They distanced themselves from rap until the latter years where they started to accept the embracing of rap music and hip hop.[9] But Crew Grrl Order made a record in 2008 called "First Lady" and also "Go Green." Part of their inspiration was Sweet Honey in the Rock.

KEYES: That's an incredible experience. I did work with Bernice Reagon. She inspired me with some things she did vocally. They [Sweet Honey in the Rock] are important to the tradition, not only just of Black women but to American music. Whether you call it folk a cappella or whether you call it a political-civil-rights-like nationalism, it's Sweet Honey in the Rock.

CHUCK D: Professor Keyes, what do you think about the growth of your fellow Louisianan Mia X?

KEYES: I was in Louisiana about two weeks ago. I have Mia X in the Sistas with Attitude category. But I was talking with somebody, and this person corrected me and said, "The first lady of No Limit Records was Sonya C." She was married to Master P, which the name comes from his father telling him there's no limit to what you can do. Mia X was a Sister with Attitude. Often first ladies became more recognized in male-dominated crews. You had Eve with DMX and the Ruff Ryders.

CHUCK D: Amil with Jay-Z and Rocafella. Shawnna in Ludacris's Disturbing tha Peace. Lil' Kim in Junior Mafia with Biggie. What's your take on Gangsta Boo from Memphis, Tennessee?

KEYES: She was with Three 6 Mafia. I had her grouped with the Sistas with Attitude.

CHUCK D: Yeah, but they end up breaking away from the crews. Mia X and Gangsta Boo ended up breaking away from the dudes and then going into some heavy "I'll put the community together on my shoulders." Same thing with Yo-Yo, Oaktown's 3.5.7 out of the Bay, under MC Hammer. They never seemed to get the respect for what they brought to the table.

ALIM: Before Eve was with Ruff Ryders, she was with Dr. Dre and Aftermath, and before that, she was out with the Ram Squad in North Philly. She opened for them at Bobby Dance's in Philly, had to be late 1990s. She would perform with Beanie Sigel later. It was really interesting to see her kind of develop and just blow up to that next level.

CHUCK D: I'd like to engage that some more. That's why I asked the question earlier about the responsibility of men in this industry and culture. How can we be most helpful to what women are trying to do in hip hop?

KEYES: I think men could stand in the position of mentors, because there are women whose skills may not be as high as yours, for example, but there is the need for mentoring and allowing her to find her space, her unique voice. Even when I think of somebody like a Clark Terry, he was a man, but it was absolutely wonderful working with someone who respected women. He had an all-girls jazz band. It included up-and-coming vocalist Dianne Reeves and a few of us from the college network. He wanted to showcase women because he felt those voices were not respected, or seen as novelties. He was a mentor. I also had women mentors, or transgender mentors. So that's important to say that "I can be a mentor," especially to those with lesser skills. On the other hand, there is a space where men have to respect, especially women who have the skills for saying certain things, and you have to get their permission. It's another one of those complex skills as a mentor, how to negotiate space and negotiate respect.

What I do want to say that complicates the Sistas with Attitude category is that this is a male-run industry. In that Sistas with Attitude category you start to see two in particular who conflated what it meant to be "a bad woman" and what it meant to be fly. What it meant to "curse like a sailor." What it meant to still appeal to a male audience. I'm speaking of Foxy Brown and Lil' Kim. To me, once that happened in hip hop—and it's nothing negative about them—but I'm talking about the music industry.

They needed to have a formula to say, "Aha, now we have the Madonnas of hip hop." You're now seeing the flesh, the buttocks, and things that appeal to male audiences. Once that happened, that's when we start seeing *My Mic Sounds Nice*, which was Ava DuVernay's documentary with MC Lyte, Lady of Rage, and others.[10] As they expressed, now they have to compete with women who look a certain way. Even though they may not look that way, they know they have to compromise the way they look. After that with Foxy and Lil' Kim, then came the Nicki Minajs, the Cardi Bs.[11] They all have this kind of template of looking a certain way and appealing seemingly to a male audience. So that's another thing that I saw happening, and this is why we don't have, in my opinion, a diversity of women voices aboveground.

In the underground, we probably do have those voices. We have Medusa here in LA. When you get more underground, there's no limit to your expression. This is what I feel may have destroyed the cultural ethos in hip hop, "It is all about skills, not what you look like." For instance, MC Lyte came out with the jogging suit unisex thing, the sneakers. "I want y'all to not pay too much attention to what I look like but what I sound like, how I flow." My girl from Texas, the statuesque Megan Thee Stallion, when I saw her at that Grammy Award celebration about two years ago, she put it *down*. But again, even having now that affiliation with Beyoncé also helped to give her a certain kind of fashionista fly girl appeal.

CHUCK D: As far as the industry, nobody ever seems to have these analytics. But in the streaming era where it's based on looks, likes, and listens as opposed to purchasing, I would say that women rappers have always been supported by women. I never really knew of guys that said, "I'ma go out and buy this woman MC based on how she looked" or even based on how she sounded. It's almost like the same issue that the WNBA has. So when they say that a woman has to dress up, I still think their support system is women more than guys. Cardi B, Nicki Minaj. . . . We're in the streaming era now. I can just press the button on my phone, and I hear it. But that doesn't really necessarily count as "I'll buy it," like someone would go out and purchase something from Kylie Jenner. The other day, I was walking into the Atlanta airport, and she got a whole cubicle in Atlanta airport selling makeup. Women are actually going there picking up something. I'm trying to figure out the demographics for Cardi B, Nicki Minaj, and also going back to Foxy Brown, Lil' Kim. Women do support this. The guys may say, "Yeah, I wanna see this," but they don't really go out there and financially support this.

KEYES: It helps to empower all the women. They are feeling that "she's doing something, saying stuff I want to say." I'm putting it like this because this reminds me of the group Bytches with Problems. When they came out, everybody was, "Oh bitches with problems . . . ," for real. They obviously fall into the category of the Sistas with Attitude. They said, "We just saying things that other women want to say. We just tell it for them." This is a reason why women are going to buy or stream these women's recordings. It makes their women listeners think, for example, "These women make me feel womanly or tough" or "I couldn't stand that guy."

Now this is the other category I haven't mentioned, the lesbian category, with Queen Pen produced by Teddy Riley. She sampled the song "Boyfriend," by Meshell Ndegeocello, turning it into "Girlfriend," like, "If that was your girlfriend she wasn't last night." Then Meshell was playing bass on there and elevating this idea about women loving women. So that category is the lesbian category. I wouldn't mind having another name for it. It's a reality that also deals with women in general, in this case another Black woman's lifestyle. We, too, have lifestyles that are not just attitudes but could also be a conflation of being a queen or being a fly girl but also women who love other women. I'm saying this because we have to understand that there are women who also enjoy the fact that there are women who enjoy and desire their bodies. This thing gets very complex when you think about what women buyers are buying or streaming and which women are buying or streaming various women hip hop artists.

CHUCK D: Another shout out goes out to the great Dee Barnes, a sister that helped my whole career with her TV show *Pump It Up!* on Fox in the 1980s.[12] Each and every week. If anything, I remember Def Jam making a mistake with ladies I knew and groups that they tried to manufacture from a dude point of view. As with BWP—Bytches with Problems—I thought the two women Michele and Lyndah were phenomenal. I admire them very much. They are friends of mine. Why do y'all have them do that when you should let them be whatever they want to be? That was a marketing mistake, and it really gave them no career. Another tragic mistake was Bo$$ out of Detroit. I would look at her and I was like, "She is the by-product of all these dudes trying to make her the queen gangsta rapper." I'm not saying it ain't in her, but she got so much to say. She was dope. But once again, everybody's trying to figure out how to make something ride along the wave of what dudes were doing. Bo$$ is a tremendous talent. And she suffered for that lifestyle. She's had three kidney transplants. She was pushed into a zone of overindulgence, just hanging out. This was the nineties going into the 2000s.

KEYES: Many years ago, you were talking about ownership and how you have been able to navigate the industry by creating alternative platforms for how we listen to and experience music. I want to know more about your Rapstation and what's called the SHE Movement Radio, the only radio station dedicated to women artists and professionals in hip hop exclusively.

CHUCK D: In this day and time, it's important to have ownership, instead of landing your content on all these platforms that you will never own, that you'll never have any input or control over. We've already seen what's happening with Twitter. Elon Musk swooped in. If you have something that you create, don't land your content on any of these public, social media areas. Get your own dot com. We build our own app system. But also I'm saying that for artists to have their ownership, you have to still get involved with some of the things where your content is owned and protected as much as possible. There's no rhyme or reason for somebody to be an artist. You're from Louisiana, Dr. Keyes. You're very familiar with the aunt or uncle that might go to the porch and just play three chords to the moon, sing some notes to the sky. There is no rhyme or reason why they do it. They feel that they got to do it to feel free. If we can get this across to artistry, everybody has art in them. To get art out of them, I think, is the goal of us curators and, like I said before, either you're a caretaker or you're an undertaker.

When I think about the future of hip hop for the rest of this decade in the metaverse, whatever you want to call it, where is the survival for the content and the creation on that particular level? When somebody wants to feel like "I want to express myself, and I'm good with me expressing myself and whatever comes my way, and I navigate it from there." I think that's the future of women in hip hop saying, like, "There ain't no rhyme or reason for me to do it other than do it, but you just won't exploit me."

So the question is, Where's the line between exploration and exploitation? Because I want to be able to explore further into that realm and not

Figure 1. Professor Chuck discusses how changes in media and technology transformed hip hop, April 13, 2022. Photo by Bad Man's Son.

Figure 2. Chuck D listens to students as the session begins, May 4, 2022. Photo by Bad Man's Son.

Figure 3. Gaye Theresa Johnson (*left*) and Chuck D (*right*) discuss the futures of Black radicalism, May 11, 2022. Photo by Bad Man's Son.

Figure 4. Chuck D (*left*) greets Scot Brown (*right*) for a conversation on hip hop and funk music, April 20, 2022. Photo by Bad Man's Son.

Figure 5. From left to right: Chuck D, Joan Morgan, Kelly Lytle Hernandez, Alexander Williams, and Tabia Shawel at the California African American Museum, June 8, 2022. Photo by Bad Man's Son.

Figure 6. Dr. Joan Morgan (*left*) and Chuck D (*right*) discuss hip hop feminism, June 8, 2022. Photo by Bad Man's Son.

Figure 7. H. Samy Alim delivers the introductory lecture, "What Is Hip Hop Culture?," March 30, 2022. Photo by Bad Man's Son.

Figure 8. Robin D. G. Kelley (*left*) and Chuck D (*right*) discuss the importance of Black geographies to hip hop, March 30, 2022. Photo by Bad Man's Son.

Figure 9. Jeff Chang (*left*) and Chuck D (*right*) discuss the impact of Caribbean immigration to New York on early hip hop culture, April 6, 2022. Photo by Bad Man's Son.

Figure 10. Davey D (*left*) and Chuck D (*right*) discuss Public Enemy's *Fear of a Black Planet*, April 13, 2022. Photo by Bad Man's Son.

Figure 11. From left to right: Chuck D, with Leroy F. Moore Jr., Maya Jupiter, and Bryonn Bain, May 18, 2022. Photo by Bad Man's Son.

Figure 12. Samuel Lamontagne lectures about French racial politics and hip hop in France, May 4, 2022. Photo by Bad Man's Son.

Figure 13. Adam Bradley discusses the intricacy of hip hop poetics, May 25, 2022. Photo by Bad Man's Son.

Figure 14. Cheryl L. Keyes discusses the continuities between Black women in hip hop and the blues, April 27, 2022. Photo by Bad Man's Son.

Figure 15. H. Samy Alim engages Chuck D about his portraits of Nina Simone, Prince, and Ice Cube, June 8, 2022. Photo by Bad Man's Son.

Figure 16. "Ice Cube," by Chuck D.

Figure 17. "Nina Simone," by Chuck D.

Figure 18. "Cypress Hill," by Chuck D.

Figure 19. "Gladys Knight and the Pips," by Chuck D.

Figure 20. "Prince," by Chuck D.

Figure 21. "Marvin Gaye," by Chuck D.

Figure 22. "Bob Marley," by Chuck D.

Figure 23. "Stevie Wonder," by Chuck D.

from a limited standpoint. I want to be able to be like, "Yeah, I'm listening to Candi Staton, 'Young Hearts Run Free,' or 'I Feel Love' by Donna Summer, or 'Pillow Talk' by Sylvia Robinson." I'm feeling all that. I don't feel like I'm invading. I feel I'm in the middle of exploration. When it comes down to songs and music people fall in love for the first time, every person does it somewhere, no matter who. But the songs and music have something to do with that connection. I don't think it should be an area where men can't explore, but where's the line of exploitation?

KEYES: You're saying exploration or exploitation, but the problem is also desperation. A lot of artists are desperate. Desperation can end up making you vulnerable or becoming exploited. So, I love what you're saying. It's very hard for artists who feel that there's no other way but to go ahead and give in out of desperation of wanting fame, out of the ego thing, and of course money. There are a lot of artists who fall prey to this kind of pressure, desperation.

For me, I'm not trying to act like I'm a big star, which I'm not, but I love doing music, and I love doing it my own way. I grew up at a time when someone made me start realizing the power of Black music. Then I decided to go on my little journey in the library. At the time, I was surprised that not too much was even written about Black music. So that's a passion I have. But I'm not desperate. What I learned from hip hop is that you don't have to go to college to learn how to be a businessman or -woman. It's all about handling your business, owning your masters. I've heard from some of the old cats, a lot of jazz cats that have masters, and they say, "You better hold on to your masters." Because the older they get, the more money they would cost if someone wanted to use them in film or television. I'll put it like this, Chuck, I still pray one day that somebody recognizes my music, but if they don't, I have something that is a part of my soul that I own and no one else. So many African American artists were exploited and continue to be exploited, musically and creatively, for the almighty dollar.

CHUCK D: In the category of women in hip hop, what about DJs—DJ Spinderella, the late great Pam the Funkstress in the group the Coup, also was Prince's DJ. DJ Jazzy Joyce. DJ Cotton Candy, RIP. I don't think that there's been a great story on women DJs. The musicianship. How do we get more representation for women? Women participate more internationally, but here, dudes have monopolized hip hop to the point where women are still far less visible than they should be.

KEYES: Female representation remains disproportionate to that of male artists of this genre. Again, we know that women have been major forces of hip hop in diverse ways, though rarely acknowledged. We need to produce more work about their prominence as performing artists and as movers and shakers in the boardroom and behind the camera in the shaping of this tradition.

Let's go back to those DJs you mentioned. I want to start with them. That's another level since we've been talking about the MCs. Let's talk about the women who are on the turntables and transitioning from the turntables into the studio. All the toughest, including the Dr. Dres and the Funkmaster Flexes, they started as itinerant DJs and spinning for folks and accompanying the MCs. But they also had access and uncanny ways of being able to check out a beat. We need to really look at who were some of the pioneering women hip hop DJs that have gone from the streets into the studios, and everybody is just knocking down a door because they really want to make sure this particular person produces their album. I want to know more about that.

Speaking from firsthand experience, though, I remember when I recorded my first CD, *Let Me Take You There*. All of this music was in my head. The producer was actually a friend of mine [Dr. Charles Moore] who wanted to watch my back because I didn't need to be in the studio, and the next thing, the sound engineer starts to insinuate himself in my production, and next to becoming the producer, all that starts to interfere with my creativity. So I had a little battle with someone who did that. Anyway, I got out of this situation when my dear friend stepped in to watch my back without interfering or insinuating himself into my creativity. But the next time was the first time that I worked with a sound engineer that was a woman. From this experience, there is no way in the world that I would *not* have this woman to mix any of my music from now on. I *got* to give props to Vanessa Parr, who mixed my double-single, *Hollywood and Vine*, a project I was hoping would be my first time getting my music in a film. Once the recording was finished, it just so happened that Vanessa Parr, then the head sound engineer at UCLA's School of Music, mixed it. I was blessed to have her to really do the mix on my project. I never heard a mix like that! And so maybe it's her sensitivity or the fact that she connects with a woman, capturing something that maybe a male engineer would not have been able to do.

CHUCK D: Would you also say that when you get into those nuances and you start reaching into the elements of things that are connected to Black music that there is something unique there? You have Black people making music, there's something there, maybe it was the hundreds of years where we wasn't able to open our mouths to say anything. But with music in the sight, sound, story, style era, one thing that's missing is that when it comes down to Black music, other than seeing it through screens, and hearing it, which is sounds, you got to feel it. Maybe what a woman will add in the mix is something that is felt and not heard or seen. This is what big business and industry, they can't figure that out if they tripped over it. There's a feeling somewhere in there that you got it or you don't. We're in the middle of academia, but when you start talking about nuances in Black folk and music and culture, sometimes, excuse the language, shit can't be explained.

KEYES: You're right about that because this is a woman who may not get those kinds of opportunities. Maybe she picked up who I was and where the mix needed to be. Let me tell you who supposedly is one of her mentors: T Bone Burnett, an award-winning music producer. And perhaps it was very odd to me that I got a woman mixing my stuff. I never thought this would have happened. So opportunities is what I'm really talking about. There are a lot of women out there who have not been discovered and may not get that opportunity because maybe other male producers may not bring them in. I was blessed to work with what seemingly may be an anomaly in the music industry today, having women in the forefront as engineers.

CHUCK D: I think today's music would take a step forward in the US if you had more women in the engineering room. If they're not engineering at the board, at least they should be three feet from the board telling whoever at the board, "No, that's not going to work." DJs, engineers, producers around the world, women are at the boards. They make that music. It's just a shame that they're held to an industry standard that's not equipped to even be able to process their music and hear and feel it.

We have to be able to build these platforms. I attempted throughout my career to play with women groups and artists on tour like Queen Latifah or J. J. Fad—we're tour buddies—and also building a platform for Crew Grrl Order. I made mistakes too because I set it up and then I kind of moved away from it thinking that they'd handle it when I should have been present. I wanted to do the opposite of what had happened to women in the industry, with men directing women—"You need to go this way, you need to do that." I didn't want to do that. But there was also a mistake in that. They imploded a little bit because they didn't have somebody being able to say, "No, that's the right road. That's the wrong road." But that's a negotiation. I tell them also in the long-term picture, I said, "Look at Sweet Honey in the Rock, how they're able to do it as women in their fifties, sixties or whatever, and they don't have a problem getting together." So, there's ageism, and there's an age limit. I think there's also women in their teens and twenties and thirties who get it. This is something I think that I can assist in—"Keep doing your thing, with no expectations. But if you keep doing it, you'll end up somewhere and let it surprise and shock and amaze you." Looking at women in other forms of music beyond hip hop is helpful. Looking at a Toni Blackman, looking back at Nikki Giovanni and Sonia Sanchez and saying, "We got to look around because we cannot look at this thing as far as the United States industry coming out of LA and New York, it don't hold us well."

Groups and collectives are the thing that makes it panoramic. Even with the screens, you can't take your eyes off it. Gladys Knight and the Pips, you can't take your eyes off it. The Pips played the back and pushed Gladys Knight to the forefront. We have those components in hip hop and rap music. I'd like to see a woman rapper up front. We got close with Lauryn Hill. We had Pras and Wyclef Jean playing in the back of Lauryn Hill. When she did *Miseducation*, she was coming to the forefront. When you have a woman to the forefront like Funky 4 + 1 with MC Sha-Rock, that's a dynamic that's hardly ever been touched. We haven't even begun to come up with the combinations that make hip hop pioneering, trendsetting, fly and just dope.

We don't need to have everybody thinking that they are soloists. As I said, solo has become the predominant artist presentation of the record companies because it is easier to negotiate, or "negrotiate" or "niggagotiate," with one person rather than five. Women as a collective. Monie Love tried it with the group Heresy with other women MCs—MyVerse, Carolina

Dirty and D. Larue. Deadly Venoms was an all-women hip hop crew affiliated with Wu-Tang. It was like, "Y'all ain't got to be Raekwon and Ghostface Killah, but be honest with yourself." What do you think about the possibility of collectives? Because I think collectives is going to save the art form.

KEYES: As long as it's not a collective that's put together, like the Spice Girls. One thing about Sweet Honey in the Rock, they had the vision. You have to have respect for the leader. You need focus. A lot of artists are not that focused sometimes. It takes a lot of discipline. Having a vision and taking risks and not doing it just for the money. Sweet Honey in the Rock also found their niche, doing something that no one else is really doing. Otherwise, human frailties, the egos, the jealousies, and all of that can consume what really needs to happen.

CHUCK D: That creates the loophole for somebody who's exploitive to come in and say, "I could give you all the direction," but it never ends up playing out for the right reasons. Again, it's good that the focus is there for the launch up period, but once you up in orbit, anything can happen. Let's open this up to questions.

QUESTION 1: A lot of music degrades women as objects, especially as a source for men's pleasure. I know that women have reclaimed this by owning their sexuality and being open about it, but is it enough for women to reclaim their sexualized bodies?

KEYES: One way I can answer that is from a parental perspective. There are a lot of folks who can offer a kind of parental guidance. How do you learn to be a critical viewer and listener? That's the kind of thing that, to me, if I had had daughters, I want to know what they're watching. I also want to be able to help them to know that this is just an artistic expression, and it doesn't necessarily mean that we have to always be overcritical. In the intellectual world, we take the Gender Studies courses and say, "Oh, this is objectifying women." But we always got to know why we are thinking that.

At the same time, as I said before, who really runs the industry? It's not always the women. The hip hop artists who we see who are partially clad, that's what they want to do. You see here again—desperation. We can look beyond exploitation, exploration. It's not their or artists' responsibility to train other women. That's where the parental thing comes in, and that's where that mentoring thing comes in. It is very complex and seemingly either representing women as meat or here they are pigeonholed into a kind of a sexualized being. But it's also how you internalize this and your perspective in being able to analyze it. When we think about back in the day, even look at the film industry, I'm sorry to say it's not fair or balanced, but it's very male dominated. It's from those perspectives that women are exploited and socialized to be those sexualized beings. Now, whether or not this is right or wrong, I know I'm way past that.

But then when you start finding out also—and I'm not trying to talk negatively about her, but take Cardi B, for example. I didn't know that it was because there was a need for her to have to be a stripper; that was bringing home bread. So once you get used to being watched and admired and gone after, it ain't no big thing. She can make much more money than in a strip club when it comes to being right there on that stage. These are decisions women make, and in a way, they should not have to be criticized for doing so. But there's something else that's happening. "Oh, she can do that. We can make a lot of money." So this thing is not black and white. There are gray areas. But it's also understanding the complexities that's behind the images that we see.

CHUCK D: There's a time and place for everything. But what we've seen in the digital age and the fact that there's access to everything at any particular time has gotten us out of whack, which has led us into a lot of these situations of desperation. When I grew up, you didn't know what was going on behind the veil of adulthood. You had to physically go through a portal to be able to engage in these things. Now, everything is out there in the open. I think the last two generations have grown up in a time where everything has been coming at them and they're unable to handle it. You have no answers at five years old, when you see something that thirty or forty-year-olds are dealing with.

ALIM: One of the things that's really powerful about this student's question is it makes me think about the constraints placed on women in relation to not just their music but also in relation to their lives. You have a lot of this cultural production happening in the context of constraints, not just the constraints of capitalism but a very sexist capitalist order. So one of the things that I hear women artists say a lot of times is that they *do* want control of images of their bodies.[13] They want to be the ones to control them. If they choose to do *whatever* with their body, then at least it's *them* doing it, and they don't give a fuck about what men care about. So they want to take that power and ownership away, as if to say, "My body is not for your consumption, period. I'm doing with my body what I choose to do for me and for other women." Megan Thee Stallion, for example, is very clear on that. It takes men almost completely out of the equation. That idea of ownership becomes a very powerful scenario. You hear Joan Morgan, Brittney Cooper, Treva Lindsay, and Kaila Story, and other hip hop feminists talk about this a lot, the politics of pleasure.[14]

But you also have a situation where those images still circulate, and they circulate among folks who already possess stereotypical ideas about Black women. So you have this push-pull, but that's the nature of being in the belly of a sexist beast. These are the constraints around women's lives and music that men don't have to deal with. I want to make this clear, I've heard countless men artists make similar claims, but in terms of race and masculinity. I remember we interviewed Onyx back in the day for *Street Conscious Rap*. They were wild, Sticky Fingaz, the whole crew. They were doing mosh pits at hip hop shows back before Travis Scott. I remember Sticky Fingaz would say, "I'm America's worst nightmare. I'm the recording industry's worst nightmare. I'm young, Black, and I don't give a fuck." He would scare the hell out of the industry folks with that. What scholars would point out was that some Black men artists were exploiting the images and stereotypes that were already circulating about Black men in order to present in their music a particular kind of masculinity because they knew that that's what folks wanted to buy. You had this with gangsta rap, as Michael Eric Dyson has written.[15] Folks would play into what they thought the audience wanted to see because it would sell records. You come from "the gutter" and you flip that exploited image into profit, so you're playing the capitalist game now, on the capitalists' terms. So you *still* have those constraints in terms of race and gender. It's also problematic for men, in the way that I just said for women, in that their images do circulate and far beyond the US, where people should know better but still don't. There's also a bit of a double standard, because these men are said to be intelligent and in control, while the women artists are believed to be ignorant and exploited.

Black women are dealing with those double or triple constraints, right? So you got the constraints of gender and race and also class and what people think about *working class Black women* to begin with, the triple threat. So as Dr. Keyes mentioned, you have a situation that is nearly impossible to navigate, unless those kinds of networks get shifted and busted up, and that women are not just the engineers, but they're also in charge of marketing, video production, and the way these images circulate. That's what real change is. That's structural change.

CHUCK D: At the same time, images can't be muted. The interpretation of the image is dependent upon the subjectivity of the beholder. The context has to be attached to the images at all times. That might seem a little bit constricting, but since everything is out there, it has to drag its narrative so close to the hip. If you have a person that doesn't know art that goes in and sees something they don't know how to interpret—David by Michelangelo, for example—they might say, "It's just a naked man statue," right? No, there's a context, but you have to learn the context.

KEYES: In terms of women being behind the camera, DuVernay has been behind the camera. She has helped us to understand all of these pressures, the shifting of images, and objectifying women in rap videos with her documentary, *My Mic Sounds Nice*. I'm just looking at some other names here that I have who were behind the camera. There's also Rachel Raimist with her documentary, *Nobody Knows My Name*.[16] She did this documentary on women and the pressures of being a woman in the hip hop world. We need more women behind the cameras to break things down and to give another narrative through the lens.

QUESTION 2: You were saying how Queen Latifah was a Black queen figure in hip hop. What social movements was she a part of that inspired women like Lauryn Hill to follow her path?

KEYES: You always have to look at an artist's background. I think Latifah's dad was a police officer, and her mother was a schoolteacher. I mention this because certain hip hop artists who are very politically inspired often come from families where they learn a certain culture of consciousness. She mentions why she didn't want to be called an MC; she wanted to be a queen, as she says in her autobiography *All Hail the Queen*. This was a political decision, a way by which she defines herself. She also has a talent for reinventing herself. When I was waiting to interview her, I waited four hours to talk to her. She was on the phone saying, "They think I'm young. They think I don't know what I'm doing." So you can see that this is a woman who will make you respect her. That's pretty much her demeanor when you look at "Princess of the Posse" and "Wrath of My Madness." She said in an interview, "They had me over at Tommy Boy Records," which was run by Monica Lynch and Tom Silverman, "and I brought in Naughty by Nature, and I started my own thing."

ALIM: Also with Latifah and Shakim [at Flavor Unit] and others, it's no surprise that their names are Arabic. When you come from East Orange, or Philly, or DC, or New York, African American Islam is a big part of the social fabric. There's all types of Muslim communities where she grew up, where she didn't even have to be a Muslim to be Islamicized, and the social movement was linked to that as well. When you're talking about spirituality in this sense, many artists that came out of that era in that time period was connected to that one way or another, whether it was half your family or whether it was the next door neighbor or the folks you broke fast with. That's a huge part of understanding the context.

The other thing I want to mention is I was with James G. Spady. I have to tell this story, because it shows that there was a Black women's consciousness around Nubian queens long before Latifah. We were at the International Association of African American Music in Philly in 2000, I think, and we were at the dinner table, and Latifah was there, Sonia Sanchez, Jill Scott, and Nina Simone, same dinner table. Nina Simone got up onstage to receive an award and began her speech to the whole entire room—I kid you not—she got up and she didn't say nothing else but "I am an Ancient Egyptian queen. I was born five thousand years ago." She was dead serious, and they didn't know what to do [*laughter*]. But I'm thinking of the queen aesthetic going back way further than hip hop, obviously.

QUESTION 3: I was wondering if during the foundational years of hip hop there were any openly lesbian MCs in the mainstream. The only ones that I know about are Queen Latifah and Da Brat, but they came out of the closet later in life.

KEYES: Queen Pen in the 1990s.

CHUCK D: Once again, it was the eighties, so people wasn't coming out, even in the nineties, because women were coming into a male-dominated, egotistical "grab my gonads" culture. Women were coming in like, "I'm identifying with myself, but there's so much crap up in here, I've got to come up with an identity. As a woman, what I like and what I'm doing, that is none of your business right now, because I'm punching you in the jaw with these bars." As it began to open up a lot more, I think women were really at the forefront of saying, "Okay, listen, this is my sexual preference." The dudes were like, "Yo, I'm not even gonna go there." The women were bolder about coming out about who they were. As opposed to guys, even if they happened to have this sexual preference, they're not even coming close to addressing that, because they feel that as an MC, immediately, they're going to be banished into this category right here. I'm like, "Well, if you hard as hell and you claiming that you the hardest MC then admit the truth." I think the women of the nineties had more courage than the guys. They were more truthful. The guys were afraid—and to this day are afraid—to really seriously communicate their full selves.

KEYES: They were not afraid of representing a spectrum of womanhood. But the person I'm thinking about was out of Queens or somewhere in New York, her name is Shä-Key.

CHUCK D: Media is funny, because media has been good at obscuring what they consider unsuccessful efforts and putting them on different measurements, like, "They didn't sell no records, so therefore they didn't count." I'm like, "What?" So what's the standard here? Now it is even more confusing because they are measuring streams, I'm like, "What the hell"? So that doesn't mean that this artist didn't exist. It's the lack of curators that's able to consider this artist as being part of the artscape, so to speak. That takes people like ourselves on the other side, as fans, saying, "That artist counts." No, they didn't sell ten records. No, they might not have a hundred streams. But what they are is revolutionary in their being. Their music is dope, and it ain't got nothing to do with numbers.

QUESTION 4: You mentioned TLC earlier.[17] Why do you think women rappers were the only ones really talking about safe sex, especially after the passing of Eazy-E? My second question is for Professor Chuck. Were platforms like BET important? What role did they play in your life, your career, and in hip hop as a whole?

KEYES: When you have the groups like TLC and "Let's Talk about Sex," by Salt-N-Pepa, this was also a period when we saw a high incidence of AIDS in the Black community. You mentioned Eazy-E, which is still controversial. We look at who he was, his stature. We have a hip hop heterosexual man—because remember, AIDS was cast as a "gay thing"—so this was a time to make a statement. These women of hip hop did do that for that reason as part of their revolution and making the Black community as well as everybody else aware that this thing called AIDS is not discriminatory.

CHUCK D: They were able to use their platform. And yes, BET was helpful. Unfortunately, before BET jumped on rap, *Yo! MTV Raps* jumped on rap. BET first followed hip hop with a ten-foot pole that was very conservative. When they saw that Viacom and MTV touched on rap more than they did, then they chased that with their own *Rap City*. I'm here to say that all of it was helpful, but once again, I have to look at what helps the genre as opposed to just what helped me. I got my help from other sources, but it's not about me. How about we? This is why when the first Grammy was won and they said that *It Takes a Nation of Millions to Hold Us Back* should have been the album selected, Jazzy Jeff & the Fresh Prince, a.k.a. Will Smith, they won it. We all paraded and protested because we were an unofficial union together because everything looked down on us as being an official music.[18] We was there on that rooftop in LA with Will and Jeff, Salt-N-Pepa, Kid 'n Play, Ice-T.

So these platforms jumped on and said, "Well, there's some money, there's some gold in there." I'm not going to say we were ungrateful. We're saying like, "We need more help to be able to lay claim to this art form and have a narrative ourselves so we could branch out into all those areas." Then the nineties came along, but did we actually help it or did the platforms actually acquiesce to the corporations that actually governed it? Eventually, the BETs and MTVs ended up being subservient to the companies and had a relationship that the artists never really had. Then when Viacom bought BET, that was the beginning of the end. Bob Johnson sold BET from being a Black-owned company in 1998, which means that he had to have some accountability and responsibility to the diversity of Black communities where the artists came from. Now the reason that you call it Black music is because when you have 99 percent of the faces and voices under the construct of Black people in the US, you got to call it Black music.

The takeover was an urban takeover, and urban would be fair if everybody within the different constructs and diversity would be included. But they didn't include it and still was Black faces, Black voices, Black males, Black females. So yeah, it's Black Entertainment Television, but they've been "urbanized," which means that they ain't got to be accountable or responsible—and they're part of Viacom. That was the beginning of losing control to big business. We're just gettin up outta that mess. We feel at this particular time it has to work for the diversity of what people feel in order for it to be connected to artistry. Because there's no such thing as loyal numbers right now. The industry is not coming to grips with that truth.

QUESTION 5: We have the rise of rappers such as Megan Thee Stallion, Nicki Minaj, Noname, and many more women artists who are currently dominating the game. With flows, stylistic choices, and identity representation in rap just completely changing over the years, has there been a new category birthed for current female artists who may not fit in the particular categories that you outlined?

KEYES: These categories are malleable. You remember I said something about Yo-Yo being a queen but also being a fly girl. When you look at Foxy Brown and Lil' Kim, I see them as the "bad girls," the ones who roll with the guys, but they also were fly. These categories are in flux. These categories in contemporary Black culture represent the attitudes of Black women who could be queens, who could have attitudes, women who love women, crossing between all these categories. So they are fluid, and there could be other categories. But what I see here is that everybody, whether or not they're on the international scene, all of these women, their attitudes, the way they present themselves, I'm wondering if they're sisters [Black women], but they might be from Pakistan or elsewhere. They all have this kind of attitude in their performances because they are watching Black women in hip hop. Black women serve as the model for how you roll with the attitude. And the other part is just language and perhaps cultural identity, where you are from. But Black women from the US to Trinidad or in the Caribbean—when you think of Nicki Minaj or Cardi B—showcase hip hop attitudes that women from around the world continue to emulate.

NOTES

1. See James G. Spady, "Mapping and Re-membering Hip Hop History, Hiphopography, and African Diasporic History," *Western Journal of Black Studies* 37, no. 2 (2013): 127–37. Queen Latifah, Sylvia Robinson, Salt-N-Pepa, Bahamadia, Eve, Trina, and other women artists are interviewed in Spady, *Street*

Conscious Rap (1999) and *Tha Global Cipha: Hip Hop Culture and Consciousness* (2006), both on Black History Museum Press.

2. See Adam Haupt, Burni Aman, Shameema Williams, and UJ Von Lyrik, "Godessa's Entry into Hip Hop in the Early 2000s," in *Neva Again: Hip Hop Art, Activism, and Education in Post-Apartheid South Africa*, ed. Adam Haupt, Quentin Williams, H. Samy Alim, and Emile Jansen (HSRC, 2019), 91–126. All the Cape Town artists mentioned here are also featured in *Neva Again*.

3. See Cheryl L. Keyes, *Rap Music and Street Consciousness* (University of Illinois Press, 2002); and Cheryl L. Keyes, "Verbal Art Performance in Rap Music: The Conversation of the 80's," *Folklore Forum* 17, no. 2 (Fall 1984): 143–52.

4. See David "Davey D" Cook, "Pioneers MC Debbie D & Sheri Sher Speak about the Important Role Women Have Played in Hip Hop," *Hard Knock Radio*, April 3, 2024, https://hardknockradio.org/hip-hop-pioneers-debbie-d-and-sherri-sher-speak-about-the-important-role-women-have-played/.

5. See Cheryl L. Keyes, "Daughters of the Blues: Women, Race, and Class Representation in Rap Music Performance," in *Rap Music and Street Consciousness* (University of Illinois Press, 2002), 184–98.

6. See Cheryl L. Keyes, "Empowering Self, Making Choices, Creating Spaces: Black Female Identity via Rap Music Performance," *Journal of American Folklore* 113, no. 449 (Summer 2000): 255–69.

7. Ava DuVernay (MC Eve) was a member of the hip hop group Figures of Speech, which also included Ronda Ross (MC Jyant). See DuVernay's documentary *This Is the Life* (2008).

8. For more on "the Roxanne Wars," see Jeff Chang, *Can't Stop Won't Stop: A History of the Hip Hop Generation* (St. Martin's, 2005).

9. See H. Samy Alim and Geneva Smitherman, "My President's Black, My Lambo's Blue: Hip Hop, Race, and the Culture Wars," in *Articulate while Black: Barack Obama, Language, and Race in the United States* (Oxford University Press, 2012); and Travis L. Gosa and Erik Nielson's, eds., *The Hip Hop and Obama Reader* (Oxford, 2015).

10. See Ava DuVernay, *My Mic Sounds Nice: A Truth about Women in Hip-Hop* (2010).

11. For more on the enduring sexism of the music industry, see the documentary by dream hampton, *Ladies First: A Story of Women in Hip Hop* (2023).

12. For more on Dee Barnes, see dream hampton, *Ladies First: A Story of Women in Hip Hop* (2023).

13. See Gwendolyn Pough, *Check It While I Wreck It: Black Womanhood, Hip-Hop Culture and the Public Sphere* (Northeastern University Press, 2004); and Imani Perry, "The Venus Hip Hop and the Pink Ghetto: Negotiating Spaces for Women," in *Prophets of the Hood: Politics and Poetics in Hip Hop* (Duke University Press, 2004), 155–90.

14. See Joan Morgan, Brittney Cooper, Treva Lindsay, Kaila Adia Story, and Esther Armah, "The Pleasure Principle: Articulating a Post–Hip Hop Feminist Politics of Pleasure," in *Freedom Moves: Hip Hop Knowledges, Pedagogies and Futures*, ed. H. Samy Alim, Jeff Chang, and Casey Philip Wong (University of California Press, 2023), 349–75. See also Brittney Cooper, Susana M. Morris, and Robin M. Boylorn, eds., *The Crunk Feminist Collection* (The Feminist Press at CUNY, 2017).

15. See Michael Eric Dyson, "The Culture of Hip-Hop," in *That's the Joint: The Hip-Hop Studies Reader*, ed. Murray Forman and Mark Anthony Neal (Routledge, 2004), 61–68.

16. See Rachel Raimist's film *Nobody Knows My Name* (1999), which features artists like Medusa, Asia One, and others.

17. See how TLC impacted sexual politics in the United States and how they fell victim to a terribly exploitative record deal, went public, and renegotiated their contract in *CrazySexyCool: The TLC Story* (2013; directed by Charles Stone III).

18. See Dan Rys, "A History of Hip Hop's Complicated Relationship with the Grammy's," *Billboard*, February 8, 2017, https://www.billboard.com/music/rb-hip-hop/history-hiphop-complicated-relationship-grammys-7684970/.

6 World Tour Sessions

GLOBAL HIP HOP CULTURE

Chuck D, Samuel Lamontagne, Mikko Kapanen, Amkelwa Mbekeni, and H. Samy Alim

CHUCK D: Tonight is a special night for many reasons. We have Dr. Geneva Smitherman in the house.[1] Much respect, peace, and love to Dr. G. I've read your writings over the years. It was always great to look at someone moving in different spaces who understood what we were doing. In the realm of hip hop language, we always needed someone to back us up, to defend our right to be able to speak, to defend what we were putting out there. It helped us know that we were not alone. You can never have enough help, although I used to box them to death! I always knew what my next move was, but the media might not properly interpret my move. At that particular time, the press thought that they could control the narrative and that nobody would combat them. But every once in a while, an eloquent academic would make the media move on to the next subject. "Damn! This professor stepped up and wrote a letter that we can't even read. So I know we can't keep attacking hip hop and rap music and create false controversies." With anything you love, you've gotta be able to deliver that logic, reason, knowledge, wisdom, and understanding. Thank you, Dr. G.

We are discussing the international aspect of hip hop and rap music. To say "international hip hop," to me, is like putting a badge on our arrogance here in the US. To a nation like France, for example, rap music and hip hop culture from the US could also be considered "international," right? If we still have that "United States of America state of mind," we fall victim to centering the US and ignoring everyone else. We're also gonna look at another thing that people blindly just say, "Well, that's overseas." I always tell people, one thing that will make you a slave is stripping the knowledge of self and stripping a sense of geography away from you. That's the one-two punch. You could make a slave out of someone if they don't know who they are or where they at. As Rakim says, "It's not where you from, it's where you at." Rap music and hip hop does its best to say, "We are ONE." Geography is a very important thing to figure out on this planet, and Samuel Lamontagne's gonna help us delve deeper into that by exploring hip hop in France.

Earlier, I broke down how the Eisenhower Interstate System works in the US on longitude and latitude as far as north, south, east, west highways and circles around it [see chapter 2]. The world is similar. The reason why geography is so important is that we gotta have a sense of migration patterns, how people travel, how culture and communication circulate, how hip hop music and culture travel. In addition to Sam, we're gonna have Amkelwa Mbekeni and Mikko Kapanen, who are headquartered in Helsinki, Finland, and will join us today from Helsinki. They're so important because for years I had rapstation.com, and Rapstation was originally born out of the need to make artists heard and seen.

This is right around the time when people were making MP3s with their music, no matter where they were in the world. Rapstation.com allowed you to upload your music, before MySpace. Later on, people began uploading music to SoundCloud. I later turned it into something that curated and took care of the culture. As I always say, either you caretake or you undertake. We wanted to caretake. In the beginning of Rapstation, we wanted to make the audience more into participants. When you're able to make something that's so infectious, then you got a cycle of energy that just spirals like a tornado to the top of the atmosphere and it don't stop.

Another one of my peers, Daddy-O, from the group Stetsasonic, is very clear on the fact that when you go visit a place, there's a hip hop energy *already* there. Now, if they're not in Los Angeles or New York, does that mean it does not exist? There are reasons why New York and Los Angeles are hip hop capitals. These places were also media capitals. Whatever happened in the vicinity of these media capitals had an advantage. If the most brilliant hip hop artist in 1981 was in Erie, Pennsylvania, for example, that person wasn't gonna stand a chance in hell of being heard or seen! There wasn't YouTube back then. These hip hop capitals positioned as LA and New York are also business capitals.

The beautiful thing about documentation of recording is that a sound on record is going to travel. If it's going to be heard in LA and New York, you damn sure it's gonna be heard everywhere else in the world, even back then. There had already been an industry that understood the power of Black music. When "Rapper's Delight" was recorded in October 1979, how quick do you think London heard that record? You best believe it was there by the end of next week! Also, you got traffic going back and forth, going from LA to London and New York on the regular. LA to Australia later on, on the regular. People move between these areas, and they're gonna carry whatever is hot in that particular area to wherever they go in the world. Add the internet to it today at the beginning of this century, and the record is heard automatically overnight. They get the same thing, same time, boom!

In terms of hip hop globally, if hip hop was the Olympics and they had to give out the gold, silver, and bronze, where do you think the US would rank? You already see that we don't automatically win in basketball without throwing pros up in there. What, because we from the US we automatically flyer? The whole automatic thing is gone. I'm here to tell you all now, I've seen African MCs spit in four languages in the same number of bars. How do you compete against that if you battling?! Let's say you're battling and you really talkin street shit. Somebody from Sierra Leone says, "Yeah, you got hard streets, but our streets is crazy in Monrovia. We have war-torn areas, dawg, for real?" So you ain't harder. "Oh, you talkin truth now? Okay." The truth is that they might have knowledge of self, but you, as a USAer, don't have it. How about DJing? Everybody got the same apparatus. The world champions of DJs didn't come from the US for about twenty-five, twenty-six years. I think it wasn't until the X-Ecutioners came along. For the longest period of time, everybody from Germany, Europe, was taking the DJ turntable prize. It's very convenient for somebody to say, "Oh, you know what, we don't do that no more anyway." But what do you do then? Because the rest of the hip hop world is like, "Yo, we do this shit for real. We'll roast you, dawg." You have no advantages. The only advantages that you think you have is the red, white, and blue flag.

I've been to 116 countries. I felt a little privileged in my early days of traveling, especially through Europe, because I felt I had "a Black badge." And I did, because all the stuff that was going on in the land that was run by R&B, Reagan and Bush, and Thatcher in the UK, and that whole alliance of the Western world was putting their thumbprint on the rest of the world's culture. I thought I had a Black badge, and I kind of did. Let me explain. I'm talking about the struggle of Black people in America who said, "You know what? We're gonna attack this derogatory look at us." This started on high overdrive after World War II. Not to say it didn't exist before World War II, but it came out of an intense period of anti-Black racism. "Damn, yo, we fought in World War II. I'm not like my daddy. I got a problem comin back and not havin no opportunity. I know when my daddy and my grandfather fought in World War I, they came back, and it was riots, and y'all even hung Black folks." That new Black consciousness after World War II made them put their antennas up on alert, like, "These Negroes ain't the same."

Raise your hand if you've heard of *Billboard* magazine. It calls itself the music business encyclopedia, the week-to-week trade paper, monitoring the recording industry. In 1949, the editor Paul Ackerman says, "Listen, we gotta change this category called 'race records' because these Negroes is different. We gotta figure out how we work with some of them in order to keep being involved with Black music." Ackerman points to a guy named Jerry Wexler, who was the head music writer for a lot of the articles in *Billboard* magazine, especially the race records, aficionado of jazz and blues and Black music. Ackerman said, "Listen, Jerry, you gotta come up with another title, man. Jackie Robinson just infiltrated Major League Baseball, which is America's pastime. Things that are comin outta Harlem is real, not just in sports but in culture. Philosophy writers are coming out, and they're being read and bought not just by Black people but white people too. We gotta call it something else." Jerry Wexler disappears, comes back, and he renames the charts. What do you think the charts name was renamed into after "race records"? "Rhythm & Blues." R&B. A term that you bring up today and nobody seems to know what it is. It's the same misappropriation because they don't know what hip hop is. All they know is like, "Oh, I love R&B." Well, the term "R&B" was created as a business construct. No, Jerry Wexler did not invent R&B. He just invented the term. He ain't invent the music.

So that old-time of forties, fifties, sixties, soul music, Black music under that whole idiom and that soul type of thing, the rest of the world knew it the next week. Ray Charles is hot in New York, recorded in New York. London and Paris want to know about Ray Charles two weeks later. The music travels, and when the music travels, you got people who will listen and say, "Yo, I like that." And if they like it so much, they're gonna end up emulating it, and then they're gonna do it in their own style.

The Rock and Roll Hall of Fame inductees were named today. Two rap inductees from the hip hop idiom. One was Sylvia Robinson, posthumously, in the pioneering department.[2] This is the first entrepreneur of hip hop recordings, started Sugar Hill Records in 1979. At the end of that spectrum, starting his career in 1997, was the induction of Eminem. So, Sylvia Robinson, a Black woman in 1979, and Eminem starting in 1997 as a white male rapper in the United States of America under that racial construct. It makes you look at rap music and hip hop and say, "Damn, that's a diverse gap between that." Black males are somewhere in the middle of that. And between 1979 and 1997, you best believe there's an entire planet Earth of hip hop and rap music contributors who've been doing it in that span of time. London. France. Benelux. What's Benelux? All these places, all chopped up for retail situations. Benelux is a territory where Belgium, Holland, and Luxembourg cooperate politically and economically. Then you got Germany.

When I first toured in Europe, we could only perform in front of West Germans, because the Iron Curtain was up. Communism was strong. They wasn't selling nothing of any note of any music anywhere. That's not to say that there wasn't fans on the other side of the Iron Curtain that loved this new music called hip hop. We would play West Berlin. But to play West Berlin, you gotta go at the edge of a city in West Germany and get ready to travel that one road to that one city in the middle of East Germany called Berlin, which was split into two halves, the east side and the west side. The west side was all the Western countries, and the east side was the communist countries. Therefore, whether you like the music or not, what dictated to you right then and there was what the OGs were doing. You know who the OGs were—original governments, gangsters. This also determined where the music was going to end up. Because them gangsters—and all governments are gangsters to me—were calling the shots. You had to find your way around it. That ain't gonna determine whether people ended up getting the music or not.

So we played in the middle of West Berlin, and there was a wall up there saying, "Y'all got plenty of fans listening to West German radio playing hip hop. But you know what? They can't come to the gig. They're on the other side." What do you think would happen if they got close to the wall back in the day? Shot dead. "We don't care. It's East Germany, that's the rules here." It ain't nothing jumping off into Russia. Yeah, they might like hip hop. I don't know when they gon get it. Yugoslavia, the former Czechoslovakia, and countries that later become the Czech Republic, Yugoslavia ends up being Serbia, Montenegro, Slovenia, Croatia here. The reason is that when you're travelling to all these places by bus, you know that you can't make a right because you'll end up in Romania. If you end up on the wrong side, you're gonna find a roadblock, and then you might find the opposition and you might be shot at.

I remember I was awakened in the middle of that bus ride going up to Berlin, and one road going there with nothing but those little communist cars that U2 used in concerts later on. There was one road that was about 340 miles, like from Los Angeles to the Bay Area, maybe a little shorter. They will wake your ass up with dogs and flashlights and ask to see everybody's passport. If your ass didn't have a passport, shit is real. Let me tell you. Any big fans of Brittney Griner in here?[3] How come she ain't here? With all the power systems we got here, where's our cultural power base? Can we get her? No. Because governments say, "You know what, we gangsters now, fuck y'all. Y'all play gangsters. We gangsters for real." It affects even the music, but the music permeates and gets to the people. So traveling around, from country to country, hip hop is the voice of the people, but some places ain't gonna be as loud as other places.

I couldn't get into Cuba, because the former Castro regime was like, "We know that you are a person of the people, but that 'fight the power' ain't workin here, dawg. You're not fightin no power, not while we here!" The number one thing when you leave this country, you gotta read the rules of the rest of the world. Anybody remember A$AP Rocky a couple of years ago?[4] "Oh, you think you could get away like Sweden is Scranton, Pennsylvania?" NO. Going to jail in Sweden is not going to jail in Biafra. You go to jail in Namibia, you might have some issues coming out of there in one piece. You go in Tanzania, like, "I'm going to Tanzania, and I'm just going to be gangster." Yeah, uhm, okay. Even in this hemisphere, you know you can't get away with too much stuff south of this border. You go to Nicaragua, Panama, Colombia, Venezuela, Chile, and you think you will get away with stuff?

But all these places got hip hop artists bringin the noise. They don't all talk, "I will get you." No, they talkin, "Yo, man, I got a problem. I just gotta figure this out. I'm allowed to breathe with my music, but I gotta be honest with my music. I can't lie to cats with my music. I still live in the same spot on the fourteenth floor with no working elevators in São Paulo. If anything, I could probably give some people hope that I'm in the community and I'm in the favela. I can't lie like that." So when it comes down to truth and winning the bronze, silver, or gold, the US ain't gettin none of those. They might get, "That's the rapper that threw the most money at a camera." That don't work well around the world, y'all.

To me, when you're talking hip hop internationally, it's got to deal with a level of truth and humility because it's of the people and should be for the people, especially if you're talking to the whole world of people. The only thing that would make you Teflon [protect you] in many cases in the past was if they realized that you come from the struggle of the US. People ain't getting the same props as they did from that period of 1945 to 1975, where everybody knew that people of color gettin their ass busted in the US. Therefore, what you had with hip hop was what they call "the Black Badge." The Black Badge is like, "Yo, man, we just like in South Africa, man. We suffer like hell, man. We just got the Civil Rights Act of 1965." "Okay, you get the Black pass." That Black pass is gone after 1995, y'all. Once dudes started throwin money at the camera, it was like, "Y'all good now. Y'all them, y'all ain't us." Now they're judging you act by act.

Hip hop is a beautiful artform all over the world, but I don't think there's any advantages here. I used to ask people all the time, I said, "Yo, man, you like the beats or the lyrics?" Cats would always tell me, "I can hear that conscious shit, but the beats gotta be right." "Okay. Just the beats?" "No, I think the flow gotta be good too." "Do you care what they saying?" "Nah, not really." "So if you don't care what they say, could you listen to an MC in another language?" The first answer back in the day, maybe it's different now, would be, "Nah, I can't hear that." "Why?" "Because I don't know what they saying." "Wait, you just said you don't care what they say, so what difference does it make if it's in a language you don't understand? What is you saying, dog?!"

Meanwhile, internationally, they're putting in the effort to try to figure out what artists are saying. We all could get English. There's places that were fundamentally slow because of the government gangsterism of that country. Traditionally, France and England would have beef between the original French and the original English. Meanwhile, African immigrants are going in there with four or five different languages, like, "Okay, we'll pick up French. It's just the slavemaster's language." Same thing with Belgium. They can say, "We'll learn a little bit of that language here, too, since y'all spreading it in the Congo with atrocities. We got code going on. We'll learn the language."

My biggest regret in my whole life is not knowing another language. I don't think I started out right. I used to take Spanish classes. Didn't do well in them. Wasn't concentrating enough. Took a little French. Didn't do well in it. It was my fault, because the US arrogantly says, "You don't need to know another language. Everybody needs to learn English." Well, we ain't speaking English here either. We speak American. That's what the language is. And thank God for hip hop infusing something into American that makes it seem like it got a little bit more flavor to it, whether they want to use Ebonics or not.[5]

Now here we are reflecting on Rapstation and how I got involved with Mikko and Amkelwa. I said we need something that's able to encompass what is happening with all this music that's going on in the world. The US is a big-ass place, two thousand by three thousand miles, the lower forty-eight states under Canada and on top of Mexico. But it ain't bigger than the damn world! Whenever somebody can't name all the continents, I'm like, "What the fuck? Where do you live, in cyberspace?" Back in the day, I come up in a time when people used to say, "Oh yeah, name the countries." "Well, you know, Rome, Africa [*laughter*]." And actually, saying Africa is one country is not really a bad thing, because once you get to naming the fifty-four countries, you start kissing the imperialist ring. Geography is a very important thing to know, especially when you're following the music, because you start going even deeper in your enjoyment of the music. Once you start following the migration of the musics, a beautiful thing that you find out is they found a rhythmic way that language will work over these beats, that there is something that could go over this music besides just singing.

Rap music has been infectious around the planet because everybody is rapping with their particular flows and dialects. Mikko and Amkelwa have been working with me for thirteen years with a segment on my *And You Don't Stop!* radio show, which is across twenty-one Pacifica radio stations and across two hundred community stations around the world, as well as rapstation.com. They do a radio station called *Planet Earth, Planet Rap* [PEPR], where they curate songs that are submitted by rap artists from all over the world, and they fit it all together in a twenty-four-hour delivery, seven days a week. Because of the different languages, you can't just throw a French song and a Korean song back to back. You have to have someone give you a prelude to what you're about to hear. What Mikko and Amkelwa do quite well is they go in and break down a song—where it's from, why it was done, where the artist comes from, what sparked them, what label it's on, where's their fan base at, what's their social media. It's called "Voice Notes from around the World." It might seem old-fashioned, but you must do that in order to get something across, especially if it's in a different language. They have broken thousands of artists around the world. I've been honored by Mikko's and Amkelwa's presence and their work. It's some of the best radio breakthrough for hip hop and rap music that there is, period, because they do like an NPR-type job on music from around the world. They treat it with the utmost respect. The dignified manner for which they handle rap music and hip hop all around the world is something that we can emulate.

This is probably going to be one of the most important classes of this ten-week course because it seriously explains where the rest of the world is at. I'm going to bring Sam in to talk about hip hop in France. He will explain the context of when I first was going to France and I tried to explain that the future of rap music and hip hop was global. It wasn't a matter of passing the baton; it was just an aspect of natural growth.

SAMUEL LAMONTAGNE: After the US, France has historically been the biggest national market for hip hop. I'm going to talk about the history of hip hop in France and contextualize it within French racial politics. Before we get to hip hop, there is a long history of US popular culture's exportation to France to acknowledge. I want to start by asking, Why—outside of immigrant communities and niche markets—is popular culture from other countries not imported to the US on an industry level? The answer is simple—US cultural imperialism, as a cultural manifestation of the US's political and economic power.

Why am I talking about cultural imperialism? How did rap music get to France in the first place? Through its commercialization in the late 1970s, rap started circulating across the globe. "Rapper's Delight" was a big hit in France, and it was a mainstream introduction to rap music there. It was distributed by the French label Vogue, which since the 1950s had been distributing American artists in France, while locally producing French artists. Karim Hammou, who in my opinion has written the best book on French rap—*Une histoire du rap en France*—showed that the French music industry had for decades been relying on practices of adaptation of American music to promote new sounds in France.[6] The early US rap hits in France quickly became an inspiration for the music industry to produce records with rap in French. "Chacun fait (c'qui lui plait)" [1981], by Chagrin D'Amour, was the first to be a huge hit. Its success pushed the French music industry to invest more in rap, and more hits came, like "Salut . . . !" [1982], by Interview, or "Le Misunderstanding" [1982] by Idris Cheba. However, early recordings with rap in French were totally disconnected from hip hop culture, as the industry treated rap as a novelty, an American trend to capitalize on. Most artists were white, and while they rapped on disco/funky instrumentals, the topics they dealt with often related to detective stories or romance themes.

If contextualizing the history of French rap within the logics of the music industry is important, there's a risk of reproducing the dominant narrative that "hip hop was born in the US and then circulated across the world through its commercialization," which is very industry-centric and US-centric. But hip hop had always been global, because it stems from a larger pan-African context that long predates the commercialization of the culture [see chapter 2]. In particular, we talked about Caribbean immigration to New York, but this wasn't just a 1970s thing. New York had been a Caribbean mecca for decades, which is why Marcus Garvey started a division of the Universal Negro Improvement Association there in 1918.[7] There were long-standing interactions between African Americans and Caribbean folks, which we have to acknowledge to understand Black culture beyond the limits of national borders.[8] For example, the significance of the Haitian Revolution goes way beyond just Haiti. It reverberated around the Black world. The first successful slave rebellion, leading to the first Black republic.... Can you imagine the meaning of this event if you're enslaved in the American South? Or in Brazil? It made the impossible possible. Pan-African thinker C. L. R. James was writing about this in the 1930s.[9]

Also, there are connections between US Black freedom movements and anticolonial movements across the diaspora. Transatlantic solidarity was built through mutual freedom visions by drawing parallels between European colonialism and racism in the US. I'm thinking, for example, of Martin Luther King's visit to Ghana and meeting with Kwame Nkrumah, Frantz Fanon's involvement in the Algerian War for Independence, or the influence of African decolonial movements and the Cuban Revolution on the Black Panthers.[10] In the realm of culture, you had the influence of the Harlem Renaissance on French Africans leading to the Négritude movement, Congolese rumba's connection to Cuban music and politics, Fela Kuti's revolutionary spirit and Afrobeat innovation as rooted in the US Black Power movement and funk music.

There are countless instances where critical diasporic consciousness was articulated through the arts. Cultural dialogues have continuously allowed for solidarities to be built throughout the diaspora. So when looking at hip hop in France, I want to center this pan-African approach, because we've been a global people since at least the days of the transatlantic slave trade. Hip hop is a manifestation of those centuries-long interactions and dialogues. French Africans have always been part of the diasporic matrix that hip hop stems from, before hip hop and rap were commercialized and ever made it to France. That's where the conversation starts. France had one of the biggest colonial empires and was deeply involved in the transatlantic slave trade. That's why there is a historical presence of Africans and Afro-descendants in France, a presence that grew after 1945, as France sought its colonial subjects as cheap labor to rebuild after the ravages of World War II. As independence movements started in the late 1950s, immigration to France from former colonies grew. As a result, there is a large, diverse, multigenerational population of Afro-descendants in France coming from North, West, and Central Africa, the Caribbean, South America, to the Indian Ocean. Given this history, we have to understand mainland France itself as part of the African diaspora, and the many generations of Afro-descendants living and/or born in France, as French Africans.[11]

I want to illustrate this point by looking at Sidney Duteil, one of French hip hop's pioneers. Sidney came up in a complex Afro-diasporic world, one that gets remixed in the context of postcolonial France. A large part of French African communities lives in banlieues, housing projects in marginalized neighborhoods on the outskirts of French cities. As second-class citizens, they deal with social and racial exclusion, police brutality, and public disinvestment. Hip hop has been a medium to define ourselves as French Africans and reflect on our ambivalent national belonging to France as Black and non-white people. Now, Sidney was born in 1955 in Argenteuil, a Parisian banlieue. His parents were originally from Guadeloupe in the West Indies. His mom was a music lover and his dad was a saxophonist playing jazz and *biguine* from the French West Indies. From a very young age, he was a dancer, multi-instrumentalist, and record collector and sang in a rhythm-and-blues band. By 1974, he DJed at the Rocco Club. Yes, 1974, a.k.a. one year after Kool Herc's original hip hop jam! Like Sidney, many French Africans share multilayered connections to their own roots and the diasporic cultures they engaged with—from Martinique to Senegal, Algeria to Congo, Madagascar to Cameroon, and so on. On top of that, let's not forget their engagement with Black American culture, which was key. Samir Meghelli wrote about this in *The Global Cipha: Hip hop Culture and Consciousness* with Spady and Alim.[12]

The Rocco Club, and the next club where Sidney DJed at starting in 1976, "L'Émeraude," gathered predominantly Black crowds who came from all over Paris and surrounding banlieues to dance their asses off. On top of a strong funk foundation, Sidney mixed soul with salsa, reggae, West Indian music like zouk and African popular music like soukous. He'd play with two turntables while MCing. From these encounters rose a pre-hip hop dance called jazz-rock. French Africans evolved in a diasporic gumbo unique to Paris and its banlieues. This gumbo was the bedrock for the emergence of jazz-rock, and hip hop a bit later. Aside from the clubs where jazz-rock took place, dancers also participated in contests or performed on the street—busking—like at the Trocadéro (facing the Eiffel) or at Montparnasse, where people also roller-skated. These spaces were especially meaningful because French Africans were largely excluded from mainstream dancing spaces. Keep in mind, this is in the late 1970s, early 1980s, *before* hip hop formally arrives in France, just as the first rap records are circulating. As hip hop arrives, it takes root in this ecosystem of places and people who had cultivated a love for funk and soul in relation with other Afro-diasporic musical cultures. Hip hop developed in continuity with this ecosystem. In an interview published by *Down with This*, DJ Chabin remembers, "We didn't really know about hip hop. 'Rapper's Delight' was the first thing that came out in 1979. For us, it was a type of funk."[13]

The Bataclan was a central place in the growth of hip hop. Jazz-rocker crews danced, soon followed by the first French breakers, pop-lockers, and rappers. As the Bataclan moved to a different location in 1983 at la Grange aux Belles, it became a straight-up hip hop space where pioneers and up-and-comers gathered and battled, like the dance crews Paris City Breakers or Aktuel Force and rappers like Lionel D. Jhonygo, and Destroy Man. In a recent interview posted by *Le Debrief*, Jhonygo said, "For me the Bataclan wasn't melting pot afternoons, it was Black afternoons. I was in my world there, because it was like I was in the West Indies because I'd see Black people everywhere, no matter what country they were from. And I felt good there."[14] As a hip hop space, the Bataclan allowed young French Africans to congregate around creative activities that resonated with them and to build community, which was significant in the context of a racially hostile city like Paris.

Before they got into hip hop, Jhonygo and Destroy Man were part of the Black Panthers (besides taking inspiration from the name, the French Panthers had no official connection to the US Black Panther Party), a street club of French Africans founded in the late 1970s who stayed in the banlieue of Pantin. They dressed in black leather clothes, trained in combat sports, and listened to 1950s rock like Chuck Berry. They protected their communities against racist violence and fought against white far-right crews like the Rebels, who listened to rockabilly and wore Confederate flags on their clothes. Before rap, Jhonygo and Destroy Man were singing in a rock band. As a matter of fact, Jhonygo's name is a reference to Chuck Berry's song "Johnny B. Goode." But when they saw the video of "The Message" and heard Melle Mel's lyrics, it resonated with them in a new way. In an interview from *Stay Tuned*, Jhonygo recalls, "They are dressed like us in the street. We were the Black Panthers, a crew of roughnecks . . . I was like, 'This is New York roughnecks just like we are Paris roughnecks.' That's why it appeals to us because they're talking about stuff we're living. It's similar, they're just in the US and we're in France . . . We were into rock because it told our thing, now it was rap, I felt it."[15]

Destroy Man and Jhonygo recognized themselves in Melle Mel. The fact that French Africans from Paris identified with Black Americans from the Bronx through fashion and music once again speaks of the importance of culture in articulating diasporic consciousness. When Public Enemy toured Paris in 1993, Chuck D actually said something that echoes that—"Black people have to recognize each other in different areas of the world, which is very important. The thing that separates us as a people is our language differences. I would like to relate to a lot of brothers and sisters over here but I don't know French. A lot of them don't know English."[16] Chuck was describing hip hop as a cultural medium to build solidarity between Black folks across the world. Hip hop has been a tool to foster diasporic connections and keep us in conversation, even when we don't speak the same language.

The transatlantic identification of French Africans with Black Americans through culture has a long history. While our West Indian or African roots were seen as primitive through the French colonial gaze, Black American culture had an allure that allowed us to imagine ourselves positively. While music like zouk or soukous referred to immigration and constantly reduced us to the outside, hip hop spoke to our postcolonial realities in France, through which we could imagine ourselves here, as French Africans. Sulee B Wax, a dancer in Atomic Breakers and rapper in Little MC crew, expressed it clearly: "We're French negroes, I'm West Indian but rap is my culture. I don't feel close to French music and Caribbean music. The only thing that resembled me was rap."[17]

France claims to be colorblind, which is a ridiculous idea considering France's history. . . . More than anything, colorblindness reflects France's denial of its racist, colonial past and refusal to address its legacies in the present. Hip hop didn't just make French Africans visible; it put race and racism in the public consciousness. France could be seen through a racial lens, and not as a "white" country. Mag3, a.k.a. Juan Massenya, explained exactly this on the TV show *Envoyé spécial* in 1990:

> When you grow up and all the time you hear about the Gauls, Gauls, Gauls. You're being shown pictures of blonde, blue-eyed Gauls. After a while you're like, "I really don't look like a Gaul so I'm going to have to know where I'm from." This movement [hip hop] allows that. People who ask this question or who feel excluded, they get together and create what they didn't have before, a culture, like our ancestors could have had but in the street. We live in concrete, well we have to make do; we're going to make our culture in concrete.[18]

Hip hop allowed us to recognize our historical presence in France and question the conditions of this presence. And to be clear, we didn't go to France. France came to us. So it's not just about recognizing our contemporary experiences with racism through the legacies of slavery and colonialism; it's recognizing the contributions of centuries of exploitation and extraction from Africa and the Caribbean and their role in making France what it is today.

It's bigger than hip hop. Through sound, style, fashion, language, ideas, movement, hip hop culture created a world where we were at the center, where we could exist in our full complexity, for ourselves. In a society that was crushing us, hip hop was oxygen to breathe. It was like flying. So of course, we gravitated toward it. It was just dope and beautiful. In *Ordinary Notes*, Christina Sharpe writes about the world-making capacity of the beauty we create and experience and the knowledge it produces.[19] A lot of times, hip hop is reduced to the explicit political dimension of rap lyrics, but it's much more than that. To return to Alim's opening framework [chapter 1], it's the politics and the poetics, the activism and the aesthetics. It's also a system of intelligence. It's epistemology as feeling. As Robin D. G. Kelley wrote in *Freedom Dreams*, "The most radical art is not protest art but works that take us to another place, envision a different way of seeing, perhaps a different way of feeling."[20] As Chuck D says, hip hop is about *feeling*.

Hip hop culture continues to grow in France to a point where it is integral to French popular culture. In many ways, it changed what it means to be French. . . . As rapper Sté Strausz writes in her book *Fly Girls*, today "everybody's hip hop. . . . Our codes became those of people who don't know their meaning, and our fashion is shown on stages where those who looked down on us are now trying to look like us."[21] Sometimes it can feel like we've been pushed out of our own space, like hip hop's been gentrified, captured, when it was rooted in opacity, as Édouard Glissant would say.[22] But hip hop is not a pure or one-dimensional thing. Its complexities and contradictions reflect our own complex existences.

CHUCK D: That was fantastic! I'm going to ask you some specific questions, because one thing I know is that there's always a bar dropped somewhere in the song that says, "This is who I am versus what they think about me." In every single song, it's like, "I'm searching for myself in this music." That has been lost in the translation over generations in hip hop and rap music, because the assumption has been filled in by industry. What you just showed has been every aspect of the original vibe of hip hop. Hip hop was always honest. "This is who I am. And this is what I'm challenging." And it could be overtly political or not, but they're born in the middle of the politic. Here, in the US, people are born in the middle of the politic, but so many things have been washed to the side. But when it bubbles up, you get what happened in 2020 with the racial justice movement, like, "I've been lied to all this time. This is who we need to be. Boom, boom, boom!" It doesn't necessarily get conveyed through hip hop like it used to, but the connectivity of hip hop around the world is still in its vibrant stage of being honest to what it is.

Turning to Mikko and Amkelwa, what got you interested in being able to take rap music and hip hop from around the world and curate it for a global audience?

MIKKO KAPANEN: The way that we got into hip hop was through you, Chuck. When I was a young person, I didn't really speak much English. I'm from Helsinki, Finland. There was something about the aesthetic. This part of the world is very sort of like heavy metal or rock and roll, so it was a different type of expression that I was drawn to. It was also a major reason how I got into a certain type of worldview. From your records, I learned about Nelson Mandela, which started a process where I ended up in South Africa.

AMKELWA MBEKENI: I'm from South Africa, mainly from Cape Town. I was born in the eastern Cape, which is the home of Nelson Mandela and Walter Sisulu, if you're familiar with South African history.[23] I didn't look for hip hop. It found me. Hip hop or any conscious music in South Africa was a very important part of our growing up during the apartheid years. During that time, we were all accustomed to being conscientized through music. We looked to our artists to speak to us about the political climate in the country, as well as what was happening elsewhere. It wasn't just about hip hop. It was about artists having the platform to be able to raise the consciousness of young people, because we used music to get us through the struggle. The protests included music. You mentioned that music travels, but also *we* travel through music and through art from elsewhere.

CHUCK D: Your work was so far ahead of its time in considering the talent level of hip hop around the globe and taking a different perspective on hip hop. For example, when they talk about gender in hip hop in the US, it's always polarized. And even women in hip hop, "Oh, it's Nicki Minaj, it's Cardi B." It becomes the only conversation after a while, because in the US, discovering new music is less of a priority than it is everywhere else, where people want to be part of something bigger than themselves. When we consider women in hip hop, explain how women comprise 33 percent of the output of all the hip hop on the planet.

KAPANEN: I think it's largely about record industry politics. They push certain kinds of hypersexualized women artists because from the industry's perspective, this is what generates money. They have the statistics to prove that. But from the cultural side, also from the US, there are a lot of great women artists, but they're not really getting the attention that they deserve because it's so narrow, and every country has their versions of Nicki Minaj. But of course, for PEPR, it's a process of selection also. That's not really something that interests me very much. We are looking for different types of artists.

MBEKENI: From a South African perspective, how we grew up, we all knew that everybody had a voice and anybody can be up there on the stage speaking their truth. Because hip hop was initially quite political, it was a space where activists would come and use that platform. Lots of us would use that space to be able to communicate important information. With respect to the gender question, it never occurred to me that it would be just men. Women, too, had the same issues, were dealing with the same ills, and wanted to express the same opinions [see chapter 5]. I've never really thought of PEPR as doing anything particularly special in finding these female emcees. There are female MCs all over the world, because there are women who are concerned about society and their communities everywhere.[24]

CHUCK D: Of the thousands of artists you've curated over the past thirteen years, what has been the biggest surprise to y'all?

MBEKENI: It's just a surprise that we're able to do a show in all these different languages, which we ourselves do not necessarily speak. I am multilingual because I come from a country that has eleven official languages. But we are able to do this show getting artists from Japan, Indonesia, Malaysia, Zimbabwe, everywhere, and every time, it seems like we find the right sound, the right message, the right spirit, and the right fire. We're looking for a specific kind of artist, maybe a specific kind of aesthetic.

KAPANEN: When we think about international hip hop, oftentimes the idea is that people listen to mainstream artists like 50 Cent all over the world. But it's a whole different ball game when you start thinking about people becoming participants. They start creating their own style. When we say hip hop is everywhere, we really mean damn near literally everywhere! I remember there was a time when I was bored and I was thinking to myself, "Okay, let me think of a place that would be unlikely to have hip hop." I googled hip hop in Mongolia, for example, and I started looking into it. Actually, at that time, there was a new documentary about Mongolian hip hop called *Mongolian Bling*. I ended up watching it, and I don't know why I thought Mongolia didn't have hip hop artists, because of course they do! They had a really vibrant scene there. They had the more street guys, the more pop artists, and the more conscious artists, the whole spectrum. You can multiply that across every country. There might be some that don't have hip hop, but I would say that would be the exception that proves that rule.

MBEKENI: Recently, we started doing this virtual world tour where we do a series of interviews with about ten artists in a more in-depth and personal way. What surprised me is that most of these artists all had one common denominator as to what inspired them to get into the hip hop game. Most of them cite you, Chuck, as the reason why they got started. Then I realized that there are common threads, even though we might not even understand the different languages that some of the artists rap in. There's a shared struggle and some pain that connects them. That's been amazing to see.

KAPANEN: It's Public Enemy and Tupac. Never underestimate the global impact of Tupac Shakur. We can have a conversation about his lyrical abilities or his flow, but the global impact of Tupac is for certain—his vulnerability, the way he was sharing his whole self, his humanity. He's a massively important artist that influenced many around the world.

CHUCK D: Also, with the video Sam played, visually and rhyme-wise, Wu-Tang Clan. They showed that collectives were welcome, eight or nine people together spittin verses, maybe sliding in and out of it. Wu-Tang came in with a force that said, "Everybody is part of this crew!" Now the collaborations that you get are incredible. Sometimes you get MCs who are bringing multiple languages, which is mind-blowing, and they can begin in one language, go into a different language, hook and chorus, and come back to it. Right now, the momentum is happening, and people are like, "I might not know your language," but I can get to know you through PEPR. You interview these people, and they give their best insights, which allows you to talk about their music. Explain some of what you do in "Voice Notes from around the World."

KAPANEN: That was an idea that came to us some years ago, because even during this time that we've been doing PEPR for your show, technology is improving. These days, everybody's mobile phone can record good quality audio. You can send voice notes in WhatsApp, for example. For Voice Notes, we are basically just asking artists to contextualize their music. When we talk to a UK artist, for example, they might talk about some incidents of police brutality or just provide the broader context.

MBEKENI: It's a progression from how we initially used to do it. We would research the artists ourselves, and then we would speak about where they are from. But now they participate in the show, and then they self-represent, and they express exactly what they are feeling from their own perspectives. I think it helps because the artists also are looking for spaces where they can connect with their audience in a much more personal way. "Voice Notes from around the World" has been beautiful in that way, because it has allowed that visibility, inclusiveness, and representation.

KAPANEN: We mentioned language. I think it's very important that we're talking about French hip hop, because French hip hop is one of the most important cultures and markets for hip hop. It's been hugely influential because, of course, language is a very important aspect of national identity. Language is central. In 1994, there was a legislation in radio that introduced a quota for French-speaking music in radio. So a lot of radio stations took hip hop as part of their playlists or became rap radio stations because it was something that they needed to do. They played music in French when French rap was readily available.

This is very important in the context of Europe. A lot of artists then, when they started rapping, they started in their own languages and not just mimicking fake American accents. They were listening to a lot of French music, so it was very important. And if you want to understand Europe, you were seeing some of those videos. This is what Paris looks like. This is what London looks like. This is what Berlin looks like, or Helsinki or Stockholm. If you want to understand Europe, you have to listen to European hip hop because the stories are told from angles that you will not get from the news. These are just ordinary people living their lives, and they are telling their stories in rhyme. If you pay attention to that, you understand a little bit more about this continent that is so complicated in so many ways.

CHUCK D: You're also floating Africa to the top because it's easy to point to South Africa, Nigeria, or Ghana. But I know for a fact that you've delivered at least thirty, thirty-five countries out of the continent and languages from the continent. It's been my prerogative and cultural priority to penetrate the psyche in this country from being isolated and self-focused. The world will liberate the free-minded people in this country and the diaspora will liberate people who feel that they're chained by this country. If you are a hip hop artist in the US, the world will liberate your art to make you look thirty years ahead, instead of year by year. If you follow hip hop and know that there's a ramp into the rest of the world, it will set you free. I've gotten so much education from your curation of the songs and conversations. I'm honored, and it's a pleasure to be able to have the opportunity to host you.

H. SAMY ALIM: Let's give it up for Amkelwa and Mikko! [*Applause.*] It's an honor for me that you all could join us. Much love all the way. I'd like to add this: every time you hear Chuck talk about global hip hop culture—he didn't say it tonight, so this is why I'm bringing it up—he will tell you all, "When you leave this room, if you don't have a passport, get one now."[25]

CHUCK D: I used to say it back in the day, too, when only 20 percent of US citizens had a passport by 2001. And when they had the Million Man March, and it's like, "Well, what could Black people do?" I said, "What I could do in the US is become connected with the diaspora by just getting a passport." Then when too many of us get it, then people beware of Homeland Security. It's like, "Why all these Black folks getting their passports for?" Right now, the conversation over where we are at in the world, it goes beyond hip hop.

ALIM: One of the things about hip hop is that you've got to engage the world. You read about France. You read about South Africa. If you're not asleep right now, you're seeing the global rise of right-wing extremism, again. What does that mean? When you see the French rappers that Sam mentioned talking about white supremacy and explaining their condition still as colonial subjects but in France, and how they're pushing back through music, that's a conversation that's been happening on a global level in terms of the rise of the right, the rise of white supremacy, the consolidation of power through global capitalism and colonization.

You can't really talk about global hip hop without talking about those issues, because what's happening in France is you have colonial subjects. France was like colonial powers all around the world, grabbing land, destroying entire countries, just taking whatever they could get their hands on in this process of colonialism. Then the people from those same places, the colonies, now want to come to France as a way out of the devastation and oppression that France itself inflicted on them. What do they do? They get to France and they realize, "Oh, shit, we're second-class citizens. We're never going to be considered French." And France says the only way to be French is to be white European and to speak French. So they look at that second-class citizenship, and what do they do? Hip hop comes along, influenced by Public Enemy and others, and joins local Black consciousness movements. Black French subjects start taking France back, reclaiming it from within.

Does that sound familiar at all? It should, because that's what Black people did in the US, and that's what South Africans did at home. In these two contexts, we're now talking about settler colonialism. Europeans land on top of you and take that shit out from under you. What Sam was saying about white people owning most of the wealth, and Black people owning almost nothing, what about South Africa? White people are 10 percent of the population and own 90 percent of the wealth. Same story. Hip hop challenges that dynamic. It decenters white supremacy and centers Blackness and other oppressed peoples. Indigeneity gets centered all over the world. What I want to point out is that you have these political ideologies that also circulate globally through hip hop culture. I'm not talking about a homogenized global hip hop nation because it's differences everywhere you go. But you must engage this now. You engage the language. You engage the culture. You engage the style, the fashion. You must engage the racial politics, the language politics, the politics of immigration and migration, capitalism.[26] Like Chuck was asking, "In the US when we deal with these issues, are we in or are we out of the global conversation?"

CHUCK D: Because it's time that we turn off the national conversation. If you ain't in the international conversation, what conversation are you in? You're talking to yourself. We are in a time of great uncertainty in the US. That's why the right thinks it can fill it up. But if you have us in the hip hop nation and you have Black folks and people of color, and all of a sudden you're not connected in the world, you're in a hot box. A hot box needs some kind of door open to somewhere else so you can get some fresh air, because this box is hot for the next two years. If I tell you who's going to be the president of this place two years from now, we don't know. Nobody knows. You got an eighty-year-old man in the presidency right now, and nobody knows what's going on with him. We know the wolf pack is out against him, and we're just watching the wolves.

Hip hop has always given me a saving grace. When I get up out of here, I hate to be selfish like that, but when I leave the US, I get IQ rehab. When I go to places where people live and we sit down and have a conversation, my conversation is worldly at this level. Like, "Oh damn, I feel like I can breathe." Now they made it to a point where if you're a "screenager," you ain't got to move out of your house to not be locked into the world. You could get locked into the world and not leave your crib but take your mind and take your communication there. Get some ideas there and open up your space. I'm not saying it's going to be easy, and I'm not here to scare you.

But I'm telling you, I've never seen anything like this in my lifetime—so much uncertainty in the US and the rest of the world. The only time I think I've ever seen a similar period in this country is when I was thirteen, fourteen years old and Nixon left office and Gerald Ford came in. Rockefeller was the vice president, and nobody knew what was going to happen in 1976. I'm fourteen, fifteen years old. My first ten years, we grew up getting accustomed to the assassinations, Vietnam War, and the obliteration of Dr. King and the Black Panthers right in front of our face. The destruction of the Black community at the top of the eighties. And here I think I'm cool. Since I got the right to vote, I'm going to vote for Angela Davis, not knowing that two-party politics is a trick. I found out later on, a vote for Angela Davis was a vote for Ronald Reagan.

We got twelve years of devastation, which rap music and hip hop grow up out of, to be the counterattack against the rise of white supremacy in the US during R&B, Reagan and Bush. All of a sudden, I seen all this stuff happening out of nowhere. There are some new drugs, and new guns to protect the money from these new drugs, out of nowhere, *everywhere*, over a span of two to three years. So here we are today, and hip hop internationally is speaking to a lot of issues that we could possibly get some inspiration from and figure out how to think *out*. The fact is, nobody could leave their crib in April 2020. Don't lose sight of that. They say, "Nobody leave your effing house or there will be ramifications." As tough as cats say they are, gangster this and gangster that, nobody moved. Nobody. The toughest, most violent cats, they said, "I'ma stay in the crib this month. Right now I don't know *what's* goin on." So I thank y'all for just being able to open me up and offer us at least an opportunity to think *out*.

QUESTION 1: Is the rise of right-wing politics in France, and in Europe generally, affecting the music and the culture?

LAMONTAGNE: France, as long as I've been alive—around thirty years, a little more—has been a racist, right-wing country. When I talk to my family, my elders, it's been a racist country for centuries. Nothing has changed, really. My grandparents were colonial subjects. My grandparents' grandparents were born enslaved. So "the rise of right-wing politics," yeah, sure, but it's always been like this for Black people. It's the same song. They're just changing the beat a little bit.

As far as how it affects the music, I'll give you an example from back in the eighties, nineties. A rapper from France, MC Solaar, one of the most well-known French rappers, especially internationally, he's put in that "conscious" box. I never really got into his music. He was too chill and too poetic, and that meant that white people loved it. I couldn't find myself in MC Solaar, because his style was too nonthreatening to whiteness. There was music that was more irreverent, that wasn't considered as poetic but that was poetic to me and my friends. That was the only space where we could see ourselves, where we could exist as our full selves. That was powerful. So the conscious/ignorant debate in hip hop is difficult, because to whom is it considered to be conscious or ignorant? In a society that wants you silent or dead, hip hop irreverence was extremely powerful to me.

QUESTION 2: The French football national team is almost entirely made of players of African descent. There's a well-known quote by French soccer player Karim Benzema, "If I score, I'm French, if I don't, I'm Arab." Is France making progress on issues of racism and discrimination?

LAMONTAGNE: Definitely not. Because France thinks of itself as a colorblind country. It erases structural inequalities and the experiences of minorities in France, because they can't see it because they're so blinded by their colorblindness. Bringing up racial issues in particular can spark controversy in France because the mainstream considers it divisive or an attack on national identity. And kind of like rap and hip hop, football [soccer] forces French society to confront racism because it's a space of racial visibility. As you said, more than half of the national team is made of players of African descent, who are some of the best players in the world, Kylian Mbappé, Karim Benzema, Paul Pogba, as well as the generation before them. I love that France won the 2018 World Cup, not because I care about football but because it gave the world a different image of France, an image where Frenchness isn't equated with whiteness. In that moment, the national pride of being world champions was intimately associated with Blackness and Africanness. That forced France to reckon with its colonial past, because why is the national team so Black? This simple question can be the start of an entire reflection on France's colonial history and ongoing systemic racism.

QUESTION 3: Could music have given a sense of false hope to marginalized people who are struggling in the diaspora?

ALIM: There's a short quote from Angela Davis: "Freedom is a constant struggle."[27] It's not about, "Will there be a point when victory will be won?" We're always going to have to fight this battle. That's just the way that societies are structured. Human beings have organized societies this way for centuries. The moment you say "Victory is won," you've lost.

CHUCK D: What are the options if you're here in the US? They say if you're a young, Black male, you are trying to get in the NBA or be a rapper. If you don't make neither, then it's the prison industrial complex. Entertainment ain't the main thing; entertainment is like a distraction from regular, everyday life. Regular life is the 90 percent that got to figure out how to make the country work, how to figure out who is going to school, how people are eating, where waste is going to go. What's the import, what's the export? I mean, real everyday grown-up shit. It is only in the US where they just like, "Okay, we got this MTV thing, or BET thing back in the day, that extend your teenage years to forty-one." That shit don't work in the regular world. Only in the US, people like, "I wanna be a baby til I'm forty-three." There's a community still. Whether it's Helsinki or Cape Town, the community says that it's gotta be some accountability from yourself or you just going to be left out. Music is a thing that you do, but it ain't going to feed your life. I mean, *you've* got to figure it out.

MBEKENI: You mentioned the word "community." Community radio was one of the places in South Africa, Bush Radio in particular, that really supported hip hop.[28] I think most hip hop artists, like Shaheen Ariefdien of Prophets of da City, have gone through Bush Radio, some actually working at the station and running programs for youth and promoting hip hop culture. In South Africa, people of diminished means from townships, they've had easier access to play their music via Bush Radio because it allowed space for them to be able to be heard. That's usually the first point of contact for artists in Cape Town. Then they go to the more corporate radio stations.

QUESTION 4: You said in Cuba that "Fight the power" was not something you could say. Are our governments always going to try to censor hip hop?

CHUCK D: Depends on where you at. There's 214 governments. Governments go through changes, or sometimes they have monarchies that say, "I've been here for 30 years and you have to kill me to get me out of there." Some governments you can work with, and some governments you can't. I remember going to Taiwan. They had a poster on the wall, said, "You might believe in smoking, but you bring one seed in this country, penalty is death." They ain't playin, fuck the music shit. You bring one piece of contraband in their country, the US will not save you. Once upon a time, Jesse Jackson saved a Black person who was abroad and brought them back.[29] I always knew if I did something internationally, ain't nobody bringing me back. Number one rule when traveling the world is know the rules. I was in Jakarta, Indonesia. They tell you very clear: "Do your songs. Do not talk to the audience." Who am I going to call? The Black nation in the US is going to save me? No. That's real talk. We can't get Brittney Griner out of Russia right now. So I got tired of the fact that being Black in America, we basically got children's power or less. Less. We ain't got no power. All the big moguls, you got money, maybe, but you ain't got *power*. The President Obama thing was cool. But at the same time, we have to understand who we are, what that man was in charge of, and what his job was.

ALIM: I wouldn't expect too much out of governments. So the party line is that governments are here to share the power, but we all know that governments are here to consolidate power. If governments *do* start to support hip hop culture, then you better start thinking about concepts like ideological incorporation and what that means to the culture and its power. Because that has happened in repressive regimes around the world, where governments now are offering grants to folks who want to produce hip hop culture and radio stations who want to play more hip hop music. Hip hop is also being produced that *supports* right-wing governments and genocides. Some Israeli rap is a good example of that.

CHUCK D: Right here in the US, yo, I'm telling you, like fifteen years ago, they would make mixtapes in the middle of an NBA game and be like, "Be All You Can Be."

ALIM: I just saw this in the park last weekend. The army was there bumpin hip hop and reggaeton in the park, trying to recruit Black and Latinx youth. As soon as you start to get that collaboration from government, you're dealing with something else entirely.

CHUCK D: We can counteract that kind of stuff. There should be somebody spittin about *Roe v. Wade* lyrics right now. Before, hip hop couldn't answer quickly, because of the limits of technology. You had to first get a record deal in order to answer something politically six months later. But now it's like, "Yo, I can go to the crib, spit, record on my laptop, and get it out there." I'm talking about words and messages that need to be out versus whatever is coming out of the government at that particular time. That's what they do in other countries. If something takes place, they answer it. That clapback is coming like, "Boom, bam!" And they don't do it for fame or commercial success. They say this needs to answer that bullshit right now, and that's when it gains traction. Then governments come and try to stop that traction. Years ago, when Sam was a shorty, there was an incident that happened in France, where two young men were electrocuted on the outskirts of one of the suburbs.

LAMONTAGNE: Yeah, it was Zyed Benna and Bouna Traoré in Clichy-sous-Bois in 2005. They saw the police, and they just ran because they got scared.

CHUCK D: Because when you talk about suburbs in France, the suburbs is basically where the government says, "We will put you all out there, and you'll have limited services. You're going to work for cheap because you damn sure ain't living in the city!" You got immigration coming up from those French-speaking former colonies like Martinique and Senegal, and they move out the motherland to get the opportunity. So when they didn't need cheap labor, they expected that the Black folk would go back to Africa and the Caribbean. Then you had another generation that came in like, "Yo, it's our home. We're here now."

When the police chased those two young men, and they got electrocuted, it was the last straw of racism that had just been outrageous in that area. The protests started, and they burned every single car that they could put their hands on. That was the method of protesting against the government and that brutality, saying, "You ain't gotta take care of us. *This* is how we gon protest this." And I think it was thousands of cars.

LAMONTAGNE: Thousands of people were arrested too. Because the police officers were let off, and the official discourse from the government was backing the cops, so people were heated. The protests lasted like three weeks. I was fifteen years old at the time. Almost every single time those protests were connected to police brutality in the banlieues. It's been happening since at least the 1970s. In 1990, in the banlieue of Vaulx-en-Velin in Lyon, Thomas Claudio was hit by a police car, which sparked several days of protests. In 2016, Adama Traoré was killed by policemen in Beaumont-sur-Oise near Paris, and a year after that, Théo Luhaka was raped by policemen during an identity check in Aulnay-sous-Bois, a Parisian banlieue, resulting in protests. These are just a few examples.

In this US, it's really the same thing, because we're all living under those legacies of slavery and colonialism, though expressed in different ways. Take the George Floyd protests in global context, and in the French context, in particular. In June 2020, Assa Traoré, who's the sister of Adama Traoré and leader of the Comité Vérité et Justice pour Adama, called for a march which gathered about fifty thousand people in Paris alone. Often I've heard Americans seeing this march only as another George Floyd–related event. There was a beautiful pan-African dimension at the heart of that march and a connection with the movement for Black Lives in the US, yes, but we need to acknowledge local particularities too. Bringing it back to hip hop, just like in the US, many French rappers have spoken out against police brutality, and a lot of them publicly support the work of the Comité Adama, such as Mokobé, Booba, Médine, and Kery James.

QUESTION 5: What does it mean when hip hop takes off in countries that are almost entirely non-Black? Are they appropriating or appreciating?

CHUCK D: A lot of it is cultural appropriation. A lot of it is also like, "Okay, now I'm on the lower edge of the classes in this country, so I'm talking to the same struggle." I would go to places like in the former Yugoslav Republic, and "Fight the Power" meant a whole different thing there. Or I'm playing in Moscow, and some people out there have "Fight the Power" in their minds, even if they can't say it. They know what they mad at. They know what they ain't got. They know what they see, how they've been lied to. This is where culture starts to jump. They're not gonna be talking about Black protests in Brooklyn. No. They know what oppression is. And that's why that song happened to resonate.

ALIM: I know Chuck has seen that resonance everywhere he goes. I could offer a couple of examples. One, you could take the Palestinian context. What are they rapping about over there? You watch Jackie Salloum's *Slingshot Hip Hop* or you listen to artists from Palestine, like DAM, for example, they were listening to Chuck and they were listening to Tupac, just like Mikko said.[30] Those are the two names that you hear over and over again. Why? If you remember, we discussed how hip hop represented what Tricia Rose called "voices from the margins" [chapter 1]. Artists were speaking back to the center and commenting on what it means to be on the margins. That political ethos globalized along with the culture, with the stance, the style, the language, the turntablism, the graffiti, the dance. All of that was globalized. Everywhere you go, you see people who are marginalized, those who got the boot on top of their neck, whether it's oppression along race, gender, class, sexuality, land, immigration, language, religion, you name it, they're resisting. Hip hop speaks to the marginalized and the marginalized speak back through it. That's a beautiful thing globally that we have seen.

The second thing that I want to point out, too, is you can have majority white countries with social divisions and fissures everywhere. Coming from the US, we might not know immediately what those fissures are. For example, most folks don't know that there are artists that are arrested and imprisoned in Spain that are living in exile because of the content of their lyrics. Imagine a rapper right now out on the street rappin, not even a major label rapper, and they say the wrong thing about the king. Yes, there's still a king in Spain. You get hunted down, arrested, or exiled. I work with La Llama Rap Colectivo out of El Raval, an oppressed neighborhood in Barcelona, and they gave me a *good* education about what happens to rappers that are too political out there. We documented that in the book *Freedom Moves*. The situation globally is dire. Even in Spain, the racism and Islamophobia faced by North Africans and South Asians and Muslims is present and growing with new right-wing movements. When you look at someone like El Chojin from Madrid, listen to the racial politics in his rhymes. Listen to the kinds of conversations they're having in predominantly white countries and pay attention to the lines of division, starting with the fact that many northern Europeans revoke whiteness from the Spanish anyway because they were colonized for centuries by North African Muslims. That's a whole 'nother story.

CHUCK D: It's easy for governments to let you become big as long as you're having beef with yourselves, and they'll just police it. That's how it works in the US. And I'm telling you, talk about "Fight the Power" working! My first time in Dublin, in Belfast, Yo! And they were serious in Northern Ireland. They like, "Yo, don't bring nothing from down here with the queen up this way because it's goin down." "Fight the Power" meant a lot to them people up there, all of them white and Irish. They go to Scotland, on the other side of the British Isles, and they're serious about Scots and Glasgow not being part of what the queen and her whole plan and the monarchy down there was about. They've made concessions.

That's what taught me a long time ago that "I made the song, but y'all took it to another place." We was in Zagreb, Croatia, with Ice-T, and they stopped war for a day. They all came to the concert to see Ice-T and Public Enemy. Pac was supposed to be on that tour, but he couldn't make it. We broke the curtain. The curtain was down, but we was a first in the area. Mercenaries were at the gig, but they said, "Yo, everybody kind of stopped for a day to get this real rap concert from the OGs." This is 1994. They said, "Listen, by next morning, y'all gotta get up outta here, man, cause we're about to bomb." I mean, mortar shells, bombs, right? We got up outta there, and sure enough, it was on the news. You couldn't go into Serbia and talk about Croatia back then, and vice versa, and the distance between them was like the distance between San Diego and Fresno! You got to know where you're going. You got to ask questions. You got to know who you talking to. And that's global hip hop and rap music 101 for today.

NOTES

1. See Geneva Smitherman, *Talkin and Testifyin: The Language of Black America* (Wayne State University Press, 1977); Geneva Smitherman and H. Samy Alim, *Articulate While Black: Barack Obama, Language, and Race in the U.S.* (Oxford University Press, 2012); and Geneva Smitherman, "The Power of the Rap: The Black Idiom and the New Black Poetry," *Twentieth Century Literature* 19, no. 4 (October 1973), 259–74, a precursor to hip hop linguistics.

2. For an in-depth interview with Sylvia Robinson about the precise moment that she decided to record rap music, see James G. Spady, H. Samy Alim, and Charles G. Lee, *Street Conscious Rap* (Black History Museum, 1999).

3. Brittney Griner, a top-ranked professional basketball player, was arrested in Russia in February 2022 for possession of less than a gram of cannabis. At the time of this lecture, Griner was still imprisoned in Russia. She was released in December 2022.

4. In 2019, A$AP Rocky was arrested in Stockholm for aggravated assault. After his release, he was found guilty by a Swedish jury, and given a suspended sentence.

5. "Ebonics" was coined by Black psychologist Robert Williams in an effort to legitimize Black linguistic practices. See his edited volume *Ebonics: The True Language of Black Folks* (Institute of Black Studies, 1975).

6. See Karim Hammou, *Une histoire du rap en France* (La Découverte, 2012); and Samir Meghelli, "'Fear of a Black Planet': The Transnational Racial Politics of Hip-Hop in France, 1990–1991," in *Hip-Hop en Français: An Exploration of Hip Hop Culture in the Francophone World*, ed. Alain-Philippe Duran (Rowman & Littlefield, 2020). See Alain Philippe Duran, *Black, Blanc, Beur: Rap Music and Hip-Hop Culture in the Francophone World* (Scarecrow Press, 2002).

7. On the ideological legacy of Garvey vis-à-vis Afrodiasporic musics, see James G. Spady, *Marcus Garvey: Jazz, Reggae, Hip Hop, and the African Diaspora* (Marcus Garvey Foundation, 2011).

8. See Kevin Meehan, *People Get Ready: African American and Caribbean Cultural Exchange* (University Press of Mississippi, 2009).

9. See C. L. R. James, *Black Jacobins: Toussaint L'Ouverture and the San Domingo Revolution* (Secker and Warburg, 1938); and C. L. R. James, *A History of Negro Revolt* (Research Associates School Times Publications, 1991; first published 1969).

10. See Frantz Fanon, *Black Skin, White Masks* (Editions du Seuil, 1952); and Frantz Fanon, *The Wretched of the Earth* (François Maspero, 1961).

11. See Samuel Lamontagne, "France through Race: Beyond Colorblindness," *Ufahamu* 42, no. 2 (2021): 99–VII.

12. See Samir Meghelli's in-depth oral history interviews with Sydney Duteil and other French rap pioneers in James G. Spady, H. Samy Alim, and Samir Meghelli, *Tha Global Cipha: Hip Hop Culture and Consciousness* (Black History Museum, 2006).

13. See "JAZZROCK la vrai histoire," https://www.youtube.com/watch?v=Ab8s0wyiFoA.

14. See "Le Monde de domain—Les erreors historique," https://youtu.be/e7l0i4sxVP8?si=yre3pNsWmAyUp1en.

15. See Jhonygo "On avait pas l'idée de faire des raps pour gagner des millions," https://youtu.be/7YSEGna96ao?si=DGrHniOLV7_hQivv.

16. See Samir Meghelli, "'Fear of a Black Planet': The Transnational Racial Politics of Hip-Hop in France, 1990–1991," in *Hip-Hop en Français: An Exploration of Hip-Hop Culture in the Francophone World*, ed. Alain-Philippe Duran (Roman & Littlefield, 2020), 29–43.

17. See José-Louis Bocquet and Philippe Pierre-Adolphe classic hip hop text *Rap ta France* (La Sirène, 1996).

18. See "1990: Génération rap, tag et NTM," https://youtu.be/VJFrDR8ew_E?si=0OF_TpK1himLIhBN.

19. See Christina Sharpe, *Ordinary Notes* (Farrar, Straus and Giroux, 2023).

20. See Robin D. G. Kelley, *Freedom Dreams: The Black Radical Imagination* (Beacon Press, 2002), 11.

21. See Sté Strausz, *Fly Girls: Histoire(s) du hip-hop féminin en France* (Au diable vauvert, 2010), 7.

22. See Édouard Glissant, *Poétique de la relation* (Gallimard, 1990).

23. Nelson Mandela and Walter Sisulu were key South African anti-apartheid activists, both imprisoned in 1964. See Nelson Mandela, *Long Walk to Freedom: The Autobiography of Nelson Mandela* (Back Bay Books, 1995).

24. See Adam Haupt, "Black Thing: Hip-Hop Nationalism, 'Race' and Gender in Prophets of da City and Brasse Vannie Kaap," in *Coloured by History, Shaped by Place: New Perspectives on Coloured Identities in Cape Town*, ed. Z. Erasmus (Kwela Books, 2001), 172–94.

25. Chuck D, keynote lecture, Stanford University, April 28, 2011. Conference in H. Samy Alim's course, "Global Flows: The Globalization of Hip Hop Art, Culture, and Politics," featuring Jeff Chang, Gaye Theresa Johnson, Dawn-Elissa Fisher, and Samir Meghelli. See https://ed.stanford.edu/events/hip-hop-race-and-citizenship-japan-franceand-united-states?newsletter=true.

26. See H. Samy Alim, "Translocal Style Communities: Hip Hop Youth as Cultural Theorists of Style, Language, and Globalization," *Pragmatics* 19, no. 1 (2009): 103–27, https://doi.org/10.1075/prag.19.1.06ali.

27. See Angela Davis, *Freedom Is a Constant Struggle: Ferguson, Palestine, and the Foundations of a Movement* (Haymarket, 2016).

28. See Tanja E. Bosch, "Radio as an Instrument of Protest: The History of Bush Radio," *Journal of Radio Studies* 13, no. 2 (2010): 249–65, https://doi.org/10.1080/10955040701313420.

29. In 1984, through negotiations with Fidel Castro, Jesse Jackson was able to obtain the return of American prisoners from Cuba.

30. See Jackie Salloum, *Slingshot Hip Hop* (2008), https://slingshothiphop.com/. See also DAM, Omar Offendum, and Ramzi Salti, "'Al-shaab yurid isquat al-nitham!': Sustaining Revolution in Palestine and Syria through Hip Hop," in *Freedom Moves: Hip Hop Knowledges, Pedagogies, and Futures*, ed. H. Samy Alim, Jeff Chang, and Casey Philip Wong (University of California Press, 2023), 83–102.

7 Prophets of Rage

HIP HOP AND THE FUTURES OF BLACK RADICALISM

Chuck D and Gaye Theresa Johnson

H. SAMY ALIM: Professor Gaye Theresa Johnson, you begin *Futures of Black Radicalism* with this:

> Amid a global wave of uprisings, Black protest against police repression and security regimes in the United States has reoriented a conversation about anti-Black racism on an international scale, generating new narratives of struggle and revealing the persistence of racial capitalism and its assault on dispossessed and working people around the world. Developing connections across multiple currents of resistance, a new generation of social actors has met the escalation of anti-Black state violence in the United States with an astonishing matrix of oppositional strategies, enlivening the intersection between domestic antiracism and global anti-imperialist struggles.

You then make multiple connections internationally between, for example, what's happening in Ferguson and what was happening in Palestine. You recall that exchange of knowledge. Then you write, "The individuals and communities who author and enact it find themselves struggling amid multiple contradictions—between neoliberalism and democratic governance, between settler colonialism and the promise of marketplace participation. Therefore, freedom seekers and cultural workers, as they have at every new political conjuncture, have found it necessary to transform this work into more than an intellectual exercise—it is a critical practice."[1]

I ask everyone here as we engage these scholars and thinkers, What does the practice of Black radicalism look like today? Why is it important to take Cedric Robinson's work [see chapter 1] as a point of entry to consider the history and ongoing struggle against racial capitalism from the roots of Black radical thought to a shared epistemology of the present moment? We are going to think through these questions and more to consider how the manifesto, the monograph, and I would add the music, can be equal yet distinct sites where Black radicalism is reimagined.

CHUCK D: I'd like to thank Dr. Johnson, because without her, this class doesn't happen. Dr. Johnson and her colleagues, such as Professor H. Samy Alim and others like Tabia Shawel and Samuel Lamontagne, said they don't want to engage hip hop without the involvement of the people within. Without y'all trying to figure out how to best understand this culture, it's all for nothing. I had to get involved with this because this circle of activity, from the academic study to the people that actually move and shake things, is very important for your future. This includes *y'all* even more than ever, because the next fifty years is yours. I want to say the next *hundred* years because they talk about "cash rules everything around us," but no, "climate rules everything around us." So when we talk about territory, displacement, migration, in-migration, and also how you have to counter all of these forces that might be coming at you, today's session is an important point on this trajectory.

Dr. Johnson's books *Futures of Black Radicalism* and *Spaces of Conflict, Sounds of Solidarity* are very much related to what we think of as "a hip hop state of mind."[2] Let's get into some of these dynamics. We've been on the other side of this, where she's interviewed me. I've been in front of a hundred thousand people, looking at a packed stadium, and not even feeling a slight bit sweaty. But today, I feel that. [*Laughter.*] How are you?

GAYE THERESA JOHNSON: I'm great. I'm just taking a moment to take in your faces and feel the presence of everybody here in this room because of the things that you hold dear and value that make this a collective. Something that is important to recognize is, when you're doing this work together, of all the places in all the world, of all of the classes that you could be in, somehow you all found your way together in this space. This class could have happened anywhere, but it had to come at the right time with the right people. I just want to acknowledge the preciousness of this moment and the presence of all of you here.

As a Black woman, I can tell you that there is always the pressure to not be as big and full as you really are in your heart and in your soul. This is something that a lot of us are all too familiar with. We learn how to be brilliant at it because there are not a lot of people who are ready for the light that we might bring. There's all this demand that we be someone else or be smaller than who we are. Where does that get us? We all have the answer to that, but there's even a more nuanced layer now. Entitlement has become a public commodity. Everybody's entitled to entitlement now. Before, if you were white and rich, a man, there was a lot of us thinking about the entitlement that comes along with that. But there's now also this empowerment that has happened over centuries, ancestral knowledges that are passed down around pride, confidence, and competence that many of us hold and possess with a lot of power. You should feel, "I feel in my soul that I belong here." Not because somebody told you in a meme that if "this" happens, then I should say "this," and "all my identities need to be present at the center." No. In your heart and your soul, in your mind, you know who you are. You know that you belong and you walk into the room like that. The public trading on our lack of confidence doesn't serve any of us. I think there's this style right now where you trade your real confidence and grounding for a performance of it. We need less words and more presence, I think.

CHUCK D: Greg Tate had this book years ago titled *Everything but the Burden: What White People Are Taking from Black Culture*, where the whole culture could be appropriated.[3] But at the end of the day, I would ask people questions like, "Okay. You love hip hop?" "I love hip hop." Then I would ask another question right after that. "Do you love Black people?" Then I'd be ready for a third question, from them, "Well, what's that got to do with anything?"

JOHNSON: You're considered racist for asking that question.

CHUCK D: I'd be considered racist today. That throws a lot of progressives into silence. The right is not going to be silenced, though. Now since we're in the technologically connected age, they're going to actually use their platforms to spew out. If you can't answer the question whether you love Black people or not, but I'm racist for asking it, where are we headed?

JOHNSON: That's why the first question is so important—"Do you love hip hop?" When you love something, you care for it by knowing it and by honoring it with the knowledge that wherever you go, you're taking stories with you. This is why I really love what I do. Because in the writing, the listening, and the telling, I'm collecting stories. Like one of my colleagues has said, it's like being a Trojan horse. You go in a place, you dress a certain way, you might have that UCLA suit on, but everywhere you go, you enter and you have all the stories inside of you that you let out because you bring in other people's histories. Now as far as the theorizing about hip hop and what it is, this class is so important because it's collective. You can't define it by yourself. Hip hop is something that has evolved in congregation and in collectivity. Working alone on the definition is not only not valuing the origins of hip hop, but it's also dangerous. You should know that about almost everything related to social movements—you don't work alone. All of the people, the living and the dead, have paved the way for where you are, where I am. We carry their stories.

CHUCK D: If you're standing on the shoulders of giants in art, culture, politics, community, how do you honor the pain? Everybody that's sitting here, you got to honor the pain from somewhere in your family that led you to sit in the classroom. As a culturalist and as an artist, I'm always naming who came before me and always trying to say to the next generation, "This is what came before me." If you don't honor the challenge, and the struggle, you're not going to recognize that you're in a struggle right now. To say that you're not in a struggle, you're kidding yourself. This world is more connected than it ever will be, but are *we* connected?

JOHNSON: It's more connected than it ever has been, but the function of racial capitalism is to have you thinking that you are not connected and that the best thing you can be is on your own and in a meritocracy where your hard work alone determines success. "I'm gonna get mine," but it's not about "we." That's one of the number one weapons of racial capitalism. One of the most important things that Cedric Robinson wrote about in his last book about film, he said that the history of racial capitalism is extremely hostile to its own display, its own history. It doesn't want you to know that it ever even had a history. It wants you to think that it was always here. It wants you to think that that's the natural way of doing things. I hear it from students all the time who say, "Oh, yeah, it's awful what's going on in the world. That's the way it is."[4] But does it have to be? Let's not be lazy about it. If you don't want to do the work—which can be as simple as being in this class and struggling through things you don't agree on—step aside so some of us can do it. Or just be here, present with one another, valuing what each other says, learning from each other, honoring your instructors, honoring the effort that it takes for the person to come in here and clean after you all leave. All of those things create a history of our time together. But the way capitalism works is that it's hostile to its own discovery. So it doesn't want you to know about all the various structures of oppression, all of the hegemonizing that has to happen in order for it to then become so natural to you that it's like drinking water. As one of my most treasured colleagues says, "Don't let your inaction masquerade as cynicism." You say, "Oh, well, that's just how it's going to be." No, you don't want to be a part of changing it. It's too scary for you, or it's too difficult for you. But that's what racial capitalism counts on, is that you won't even stick your toe in the water because you're too afraid to figure out what it is.

It's not easy when you're talking about hip hop and how much it's evolved over these decades, because it has become something that is at once both extremely commodified but also still reflective of a particular kind of situated knowledge that is happening on the streets and in the suburbs and in the country and is also an echo of the blues and rock and roll, folk music, bluegrass. You can hear Appalachia in certain forms of hip hop. You can hear different regions. You can be in one part of the world and listening to another. You can be at a crossroads. As my friend Clyde Woods used to talk about, you could be in Chicago listening to the Mississippi Delta from a migrant who's singing a song and be right back there.[5] Think of all of the forces and the powers that hip hop effects and animates, the places that it can take you, the spaces you inhabit together, sonically, visually. The power there is immense. Coming back to your first question, if we don't know what hip hop is, then it's very hard for us to sit in its power and also then take hold of ours.

CHUCK D: How do they keep this experience with them when this is over, post-UCLA?

JOHNSON: I coach movement leaders to have more capacity to do grassroots work. The only way we can answer that question is to ask for your participation. So the question is, How do you take this with you right after this? Just for a moment, try to minimize your distractions. If it's available to you, put both your feet on the floor. If it's available to you, create a posture in your body that makes you feel whole and at your best. Now I want you to think about this course at its best and think of one word that embodies the feeling that you have when this course and you are at your best and those two things meet. You come in here at the end of the day, beginning of the evening, and you hear a legend but also someone with a good heart and who is powerful. You have these incredible instructors and organizers of this course. You have each other. What is a word or phrase that comes to mind as you sit here?

AUDIENCE: Insight. Unity. Community. Uplift. Illuminate. Gratitude. Grateful. Evolution. Relief. Perspective. Wisdom. Fearlessness. Symphonic.

JOHNSON: Let's marinate in that for a minute. Let's try to bring these into our bodies not just into our heads. These are all shared values that you've made here, and they reflect the energy in the room, the people and what they're bringing to it. These values are what you take with you when you leave. Wisdom. Gratitude. Insight. Perspective. Unity. Community. Relief. Fearlessness. Symphonic. You take those with you, but you gotta feel them and remember that when you show up, anywhere you go, that hip hop was the subject. There are all these reasons why these particular words came to the surface, but that's what you really felt and in that you had power. Every space you go into, no matter who you are, you feel those things and you know you belong because you share this with these people.

CHUCK D: That's incredible. It goes back to the book *Futures of Black Radicalism* with Steven Osuna's essay "Class Suicide: The Black Radical Tradition, Radical Scholarship, and the Neoliberal Turn," where there was a Frantz Fanon's *Wretched of the Earth* [see chapter 6] quote: "Each generation must, out of relative obscurity, discover its mission, fulfill it, or betray it." Also, our good friend and mentor Harry Belafonte told me personally [see chapter 3] that in his final days, Paul Robeson told him the exact same thing. When Mr. Belafonte asked him, "What am I doing wrong? What should I do?" Paul Robeson said, "Every generation has got to work and fight and grab every piece of information to fend for itself."

My next question is, What is art that's over the line, and what art crosses barriers, boundaries? When is the protest over the line, as far as art is concerned?

JOHNSON: That's a dangerous question.

CHUCK D: We're in a dangerous class! [*Laughter.*]

JOHNSON: I can't say "Oh, this is art. This is not art." I'm somebody who loves and appreciates art. Can you give us an example?

CHUCK D: Travis Scott got in crazy trouble [see chapter 2]. Packed stadium, kids died, and everybody's swirling saying, "His music is filled with Satanic verses, that's what he do." In the cultural world, which floated to government, media, and business, it was like, "He made money." Everybody knew this, but then all of a sudden they treat it like the casualties due to the stampede at his concert are all his fault.

JOHNSON: That is definitely not the most controversial example I have heard you say!

CHUCK D: I know, but I'm just starting with baby steps here.

JOHNSON: That's such a softball.

CHUCK D: Or like the MC from Spain, Pablo Hasél, that they locked up.[6] I think that's art making a statement inside of a fascist situation. It's still art, but now I don't even know if that's art or you're just doing something else. Is drill music political, reaching out and crying for something, or is it just used as a portal so somebody can get somebody back on some street code? We're in a system where they can take your words in the so-called United States of America and throw you in jail for fifteen or twenty years. Real is real.

JOHNSON: Real is real. That's right. There's also the question of what do you need from art in order to increase your capacity, your community, and your unity and all of the words that you all mentioned. This is so random, but yesterday I was watching Perry Farrell, who was a singer in Jane's Addiction. He started Lollapalooza. It was his tribute to Taylor Hawkins from the Foo Fighters. I was thinking about what a strange guy Perry Farrell is. He said, "Taylor Hawkins was one of the best friends I've ever had in the whole world." In fact, apparently, the last words that Taylor uttered were a voicemail to Perry Farrell. "So for the rest of my life, I'm going to make music the way that Taylor Hawkins and I used to make music, like in my den." That is an art thing. That's an artist thing. It's just that some people look at Jane's Addiction or punk music or Travis Scott or whatever, and there may be elements of that for whatever reason. But there's the artist conversation about that and what is possible, and then there's the observer's conversation about that. And many of us who are observing and writing, we really don't know shit about it.

CHUCK D: So when somebody catches a case and then it's all in the court of law, then you got lawyers and a jury and a judge talking about shit they don't know about, which means that art . . .

JOHNSON: That's what we see with Young Stoner Life Records right now in Georgia, the RICO [racketeer influenced and corrupt organizations] charges with Young Thug and Gunna, because the laws that they put in effect to crush Black people are 100 percent real. We have artists imprisoned. Art can be everything. It can be real. It can be abstract. RICO is going to charge one person with fifty-six crimes at once and put you in jail for all fifty-six of those crimes, even though you might have committed one, or might have just been there watching. That's real. I hear what you're saying about the future.

CHUCK D: Art is now on its way to being the new Willie Horton.[7] It's the Willie Horton map of rappers' faces. Willie Horton was used in a political campaign. Bush was running for president, and they used him in the campaign, like, "Here's a guy that has a felony. This is America if you vote for Michael Dukakis," who was Bush's opponent. This Black man was let go, and they seemed to make him really dark in the ads and made him look like and called him a monster. I saw a list of twenty-five well-known rappers who are now in prison from court cases, and every single one of them was Black. Eminem just got inducted into the Rock & Roll Hall of Fame and God bless the dead Mac Miller, but I'm lookin at a wall full of Black faces. At the same time, we can't afford to be scared, which brings us to the question, What is radical thought right now?

JOHNSON: I think you can be scared because fear is human. I think you can be scared and also know that people who have made changes have been afraid, but they didn't let that rule them. There's nothing scarier than having some hounds after you and trying to keep a baby quiet in the middle of the night in 1856. This is something Toni Morrison said, one of the very basic functions of racism is distraction, is to distract you from who you are, from what you need to do, which you already have right here.[8] You don't need somebody else. You don't need a different community. You have it *right here*. You've got the soundtrack for it, the tools for it, the ancestors for it. You've got the future for it. You have it. So if you get distracted . . .

CHUCK D: You have weapons of mass distraction out there.

JOHNSON: That's all it is now.

CHUCK D: They want that distraction more than ever, and they're getting it. You can look up "radical" now in the dictionary, but what is radical thought right now for these students or people in society today?

JOHNSON: Radical right now is being able to center yourself and know who you are and decide that nobody's going to throw you off of that mark and that if somebody does, you have some people around you to remind you of who you are. Because these weapons of mass distraction are designed to get you so out of your body that you're just always anxious all the time. It's not your fault. That's the function of the moment—it is to distract you and make you doubt your own intuition, make you doubt your own confidence and worthiness. Like, "Do we even deserve to be here? Do we deserve to be free from surveillance? Do we deserve to say what we want, to do what we want with our own bodies?" Hell yes, we deserve that! That should be default number one, always there, underneath everything. But the very function of this moment is to have you question your intuition and whether or not you have a future that you can make. If you can stay grounded and centered on the fact that that is well within your grasp and you are powerful enough to do it, that's radical.

Two, you've got to recognize the power and support that you have and the particular gifts that you have. This is a very transactional moment where people are like, "Oh you're beautiful." What does that even mean anymore? What is beautiful about me? Tell me what is powerful about me? The reason this is powerful to me is the accumulation of years we have among all of us here, the way that there are people here in the audience that I've seen and known for a long time who I admired, even though they are students who I think are brilliant. The accumulation of all of that, that's power. This is beautiful. This is powerful. Being clear about what it is that you have instead of, "Let me just exchange compliments with you real quick." No. Right here in this moment, this is powerful to me because you showed up and did your best. "Let me be here in this with you for a moment." That's radical in this moment of distractions.

Three, slow down. That is the worst to say, because it sounds so old. I remember my grandmother used to say to me, "Don't be in a hurry to get everywhere all the time." This is true especially as a Black and Latinx professor. Black women professors are so overrepresented in all the brochures and the websites. You would think from Twitter that we are just everywhere, that we just came up and there's a whole gang of us. No. The number of tenured Black women in the US is still well below 2 percent. The overrepresentation of Black women in brochures and websites leaves you thinking, "Oh, we have done this!" I was on that hamster wheel for years, like, "Write, teach, service." Always just running. I remember when I first came to UCLA, there was a Black woman professor who stopped me one day and was like, "We haven't met yet, but every time I see you, you're running to your car." This is the truth for so many of us. This culture of urgency, it doesn't serve us. So slow down a little bit, especially when people tell you there's not enough time. "I'll make a little more time." You will notice other things that actually are all around you and give you life. Look at the trees. When you slow down—and you can—this is part of an anticapitalist, anti-racist practice.

Four, study and observe closely how systems work. For example, mass incarceration has this trick of, like, "Oh we're closing down the prisons." Yeah, but Microsoft, Amazon, all these places are investing in surveillance in a different kind of way. The ankle monitor that you have to pay for, you will go into constant debt for it. Somebody told me the other day about a friend who was a sponsor for someone who was seeking asylum. When you're a sponsor for someone who's a refugee, you take on responsibility for everything. This person had to wear an ankle monitor as a condition of his release to this woman who agreed to sponsor him. I think he was there for like a few weeks. Then he went on to live his life. The fees for the ankle monitor now are at $11,000. She owes this, can't buy a house. This is how they get themselves into your life. This is the reality. But then you are centered enough, studied enough, to know that's not it.

It can feel overwhelming like, "Oh, my God, there's so many layers of oppression," but honoring the pain is also honoring the joy you make in spite of it. Despite some of the worst circumstances, you still see people endeavoring to bring humanity to whatever situation. That's a triumph. Slow down and feel that.

CHUCK D: Yes, slowing down is radical. At this point, artificial intelligence is not going to get slower or dumber. If it's going to come at the average mind at a speed that just speeds up, you must be able to slow your clock down. Supposedly, post-pandemic, everybody is on go right now, like "I missed the last two summers. I'm getting it this summer right now. We goin for it!" My desk is so full of requests. And I'm like, "Give me eighteen months."

JOHNSON: Who's making this urgency?

CHUCK D: Whose clock is it?

JOHNSON: What's the function of it? It is to get you off your mark.

CHUCK D: That's one thing you take away from this, the ability that you have to gain within yourself to slow down.

JOHNSON: This is a Black radical tradition, like chain gangs when people would sing to mark the pace. Old songs that you would hear folks who were working on a railroad track or digging something. There would be a song and there would be somebody who is leading it and then people would be responding. That person who led the song led the pace. Toni Morrison writes about this too.[9] She talks about the high man who was the one who called it when people had too much, and everybody put their pain into that movement, into that motion. This is part of an ancestral instruction.

CHUCK D: Do you feel that in 1968 Dr. Martin Luther King was that person at the top, but we didn't have enough of whatever we needed to have to go on after that assassination? It derailed us for a time.

JOHNSON: It derailed us, and it wasn't the only one. There was a series of assassinations. We could bookmark it at '63, '65, and '68. I don't think that was the only thing, but it was huge. I think that what was happening also in '68 was that there was this crisis of confidence in what was possible because King had a certain knowledge and demonstration of entry into the American community. There seemed to be a way, whether through respectability, whether through nonviolence and persistence like the peace movement, an understanding of how Eastern religion was synonymous with a lot of the Southern Black Baptist traditions, an affinity with people who were considered more hippies. He had a way of being that seemed to include everybody in the possibility of stepping into a democracy that was going to be redefined after voting rights comes and all these really serious fights for the things that were already in the Constitution that end up being realized in the sixties. What's so debilitating about that?

And then also this moment now where so many people's rights hang in the balance. This is a really critical time. Some people still believe that this democracy, the way they see it, is possible. But your body will tell you differently, because you could say those words, but inside you're like, "Oh, what's really going on?" That's your intuition telling you, "No, no." This society is in the crumbles. I heard a journalist say the other day, that's the stage we're in right now—the crumbles.

CHUCK D: Journalists feel that they can't write anymore, because they know that people don't have the patience or the tolerance to read anything lengthy. In the past, you would have an arts community that would immediately respond, although they wouldn't be able to record right away. Now you can record right away and release your message into the world. But you would think that even a question about *Roe v. Wade* would be answered to by an artist community, like there would be pressure from the arts community. Today, it's the fiftieth year of hip hop, which okay, celebration, whoop-de-do, bring out all the great pomp and all that. But what does that mean? I know even looking back in my life, being eight and nine years old and living throughout the whole sixties, that real people were doing real things. Activists were real heroes. We knew entertainers and Motown and Stevie Wonder and James Brown and Maria McKee. But we knew they were entertainers, like these are entertainers and these are people that move something. We were like "Free Huey!" Black Panther lunch program. I was in it as a shorty at eight, nine years old. I happened to meet Huey Newton like twenty years later in Oakland. But these were like straight up superheroes.

What happens at that time? Well, Marvel Comics puts out *Black Panther* [see chapter 3]. Stan Lee didn't even get permission. The assassinations. Vietnam War. Then you had the placement of fictional heroes in place of the real heroes. And then you had what? *Shaft*. You had blaxploitation films. You had people leaning onto musicians for having the dominant voice because they were unsure about what politics was. This is fifty years ago, which covers the whole gamut of hip hop and rap music. We almost know that in this country that we had to whisper to answer to the audacity of what happens in this society, but it's almost like, even if it is screamed out, it ain't really going to get heard.

Is hip hop radicalism overblown? We praise martyrs like Pac and Nipsey Hussle, while real activists die in prison and obscurity. A lot of them still living. I'm not bashing President Obama. I have my own feelings of who he should have pardoned, and especially after Trump pardoned Lil Wayne. There's a fear factor that even goes up to the point where President Obama felt that he couldn't get close to maybe pardoning Mumia Abu-Jamal.[10] That fear factor from your high man trickles down to a society like ours, like, "If he doesn't do anything I'm not going to do anything either."

JOHNSON: Maybe it's not as important.

CHUCK D: Or maybe some of the pardons that President Obama did do is something that we should have paid more attention to.

JOHNSON: Or the number of judges that were appointed during his time, Black women judges.

CHUCK D: Hip hop says that younger heads have as much power as the older demographic. Whenever you have a society like that, you're in trouble—when the young people say, "I got as much power as you. You ain't got no power, old head." The only thing that will save you as a collective is a collective unit organization. You can afford a little bit of fearlessness when you are together in a collective. But if we're going to call out our radical artists that died in the middle of the art battle, and we could say causes are connected to them. But I'm saying back in the day, the ones who were eradicated from society, I don't think that we can compare to that. People say, "Oh, Chuck D, you did this," but I'm not comparing myself to somebody who was in the trenches every damn day making sure a community was fed. When you actually point to these people, there's less of an acknowledgment from the society.

Years ago, I made a statement that hip hop was the Black CNN, and I was giving CNN too much damn credit. But understand this. This was not done in the context of today. It was done in the context of the 1980s, when they thought CNN founder Ted Turner was crazy, "No way in hell is it gonna be a news network twenty-four hours a damn day!" Back then, in the sixties, seventies, news was an hour, thirty minutes for local, thirty minutes for the world, and back to regular programming. Ted Turner came along in 1981 coincidentally the same year that MTV started, saying, "I'm gonna do twenty-four-hour news per day." Black News Network in 2020 came out and said, "We're Black news." This is a Black twenty-four-hour TV network. They filed for bankruptcy in March. But right now, right here, if the music cannot communicate on its own terms, with clarity and address issues, and you don't have it in news either, what do you have?

JOHNSON: I've spent a lot of time with movement leaders and organizers, and let me tell you, they're doing it. Just because we don't know about it, or we're not in the middle of it, doesn't mean it isn't happening. They're out there dealing with every kind of possible connected issue you can imagine, from evictions to incarceration to single moms that are struggling to buy baby formula in the richest place in the world, and people making you have to have contraception or not have any, depending on what state you're in to be criminalized and stigmatized and all of these things. Movement folks are like, "We're on it. We're fifty places at once. We're doing this thing." A lot of women are leading these incredible mobilizations. It's happening in music too. Just because it's not on the news doesn't mean it isn't happening. You could look at hip hop, but punk too, the way that it's not even sometimes meant for big business, it's just meant for community. The politics are there, but where are we? That is the question, where are our eyes?

ALIM: I'll start with some comments to get the conversation going. You all have been hearing the conversation about slowing down. We've been hearing the conversations about rest. These anti-capitalist conversations became really important during the pandemic and have gained traction. This is important also in Indigenous theorizing, the politics of refusal, withdrawal from the systems that ultimately crush us into the earth for their profit and their gains, not ours.[11] How do you withdraw from systems that are meant to crush you into the earth while at the same time knowing that the devil never sleeps? We have this kind of tension that we have to navigate. I think that's where the hard part is, because Gaye was talking about activists working around the clock. What happens to activists is that eventually, they burn out because the struggle is real in that very exhausting sense.

CHUCK D: But "activists" is definitely plural. It has to be. Burnouts are always going to happen to any individual at any given time, trying to always overtake the obstacles. You have to pluralize all of the efforts and that's what the movement is.

ALIM: That's a really important thing to think about how to navigate—never being alone, pluralizing the effort. In terms of movements in hip hop culture, I got a historical question about the Black Arts movement [BAM]. I've had conversations with Sonia Sanchez, Amiri Baraka [RIP], and James G. Spady [RIP] over the years. We would read all of these works by the BAM poets. The thing that they would say repeatedly is that Black poets and Black artists in the BAM were the cultural arm of the Black Power Movement, so they saw themselves as part and parcel of the movement. As we saw Chuck and Public Enemy and others come along, that conversation continued, and then it took a turn. Do we think about hip hop being the cultural arm of a particular movement today, and what has happened that has shaped how we think about that?

For Chuck, I remember reading Larry Neal, Leroi Jones/Amiri Baraka. I remember reading Nikki Giovanni, Sonia Sanchez. Also, the artists and poets themselves would write these works about the movement, and theorize the role of the artist, and what the BAM meant. The conversation was there in written form, and the artists would have these conferences. I know you've written a lot about the culture. I know you're doing it now because you're teaching. But is there a conversation to be had among the major figures of the movement about creating that kind of body of knowledge to help folks understand hip hop the same way the BAM writers did for previous generations?

JOHNSON: Outstanding question. Things have changed a lot. First of all, the proliferation of digital media makes everything feel a little bit more dispersed. It's harder to capture what appears to be like a unitary subject, Black people. Like what does that mean? Latinos, what does that mean? Women, what does that mean? I think there's been in many respects, in terms of right now, this kind of overwhelm that I think a lot of people feel. What is actually happening? So much moving alone, not being connected to all of the different things that are happening. Let me give you an example. Reproductive justice [RJ] workers, warriors—to them, the Supreme Court leak was no surprise but still a punch in the gut. They know that the abortion issue is just a thinly veiled attack on poor women and women of color. It's really a very racist thing to ban abortions. My best friend, who is a RJ worker, says, "These questions are so lazy, like 'Why should we let somebody who has eight kids not learn the lesson of what it means?'" I love how she just looks at you dead-ass, like, "Ask another question. Ask about the resources that they had, the availability of birth control, whether or not this was consensual sex. Ask about what are the circumstances that this person is in. Ask whether or not this person should be able to know that they're more important as a human being than this pregnancy. And how related that work is to the work of getting people what they need to be human in their circumstances. When did they cease to be a human being that you asked them to give birth in shackles in a prison?"

I know I'm going a little far afield, but I can bring it right back here. In these circles, one, people know that their struggles are intertwined. Desmond writes about this in his book about eviction.[12] There's a reason why there's childcare in the courts and eviction courts. Men and women are locked up. RJ workers know that without mass mobilization for housing, that RJ can't succeed and vice versa. So there's an understanding already of the intersections of these pieces. The ways that people organize nowadays are becoming even more connected to somatic experiences. People know that if you show up to organize people on a corner, day laborers, you got to have a guitar, some kind of song ready, right? Not everybody on the corner speaks the same language. So you better be ready. All of those things are interconnected.

That's what I think the BAM saw and felt. But we can also do that too. We can't let somebody else determine what is too much for us to deal with. No, you don't have to be everything to everybody. You just have to know, I'm good at this. I feel connected to this. Art and politics, they're very reciprocal in the sense that you reflect a lot on what's going on. You give voice to it. And most of us are not going to the archives to figure it out. We're not going to the library as much as we used to; we go to YouTube. But artists are reflecting what's going on, and the information and the way that people learn it is different, but it's still the same kind of relationship of reciprocity, reflecting back on the good and the bad.

When Chuck said *Shaft*, for example, art is complicated. There's a lot of things about that that were wrong, but there's also a lot of things about it that were right. The music was right. It was an interesting commentary on how under a capitalist, white supremacist society, how can we be men? Which turns out to be really toxic and hypermasculine but is a reflection of that kind of toxic masculinity and race all mixed together. And then Gordon Parks and Melvin Van Peebles make something beautiful in this moment, you know? So there's a lot on both ends. And we have to be comfortable with that, as critical thinkers, to never let somebody else take this, like, "It's the end of the story, punto final." There's always some other question.

CHUCK D: We also have to revamp schools. If people are going to be a captive audience in these school systems, some definition got to come out of there. That's why I always thought that K–12 curriculum, at least 33 percent of it, should be embedded in the arts, allowing the students to really involve themselves in not only listening and studying it, but also creating arts. I think 33 percent of your curriculum as arts would be healthy, a way to spark the curiosity to figure out things like history, geography, and philosophy.

Regarding the BAM, family and community connects us to our traditions. What has happened in the last 30–35 years out of the fifty years of hip hop is the destruction of the collective for the sake of the solo individual, and the solo individuals are isolated. Collectives were defining the art. If you're not even going to connect with your peers, ain't no way in hell you gon connect to the great poets that laid out the groundwork, philosophies, the logics, and the histories. It used to be that way. The first fifteen years of hip hop and rap music is connected to Gil Scott-Heron, The Last Poets. Even when they said, "On and on til the break of dawn," that came up out of The Last Poets and Lightnin' Rod, people like that. That vernacular started out of that era. That disconnect of going back to what Amiri Baraka was doing, and then the Beat Poets in the late fifties, you have to teach this education. You'll find out that there are flyer bars [better lyrics] than you can imagine!

I was talking to the great Oran "Juice" Jones last night on a podcast. He was a singer that was with Def Jam early on. He said that the person that kept him speechless for the longest period of time was the great Sly Stone. I heard this twice. The other person that told me this was the great George Clinton. He said you could go behind Sly Stone with a tape recorder and get things that you never heard before, like he spits automatic bars. Oran "Juice" Jones said he spit what Sly Stone told him. I was like, "What did you just say?" He said, "Yeah, man, I want to own it, man. Sly Stone taught me this. He was comin up with fly stuff." Before MCs said, "I'm not making this stuff up, I just got it from the poets before me." Because ain't no way in hell I'm seventeen and I'm going to be flyer than some dude who's thirty-five who is in the middle of pimp streets in 1957 Harlem. There is no way. No way you could get that amount of lingo, life skills, survival skills in three or four sentences, like somebody from 1961 on a street corner of Philly. They were able to knock it down to three or four sentences. Today, if you're isolated from your peers and you think you're doing it solo, ain't no way you're going to lock into something from the past. It's just not there.

All these things had to be taught, which means that academia has its purpose. But they just can't be "poor righteous teachers."[13] They've got to be rewarded. Ice-T said this years ago, "I'm living in a great society if my teacher has a private jet. But if my teachers and my professors, if they're not rewarded by that society, if they are struggling, you're not getting no movement off that." You need thinkers.

QUESTION 1: Many artists are being controlled by record labels to maintain a certain image or type of music. Black women specifically tend to not fully present themselves. How do you propose that these artists combat this while still trying to stay relevant and true to themselves?

CHUCK D: I always would tell women in the arts, you have to be 100 percent of yourself. As I said earlier [see chapter 5], for the whole tenure of hip hop and rap music, there's always some dude in the background trying to tell them what's going to sell to people. And I'm like, "Says who?" Whenever you have people changing up who they are for the sake of the sale, that means that the industry that contracted them, they're like, "Look, we contracted you. We gave you this money, and we want it back with interest." Simple as that. I never believed that a woman should listen to a male's point of view on how to market their art towards a public space.

JOHNSON: We have a lot of opportunities as mascots of success, even though we really aren't truly as a whole always successful, in the ways that white America will define it. Still, people assign to us certain roles and performances. We have to ask ourselves, what's the cost of this opportunity? If the cost is that the only way you're going to make money is if you are not being yourself, that you are catering to this audience that somebody says you got, you gotta ask yourself, is success making a ton of money? Is it being whatever I think is my authentic self? That also can sometimes be a trap in its own way, because we have a lot of different people inside of us.

We have to remember that this is part of the distraction thing too. People want you to feel like, "I'm this one thing and I got to be true." But you have a lot of things inside of you, a lot of experiences. So what's the cost? But also, if you decide, "Yeah, I wanna be a billionaire. I don't care what it costs me," that is a perfectly fine choice. The moment you start feeling that piece of your heart that got you into it in the first place slipping away, that's when you hope people wake up and say, "Wait, wait, hold on. I made this much money or had this much success, it is enough." Again, slow down, figure out what success is to you. Who are you right now? Does it all align?

Coming back to Samy's original question about burnout, some of the most successful movements recognize that there's like a cycle of action. You identify the issue, you prepare, you meet, you organize, then you have a protest and do some kind of action. You win, you lose. Then you rest. And just like you said, the devil doesn't sleep. The devil has about five million accountants working too. So the devil *can* sleep, you know? In our movements, we have to figure out who rests when, and who keeps going. The beauty there is in that resting place and what you can do with capacity. If you're always stressed out, freaked out, you can't really be that effective. You've got to remember why you got into this in the first place. Where's my heart in this? If it's not here anymore, then I made a wrong turn. Let me come back and stop.

QUESTION 2: What does radical work look like within hip hop? Does it need to look like Kendrick Lamar or J. Cole, or can it look like Pop Smoke?

CHUCK D: Radical thought right now is slow your ass down! That to me is like one of the most perfect statements for today, because everything that's coming at you is sped up. The thing about it, Kendrick Lamar's latest video/song, today, you gotta judge it by the video. People listen with their eyes. If the video never happened, would you treat the song differently? People might talk about how Kendrick Lamar and his team bit off of an artist because he had that first look for his video. But then a real full 360-degree flip, a hip hop head is like, "Yo dawg, it's about the song. It ain't about the video that you had." Anybody could do the video, man, but not everybody could do what Kendrick Lamar did with the song. That's the brilliance.

Right now we have this transfer that goes back and forth from different generations, which is good because you got what they call two-way traffic. So if the radicalism is going to come posthumously from a Pop Smoke and there's something in the bars that somebody else could take and run with like Kendrick did with Nipsey, then you got something that speaks right to the moment. I think it could go one step further, even with Amiri Baraka or Gil Scott-Heron. When that starts happening, then it's like, "Okay, we got the tools to go deep fake with these lyrics from here." Kendrick Lamar introduced a thing that says, "I gotta blow your mind visually to sweep you into my lyrics." That's the state of time that we're in today. Radicalism will raise its head in hip hop lyrics with the use of these tools.

JOHNSON: Yes, but also, I'm really interested in things that aren't meant to be seen. So who's the teacher? Bryonn Bain is a prison educator [see chapter 8]. How are they using Kendrick Lamar? How is the person who is never going to see freedom again inspired by Queen Latifah or Missy Elliott? Missy could sing, she could dance, she could produce, she could do almost anything in rap. You don't always know that, but sometimes, if you learn to listen for it you can hear her in her signature style. I'm really interested in those radical things. What is the occasion? What does it make? What does it animate? One of the first times that we did this kind of dialogue, there was a guy who sat in the front and he stood up at the end. He was like the last question. He said he had been teaching in a prison for about twenty years and that he just wanted to let Chuck know, like, "Your music meant so much to me and my students in prison." It was like one of the most meaningful interactions because you're this guy who himself taught for twenty years in a prison that he had been incarcerated in. That's radical to me. So what's behind the glitter and sparkles? Like what made him write that piece? Who's he writing about? Who is he listening to? What records did his grandmother play for him? That's what's more interesting to me, those things that are not meant to be seen.

CHUCK D: At the same time, whenever you detach the past and the story, it could lead to other things. Like I said, there is a flipside. Did I tell the story about Eazy-E? 1988. Myself and Public Enemy, we were kinda like uncles back then. We were six, seven, ten years older than a lot of rap artists. We just happened to look young. In 1988, which was the year that I was allowed to talk to prisons, I wanted to do like what Johnny Cash did. I'd go and do prison shows, and we did Rikers Island in New York. It was big news. But the minute that we did that successful prison tour and Rikers Island in the summer of 1988, they sent an all-points bulletin to all the prisons across the US: "Do not let them do any more prisons."

Our time with those in prison was very enlightening. Everybody remembered it for the rest of their lives and the rest of their sentence and said, "We're in prison in New York City, but we will try to do our best to get outta here."

During the summer tour of 1988, we made it a part of our plan during the time of *It Takes a Nation Millions to Hold Us Back*, to go to as many prisons and detention centers across the US as possible. About seven to eight of them that we did across the US allowed us to go into their maximum or minimal security situations. And we're in Kansas City. At that time, Kansas City was a wild town, because in the eighties, all of a sudden, all these areas, the Black side of the town, it was once again a plethora of guns and drugs out of nowhere. By 1988, not only did the crack move out there, but the drugs and the gun game, and also gangs that were choosing sides and what gangs took what territory. All of a sudden, they became gangs with names that came from other places. Basically, some of the gang members, since it was based in Los Angeles and New York, were able to go to these spots like St. Louis. Denver was a spot from the west. Kansas City was one. By the middle of 1988, Kansas City was a wild, wild place. You did a gig and afterward—there was an arena there called Kemper Arena—as the cars are moving out of there, you'd hear gunshots, and that's how crazy it was back then.

On that particular tour, it was EPMD, Jazzy Jeff and the Fresh Prince, Public Enemy, N. W. A., and Daddy-O from Stetsasonic. As we're getting ready to get in the van before the concert, Eazy says, "I want to go with y'all." I'm like, "Aight, Eazy, come on." So we get to the prison, and I usually open up the floor. I'm twenty-eight years old at the time, so that's OG age back then. I opened it up and said, "We're hip hop. We try to tell you all that this ain't the place to be but keep your head up." Then Will Smith talks, like, "I'm from Philly," shares about his background, "all love, it's about perseverance." Jazzy Jeff speaks, Erick Sermon, Parrish Smith speak. Then Eazy talks. He's saying the same things that we're saying, "I want to see y'all come up out of here and keep your head up." And this young man gets up out of the back and says, "I hear what you talkin Eazy, but I'm in here because of your ass!" Eazy freezes, looks at me, goes back to the van. It was the last time you saw him in a prison.

I'm just saying that whatever you say that you are, you will end up looking in the mirror two fold. You're a revolutionary? You're gonna run into revolutionaries that are gonna look right at you like, "You're a revolutionary activist, huh? We do this. Oh, you want to go gangster? You're the toughest dude?" You gon run into twice what you think you are. Now, of course, all these other things could save you. You could take a private jet all over the place. You got security. All these things that keep you from seeing yourself. This is why activism is important, because you be who you are, and you can help grow what you want to see in yourself, manifest. You gotta also give a damn.

QUESTION 3: We talked about the importance of slowing down, and something we can't ignore obviously is how COVID slowed down the entire world. It made people realize that they have more agency over their own lives—for example, workers forming unions in places like Starbucks and Amazon. Do you see any future lasting impacts of this?

JOHNSON: I'm glad you brought up the Amazon and Starbucks workers, because this is a point that I was thinking about earlier when we were talking about history and the connection to different kinds of movements. These workers are doing something really powerful, which is that they're not just looking only to civil rights activism as an inspiration but to the labor movement, which precedes that. If you're unionizing, you can't just focus on one aspect of history. There's so much that has come before it, so many organizing strategies and victories that occasioned this present moment. I think that's one thing that has come out of this, people's desire to do more than just look at surface value stuff. A lot of good is going to come because even though COVID was what it was, many essential workers who didn't have a choice, a lot of people chose to go into movement building. There's a lot of good work that's happened.

The people that save the elections every time—and we saw this with Biden—it's Black women. Black women go to the polls. They organize all the time. We're going to see this happen again in the midterm elections when folks are going to be like, "Okay, let's go, twelve hours in line, no water." It's a felony to give a bottle of water in Florida to somebody who's waiting to vote. The reason I bring that up is because people are tired, but they're also more determined. So we're going to have an acceleration. I mean, we got Trump-appointed justices Brett Kavanaugh and Amy Coney Barrett on the Supreme Court, and now we got the overturning of *Roe v.*

Wade. There's that acceleration there, and then there's also some pushback. I think it's going to be both.

A lot of people say we can't imagine what's after capitalism, but we have to imagine it. For hundreds of years, the people who were enslaved, their grandchildren never saw emancipation, but they envisioned it. They sang about it. They talked about it. They made stories about it. That's what we need to be doing, is to be dreaming it up because it's not conditional. It's not called a democracy anymore unless these basic things are met. The thing about COVID, there's a lot of slowing down, but also a lot of realizing that the rich got much richer during this time. The poor got much poorer. And now with the rent forgiveness and loan forgiveness going away, believe me, the right is ready. But we're also ready.

QUESTION 4: You mentioned the intertwining of struggles. I think about the lack of representation of Mexican people in West Coast music. They are such a large population in Los Angeles, but I feel that the powers that be were about dividing Black and Brown people. Why was there this lack of Latino representation when hip hop was exploding on the West Coast? I know we have different histories with colonialism and racism.

CHUCK D: The powers that be can't crack the Latino code. They cracked the Black family code of father to son. What I've seen is that the connection of Black father to son is a little more broken, where a Latino, and even especially I'm going to say Mexican in California, you see a Latino father and their son working on the roof, both of them. They're gonna eat lunch together. It's a hard thing to crack. You're not cracking la familia without unbelievable pushback. Black America's scattered in so many different places, and the scrutiny, the assassinations, the kind of the B. S. acceptance, but then the splitting up and dividing us, for hundreds of years, going back to slavery. Self-hate up in there. I'm not saying it hadn't been on the Latino side because all the games have been played there too. I'm saying where we are in hip hop and rap music, they could not crack the code of Latinos with that B. S. as much.

I traveled the world with Cypress Hill, good brothers of mine. B-Real is my brother from the group Prophets of Rage. Brother for life. As we go down to South America, Central America, it's a whole different dynamic when he's spittin to them. It's a whole different solidarity. The movements in this hemisphere, in Central America and South America, you cannot play around with that. That movement is going to be strong no matter where you go. That pipeline carries right up into the western part of this country.

The Black family was one of J. Edgar Hoover's targets in the US COINTELPRO program [see chapter 3], and it carried right up to Reagan and Bush in 1980. And then the guns and the drugs, which manifested in all these other things. Black America still reeling off COINTELPRO going into its third phase. Rap music can only be a little bit of pushback with the dialogue and bringing together a Million Man March with the Nation of Islam in 1995.[14] Even fighting through the naysayers saying, "Okay, we got a million Black men march." At least for one day, that code couldn't be cracked. I was there. You could not crack that code on that one day. A brother wasn't even taking a pee on a tree that day. We was in Washington, DC. They were like, "Oh, it's not really a million people. And Farrakhan is this and that." It's like give us one day to at least show the world that we're together. Afterward, they questioned its effectiveness. It's always an attack. And that was that one day.

JOHNSON: I love your question. I was thinking about the group Lighter Shade of Brown from Riverside. Representation does matter. It means something when you see someone up there singing/rapping your soundtrack. And there have been connections. R&B on the West Coast, it became oldies among Mexicans. In a lot of ways, that's why R&B in California becomes so important, because Mexicans have it blasting on Whittier Boulevard, going to the shows like it's a sea of brown faces when they have people who are usually on the chitlin circuit who are actually coming out to the West Coast, maybe for a little run. It's never going out of style. Going together as family. So while representation matters in terms of who is famous, the whole reason why Black music in California becomes what it is is also in large part due to Mexicans and Chicanos. Rock, too, punk for sure. If we switch the lens a little bit to think about how important then some of these venues become, like who's organizing the shows? Where are they? Who's doing the art? A lot of incredible Mexican visual artists are doing art, invitations, and the fliers for hip hop and punk shows. We see that throughout the decades.

In terms of the Latino unity Chuck was talking about, part of that, too, is Catholicism. It's not always the best reasons that bring people together.

There's a power in the proximity to migration as well. So there's a lot of things that I think bring us together to make us really important in the story of hip hop, but it's not told. Maybe you gotta tell it.

QUESTION 5: I want to ask about the show you did in Croatia where they stopped the war for the show. I also want to ask about radical, anti-capitalist movements globally.

CHUCK D: Yeah, it was in Zagreb, Croatia, and they stopped the war for one night. So everybody was there. Serbians were there on the low [see chapter 6].

JOHNSON: It's funny, because when I saw you perform in Serbia, a lot of people didn't even know English, but they knew all the words of the Public Enemy songs. It was incredible to see these folks. What they were getting from it was something that in many aspects was verbal, but it's more like a corporeal syntax and what your body does when you say the words and this performance of what it means to be powerful. I want to also encourage that kind of sight. Because with movements, so much of what becomes important is the soundtrack, what people may not understand, but they get in their soul.

I think we saw in 2020 people who were in solidarity with protesters here, marches in the UK, marches everywhere around the world that were animated by this idea, "This is just enough!" Black deaths become this awful, trauma porn, and folks are like, "No, not any more, not on our bodies." Returning to Samy's opening comments today, there are so many people around the world who can identify with that and people sending each other helpful information. "This is what you do when you get tear-gassed. This is what we do in Palestine." This is the kind of information that travels around liberation networks. There are so many people that are communicating internationally with folks around community gardens, climate change. We better learn how to grow some stuff. We better learn how to preserve some water. We better learn how Indigenous people figure out not just taking the land back, but what are we going to do with it? Where's the resources? So people are learning all the time from other folks, the struggles. We just have to see it. We just have to ask, Where are you drawing your inspiration? People in Guatemala who are trying to organize folks in coffee plantations are like, "Oh, let's talk to the organizers in Kenya because they had the same struggle." They're doing it. It's happening all the time. You talk to any movement folks. You get in conversation and community with them, and they will teach you. It's incredible the knowledge you can get in a place like this. There's also a whole world of liberation. So there's countless ways.

CHUCK D: Is there a possibility that all these collective movements can be made more known? But then again, if everybody's privy to the movement, then your enemy is privy to the movement too. It's also not so great that it's isolated to itself either. Where we are right now, it's chopped into small regions of thought and demographic. What could be that spark plug to help people know what movements are happening elsewhere?

JOHNSON: One of the foundational pillars we were working with in *Futures of Black Radicalism* was this observation that Cedric Robinson made about abolition movements promising freedom like, "This is the promise." But it was only the promise of liberation. The beauty in liberation is in the practice and the community and how we come together. It is not a destination. Because even Harriet Tubman, she gets all these people, her parents, everybody, right across the Mason-Dixon Line. Then she opens up a home for elderly people who were formerly enslaved. Her work was never done. So it's not a magical place. This is one of the tricks of racial capitalism like, "Oh, are we going to get to that point?" No, this is the struggle that is beautiful and bitter. It's what you make in that together. It's the backyard barbecue. It's the soundtrack. It's the car that you and your *tíos* work on every Sunday. It is the *panadería* that you've been going to for generations. It's your grandma's *menudo*. It's the ribs, the mac and cheese. It's all of the things that give you the capacity to struggle and think about freedom together. It is not a destination. It's just a promise. But what we have is each other. Always, always, always. So knowing that, and adjusting. Don't let other people tell you what freedom is as a destination but instead find freedom in the slow down so that you can recognize. "I see you." "Oh, I didn't know that you knew so much about Mexicans in hip hop." "I didn't know that you were so into unity and community." I didn't know that until I sat here in this conversation about freedom, which will never end. I did the work of listening and participating, congregating.

ALIM: We quoted Angela Davis earlier on freedom being a protracted struggle [see chapter 6]. And we are hearing it again. Angela Davis also said that radical was just "grasping things at the root."[15] When you start thinking about radicalism, start with that, grasping things at the root, understanding why things are the way that they are. Understanding how things are formed is the first step to understanding how they can be transformed. There's no substitute for the work, for the scholarship, for the knowledge, for the reading, for the studying. That's point number one. I don't just say this to you because I'm a professor. I actually believe this wholeheartedly.

Point number two. When you think about everything that you're doing in this class, one thing you have heard Professor Chuck do over and over again in his own pedagogically smooth way, is that he takes your questions and slightly reshapes them in conversation, in humorous tones, in a joke, in an aside, and reframes them back to you so that you can think about your own responsibility moving forward. Professor Johnson has done this too. Why I say that is that radical and being radical is in your everydayness. You don't have to be a version of what you think radical is, but radical is how you move through the world. Everybody that you engage, everything that you involve yourself in. Are you coming with the generosity, with the genuineness, with the community building, with the love, with all these values that we have in here formed together, as Professor Johnson showed us? Are you bringing that into your everyday? That's radical, too, in a big way. It starts with us.

NOTES

1. Gaye Theresa Johnson and Alex Lubin, eds., *Futures of Black Radicalism* (Verso, 2017), 9.

2. See Gaye Theresa Johnson, *Spaces of Conflict, Sounds of Solidarity: Music, Race, and Spatial Entitlement in Los Angeles* (University of California Press, 2013).

3. See Greg Tate, *Everything but the Burden: What White People Are Taking from Black Culture* (Crown, 2003); and Greg Tate, *Flyboy in the Buttermilk: Essays on Contemporary America* (Simon & Schuster, 1992).

4. Cedric Robinson, *Forgeries of Memory and Meaning: Blacks and Regimes of Race in American Theater and Film before World War II* (University of North Carolina Press, 2007).

5. See Clyde Woods, *Development Arrested: The Blues and Plantation Power in the Mississippi Delta* (Verso, 1998).

6. Anti-capitalist, anti-fascist Spanish rapper Pablo Hasél, among others, was imprisoned in 2021 for insulting the Spanish king in his rap lyrics. See the introduction to H. Samy Alim, Jeff Chang, and Casey Philip Wong, eds., *Freedom Moves: Hip Hop Knowledges, Pedagogies, and Futures* (University of California Press, 2023).

7. See Tali Mendelberg, *The Race Card: Campaign Strategy, Implicit Messages, and the Norm of Equality* (Princeton University Press, 2001).

8. See Toni Morrison, "A Humanist's View," delivered on May 30, 1975, at Portland State University, https://mackenzian.com/blog/transcript-morrison-1975/.

9. See Toni Morrison's Pulitzer Prize–winning novel, *Beloved* (Knopf, 1987).

10. See Marc Lamont Hill and Mumia Abu-Jamal, *The Classroom and the Cell: Conversations on Black Life in America* (Third World Press, 2011).

11. See Leanne Simpson, *As We Have Always Done: Indigenous Freedom through Radical Resistance* (University of Minnesota Press, 2017).

12. See Matthew Desmond, *Evicted: Poverty and Profit in the American City* (Crown, 2016).

13. This is a play on the phrase "poor righteous teachers" from the Five Percent Nation of Islam's philosophy on spreading knowledge, wisdom, and understanding. See Felicia Miyakawa, *Five Percenter Rap: God Hop's Music, Message, and Black Muslim Mission* (Indiana University Press, 2005).

14. See Haki Madhubhuti and Maulana Karenga, eds., *Million Man March/Day of Absence: A Commemorative Anthology* (Third World Press, 1996).

15. See Angela Davis, *The Meaning of Freedom: And Other Difficult Dialogues* (City Lights, 2012).

8 Black Steel in the Hour of Chaos

HIP HOP, JUSTICE, AND THE PRISON INDUSTRIAL COMPLEX

Chuck D, Bryonn Bain, and Maya Jupiter

CHUCK D: We are continuing the theme of the social meanings of hip hop and its connections to social movements. This time, we consider the prison abolition movement. The average person in society today will usually go off the top of their head and say, "Oh, yeah, you know, like, there's three million Black men in prison." No one ever seems to do a cross-examination of those statistics. When it comes to facts, there's a lot of freestyling out there. Freestyling is fantastic when it's an art form on a stage—MCs battling back and forth—but when it comes down to statistics and evidence, freestyling really doesn't end well.

We will introduce Maya Jupiter shortly, but my first question is for you, Bryonn Bain. Bro, how did you get into all those prisons? Because in 1988, we played at Rikers. It was groundbreaking. It was inspirational. It was also heard around the world. From that point on, COINTELPRO part three kicks in, and I found out I'm banned in all prisons [see chapters 3 and 7]. I even had Crew Grrl Order, an all women rap group on my label, try to go into the prisons. We was gonna go to a women's prison in Merced and have a full performance and lecture and school them on how to present yourself and do your music. I got the flights, got the vans, and we're getting ready to drive to do a prison show that we were going to record on video. At the last moment, Sacramento called: "Can't do it. Chuck D's involved. Hell no!"

BRYONN BAIN: They did one internet search on you and they saw "Shut 'Em Down," "Fight the Power," and heard, "I got a letter from the government the other day . . ."

CHUCK D: . . . and they don't read. So they haven't read your books.

BAIN: Straight up. There are thirty-four state prisons in California. For seventeen of them, last time I checked, the highest level of education for the wardens is a high school diploma or GED. So some folks push back on colleges coming in because they're like, "I don't want these people in here to get more education than I have." They definitely search you. There's one prison where I've done a lot of work with a brother, Nanon Williams.[1] I got a whole show about his story. The Texas prison that he's in, for thirty years this month, banned my book. I can't do a lot of stuff in prisons in Texas, especially Harris County, where they've executed more men than many states.

But there's a key difference between us. I don't have the reputation of being the Malcolm X of hip hop like you. I don't raise the same red flag. I send my CV. And they say, "Oh, he went to this school and that school." I got the best white boy education money can buy! So they're like, "Oh, let him in." I say, "We're going to do poetry, and it's about spiritual growth and development." All that is true, but I don't say I'm also going to bring in Maya Jupiter's video "Crumble," which is about abolishing the prison industrial complex, disrupting the school-to-prison pipeline, and overthrowing the system and rebuilding a new one.

That works most of the time, but we've been shut out of some prisons, like the California Institution for Women prison. I've had to become the "spook who sat by the door."[2] I had to really read Sam Greenlee and take note and be like, "Okay, I just got to know who I'm speaking to at different times." In some prisons, the juvenile halls, they'll leave you, and it's just you and the young folks. I did lessons at the juvenile hall here where we taught the young brothers how to make picket signs and how to organize a demonstration. We marched around the cafeteria showing how you could actually protest, but we framed it as a lesson about civil rights history, about what Dr. King and Rosa Parks were doing. If we frame it the right way, the medicine goes down a little easier.

CHUCK D: Some places are easier than others. This country is really made up not of states but of counties. When it comes down to voting time, what people don't understand is that those counties really matter to the end result. It's an outdated system, but it's the system, nonetheless. We have to be aware of this, just to begin doing the dance. In terms of prisons, there was an unclear statistic that in 1970 there were a hundred thousand Black men in US prisons. I don't know if there's any truth to that statistic, but there's a lot of freestyling on that statistic. I'm going to ask Maya about what the statistics are when you get down to Australia too.

BAIN: Maya dropped jewels on me that I had just not come across at all in terms of the history of both Australia and the US, which have their own settler-colonial histories that created distinct prison systems. I learn so much from her. The statistic that from the years 1975 to 1977, between one hundred thousand and two hundred thousand people were in prisons, comes from a number of places. Most famously, from Michelle Alexander's book *The New Jim Crow* in 2010.[3] She does a good job of breaking down the history and the growth over the last forty, fifty years of the prison industrial complex. Before that, we had the Sentencing Project, Marc Mauer's organization, that crunched the numbers out of DC.[4] Then there's the Bureau of Justice statistics, which can be a bit late in terms of releasing information but is a federal database. Those are some solid sources that I recommend.

Lastly, my mentor recently passed, the brilliant warrior-lawyer Lani Guinier. She wrote a book, *The Miner's Canary*, with Gerald Torres.[5] She did a lot of that work before Michelle Alexander's book came out, when she laid out that framework and the statistics and how it's grown—really paralleling the growth of hip hop. Hip hop is going to be fifty years old in a minute. Since the early seventies, from Nixon to Reagan, there's some touch points along the way that have shown the rise of over two million people being incarcerated across the country. If you count the number of folks who are not only in prison but also are under the jurisdiction of the criminal justice system through parole and probation, it's between seven and eight million.

CHUCK D: Business as usual, or *unusual*. We're definitely going to get back to that, because like I said, I was trying to come up with an answer to address the droves of Black men that were going into the prison industrial system in the mid-eighties. Y'all know my saying for the mid-eighties: the R&B era—the Reagan and Bush era. In terms of a switch, it was like a lava flow of Black men, guns, drugs. When we fast-forward to today, we have a lot of people from our communities who basically call hip hop a galvanizer and a one-stop shop right into the jails. How do we answer that? That's what brings us to this classroom. How do we diffuse the hype? What are the real statistics? How do we counteract that stereotype between Blackness and criminality that has traveled around the world as being something that's inherent in us?

I did a song, "Black Steel in the Hour of Chaos," in 1988, and it was about the prison industrial complex, but it also alluded to being a conscientious objector—"I refused to go to war and I was imprisoned." At that particular time, it was like, "What are you making up a war for?" Actually, the song was answering a letter that my uncle got in 1967 when he was drafted by the Marines to go to Vietnam. My mission in the song was to compare the prison system to a slave ship. This is 1988, when they thought rap music was about figuring out what your latest dance is. And I'm like, "Well, jails is becoming all too familiar, and hip hop is not gonna be a viaduct into the prison system. This is going to *answer* that." Here we are almost thirty-five years later with some questions I'm going to ask. Let's bring Maya in.

MAYA JUPITER: First of all, Chuck, your music and hip hop was my critical race theory education growing up in Australia. When the anti-police brutality uprisings happened last summer across the US and white people started talking about, "We need to learn how to be antiracist," I thought, "These conversations have been happening for decades through hip hop." I learned about all this while I was in Sydney. Aboriginal and Torres Strait Islander people make up 3.2 percent of Australia's population but account for 32 percent of those incarcerated. It's the same thing that we're seeing in America with Black and Brown people. My father is Mexican; my mum is Turkish. I was born in Mexico, and we moved to Australia when I was a one-year-old. I fell in love with hip hop as a culture. It was the culture that I identified with as a teenager.

I grew up in Sydney's west, which is very multicultural. It's where a lot of immigrants settled and where I spent my high school years. Let me paint a picture for you. My best friend who lived across the road, mother is Eritrean, father is Sudanese—half-Egyptian, half-Italian. Our surrounding neighbors are Fijian, Greek, Serbian, Argentinian, and Chinese, among others. It was a very multicultural community. Hip hop is what we listened to. Many people from non-English speaking backgrounds gravitated toward hip hop because it was not white. It was not the white experience. It was a music of struggle and oppression, which is what we felt.

Turning to Australia's history, Australia had a white Australian policy until 1973. If you were not white, you could not migrate to Australia. You were locked out. My friend, who's Tongan, recently posted about when Australia was colonized in 1788. After slavery was abolished in the US, white Americans went to Australia and created cotton plantations and enslaved Aboriginal, Torres Strait, and Pacific Islander people. I didn't know that, because we did not get that education in primary school. It was all about "Captain Cook discovering Australia and everybody was happy." We have a very racist history that we need to deal with in order to face our current issues.

I have memories of experiencing racism as early as six years old. They didn't know what a Mexican was because there were only a thousand of us in my state at the time, so they called me the derogatory terms they would call Aboriginal people. Then they would say, "Where were you born? Go back to your own country!" I remember being in first grade, coming home crying. That was kind of the roots of my childhood. By the time I hit thirteen, fourteen, I started hearing Salt-N-Pepa on the radio, De La Soul, Naughty by Nature, eventually Ice Cube and, of course, Public Enemy. I was like, "Okay, what's this?! This is what I want to be a part of!" Because I wanted to talk about what's happening around me, the injustices that I was seeing every day. People's stereotypical version of an Australian person is a "blonde-haired, blue-eyed surfer," and that's not who we are. We're very multicultural, and we're Indigenous.

CHUCK D: The whole melting pot of the US has melted somewhere in the bottom of the crock pot. This classroom is open to the world and not limited to California and the US, as far as hip hop culture and rap music [see chapter 6]. Based on what was coming out of the US, Maya, were you ever like, "I got more to say. I can do it better"? You hosted a hip hop show on a radio station that I've appeared on many times throughout the years, so obviously everything is coming through you. You know what's being said, but more importantly, you know what's *not* being said.

JUPITER: In hip hop, we have the underground and the commercial, which have always coexisted. It's interesting how people don't realize how much American culture has an influence on countries around the world, for better or worse. I say that because gang culture also translates down under. In New Zealand—or Aotearoa, which is the Māori name—they have the Bloods and Crips, street gangs that started in LA decades ago. They learned that from the US.

Being the host of a show, I would always play 50 percent Australian music because I wanted to make sure that our voices were amplified. But I would come across some kids rapping in an American accent, and there's a huge debate in Australia around that. There are literal fights over MCs who rap in their local accents and the ones that rap in an American accent.[6] It's a big no-no. I would get kids sending me their music. They have skills, but they're talking about, "I've got a gun in my car . . ." We don't have guns like that in Sydney. That's not how it is. We had a horrible mass shooting in Tasmania in 1996, and the government immediately created a buyback program, made very strict laws around it, and we haven't had one since.[7] That was an incredible reaction, but we don't have the National Rifle Association lobbying us. My heart is with the people in Buffalo, New York, right now.[8] I just want to acknowledge the families. We're all touched by that loss and the devastation of what just happened. And also in Orange County, California.[9]

CHUCK D: That plays into conservative-right talking points right now in the US—"Oh, you're killing each other, so why should we have you live near us?" They're blaming the music. We have to follow the breadcrumbs to the sources and find out who's manipulating this situation. When it comes down to prisons, if they know they're going to quadruple their investment, who's investing in prisons?

BAIN: It's an over $80 billion industry. If you think about police and prisons together, it's an over $300 billion industry. It's always been profitable from its roots.

CHUCK D: It's always been that, but there are also new mindsets, new people, new generations that might just look the other way like, "Yeah, I don't know my business man. He just dropped a hundred G's into something I didn't know."

BAIN: This is definitely the remix.

CHUCK D: Which brings us to your book, *Rebel Speak: A Social Justice Mixtape*.[10]

BAIN: Yes. . . . I was so blessed to have Angela Davis write the foreword. I never imagined that would happen. The best response I've heard to those who blame Black folks for the violence that's happening in our communities comes from Angela when she was incarcerated.

CHUCK D: We're talking early 1970s. I was part of a program called Free Huey and Free Angela.

BAIN: Exactly. There was an international movement to free her. She joined the Black Panther Party for a little while. She left when they said you could *only* be in the Black Panther Party because she wanted to maintain her alliance with the Communist Party. She taught at UCLA until Ronald Reagan ousted her for being part of the party. When she was incarcerated, a Swedish film crew interviewed her and asked, "Why do you and the Black Panthers support all this violence and carry these guns?" She said, "Is that the question? You're asking *me?* I'm from Birmingham, Alabama, where four little Black girls got blown up in their church. And you want to ask me why *I'm* violent? My father had to have a shotgun to protect the family."[11] I thought that was a brilliant response then, but also today for thinking about hip hop being the cause of violence. Now, does it excuse misogyny, hyper-capitalism, and violence when you see it in our culture? Absolutely not. We need to call that out for what it is and make sure that we talk about that. It is not a free license to be antihuman or antisocial at all, but we have to talk about the origins of these things.

CHUCK D: That was some of the reasons for this class. We've talked about the fact that it's one thing to have a clapback on social media, but academics are necessary. A lot of times, academics, too, understand that you need the culture creators to cosign the work, because if not, the ones that's going to cosign the academics is going to be a corporation. And once everything's corporate . . .

BAIN: There's a whole lotta corporate scholarship going on. But one of the connections I want to make is, I'm from New York City. My cousins were the Fu-Schnickens from Flatbush, Brooklyn. So I wanted to be like Poc Fu and Chip Fu—like my big cousins, Lennox and Roderick. They were going on tour with Digital Underground. There was some dancer that nobody heard of called Tupac Shakur. [*Laughter.*] I was like, "I want to be like y'all!" But we didn't have the same opportunity they had. We got offered to do the holiday shows in a prison in upstate New York. So we were like, "We're doing that!" And we kept doing that over and over again because it was the door that opened for us.

CHUCK D: The Fu-Schnickens, those guys are scholars. They were geniuses. Shaquille O'Neal is an unofficial Fu-Schnickens, with the song "What's Up Doc? (Can We Rock)."

BAIN: Word. Even before Wu-Tang was doing the Afro-Asiatic thing, right? We were trying to be like them. Then we saw *Do the Right Thing*, and we were trying to be like *you*. Those were the influences that we had. But I remember clearly the year Mayor Rudy Giuliani came into office. This is the guy who became, in some people's mind, "America's mayor," after September 11th, 2001, but we never thought that. He was gonna "clean it up." That was some bullshit. I remember seeing things change. Up in Harlem, there were all those African markets up on 125th street. They swept them all away. They were gone overnight.

CHUCK D: They started with the cassette tape cats in the nineties. They said you gotta clean the streets of merchants, because they are selling black gear because the merchants can't own or work inside the buildings. The rent is too high, so they gotta be in front of the buildings. That was part of Giuliani's first steps to clean up the streets.

BAIN: That's why we went to Harlem to go see the brothers and sisters selling mud cloth, CDs, and tapes. Then Giuliani put them all into a little kennel, a gated space. They called it Shabazz Market on 116th and Lenox. It was nonsense. The year before he came into office, there were five thousand arrests for marijuana in New York City. The year after, there were fifty thousand. Did the number of people smoking weed explode overnight? No. The mayor and cops used marijuana as a pretext to fill the prisons with Black and Brown bodies.

This has a long history. In the book, I say it is "the remix" because right after slavery was abolished, one of the people I interviewed in the book was a brother named Albert Woodfox, one of the Angola 3.[12] Albert

Woodfox is the longest-held solitary confinement survivor in this country. Forty-four years in a six-by-nine box in the largest prison in the country, the Louisiana State Penitentiary. They call it the Angola State Penitentiary because before slavery was formally abolished, it was four slave plantations that became the Angola State Plantation. After the Civil War, they literally just changed the name of the sign on the door from "Angola State Plantation" to "Angola State Penitentiary." That's what they did! But it's still got white men on horseback with shotguns overseeing Black people as we work in the fields. They continued the same plantation economy and politics.

It's important for folks to know that after slavery was abolished, the slave codes became the Black codes. We had vagrancy laws all of a sudden. What was a vagrant? A vagrant is somebody who doesn't have a job or a place to live after slavery was abolished. A whole lot of Black folks were looking for a place to live and for some work, so that was instantly criminalized. Vagrancy, joblessness, homelessness were criminalized. So you, by virtue of being in your Black skin, moving around, were a criminal. They filled these plantations with Black bodies, and they leased us out. The convict lease system was created, and that was the precursor to the war on drugs for the last forty, fifty years. If you could use vagrancy as a pretext, you have a bullshit excuse to lock people up, exploit them for their labor, treat them with wanton violence, and warehouse them.

CHUCK D: This is why the city of Los Angeles is teetering on the edge, with the largest population of homeless people in any city in this hemisphere. When that tips over, then you have a prison industrial situation coming, unless we go further into the digital age and they come up with something that they can implant.

BAIN: That's the future. Folks will say the implant is a conspiracy theory conversation, but the ankle shackles is the slick trick they've used to say, "Oh yeah we have bipartisan support to end mass incarceration. We want people to get out of prison. We want people to be on 'home confinement' and wear an ankle monitor so that we can continue to make profits off of their incarceration in their home" [see chapter 7].

CHUCK D: "No, I don't want the ankle monitor, just give me an implant in my tooth."

BAIN: There you go.

CHUCK D: At first, you'll have some resistance to it, but then it becomes almost like a volunteer program. "Once I get this little implant, I'm able to go to the supermarket. I ain't got the ankle bracelet anymore." Maybe we need to, every once in a while, check out the technology department at UCLA. But you cover all of these issues in *Rebel Speak*.

BAIN: The book centers the voices of folks who have been impacted, folks who have family who've been behind prison walls. People like Susan Burton, who folks called "the twenty-first-century Harriet Tubman—Harriet 2.0," right here in South Central, helping women to get their lives on track.[13] This is a sister who the LAPD killed her five-year-old son and then were shocked that she spiraled into alcoholism and drug addiction. The white folks in Santa Monica, Bel-Air, and Beverly Hills get treatment for that. But Black and Brown folks, or folks who don't have the resources, get prison time. They get the California Institute for Women. Those racial disparities have a long history. We are seeing them reimagined in different ways right now.

My hope is that by centering the voices of folks who are incarcerated, formerly incarcerated, system impacted, bringing them into the heart of the conversation, we will actually get some different results than we got for the last four decades of a bunch of experts who are not rooted in community or the realities of folks who are experiencing what you showed us in your video for "Black Steel in the Hour of Chaos." You should know that I recorded that on *Yo! MTV Raps*. I got the Betamax tape in my mom's basement. I remember the scene where you're in the cell . . .

JUPITER: Public Enemy was visually very provocative. I just read in Will Smith's autobiography about going on tour with you in the early days and how you had somebody hung onstage.

CHUCK D: Yeah, that was later on in the nineties when we hung a Klansman. I couldn't do that in the eighties, because we'd go to different cities and states, especially places of nonunion. A rap show coming to Albany, Georgia—who do you think is going to be the crew working the stage? I wanted to do it on the Run-D.M.C. tour with Jazzy Jeff and Fresh Prince and EPMD and J. J. Fad. As a matter of fact, it was a civilized but heated conversation with Jam Master Jay, who basically told me, like, "Chuck, you do that on *your* tour, you not doing it on *our* tour. There's a lotta cracker towns we're rolling into. Anything can happen." Jay was like our union leader. I was like, "I got it Jay," and we did it on our tour three years later, but it was a slightly different climate with Public Enemy going into it. The heat was on every place we went, but we was coming in, and we had twelve thousand people out there on our side. So it was, "We just want these negroes to do their thing and get the hell up out of town."

I got what Jam Master Jay was saying, but the point is that hip hop as a culture and an art form was a springboard for dialogue. Both of you come out of that whole idiom and poetry, performance, presentation, curation. We have a saying that "it's a difference between the caretaker and an undertaker, and a museum is different from a cemetery." How do we come up with a clear and direct message and path for hip hop? One thing that was definitely out there in the past was nobody wanted to be called fake. If somebody would say, "Yo, I'm gangsta," but if you're not, then you're fake. Fast forward twenty years later. It's like, "If I'm fake, it don't matter. I'm good. I got fame. I got money. And you conscious people is broke."

The other subject we've touched on is that a lot of the music is in code. Code runs so deep. If you're in Chicago and somebody's in the middle of a drill record, there's some code in there like, "Yo, I'm *gettin* this cat." Then what? Trust me, there's a reason why code is code. Even if everybody don't hear it, the adversary heard that code up in there. Eric Adams, the mayor of New York, whatever we think of him, is a Black man in his fifties from Brooklyn. Regardless what anybody says about him or what he's ever capitulated, he ain't no corny, fake, wack dude. Now he's got to make concessions. When he said, "Look, man. I'm not one of those cats giving excuses. These cats got codes up in there. We want to just get them to get out of that code thing and using the delivery of the music because what's going to happen is something that I can't stop." Now we've got a Black woman police commissioner. We got Black people in the head of these situations, but the whole infrastructure of it is still going to have the same result: "Lock these little niggas up or shoot them."

BAIN: I think you gotta bring those folks to the table. I'm no fan, but he has the power to bring folks to the table in ways that other mayors couldn't. My brother does violence interruption work in eighteen projects across New York City, so he's met with Adams many times.

CHUCK D: How did it go?

BAIN: It's a dance. They had to write a letter afterward saying, "Listen, don't misrepresent what we said in this conversation." So my brother's organization has projects like Queensbridge, largest project in the country where they stopped shootings for 365 days. But it's all dudes who used to be shooters. My brother hated conscious hip hop. He didn't like Talib Kweli. He was like, "That nigga's corny." I was feeling Mos Def, Blackstar. I got three brothers. Two of them were locked up a whole lot. The one I'm talking about is a year and a half younger than me, and he didn't want to be exactly the way I was.

CHUCK D: So there was a little bit of rebellion there.

BAIN: He loved N. W. A.

CHUCK D: There was a gap between you and your brother. It was a gap between me and my brother. My brother served a lot of time in US prisons and New York prisons. That's why we worked on these things. Looking back on your early days, how would you change your technique now if you had that audience using rap music as your tool to open them up?

BAIN: I think about his transformation. He's one of the dopest MCs. He's mad *lyrical*. I called him up years ago. He wasn't rhyming as much, wasn't in the streets as much, and it sounded like he was crying on the phone. I said, "What's wrong, K?" He's like, "Yo, man I'm watching this documentary, and it's just fucked up how they treat these sisters in Pakistan." I was like, "What?" He was like, "It's fucked up!" All of a sudden, bitches and hoes wasn't as much a part of his vocabulary in his lyrics anymore, you know what I'm saying? He had two daughters! It's a shame that's what it takes for some folks to have a realization of how powerful their words are. But to his credit, since then, he's realized that power, and now he organizes formerly incarcerated folks, former gang members, to go into the projects to de-escalate beef before it becomes fatal, to stop shootings, and even intervening to stop domestic violence. The NYPD stays out because they don't really want to be there anyway. So K and his team, Community Capacity Development, talk to the young brothers and de-escalate because they are "credible messengers."[14]

CHUCK D: There's a lot of OG wisdom out there in the world right now that is underutilized. If we think about the education of the disenfranchised communities that we come from, how do we put that mindset in the right teaching form?

JUPITER: I've facilitated a lot of collective songwriting workshops, that is, we would be all here together, and we would talk about what's going on in your world right now, the issues you're facing. As we discuss, we throw words up on the board, and then we put it together into a song. I've been doing that for the past twenty years. I think that's community building. It's listening to one another, being present, witnessing a person's testimony. It's about having these discussions, and I think that helps bridge that gap between the generations.

I also always say, to paraphrase you Chuck, "Hip hop is the CNN of the streets," and sometimes, the streets are problematic in some ways. . . . I'm always asked this question: "What is it like being a female in hip hop when hip hop is so misogynistic?" [see chapters 5 and 10]. Hip hop is a reflection of our culture and our society right now. That's who we are. As Yasiin Bey [Mos Def] says in "Fear Not of Man" on *Black on Both Sides*, "Hip hop is not a person living on the hill. We *are* hip hop." If there are homophobic or misogynistic lyrics and people are discussing violence, it is because that's where society is at.

My experience with my radio show is a beautiful one, because I personally got to produce and program three hours of radio. This is National Radio in Australia. I didn't have to censor anything. I got to choose what went out on the airwaves. That does not happen on commercial radio in the US. Good luck trying to get songs played. You have to pay a radio promoter $50,000 to get your song played on the radio here. There is no free radio. That's why it's almost impossible to hear more diverse perspectives on commercial radio. This is the question we need to dig deep into: Who is deciding what messages are coming out? Who benefits from the system that continues to oppress us?

CHUCK D: I think, in fairness, we say that they're not the radio generation. The radio is still very powerful, but they're part of the generation that listens with their eyes. We have a saying, what is it y'all?

AUDIENCE: Screenagers!

JUPITER: I've had people say, "I saw your music."

CHUCK D: If they don't *see* it, they won't *hear* it. Listening is at an all-time low because this comes out of the generations that felt that they hadn't been listened to. We're in that generation now where people might feel like they have something to say, but the only area where they can say something is in the comment section on YouTube. Back in the day, the comment section used to be laughed at, but if this is the only area where your voice can get out, who feels excluded?

BAIN: I just read an article today on krip-hop, and I appreciated Leroy Moore's perspective [see chapter 1]. He came at you, Harry Belafonte, a lotta folks. It was a blessing to hear him thinking out loud about disability rights, disability justice, ableism, these things that existed in hip hop's early formation. As we have expanded our vocabulary, I think about intersectionality, how our different kinds of oppressions are related. Moore highlights it in Kendrick Lamar, in his videos and music. I mean what rapper have you heard before this week to have an album listened to by millions of people that has lines like "My auntie is a man now. . . . Demetrius is Mary-Ann now."[15] So I think there is some wrestling with not having a voice. Kendrick is also like Jay-Z, "Che Guevara with bling on—complex." We all have contradictions. He's also trying to wrestle with his own demons, his own misogyny, and dealing with being abused as a child. I think all of those complicated themes, I see them in certain artists. I see it in Vic Mensa. I went to college with Lauryn Hill. She was doing it before a lot of these folks.

CHUCK D: Artists give you a *slice* of their life in their art. When you teach the arts: art can be short for *artificial.* It's a facsimile. It's not the reality. But if you ain't got your realities in place, then there's a haze between the two, where fantasy and reality are all mixed up. To return to something Maya said, when corporations control the arts, that leads us into consumption. People are led into numbers, views, likes—consumption. Also, you get indoctrinated to the negativity of it all online. This is where we are right now.

JUPITER: I always say social media is not real. On my Instagram, you're gonna get like 5 percent of who I am. I don't post pictures of my kids, and my kids are my life.

CHUCK D: Your kids are growing up as twenty-first centurions, but you are a twentieth-century centurion. Therefore, the ability to see what's real and what's not real is different.

BAIN: You talked about art having one of its origins in "artificial." It also has etymological roots in "artillery," which is the big guns that an army carries or the firearms that are moved by a carriage. In some ways, the mic stand might be the carriage, and the microphone might be the firearm. Like Toni Morrison and others have said, art can be dangerous.[16]

CHUCK D: Or it could just be symbolic, like Run-D.M.C. used to hold their Johnsons [male organ] because they took everything else away. That used to be, "Oh, Run-D.M.C. is just holding their whatever." They were on the mic, but it was like a lot of that, "Ohhh!" coming out.

BAIN: There's a history of white folks gathering around as Black men and women are lynched from trees, and their genitals and other body parts severed and carried around like trophies. That's part of this country's history of racial violence. We can't divorce mass shootings from this country's history of racial violence. South Africa is still in apartheid. They ain't got over it, but South Africa attempted to have Truth and Reconciliation tribunals. Germany, after World War II, after the Holocaust, attempted to have the Nuremberg Trials deal with some of their history of racial violence. These attempts were flawed in many ways, but the US has never had a real reckoning to deal with its history of racial violence born in genocide and slavery. And they're surprised there's racist mass shootings happening on a regular basis?

CHUCK D: With this recent mass shooting, the media narrative tried to make it seem like dude traveled from two hours away to bring his racism to Buffalo. Like it ain't racism in Buffalo. Wherever he drove from to Buffalo was a strike *full* of racism all the way up into Buffalo, which is the reason why Buffalo is Buffalo. Don't play the audience for being stupid. Griselda Records, small independent label in Buffalo. . . . We got Benny the Butcher. We got Conway the Machine, Westside Gunn. We got gangsters in Buffalo. We got Black gangsters everywhere. For like a hundred years we've had that. They're a small voice speaking some reality in Buffalo. What changes is that Eminem and Shady Records sign them to a distribution deal, which means the gangsterism got muscles in it now. Nobody answers to that, and they say all of a sudden, "They blew up because they're the hot shit." For everything that ends up going unexplained, there's somebody that presses the executive button. This is why we cannot do this in the future without academic discourse, thought, and dialogue. The academic discussion is gonna hold the bullshit on its heels, so to speak.

BAIN: I think this is what critical race theory is attempting to do. Hip hop was our critical race theory back in the day. There's such a strong pushback against it because white folks don't want their children to learn how they are complicit in the oppression of people of color. My sister Esther Armah has written a book on "emotional justice."[17] I want to shout her out as one of the most brilliant minds of our generation. We need to reimagine justice in radically different ways. Justice as punishment, as retribution, is not going to work. We have been locked in this model of justice as retribution, justice as punitive. We need something that goes left of center beyond even rehabilitation as justice, beyond even restorative justice. Restoring to what *was* is not good enough. We can do better. We have to.

Arundathi Roy says the pandemic should be a portal to something better.[18] We don't want to go back to what was, because normal was some bullshit for us in the first place. How do we transform ourselves into a whole different situation? Transformative justice. Or what formerly incarcerated folks in Brooklyn call human justice. The equation for that is *human rights*, which means defending our basic human dignity, plus *human development*, which means creating the opportunity and resources for folks to develop their full potential, equals *human justice*. That's a vision and framework for justice that gets us out of this tired and backward retribution mode: human rights + human development = human justice.

We know white folks push back against Black power and Black freedom. The Black freedom struggle comes from a place of deep guilt from the racial violence that was happening all across this country. Brother Justin Dunnavant in UCLA Anthropology just excavated a slave ship, the *Clotilda*.[19] They don't want to deal with that history, but we need to deal with it. That means it's not just about Black and white, because it means men have to deal with patriarchy, sexism, and our own complicity in not only the oppression of women but the oppression of other men. 50 Cent shut down Ja Rule back at Summer Jam when he said, "There's been a whole lotta talk about niggas, bitches, and bitch-ass niggas," and he put up a picture of Ja Rule crying. Has Ja Rule had a hit record since? Now, I am inspired by 50's survival story and resilience. Anyone shot nine times who lives to tell the tale and makes his living processing that trauma is a phenomenon. That said, he also used his platform to turn the volume up on heterosexist feminization by attacking Ja in a way that was deeply problematic. We need to think about not just white supremacy but patriarchy and capitalism.

CHUCK D: You gotta watch out for what you think a victory is. 50 Cent got a win, but was that really a victory?

BAIN: In a certain way, that kind of toxic masculinity locks men in a prison of another kind. It limits our ability to express our full humanity. "I can't give you a hug. I can't show you love, because I gotta be this stone-faced, ice-grill version of myself that is as cold and dehumanizing as anything that I could think about doing to any man or woman."

CHUCK D: It comes with a lack of communication and connection. Once you box everybody into being "an individual," then you can turn a cluster of individuals into anything you want if you just show the money. The question to y'all is, Y'all fighting battles at seven hundred thousand feet, but what makes you tired?

JUPITER: My kids.

BAIN: Amen.

CHUCK D: Because you can't have day and night at the same time. To do that, you gotta shut the world off, especially now.

JUPITER: I didn't know it before, but I really believe that parenting/mothering is a revolutionary act. Raising children to be kind, compassionate people who care about the world and want to make a positive impact. Everything we're talking about is mental health. It's all about the trauma that BIPOC and poor people experience in this country and to constantly have to face the world in a way where you have to show up without having all the privileges and resources and also dealing with racism and all the other shit that goes along with it. What worries me is that there's a sense of hopelessness now. The suicide rates among teenagers and children are going up. The CDC [Centers for Disease Control and Prevention] just declared it a national crisis. This scares me. The high rates of depression and anxiety, medicating our youth. All of it. Kids know too much. The internet in the palm of their hand is overwhelming. I don't think, as humans, we're supposed to know about all the atrocities that happen in the world at the same time, especially as a twelve-year-old. I don't just mean the big issues of climate change and mass shootings, but knowing about all of the pain and suffering around the world all at the same time can be too much for us.

In this moment of reimagining, we don't want to go back to the old way. I'm a big advocate for all of us reimagining the future. What does it look like when we abolish the police? What does it look like when we get rid of prisons? Who are the members of the community that are gonna look after each other? When someone's having a mental health crisis, who do we call rather than the police? When someone has committed a crime, where do they go instead of jail? How do we circle up around them and tell them about the harm that has happened to us and implement these transformative justice practices? How do we have those conversations so that we're not throwing people away? I don't know if I'll ever see it in my lifetime, but this is something that I'm thinking about, the way Native Americans think seven generations ahead. What are we doing now that's going to affect people in seven generations?

BAIN: I think self-care, community care, and mental health are languages this younger generation coming up has that we didn't have. I say this as a father of a twenty-year-old. He's an artist at the Chadwick A. Boseman College of Fine Arts at Howard University. Super proud. I've seen some things I don't want him to have to suffer through. I survived the London Bridge terrorist attack. I was about to go onstage. I saw people killed. I came home, couldn't sleep, had nightmares for months, you know what I'm saying? So I see him walking the streets of Brooklyn, DC, or LA, and I want to be able to protect him from that. But I also realize that I can't stop him from living his life and experiencing the world. That's challenging for me because it's a nonstop paradox.

There's a third way of thinking about art that ties into this. We talked about art as artificial. We talked about art as artillery. There's also art as medicine. I always think about you and Malcolm X in tandem with each other. Brother Malcolm said, "When you go to the dentist, they put Novocain in your mouth. So you bleed all over the place, and you don't even feel it. You suffer peacefully." Novocain is an anesthetic. It numbs your pain. It makes you feel less. I think art should be the opposite of that. You should hear better. You should see more clearly. You should feel your human emotions more deeply, and your sense of connection to other human beings should come alive. Art should be an alarm clock to wake us up. This language of being woke comes from that way of thinking about art as something that enlivens our senses so that we realize that old Buddhist, Indigenous, and African philosophy that says our separation is an illusion and our interconnectedness is actually the reality.

There are no individuals without community. The Western mythology, the American mythology of how we exist—Descartes, the Cartesian idea—is "I think, therefore I am." But Audre Lorde says, "Those white men are wrong. Because the Black woman, the Black goddess in each of us tells us: I feel, therefore I can be free."[20] With that idea, we actually feel connected to each other. If COVID didn't teach us anything else, we're breathing the same air, y'all. We are part of one organism. If our consciousness could be imbued with that way of thinking, then we would act like we know.

CHUCK D: That comment goes alongside some deep conspiracies within society. "If we could get human beings in a matrix where they are more like gadgets, and people worship the machines and gadgets like human beings, then we have a process where everything has to be literal." You see, you may hear, but you ain't never gonna feel. This music was always born out of the idea that you gotta feel this music to get into it. Having the soul of a gadget means that you will fall into the temptation of being a lifetime consumer. It'll be part of a game plan that says, "You could be woke if you sleep. We try to make your ass dead." You can't get woke after you're dead.

I think hip hop is termed out. It may be the original term, but whatever is happening now is sorcery through a gadget. They just happen to brand it, just like they happened to brand us as slaves. Hip hop brand. NOPE. They're doing something, but that's not hip hop. Maybe the beginning of academic discourse on trying to fix some of this has to be like, "Well, that's something else, man. We gotta remove it out from the hip hop vernacular." A jazz cat will beat you over the head with an instrument and say, "Oh you think you jazz just because you got a trumpet? We will beat your ass."

BAIN: The Navajo Indigenous people welcomed Europeans here. Africans did it too. We welcomed folks in and got kidnapped. Hip hop has this openness that has invited folks in, but now we have centuries of lessons. My mama has a protocol when you go into her house. You have to take off your shoes. Now if you don't like taking off your shoes because you're wearing funky socks with holes in them, that's fine. You just ain't coming into my mama's house! I think there needs to be some protocol. Now, how you figure out what that protocol is, that is a whole other question that I'm not prepared to get into right now. But yes, I do think the volume is turned up on a whole lot of stuff that is dressed in the drag of hip hop.

CHUCK D: And you cannot detach academic scholarship from it, because an academic might be the saving grace in there. When I hear people like, "Oh, they're an academic, man. They don't know nothin about these hard-ass streets." I'm like, "You don't know nothin about the hard-ass streets either. You make music, dawg. How hard can you be? You know the real cats, and you know you're not one of them." We have academics that could be the last saving grace saying, "We're not trying to destroy you, but the next set of people coming in, it's going to be easy for them to press the button, destroy you, and get paid for it. They'll get paid for your execution."

It happens in other places. I was in Beirut, Lebanon. This cat said, "Yo, Chuck, I'm part of an MC coalition of the whole entire Middle East, from Syria, from Dubai, you know, a fifteen-nation, Arabic-spittin hip hop contingent out here." Big Hass that we played on Planet Earth Planet Rap, he says, "Tell these dudes in the US they don't want none of this. I had to walk from Damascus thirty miles. This is right over a mountain, right into Beirut, with my surviving son on my shoulders. My wife's wiped out, my other child's gone. And we had to pick through the rubble for food. Tell everybody in the hip hop community, 'Stop fuckin around and talkin war shit.' They don't want this." So I come back to the US, and I'm lookin at cats who claim to be hard asses like, "Really?"

I want to tie this to the realm of politics, because it's so crazy right now with an uncertain government in 2023, '24. The world talk on President Biden is like, "I don't know what the US is doing, but dude is half sleep half the time." It ain't even funny right now. He was the only dude to stop fascism in the US right here right now. And this isn't a Joe Biden speech. I'm saying that in this case, we don't even know what 2024's lookin like. It is always in these breadcrumbs. These seeds are all over the place with atrocities every other week, with the rise of white supremacy. That faction feels like it's got a groundswell. I'm not preaching fear right here, but y'all are the demographic that's growing into this madness, watching the chaos unfold right in front of your face.

It's very easy for them to say, "It's hip hop's fault!," while this other thing goes on. There's growing animosities out there right now. We know that social order already got these things taking place, manifesting and bubbling up. It's almost like, "Damn, man! I'm seeing the swelling of fascism happen right in front of my eyes." What happens in the next three years to

2025 and beyond? Do we also factor in the fact that we have a Black vice president, Kamala Harris? Does that animosity get crazier if the dude who is eighty years old says, "I can't do it no more. It's her turn?" Then what happens? And let me tell you, young people twenty-five and under, you won't be able to hide.

JUPITER: I think we're in danger of Trump coming back into the presidency. He even said he could shoot someone on Fifth Avenue and nothing would happen to him. There's no scandal for his fan base, because there's nothing he can do that they won't excuse. We saw the rise of fascism, but it already existed. It's just people have come out of hiding now. It's like they're proud to be racist rather than trying to hide it in their communities.

In terms of technology, I think what's scary is that we're in our own silos. Our algorithm just lets us see what we already like to see. We're not seeing alternatives. People that watch Tucker Carlson are listening to him and Candace Owens. They're just seeing the same shit over and over again. I'm worried about what they call Web 3.0, and how everything is going to be AI. We're going to chat with each other, but through fucking avatars? We're going to be a cartoon character of ourselves and talk to each other through goggles? Deep fakes exist now. They're making content where your eyes are deceiving you. Is it real? It's not going to make our job easier to discern the truth.

In these conversations, I always return to cultural healing practices. We've got to get back to the ways that humans came together. Every time I look for an answer to my question, I go back to Indigenous practices because they highlight how to heal as communities, to live in harmony with the earth and with one another. And it just goes back to circles. The cipher. It comes back to this always—having conversations. I'm looking forward to the Q & A, hearing from you guys as well, being part of this conversation and hearing your experiences and your voices.

We have to make a conscious, intentional effort to say, "Yes, we're going to use technology because social media helps us spread the message around the world." When everyone was shouting Black Lives Matter in the US, Aboriginal communities picked that up and said, "Black Lives Matter! We need to stop the Aboriginal deaths in custody [of police and prisons] and in Aboriginal communities." All of a sudden, they had a massive international voice and platform because they participated in the Black Lives Matter movement, which they got instantly because of social media.

BAIN: That really resonates with me. First, what's going to make a difference? Presidents are significant, but movements make lasting change. Community organizing work is the thing that has always made change. It'll be informed by technology, certainly, but you know what my peoples in For Freedoms calls the original AI?[21] Ancestral Intelligence. That has to be a part of what informs our movements.

Every week, I get on a bus right outside this building with ten UCLA students. We drive a hundred miles to Victorville Federal Prison, and we have class with ten women at the federal prison. Nobody can bring their cell phones or laptops in. Everybody is unplugged for three hours while we're in a room together. As much as I am an abolitionist and working to end the prison industrial complex and racialized mass incarceration, I find great value in this space where everybody is unplugged for a brief bit of time every single week. This is my seventh year teaching at UCLA. For the last three years, I have not taught a single class on this campus. Every class has been in a juvenile hall or in a women's prison or in a federal prison. The incarcerated women and youth appreciate the opportunity to have access to education ten times more than the average UCLA student. No shade on y'all. I'm just saying facts. They see it as a passport to their liberation. We changed the laws with the referendum. So you can take six months off of your sentence if you complete a certificate of degree. This education is liberation in a real way.

Like others, I also recognize hip hop is good operating software—it goes with a lot of things. It can go with fascism. It can go with hyper-capitalism. It can go with misogyny. But it can also go with disability justice. It also can go with hip hop theater. Lin Manuel Miranda's *Hamilton* made people aware of that, but there's so much beyond that. The point is, hip hop can go with a lot of the ugly, but it also can go with a lot of the beautiful. We have to negotiate that through our movement-building work.

Lastly, part of what this generation has brought to light is the genius of our best hackers. Hackers understand a system so well they can make it do things it was not designed to do. We have to embrace that lesson from this generation. How well do we understand the system? How can we hack it to get free? The Qur'an says, "If you save one life, it's as you saved all humanity." There's a lot of investment in symbols and not really changing the systems and structures that maintain the subjugation of masses of people. For example, I voted for Obama twice. I probably would've voted for him a third time. However, I also recognize that a Black face on a white power structure is still a white power structure. I also recognize that he deported more people than presidents before and after him. I also realize he didn't do a whole lot that he should have done for all of the celebration he got, including the Nobel Peace Prize. Dolores Huerta needs a Nobel Peace Prize, as far as I'm concerned.[22] If Obama can get that, so should folks who sacrifice their bodies and put themselves on the line, especially women of color, who lead all these movements and don't get the credit for it. We need to rethink how we look at the symbols versus the systems and the structures.

SAMUEL LAMONTAGNE: We've been talking about how hip hop can be a powerful tool to critique systems of power but can also promote violence and systems of power. Hip hop scholar d. sabela grimes thinks of hip hop not in terms of content but in terms of practice and community.[23] I think this idea really resonates here because thinking of hip hop as a thing, then it easily fits within a capitalist framework which captures and commodifies it as a product or as an experience. But if you think of hip hop as practice and as community, then you can step outside this capitalist framework and look at how people use hip hop on the ground and what it means to them, and what they express through it, and what they build socially through it. We need an approach that makes room for our agencies, creativities, experiences, and critical perspectives. That's what hip hop has always been, a practice where we could reclaim our humanity, and create space for Black life in an anti-Black world.

QUESTION 1: Maya, you talked about doing collective sessions with community members. Have you noticed differences in how those sessions work in the US versus Australia?

JUPITER: Back home, I used to work with a lot of young women through community centers, mostly Aboriginal, Pacific Islander, and culturally diverse youth, usually around high school age. There was one group—the course was called "Hip Hop 4 da Ladies"—that was an incredible experience. I was in my early twenties, but hip hop taught me "Each one, teach one" [see chapter 3]. I was always drawn to the idea that if you know something, you pass it on. It wasn't about teaching kids how to rap and then say, "You're all gonna be superstars." It was more about facilitating a space where people felt safe to talk about their personal struggles. A lot of the conversations, because they were all women, were always around issues like, what does a respectful relationship look like? We didn't have the language of affirmative consent back then, but we discussed what happens when someone crosses a line in that relationship into domestic violence.

It was really about them finding their own voice and the confidence to know that they can do more than what they thought they could do and be more than what the idea of themselves was. The reason I'm mentioning this specific course is because that was a pathway into tertiary education. It was a hip hop course, but it certified them with a certificate from a federally funded technical college in Australia called TAFE. They could take our course and enroll into another course and further their education.

In the US, I've facilitated workshops, mainly with the Chicana/o community, with Spanish-speaking folks, and just talking about issues that face our community in terms of immigration, deportations, and family separations. I think there are a lot more similarities than there are differences between the work across the US and Australia. A lot of the times, people say, "Well, I've never written a song in my life. I don't know why I'm here." Then they leave very inspired and realize that it's about the connections made and not how good you can sing. We bounce off each other. Someone says one line, and then a person who's never written a song in their life has the most poetic, beautiful line that you could ever dream, that I could never write. And that line was inspired by the person sitting on the other side of the room. When you're a part of something like that, it's healing. It shows you that there's a wealth of knowledge and wisdom in our communities. Look around you. I think we need to value what's in ourselves and in each other more, and I think this process allows that to happen.

CHUCK D: The fact that you are curating and caretaking the art out of people and bringing them together, that's really where it all comes from anyway. You said, "We got three hours of focused time and I want to hear some poetry out of y'all." Nothing gets better than when the audience turns into the participant and the teacher or curator turns into the audience. That's the give and take, the exchange. It's not about "My art is better than your art." That's not how the bars are raised. That's where consumption comes into being the by-product of industry, messing it up. To me, it was never about that.

BAIN: I took my son on a rites of passage trip to Cape Town, South Africa. They invited me to do a performance in a shanty town outside of the city. They said, "Okay, before you perform, we're going to perform for you." It was young folks. They did this whole show, singing, telling stories, dancing. Then they grabbed my son and this other sister that was on the trip with us, Rosie Rios, and said, "Now tell us what you saw in our performance." Totally put them on the spot. They were like, "No, you don't just passively sit there and observe us. What did you see? What did you get from this?" Each of them had to break down what they saw, and then they were like, "Okay, cool, now you can perform." It was this give and take. It was a call and response. The kind of theater that I trained in, Theater of the Oppressed, comes from Rio de Janeiro, Brazil. It's participatory theater. It critiques what they call the Aristotelian notion of theater, where you sit there and you just passively take in everything. Back in the day, everybody was involved in theater. Indigenous folks. African folks. Somebody's singing. Somebody's playing the drums. It's call and response. It's back and forth. It's the church experience: "Can I get a hallelujah? Hallelujah! Can I get a amen? Amen!" The concert is the same energy.

We actually do "legislative theater." We do theater where you dramatize your experience of injustice and oppression and then you create legislative proposals and go lobby for them in Sacramento or City Hall. That's the kind of rich back and forth that we can create. It's been the most fulfilling experience for me in these workshops, mostly with Black and Brown youth and incarcerated women on the West Coast, men in Sing Sing and Rikers on the East Coast. I will never forget one of the first cats I interviewed for one of these programs. I said, "Why do you want to pursue this arts education while you're incarcerated?" This young cat looked at me and said, "I need to pursue this while I'm in here because prison is like Medusa, and it will turn you to stone. I need something else to feed my spirit. To keep me alive."

One of the first times I had that experience was with incarcerated white folks in the Midwest—Clark County Juvenile Detention Center. There was this fifteen-year-old Polish kid named James Kalinowski, who was sentenced to ninety-eight days. I did a performance. We did the workshop. I said, "Boom! I'm coming back on Wednesday, and we're gonna do a poetry slam, and y'all will win gift certificates and books." James Kalinowski requested to stay in the prison a ninety-ninth day, just so he could be in the poetry slam. And then he won! He left the prison with the wind at his back, as a poetry champion, and with this new relationship to language and the power of his words to actually be about his own sense of agency.

CHUCK D: He'll never forget that day.

BAIN: I still remember it myself over ten years later! But it wasn't about the individual; that all happened within a cipher. Historically, to nerd out on y'all a little bit, the cipher is something that Africans brought to Europeans because they didn't have the concept of zero before we came for eight hundred years and the Moors occupied Spain, anyway. The cipher, the 360 degrees which got us out of Roman numerals, actually is the circle in which everybody stands and has the opportunity to engage and to have respect. Your skills, your willingness to be vulnerable, to step into the cipher is a part of that at its very best. Some ciphers go sour, but at its very best, it offers the opportunity for folks to sit in a circle and to engage in sharing a part of themselves and to be affirmed. That interconnectivity is part of what hip hop can bring into all of these spaces.

QUESTION 2: Maya, should these workshops start at a younger age, before children get to these detention centers?

JUPITER: I think I'm a radical parent, but I say, "Hell no." I'm a mother of two Black children. I'm very aware of the country that they're being raised in. I have a mentor, a Black woman, Kikanza Ramsey-Ray, who was in the movement, the Bus Drivers' Union. She started an early childhood program in Altadena called Village Playgarden. It's an amazing space. I want my children to have the privilege of a childhood the way that white children get to have their childhood. It's not stolen from them.

I am very aware that this stance is not the mainstream way of looking at it, but the way my mentor described it, she said, "We don't need no child soldiers. We don't need children in the streets, fighting for their lives before they even understand who they are." I used to be in the protests with my child in the stroller. We were in the front. And bless AF^{3}IRM [Association of Feminists Fighting Fascism, Imperialism, Refeudalization, and Marginalization], a transnational feminist organization. I love their work so much.[24] They put all women, families, and children in the front of the march, protecting us. I thought that was amazing. Then I thought, "Why do I have my children in the march?" They were toddlers at the time. I really want to protect their innocence, and it's important for their development that they feel safe. I also want them to have the magic of dreaming and imagining. They will learn about this country soon enough.

BAIN: I love building with you because I'm always forced to rethink my positions. Living in Brooklyn for most of my life, in some ways, we're spoiled. "How diverse was your kid's school?" Oh, it was very diverse. It was Jamaicans, Trinidadians, Belizeans. My son, when he went to first grade, it wasn't called "first grade," "second grade," "third grade." It was called Ghana, Mali, Songhai. The grades were named after our people. Trying to recreate that experience in LA has been challenging. We go to Capoeira, so they get that cultural and spiritual experience of being around our folks, and African rhythms. But then I may go to the extreme other way. I'm thinking now that maybe reading my ten-year-old *The Autobiography of Malcolm X* as a bedtime story was a little much. We didn't finish it, but I was like, "Yo, you should know that soon!" I'm constantly wrestling with that.

JUPITER: The reality is that by the time Black boys are twelve, thirteen, they're looked at by police, especially in this country, as a threat. We've seen that with Tamir Rice.[25] My son just turned six. My daughter is eight. She's at that point, though. There's a change coming.

CHUCK D: Math is real, and time is short. You look at childhood years from when I was in my teens, from 1970 to 1980, and we still found a large block of time to be kids. We knew what was out there, what was coming. I was in the African American experience as a ten-year-old, a nine-year-old taught by Muslims and Black Panthers and radical students, on the campus of Hofstra in 1970 and 1971. In those years, it was coming at you for real. So we had that for the summer months, but it also was mixed in with going to the pool and having madd kid fun. Then we went to the fourth and fifth grade.

That was the last decade in this country where Black childhood had a large span of years. I would say from zero to sixteen or seventeen years old, depending on where you was at. Then it was, "Okay, you're gonna grow up into adulthood and you're gonna catch up on things that were hinted at you." Because you had things that automatically came to you in the sixties, whether you liked it or not. You saw Dr. King get murdered, the Black

Panther Party get eradicated, and Vietnam. You saw these things, so you couldn't help but ask questions about it. The whole key of the seventies and the sixties was to have as much fun as you can, but you better know who you are. That disappeared in the eighties when there was guns and drugs in Black neighborhoods across the map. A lot of parents at that time had the ability to shield a lot of that, but it was right there. In the nineties, there was a bit more escapism into hip hop, so we could kind of see it and know about it but not see it across the board in this country. Right now, what would we call true childhood years? Zero to six. And then what? You got from seven to twenty. You got a barrage of trauma. You got depression at thirteen and fourteen.

JUPITER: That's why you have suicides happening at nine years old. There's so much of these "teach anti-racism books," etc. Kikanza was telling me the other day, "People ask me to come to their school and say, 'Can you teach our kids not to be racist?' And it's like, 'You don't be racist!' Your children mirror you." Doesn't matter what you say they're gonna act the same way you act. We can't escape the actions of our parents. We see and hear what they do. If you don't want your kids to be racist, then start doing the work. Babies are not born hating other people. They learn this.

BAIN: I think about my own complicity in reproducing these cycles of violence and trauma. I think for all of us, that is part of the lesson. But I wrestle with this so much—this idea of balance—because we don't celebrate a lot of holidays. Because there's no way I'm telling my kids the toy I couldn't afford to get them come from some big, fat white man from the North Pole who came down the chimney to give it to them. I'm just not doing that. I can't send him to school and be like, "Yeah, that white man on the cross is your Lord and Savior." No, I'm not doing that. We have to find ways to challenge these narratives that we're constantly bombarded with, which is a kind of violence. Violence is not just shooting 'em up at the mall or the grocery store. It is violence that is coming at us in every which way in the messages we're hit with, the negative programming. Radio programming is just that. Television programming is just that. Programming. We're being programmed to see ourselves or to not see ourselves in certain ways. I'm constantly trying to figure out how to balance all of that out. But the kids also need magic and imagination and creativity. You don't want to squash that.

CHUCK D: They got this kid who just did this atrocity in Buffalo, and people have already forgotten the name Dylann Roof.[26] Dylann Roof was in South Carolina, wiped out a church, and all of a sudden, that was forgotten about. Kyle Rittenhouse too, who shot protesters in Wisconsin, and then was invited by the Dallas Cowboys to visit the facility and enjoy the Super Bowl trophy.[27]

BAIN: Look, I'm reading this brilliant Muslim brother, Hanif Abdurraqib, *A Little Devil in America*.[28] He has a passage where he told his friend, "I'm not writing about police shootings anymore." His friend responded, "Do you think by not writing about them that they're not gonna happen anymore?" That stirred up so much for me. Ten years ago, the Malcolm X Grassroots Movement, an organization in Brooklyn, started doing cop watches before we had phone cameras walking around policing the police. They were inspired by the Panthers. They issued a report called Operation Ghetto Storm, and they found that a law enforcement officer, not always a cop, sometimes the George Zimmermans, but a law enforcement officer or a security guard of some kind, kills a Black person every twenty-eight hours in America.[29] Every twenty-eight hours. That was their count in 2012. We're capturing what has always been happening. The body count been high. First fifty years after Columbus arrived, there was a 9/11 every single week. A million people died from COVID since it began in this country. Fifty million around the world documented. The numbers are higher than that. The violence is real. The violence is raw. Over two hundred thousand people are raped in prisons every year in this country. It is happening, whether we look at it or not.

I do think there's a danger to becoming desensitized to it, but I think paying attention to how what's happening here is related to the globalization of the world is important because the good and the bad are being exported with hip hop. My time in Palestine helped me to see that. I went with dream hampton and Jasiri X. It was the first time I felt like I was in Rikers Island out in the open air. Seeing eighteen-year-olds walking around with M16s and rush out of a van ready to attack when somebody's blowing the whistle. This violence is real, and we are complicit in it. It's not just "those people out there." We are complicit and our tax dollars are being utilized to send weapons to Israel, to Ukraine, around the world.

I think the investigation to do is starting with ourselves. How do we examine how we participate in the oppression of ourselves and others? How do we try to reconcile that? Those are the tougher questions. The easier questions are to point the finger and say, "It's them!" No, it's us. We play a role in this. I think we can work to try to wrestle with how we play a role in it and how we can undo and unravel that. The state is made of people. These institutions are made of people. Whatever can be constructed can be deconstructed.

That is the work that lies before us.

NOTES

1. In 1992, seventeen-year-old Nanon Williams was wrongly convicted of murder and sentenced to death in Texas. After much advocacy, his sentence was reduced to life in prison. See Bryonn Bain, "Free Nanon Williams Movement," https://www.bryonn.com/advocacy; Williams's autobiography, *Still Surviving* (Breakout, 2003); and *Lyrics from Lockdown*, executively produced by Harry Belafonte. Three separate judges have overturned his conviction, yet he remains behind bars.

2. See Sam Greenlee, *The Spook Who Sat by the Door* (Wayne State University Press, 1989), a story about a Black man trained as a CIA agent who uses his training to lead a revolution.

3. See Michelle Alexander, *The New Jim Crow: Mass Incarceration in the Age of Colorblindness* (The New Press, 2010).

4. Marc Mauer directed The Sentencing Project for thirty-three years. Kara Gotsch is the current director.

5. See Lani Guinier and Gerald Torres, *The Miner's Canary: Enlisting Race, Resisting Power, Transforming Democracy* (Harvard University Press, 2003).

6. See Ian Maxwell, *Phat Beats, Dope Rhymes: Hip Hop Down Under Comin' Upper* (Wesleyan University Press, 2003); Chiara Minestrelli, *Australian Indigenous Hip Hop: The Politics of Culture, Identity, and Spirituality* (Routledge, 2016); and Sudiipta Dowsett, Lucas Marie, Dianne Rodger, and Grant Saunders, eds., *Representing Hip Hop Histories, Politics, and Practices in Australia* (Routledge, 2023).

7. In 1996, Port Arthur in Tasmania was the site of a tragic mass shooting that took the lives of thirty-five people. The government bought back and destroyed over 640,000 guns.

8. Ten people were murdered in an anti-Black rampage in a supermarket in Buffalo, New York, just days before this lecture. See Hurubie Meko and Dan Higgens, "Buffalo Gunman Pleads Guilty in Racist Attack that Left 10 Dead," *New*

York Times, November 28, 2022, https://www.nytimes.com/news-event/buffalo-ny-mass-shooting.

9. The Orange County church shooting occurred just days before this lecture. See Caroline Linton, "1 Dead, 4 Wounded after 'Politically-Motivated' Shooting inside Orange County Church, Police Say," CBS News, https://www.cbsnews.com/news/laguna-woods-shooting-geneva-presbyterian-churchorange-county-california/.

10. On UC Press's hip hop studies book series, see Bryonn Rolly Bain, *Rebel Speak: A Justice Movement Mixtape* (University of California Press, 2022).

11. See *The Black Power Mixtape: 1967–1975*, directed by Göran Hugo Olsson in 2011, starting at 56:23, https://www.youtube.com/watch?v=e0bWTh74m6c.

12. See Bryonn Rolly Bain, "Track #2. Panther Rising: How Alfred Woodfox Survived 4 Decades of Solitary," in *Rebel Speak: A Justice Movement Mixtape* (University of California Press, 2022), 35–60.

13. See Susan Burton, *Becoming Ms. Burton: From Prison to Recovery to Leading the Fight for Incarcerated Women* (New Press, 2017). See also Bryonn Rolly Bain, "Track #3. Twenty First Century Harriet Tubman: A Dialogue with Susan Burton," in *Rebel Speak: A Justice Movement Mixtape* (University of California Press, 2022), 61–78.

14. Community Capacity Development (CCD), established by K Bain, is a non-profit organization dedicated to fostering growth and healing in historically disenfranchised communities. See https://www.ccdworldwide.org/.

15. On *Mr. Morale and the Big Steppers* (2022), which was released the week of this lecture, see Kendrick Lamar, "Auntie Diaries."

16. See Constance Grady, "'Art Is Dangerous': Ta-Nehisi Coates, Toni Morrison, and Sonia Sanchez in Conversation," *Vox*, https://www.vox.com/2016/6/17/11955704/tanehisi-coates-toni-morrison-sonia-sanchez-conversation.

17. See Esther Armah, *Emotional Justice: A Roadmap for Racial Healing* (Berrett-Koehler, 2022).

18. See Arundhati Roy, *Azadi: Freedom. Fascism. Fiction* (Haymarket, 2020). Watch Roy discuss the idea of the pandemic as a portal with Imani Perry at https://www.haymarketbooks.org/blogs/130-arundhati-roy-the-pandemic-is-a-portal.

19. The *Clotilda* is believed to be the last ship to bring enslaved Africans to the United States. When they were freed, they established Africatown, which Dunnavant argues will be one of the most significant archaeology sites in the twenty-first century. See Tara Roberts, "The Search for Lost Slave Ships Led This Diver on an Extraordinary Journey," *National Geographic*, February 7, 2022, https://www.nationalgeographic.com/history/article/a-divers-hunt-for-lost-slave-ships-led-to-an-incredible-journey.

20. See Audre Lorde, "Poetry Is Not a Luxury," in *Sister Outsider: Essays and Speeches by Audre Lorde* (Crossing Press, 1984), 38, first published in *Chrysalis: A Magazine of Female Culture* (1977).

21. For Freedoms is an artist-led organization committed to activism, healing, and justice through creativity. See https://www.forfreedoms.org/.

22. See Bryonn Rolly Bain, "Track #1. The Blueprint: The Radical Solidarity of Dolores Huerta and Harry Belafonte," in *Rebel Speaks: A Justice Movement Mixtape* (University of California Press, 2022), 3–34.

23. See Shamell Bell and d. sabela grimes, "Street Dance Activism & Black Liberation," facilitated, recorded, and edited by MiRi Park and grace jun, May 24, 2021, https://hdl.handle.net/2027/fulcrum.jm214r214.

24. Learn more about AF^{3}IRM at https://af3irm.org/af3irm/.

25. Tamir Rice was a twelve-year-old Black child killed by a white policeman in 2014 in Cleveland. He was playing with a toy gun. The US Department of Justice refused to pursue charges against the officers who murdered him. See "U.S. Justice Department Declines Charges against Officers in Tamir Rice Case," *PBS Newshour*, https://www.pbs.org/newshour/nation/us-justice-department-declines-charges-against-officers-in-tamir-rice-case.

26. Dylann Roof is a white supremacist who murdered nine Black Americans in the Emanuel AME Church in Charleston, South Carolina, in 2015. See "Dylan Roof Found Guilty in Charleston Church Shooting," *The Guardian*, December 15, 2016, https://www.theguardian.com/us-news/2016/dec/15/dylann-roof-convicted-charleston-shooting.

27. During Wisconsin protests that erupted in 2020 after Jacob Blake was left paralyzed by a white police officer, Kyle Rittenhouse shot and killed two protestors. He was found not guilty. Not only did Rittenhouse visit the Dallas Cowboys, but he also was welcomed to Mar-a-Lago by President Donald Trump and became a darling of Republican conservatives. See Teaganne Finn, "Trump Says He Met with Kyle Rittenhouse after Verdict, Calls Him 'A Nice Young Man,'" NBC News, https://www.nbcnews.com/politics/donald-trump/trump-says-he-met-kylerittenhouse-after-verdict-calls-him-n1284513.

28. See Hanif Abdurraqib, *A Little Devil in America* (Random House, 2022).

29. Read Operation Ghetto Storm here: https://www.prisonpolicy.org/scans/Operation-Ghetto-Storm.pdf.

9 Harder Than You Think

THE POETICS OF HIP HOP

Chuck D and Adam Bradley

CHUCK D: We are going to talk about hip hop poetics. A lot of times people say, "It's about the flow," or "It's about the lyrics." There was a time period when people were saying, "I only like rap because of the beat." I think everybody here has a thorough understanding of this art form as coming out of the creativity of a people throughout the course of their history, from the griots to the streets, beating on the lunch tables or street corner doo-wopping—the creative impulse of a people and their traditions. We've been doing it on the strength, but we also have been helped out by the fact that this has been a recorded music. We're also going to talk about the international aspects of lyrics. In terms of the beauty of the lyrics, if you don't hear it in the language, do you really hear it at all?

Many artists read your works like, "Wow, I didn't know I did it like that. That makes sense to me." Logic is the thing that rap music and hip hop needed from day one. It was always gonna be dope, because that's what we do. You actually explain *how* and *what* we do. Professor Adam Bradley, as the poetic chief that you are, can you break down what got you into the study of hip hop in the first place? What is it about the lyrics?

ADAM BRADLEY: First of all, I'm grateful for your words and your inspiration. So many things you said struck me. One that I wanted to tend to right off the bat is that tension inherent in what rap is. It manifests as flow but also as language. We can talk about having a book of rhymes and where rhymes are born, for example, back in the days when people wrote by hand more than on their phones. But there's a kind of literary art that rap music, and rap lyricism in particular, has at its roots that stretches all the way back, for millennia, across cultures, not just in the Western world, but in the Eastern and African contexts, and in so many global poetic forms. What happens when that also meets with performance on record?

Chuck, you've talked about that transition point when rap went from being something that was an event where you had to be on-site to participate in it to all of a sudden being on the radio [see chapters 1 and 2]. That was one of the most poignant things that you said about the early years of hip hop. Whether it's the first recorded rap record, the Fatback Band's "King Tim III (Personality Jock)" or obviously the Sugarhill Gang's "Rapper's Delight," which went national and then global, by 1979, rap was making that move from a participatory thing that was bubbling up out of the culture to being something that had a structure and a form [see chapter 1 on these early records]. Being able to study rap both musically and then lyrically, on the page, speaks to the breadth of the art form and the different ways that we can enter it as well. Can you take us back to that moment when you first heard early recorded hip hop, and what that did to your head as someone who knew it as more of a grassroots feeling?

CHUCK D: In this class, I discussed that when we get down to what we hear as recorded hip hop, if we're gonna talk about rhymes on record, I can't leave out the fact that when I was eight years old, in 1968, I heard Pigmeat Markham with "Here Comes the Judge." That was in a format that ten or twelve years later on we understood as rap records. We also broke down rap as vocals on top of music. The music's already been defined. If you want to point back to the Jamaican toasters and DJs, dub plates were instrumental, so when the DJs got on top of it, that was the overdubbing process of a voice on top of music. If it wasn't a band like Bob Marley and the Wailers or the Upsetters, they had DJs that would make sure that the beat goes on and on with those two turntables. As I said, any pauses or stops in a party in Kingston, you might have a *problem*. You gotta keep the rhythm flowing, and the microphone kept flowing, although in a different patois. So that was rap on top of music. Also, we've been a creative people for millennia, so the fact of our creativity makes that hip hop and then rap on top of music. That vocal style is something underneath that umbrella.

In this class we said, "Don't be in awe of the elements of hip hop." As they sell the elements like "hip hop is MCing, DJing, breakdancing, graffiti." We discussed that MCing is vocalization. DJing is musicianship. Graffiti is art, hieroglyphics and art expression, which goes back to the beginnings of time. Breakdancing is dance culture. So we're not in awe of the elements of hip hop. Hip hop is a terminology. When you study the culture of people who have been disenfranchised, Black people in the US were basically told, "I don't want you saying nuthin. If you're upset, sing it to yourself while you die. If you got a point of view, you keep it to yourself." We were a silenced people. Out of that silence comes our creativity with music.

Hip hop is going into its fiftieth year, but we go back a little bit longer than fifty years. I remember in 1968, me, my brother, and my sister listened to this record off of Chess Records, home of the Chicago blues, by Leonard and Phil Chess. They made this record produced by Gene Barge, "Here Comes the Judge," by a comedian by the name of Pigmeat Markham. In the middle of that record, Minnie Riperton appears. What I am saying is that the beat, the boomboom-clap, was *funky*, as we would say in the vernacular of James Brown. Add to that the fact that he's staying on the one and the four and rhyming with "Hear ye, hear ye, the court of swing / Is just about ready to do that thing / I don't want no tears, I don't want no lies / Above all, I don't want no alibis / This Judge is hip, and that ain't all / He'll give you time if you're big or small." He's comin with the flow on top of the beat and not straying off the beat. *That's* when I first heard it [see chapter 4 on funk].

Later on when I heard "King Tim III" in 1979, it was a similar feeling. I didn't know if I could call it a rap record, because it was with the Fatback Band, but I knew that it was different from what Gil Scott-Heron, the Last Poets, and the Watts Prophets were doing. Those were older people's records anyway. If you looked at the Watts Prophets or the Last Poets [see chapter 7], it almost would go into Richard Pryor's section. By that I mean that the way they were breakin it down, it was grown folks music. But "King Tim III" brought this thing that was happening in New York and almost got it. Later that year, in September 1979, "Rapper's Delight" comes out, and that's the big bang theory. When I heard it, I was like, "Wow! What we thought was a three-hour party thing, they got it down to fifteen minutes. They put rap on a record!" It was inconceivable to me until I first heard it in that particular way.

BRADLEY: Meanwhile, radio DJs are getting it, and they're saying, "Fifteen minutes?! We play three-minute songs here." There's a tension there. I love when you emphasize how short fifteen minutes was to people who were used to experiencing the music over a period of hours.

CHUCK D: That's the irony, and how short it is today. Let me ask you, what do you think makes rap different from other forms of poetry? Shakespeare had his poetry. You covered Ralph Ellison in the 1920s and 1930s, great writers and poets, and the Harlem Renaissance poets. What makes rap different?

BRADLEY: Part of the answer lies in something you already suggested. Rap is vocals over the music. The term "lyric" has its roots in Ancient Greece. The word derives from the stringed instrument of the lyre, which was used to accompany the songs of poets. Both the idea of lyric poetry and the idea of song lyrics spring from the same ancestral context. It's knitted into that very word in English at least, that we give to both song lyric and to lyric poetry, of which Shakespeare's sonnets would be an example. T. S. Eliot, Emily Dickinson, Langston Hughes, whomever you might name in the canon are all writing lyric poetry. In that sense, MCs and poets who write for the page draw from a common toolbox of poetic language and form. They use the same tools of rhythm and rhyme and figurative language of all types, doing so in ways that are sometimes conscious and sometimes not.

It's really not the artist's job to tell you that they're using onomatopoeia. That's our job as students of it, to break that down and recognize it. They may just be like, "Yo, that sounds right," or it may be somebody who has studied consciously and is trying to achieve a mosaic rhyme, as Dr. Alim references in his reading for this week on Pharaohe Monch.[1] There may be a conscious craft that's involved, but there's something remarkable and distinctive about rap from other poetic traditions, and I would include other songwriting traditions here too. You talked about other Black American traditions of the blues, or R&B and soul music, or rock and roll that emerged out of the Black American musical context. Rap's defining difference from them all is the density of its language. There are simply more words per bar in the average rap song than there are in a rock, pop, or R&B song.

CHUCK D: For years, nobody said that Bob Dylan couldn't sing. They said, "Okay, that's Bob Dylan. He's Bob Dylanizing this song, but we're gonna give him credit because he's deep." I don't think they really gave him credit because he had a flow. When it comes down to bluegrass poets in country, they're flowing over bluegrass. Or even auctioneers, or play-by-play announcers doing hockey. I was influenced by the way Marv Albert would flow. Nothing broke his flow. How does that figure in?

BRADLEY: That's an amazing question, because I think all artists are sponges. They soak up what's around them. I had a student of mine in my hip hop poetics course earlier today. She did a presentation on Baptist preaching, and she put some examples of preaching from her own community here in Compton, Los Angeles. The thing that you heard was a rhythmic sensibility, a sense of flow. So we have one type of flow going on Saturday night when we're out partying and another on Sunday morning when we're at church! You're surrounded by flow wherever you go.

CHUCK D: Is flow overrated, though? Also, does the flow have to ride the beat?

BRADLEY: I think we're at a moment right now in hip hop where flow reigns supreme, at least in the melodic kinds of approaches that artists are taking to a beat. Who knows what Young Thug's talking about half the time, but you feel the flow. Generally speaking, at least in the rap music that bubbles up to the mainstream, there's less of the wordsmithing of the eighties and nineties, where we would break down a Rakim bar and we'd see the intricacy of the balance of his internal rhymes and multisyllabic rhymes and flows on top of flows that are based in wordplay. I think part of it is a shift in our artistic approach, which has to do with the blending of genres. I don't think artists think of genres as boundaries. They think of the art that they want to create and the people they want to work with and they make music in those contexts. I think genres are imposed on the music from the outside. What we're seeing now are artists saying, "You know what, I have lots of styles and I'm going to tailor a style that draws from many influences." For the moment at least, this seems to be privileging a certain kind of flow that sometimes comes at the expense of other aspects of the art. But at any given time, the art of MCing contains it all.

CHUCK D: When I first started, the thing that dictated an MC wasn't necessarily the flow. If you didn't have a voice that stood out, especially with records, then anybody could take your style because they had the same voice. Today we have similar flows but also similar voices, and also similar topics. One of the theories that we have in this class is that today, people listen with their eyes maybe a little bit too much. They see a visual aspect of the presentation of the flow, the voice, the topics, and they see that person. That first sight is what dictates to them what they're looking at as opposed to what they're hearing. All those other things come into play only if they agree on what they're seeing first.

BRADLEY: I think we had a profound example of that with Kendrick's drop a couple of weeks back, when the video for "The Heart Part 5" came out.[2] It features this masterful morphing of famous and infamous Black men's faces—O. J. Simpson, Will Smith, Jussie Smollett, Kobe Bryant, Kanye West, and Nipsey Hussle—all knitted into the content of Kendrick's lyrics and delivery. The music and visuals were a work of art in their entirety; it's kind of irreducible in that sense. I can listen to the song as I drive around, but it's different. I think there is something to be said for that. I wonder though, I recently played the "Fight the Power" video that Spike Lee did. After it came out, when I heard the song, it conjured the video. How closely do you think image and song are bound in that?

CHUCK D: When people ask me about "Fight the Power," I'm not saying that song is nothing, but without Spike's movie and people seeing it that much, it wouldn't have been what it was. He embedded that song in the movie. So the visual aspect of that song is, to me, beyond the lyrics and the flow. But getting back to the topic, it's like, "Okay, it might not be the main thing, but it better be the anchor that brings it all home."

BRADLEY: No doubt. I think that's almost irrefutably true. I wonder where we go from here, though.

CHUCK D: We go to your books to get a guideline on what's happening. You were at Harvard, but what moved you into the study of hip hop poetics in the first place? It's the 1990s, rap music is going into its third phase, embedding itself into album-oriented music. It was an industry, but it was like the wild, wild west as far as theories and infrastructures is concerned.

BRADLEY: I set foot on Harvard's campus in between Tupac's death and Biggie's death. I was on campus when Biggie passed away, and I was still in college when Tupac died. That was an era in which we very powerfully saw a demonstration of young geniuses at the forefront of the culture but not appreciated fully for the art but seen as a sideshow. It was a powerful moment in that period from '94 to '96, because as we moved through that era of hip hop, we had the emergence of some of the voices that now a lot of our students would refer to as "old school." With Nas and Jay-Z, Lauryn Hill coming out of the Fugees in '95, '96, and then '98 with her solo album *The Miseducation of Lauryn Hill*. This is the era when I was walking around with big-ass headphones. They were not Beats by Dre! They were just big old generic headphones. I was bumpin all of this music that now we look at as classics, but to me, it was just what came out on a Tuesday. That's a very privileged place to be in relation to hip hop. I look back at it now with great reverence, being present in a moment like that, going to shows and seeing The Roots and the Wu-Tang Clan and all of these folks that would come through.

CHUCK D: Were you the main explainer to your surroundings at that particular time?

BRADLEY: We had some folks. There was a small cohort of us that were so dedicated to hip hop, foremost among them my friend and collaborator on the *Anthology of Rap*, Andrew DuBois.[3] During the day, I'm going to these classes, learning stuff all the way back to Beowulf and Geoffrey Chaucer and Shakespeare, all the way up to Toni Morrison. Then at night I'd listen to this music, and I started saying, "All of these things that I'm learning in class apply just as much, if not more, to this music and the lyricism on top of the music that I'm hearing." That was the "aha" moment. That was the chocolate and peanut butter coming together where I said, "Man, this is what I gotta do for my life. I have to explore this." I started working on what would become *Book of Rhymes: The Poetics of Hip Hop*.[4] I started dreaming up, along with Andrew, what would become *The Anthology of Rap*.

I began that process as a student, and it took a lot of struggle to get publishers to believe in this kind of work. I know Dr. Alim will tell you that he had to fight to get credibility to do the hip hop linguistics work that he was doing. I know that Dr. Cheryl Keyes coming from ethnomusicology also faced the same sort of thing. I think if you talk to most hip hop heads in the academy, they will tell you it was a struggle in their various fields. For me as an English professor coming into literary studies and poetry, I had to fight my ass off for this work to be considered legit. I already knew it was legit. I didn't need anybody to give the stamp of approval. What I had to do is be stubborn and forceful and keep at it until I broke through.

CHUCK D: That has to do something to you, too, because it seems so easy. It seems understood by everybody, but once upon a time you fought to pioneer and open up people's thinking. Today the average person would say, "Your book is one of a thousand books," but your book to me is foundational. The books that you have written are so necessary because they organize our thoughts around these issues.

BRADLEY: That means everything to me, Chuck. It all goes back to what you say about building on the foundations. I'm fortunate that by an accident of history, hip hop was born at a time that allowed me to write one of the earliest books that dealt with rap's poetry. People are going to build on it. I hope people in this class will build on the work that I and others have done in studying hip hop poetics. That's how we build something like a lasting tribute to this art form where we as people who don't rap, who don't DJ, who don't participate in other ways in the culture, can contribute to it. Because, Chuck, I tried all the other stuff and I couldn't do it! So I found my lane. I found my way to give back to something that I loved and to pay tribute to the artistry that I loved in a way that I felt could contribute to the world's understanding and appreciation of this culture.

CHUCK D: We appreciate that lane, because the lane is necessary and there's many more lanes that have to be found to make it easier. But when the explanations come in and say, "Well, sometimes honesty could be a little bit greater than parody and popularity." That's a crossroads that hip hop is starting to get into a little bit more now. Kendrick came out with a breath of fresh air, even if people might not know or believe what he's saying. But one thing Kendrick comes out with is a sense of balance. Me, coming up in the art world, as an art student from the late seventies and the early eighties, we were taught that art is subjective. We were taught that there is no better or worse art; art is in everybody. It just comes down to developing ways to get art out of everybody. In *Book of Rhymes*, you hit from a bunch of different vantage points and artists. You don't get judgmental, per se. You just let people flow in the book.

BRADLEY: I think both the *Anthology of Rap* and *Book of Rhymes* were occasions to start by just doing what every hip hop head loves, which is to put together your favorite mixtape. For the anthology, for instance, my partner, Andrew DuBois, and I came up with a list of five hundred songs. This is from 1970-something, before recorded hip hop, all the way to 2009, when we were doing the work. Then after spending a lot of time with all of those songs, we sought the opinion of twenty people in different sectors of hip hop, although decidedly and crucially not MCs. We wanted to get a sense of people who could step outside of the craft itself and look from the outside in, who were inside-outsiders to the art of MCing. We had some DJs, scholars, writers, and journalists. We told them, "Take that list of five hundred, and cut things out and add things in as you see fit." We got the lists back. People had cut out maybe three songs and given us another five hundred! Now we had almost a thousand songs. Then we started listening and cut it down to five hundred again, but it was a radically different five hundred from the one we had conceived on our own, which speaks to the importance of the collective work, which is why a class like this is so crucial to be able to talk through these issues, listen to the same music, watch the same images, have these kinds of conversations. It shapes one's perspective and attunes one's ear to the art.

With *Book of Rhymes*, I had some songs I was listening to, but then I also just asked a lot of people, "What should I listen to?" Luckily, I was a professor at the time, so I had a fresh crop of eighteen-, nineteen-year-old students coming in every fall. I'd be pulling back their headphones, like, "What is this? Let me get in on this." I still do that to this day to keep my ears fresh, to keep expanding what I listen to, and to find a way to relate these basic tools of analysis to what's happening in the moment.

CHUCK D: How do your books deal with the complexities of language? Hip hop and rap music have been around for fifty years. I've been to countries mimicking English and adding the language onto whatever languages they were already speaking. Going into the nineties, going into the new millennium, where American rap is a language and a subculture that they keep on their hip, but also, they bring in patois and other languages. Does this make the next Adam Bradley venture even more expensive as we get into these different languages?

BRADLEY: Right behind my shoulder here is the Korean translation of *Book of Rhymes*, and that symbolically speaks to what you're saying—the globalization of the art form [see chapter 6]. The engines of commerce in the US have done a lot of damage to the world. One of the things that has been a silver lining of that, though, is the way that it's helped accelerate hip hop's dissemination. American corporations with advertising campaigns and even with T-shirts, for example, going to places around the world. Combine that with youth and other artists touring and going to these countries where some folks had never heard of rap music, and it's so powerful. I was talking to a friend of mine from Poland, and he told me that they still talk about Ice-T performing there right after the fall of the Iron Curtain in 1989. When that happened, that was their "Rapper's Delight." There were all these kids who didn't know anything about rap because they'd been behind the Iron Curtain. Just a few had access to some of the music. But they saw him perform, saw the love that he was giving to the crowd, and all of a sudden, there was a generation of MCs that emerged out of that moment. There are stories like that across the globe. That is one of the things that demands that we listen to the breadth of the tradition.

Right before the pandemic, I had an amazing couple of experiences. I was onstage with Rakim in Denver, and then a little bit later, I was down here in California, in Irvine, at the first Afro-Korean hip hop festival and conference. I keynoted that. I should have known something dope was up when the keynote, which is usually the finale of a conference, was at 9:00 a.m. Fast forward, and at 9:00 p.m., I'm in a crowd surrounded by a few thousand strangers listening to hip hop in a language I didn't understand yet feeling every pulse of it. That goes back to something you said earlier about the way that rap can travel as a musical form, as a literary form even, without even full comprehension. One of my poetry teachers, Helen Vendler, said to me, "Poetry can move you even when only partly understood." I would push that even further and say hip hop music can move you even when not understood at all, because I could feel emotionally what those artists were feeling when they were spittin. I could tell when it was a party rhyme or when it was a more reflective tone. I could also tell by the energy of those around me who spoke the language, the cues for what it is to connect on those multiple levels. I'm really hopeful about the future of hip hop, and of rap music lyricism in particular, because of that hybridity of language that you referenced. Folks being able to flow in multiple tongues, sometimes on the same track, sometimes on the same verse, it's amazing.[5]

CHUCK D: Women in hip hop and rap music are a mighty force worldwide. When you get three or four, or even two women rhyming back and forth, there ain't nothing that matches that—the execution, the style, the voices. There's some energy, something electric there, lyrically, flow-wise, harmony-wise that can't be reached.

BRADLEY: We could take it all the way back before your time in the industry with the Sequence. We featured them in the anthology. One of the most meaningful communications I've had about the anthology with an artist—present company excluded—came from when Blondie, a member of the Sequence, reached out to me. She was like, "Yo, people don't include us a lot of times in the conversation about this moment with Sugar Hill Records in 1979" and their importance in that foundational story. When you go back and listen to, "Funk You Up," and some of those tracks . . .

CHUCK D: You could play "Funk You Up" right now and it'd hold up. I mean flow-wise, rhyme-wise [see chapter 5].

BRADLEY: Same with J. J. Fad on the West Coast with "Supersonic." The flows, particularly at the end of that song, are just crazy. It is literally twenty years ahead of where we're seeing certain other male artists like Eminem attempt some of that kind of speed rapping with a sensibility of play. There's such a virtuosity in that moment and such a "Look ma, no hands" type of swagger in it that I just love. That's old school. Fast forward to this moment, and there are so many women artists who stand out in the rap game. It goes without saying that one of them is Rapsody, who I had the pleasure of interviewing at length for the story I did in the *New York Times* last year.[6] Her entry point into hip hop was when she was a kid in junior high and high school who would be just journaling and writing poetry. Then she goes to college, and she starts trying out the whole slam poetry scene, but yet not on a beat. Then producer 9th Wonder gets to her and is like, "Get in the studio. Let's see what we can do!" Within a short period of time, from what she explained, she had learned the science of moving what she was doing on the page and in spoken word performance into MCing.

CHUCK D: Tell us about that bridge. Do you think Countee Cullen would have been a dope MC? Am I going over everybody's head? [*Laughter*.][7]

BRADLEY: For real, hip hop heads should look at Countee Cullen because I think you're right about him. He has this poem called "Heritage."

It's so driven by this beat. You could just count the beat off, and it's so fluid and playful where it's both patterned but then offers just enough variety and breaks patterns. People don't want a metronomic, perfect flow. They don't want a metronomic perfect beat. Some scholars did a breakdown of Pharrell's huge hit "Happy," from several years ago. They talked about micro-rhythmic imperfections that Pharrell knitted into the beat. Those imperfections give it a sense of swing, where you find you can dance to it. If it had been perfectly computer-driven, it would have left people cold. I think we've known that, as Black artists, for the longest time. It's one of the things that I think knits the experience from talking about these early women MCs with some of the innovations of the present moment in the way that artists, both in the international context and domestically, are pushing rap forward.

CHUCK D: What are some of the criticisms that you've gotten for your work? Because if you criticize anybody in hip hop, there is always that little, you know, "Yo, listen, you better watch your words. I'll shank you. I know I'm a professor, but yeah." [*Laughter.*]

BRADLEY: Exactly. You can go too far. There have definitely been moments. As an English professor, you're not much in the public eye. But you start doing something hip hop related and all of sudden there's some cameras in your face and microphones in front of you, and you gotta deal with all of that. When the anthology came out, there was an article that attacked some of the transcriptions. Transcriptions is one of the most difficult things in moving an art form from oral to written. You can ask anybody, going back to people who transcribed medieval ballads to the Harlem Renaissance era, with people like Zora Neale Hurston, who did anthropological work in Haiti and in the American South and documented these songs that were part of the oral tradition.[8] Anytime you move an art form from oral to written, it's going to introduce imperfection.

There was a level of scrutiny on our effort more than on any other before it or since. I understand why. The book was coming out on Yale University Press, so people had this idea that somehow it's elevated because of that. It was on the printed page, so that sets out a different set of expectations from online. Nobody holds Genius.com up to as high a standard. But the thing that was so fascinating for me is that *Decoded* came out the same year and Jay-Z is breaking down his lyrics.[9] Somebody wrote an article that was so amusing to me where they compared Jay-Z's lyrics from *Decoded* to our Jay-Z lyrics from the anthology: "Actually, the anthology gets the transcription right on this part. Jay-Z has it right over here." Now, of course, Jay is not himself transcribing his lyrics. But nonetheless, it speaks to the fact that there's that indeterminacy. That was a moment that really challenged me, because it challenged my sense of pride in the effort. I knew how hard I worked to get those transcriptions as good as we could. I stand by the fact that they are the best available, even to this day. But it also hipped me to the fact that these are the kinds of debates that people are going to have, so bring them on. I'm preparing a new anthology right now actually that's focused on 2010 to today, and it's an even greater challenge on transcription. Have you ever tried to transcribe an ad-lib?! [*Laughter.*]

CHUCK D: Genius comes up and they put the lyrics online and that's their service. But what gives us a description of what the lyrics are about? What cuts through the code? I mean Genius does it, but . . .

BRADLEY: They do the crowdsource annotations that go toward content, but what I've always been about is creating a space to give attention to the form and to the artistry of the MCs in the language itself. It's dope to have all of the references that people have and the triple entendres whenever Lil Baby is talking about his particular neighborhood. Genius is great for finding all those details, but when you want to actually understand the difference between a particular kind of texture of rhyme or a particular form of figurative language that may have its roots in a tradition that goes back to the Bible and beyond, then there's another lane that you need to open up. That's the one I've tried to travel through.

CHUCK D: There's a tendency in the last thirty years of saying that a rapper doesn't want to be too preachy. But I've been able to see the advent of the forty-year-old MC, and there's tons of them and more coming. They're having real conversations about driving a Mazda that's breaking down or not being able to pay that school bill, but they are yet to have huge audiences like artists who make songs about, "I'm gonna rap like I have the things I wish I had," or "Here I am thirty-seven years old, but I only could drop my lyrics from my nineteen-year-old self because I know you probably not gon feel my thirty-seven-year-old lyrics."

BRADLEY: The thing that you and your generation, in particular, and a few artists before you, have done is to show that rapping is a form that can contain any damn thing you want to say within it, and it can be something that doesn't have to be fixated on youth alone. We love that the power of hip hop in its original format and the power of rapping, in particular, was to give voice to young people who often weren't heard. This is something we hear constantly from the first and second generations of artists. KRS-One says that hip hop was the final conclusion of a generation of creative people oppressed with the reality of lack. MC Lyte says something like, "How else was a young Black girl going to be heard around the world? I had to rap." So there is a way that rap has had an important place for young people, but I think now it belongs to the world. When my students mention Childish Gambino, for instance, and artists with academic backgrounds, it opens up a new zone too. I think that speaks to how suffused hip hop is into our culture at all levels. You and I just spent time working on *The Smithsonian Anthology of Hip-Hop and Rap.*[10] The Smithsonian would have never spent time with hip hop a generation ago.

CHUCK D: Once the team was assembled and everybody had to choose those records, I ran outta that room! I didn't want to be part of that, but thanks to you, following it through, taking the baton to the finish line, there is such a thing as the *Anthology of Hip-Hop and Rap* in the Smithsonian and we're thankful for that.

BRADLEY: One of my most vivid memories is that day when we were all in that room and we're just going back and forth on this huge list, track by track. There was a surreal moment—and I've mentioned it to you before, and you had forgotten it, and I'm glad that you did—where I found myself pushing back on something you were saying. Then I realized you had actually been in the studio when it was recorded. I don't even remember what the track was. It wasn't yours. That just speaks to the fact that there are all sorts of points of entry into hip hop, and yours is very different from mine. I grew up in Salt Lake City, Utah, of all places, where hip hop took a minute to arrive.

CHUCK D: My first time coming to Utah was with the metal group Anthrax in the early 1990s. That was my portal into Utah. What did you hear growing up? Most people hear Americana growing up anywhere. Especially when I was growing up, Black kids heard everything the white world had to offer in music and culture. It's just that we also heard our thing. When I went to a white high school, they were surprised that I knew their thing, but they didn't know my thing. Growing up in Utah, I'm pretty sure you know both worlds.

BRADLEY: You had to. If you listened to the radio, you would hear all of it. I wouldn't change it if I could. I'm glad I know who Winger is, who Siouxsie and the Banshees is. I'm glad that's part of my education. One of the things that probably would surprise some Tupac heads in the room is that when he was in high school going to the Baltimore School for the Arts with Jada Pinkett Smith, they were huge rock music heads. They were listening to Metallica. They were listening to stuff that was bubblin up in the Pacific Northwest at that time. He really had an encyclopedic knowledge and love of all music. One of his favorite artists was the singer-songwriter Don McLean, who wrote "American Pie" and "Vincent (Starry, Starry Night)." This is music that came out around the time that Tupac was born. His mother would have played it for him, along with all the music that you'd imagine that she loved, like Roberta Flack and others. For Tupac, that helped him access a part of his emotions that otherwise he might not have been able to get to.

CHUCK D: Before Pac, I'm not gonna say that emotions were not there in hip hop and rap music, but Pac came along in a period of time where you knew you could spread your emotions, because you had an album to present your emotions on. Public Enemy was really one of the first groups that was an album-oriented rap group just like rock. "We're gonna give you a bunch of different feelings and a diversity of attitudes and ideals and points of view." Rap artists in the nineties were album-oriented. They could actually go and give a whole host of different emotional outlets to the music and rhymes and vernaculars. You had to come from a perspective where you understood other musics, not just a perspective about the next hot single. When I was comin up, or people like Tupac were comin up, we had to know about American culture. We had a big dosage, and it wasn't an uncool thing to get, because it's just how it was. At that turning point when Tupac comes out, then you start to see it polarizing into a Black or white upbringing. White American youth, all of a sudden, become hip with Black culture. But also at that time, it seemed like our culture was being promoted and projected, and now twenty years later, in Black culture it's not a hip thing to pick up on this aspect of American culture and musical contributions.

Tell us about Common and your book *One Day It'll All Make Sense.*[11] He's one of the greats.

BRADLEY: How do you write with and for somebody who has such a recognizable voice? And I mean both the vocal instrument itself and the things that he says in the world. It's the same thing with you. You have one of the most recognizable voices, not just in hip hop but in American culture. Common is a bit like that. The biggest challenge as a writer was how do I find a way to inhabit that voice to make it both mine and his and yet neither of ours? I found it in a very unusual moment. I would carry my phone around in my pocket with the recording on, and we would just vibe. We would hang out. We'd go to the studio, because he was working on an album at the time. We would drive up and down Pacific Coast Highway and just talk. We were just cool, and we became friends very fast. In the process, I came to know his voice.

One night after hangin out with him, back at my hotel, trying to fall asleep, the opening lines of the book came to my head. "When I was six months old, my mother and I were held at gunpoint. My father held the gun." It was off to the races after that! I had the voice locked in. I could write in his voice. I would listen to his stories. I wouldn't even look at my notes. I would just vibe off of what he said in the voice that I had fashioned. By the end of it, his mom read the book and said, "That's my son." That's better than any accolade or *New York Times* best-seller recognition.

CHUCK D: It's one of the great books. We're in a genre where we need a thousand books. We also need a great directory of all the hip hop books ever that would actually let everybody know where something is at.

BRADLEY: Particularly for a culture like ours that was born outside of recorded history in a sense—in the oral tradition, born out of rumor, myth, and legend. It is still all of those things, even as it's also captured on wax and in print. That's where the academy's influence on hip hop can be, as students, professors, and staff members at universities, not to try to cage rap music or hip hop culture but rather to do that descriptive work you talked about to enhance people's appreciation and understanding. We need to create foundations that will never erode, that won't get lost to time. As writers, thinkers, and scholars, that's how we can contribute to the culture.

CHUCK D: With all that's going on in education, post-pandemic sadness, depression, even in the school system, they're not really able to have students' souls connected to what they need to learn or embrace. They're not able to deliver the knowledge and have meaningful interactions. We see these schisms growing. You have the RAP Lab—the Laboratory for Race and Popular Culture—and it is something that uses the art form and lyrics to open people up a bit.[12]

BRADLEY: I founded the RAP Lab almost a decade ago now, and the vision at the time was to galvanize young people, incarcerated populations, folks that are often cut off from the flow of the culture to connect them to the best, cutting-edge scholarship. The goal was to connect them to it in an organic way and to be receptive to the knowledge that was coming from the outside in. That often took the shape of onetime engagements with classes. Other times, it would be more long-term, embedded experiences. I have my graduate student, Alexander Williams, in the crowd right now, who was at University of Colorado Boulder with me and has come out to UCLA to help me build this lab. He and I share this vision that hip hop is something that can radically open people's minds and create new foundations for confidence. For instance, I did a shadow class at a Colorado penitentiary on Tupac as I was doing the same class on campus. The guys behind bars got the same materials. They did all the homework, all the writing, and got the same feedback. That was a powerful thing for me as a teacher to see the poignancy and the eloquence that these young brothers, mostly brothers, were doing in response to Tupac.

Right now, I'm looking to connect the RAP Lab to what's already going on here with the UCLA Hip Hop Initiative, which is really something special with what Dr. H. Samy Alim, Samuel Lamontagne, Tabia Shawel, and others have done here to create something that is going to be a center of gravity for the study of hip hop music and culture. For the RAP Lab to be part of that, I'm just so blessed and fortunate to join the faculty here to help build the next generation.

CHUCK D: Let's open it up to Q&A. Let's go.

QUESTION 1: Professor Bradley, in your foreword, Professor Henry Louis Gates Jr. mentioned how rapping was originally something else. Could you talk a little bit about that? Professor Chuck, you mentioned the

Smithsonian exhibit, and I noticed you donated to it. I noticed there's a big, beautiful book for sale too. Who benefits from that sale?

CHUCK D: Adam benefits from it! Nah, I'm just kidding. It's an unbelievable piece of work. Dr. Bradley and so many others contributed to look at hip hop from an academic point of view as something that's culturally misunderstood. The fact that we have people who have grown up in the culture that will play an important part in narrating the culture, I thought was the best thing that could ever happen. The culture is in good hands and good minds, and not as just a beginning or ending, but something that continues the narrative in the best manner. My donation to the National Museum of African American History and Culture [NMAAHC] was just a bunch of things that I had in storage like Public Enemy banners and so on. Timothy Anne Burnside, at the NMAAHC, was of tremendous help to me when I was looking at the museum, when it was a cardboard model, so I immediately got on board. Then after you build it, what are you going to put in it? I was one of the people that said, "Well, if we're gonna put African American culture in this museum, you gotta include hip hop." I was at the right place, with the right person, at the right time. But then it doesn't start with me.

BRADLEY: To the earlier question about Gates's foreword, he started it off by connecting rapping to the larger Black tradition of the toast, these long narrative poems that were often extemporaneous expressions based on some common stories, "Shine & the Great Titanic," "The Signifying Monkey," for example, that would be passed down in the oral tradition.[13]

CHUCK D: You convinced Dr. Gates of the strength of this music. He's always been a pillar in our culture, but you really brought it home to him, and that's important.

BRADLEY: He's a big Pigmeat Markham guy too. He's all along that tradition. There's something about the improvisational quality that's so key. That's the through-line of all of this and inspired by repetition with a difference. That's the hallmark of Black expressive culture and the thing that knits the toasts and these comic routines with rapping.

QUESTION 2: What's the importance of having hip hop practitioners be part of this movement to not only advance the conversations around the music but also in terms of trying to penetrate the gatekeeping in academic institutions?

CHUCK D: It's important. For a long period, maybe a fifteen-to-twenty-year period, the media covered things like this, "The person that was caught robbing and knocking over the ATM machine was an aspiring rapper," or "These people were shot; they were aspiring rappers." To be called a rapper was used against you. When I was comin up, you couldn't use the word "rapper." You had to use something else. But now, it seems like that threshold has been broken and you can say you're a rapper and almost get the same respect as a guitarist.

BRADLEY: I think increasingly within the academy, too, there are folks who are bringing the performance element to the work that they do. We have artists moving into the academy. You're here at UCLA. I saw that Lupe Fiasco is going to be at MIT, for instance. Bun B's been down at Rice University, and 9th Wonder has been at Duke. You get all of these artists in the context of the classroom, and you also get folks from doctoral programs going into hip hop as part of what they do. There's a guy at the University of Virginia named A.D. Carson.[14] He was the first person I know to have his dissertation be an album. He's literally a professor of hip hop at UVA. Now, for my generation of academics, that wasn't an option. I've been called at times a "hip hop professor," but I still report to the English department. So things are changing.

QUESTION 3: More than ever there's a need for the oppressed to be heard. At the same time, corporate influences dictate what is heard by the masses. I'm not really an active artist. I'm a writer now, an academic. How can my voice be heard? We have very limited audiences, and oftentimes our work seems impenetrable to those outside of the academy.

BRADLEY: What it is to be an academic is changing in this moment, and our audience is changing. As an academic, you used to write to the twenty-five people in the world who happened to study the same little thing that you did. It is not the same anymore. I think hip hop is one of the influences, maybe one of the main influences, to expand the scope of academic discourse. My first book was on a trade press, that is, a commercial rather than an academic press. I write routinely in spaces that reach millions of people. I'm not saying that everybody's going to follow that path, but that path is open.

It is helpful to think about the moments in which voices get suppressed and the structures that govern our societies, but we also need to look at the loopholes that are available in this moment. There's so many ways to get your voice out there. This is true both for artists and academics. It's one thing we have in common. It used to be that there was a very narrow way to get your music into the world. You had to go with a major label. On the academic side, you had to go with a handful of academic publishers. Now there are all these open-source journals. There are other ways of getting your voice into the conversation. The gatekeepers, although they still exist, can't block all the gates of opportunity at once. We can bum-rush the show! There's something that someone from the Wu-Tang Clan said, "They can't stop all of us. If we all rush to the front door of the club, they might get three or four of us, but there's gonna be twenty of us that get in." I think that's what we gotta do. We just gotta bum-rush the culture and get our voices in there.

QUESTION 4: Professor Chuck, we talked about the creative impulse. How healthy was it that your anger informed your early artistic expression with the first three albums of Public Enemy?

CHUCK D: My anger came from knowing that I had to be a spokesperson for more than one or two individuals. It came from a collective look at how we as Black men were looked at in the 1980s especially. We come from the sixties and the seventies, so there's already a collective anger and political awareness that takes place. I was able to be the wordsmith for that and put the emotion verbally in the words, help out on the music, and create that atmosphere. We were kids in the sixties, so we knew the vibe. A lot of the samples even reflected some of that vibe too. That was transferrable. When they're closing the door on your face, how could you not transfer that anger into artistic expression? I was angry, but I was never confused. I was too old to be confused about what was happening to us.

I think you have to do more watching and listening when it comes down to expressing yourself. One thing is what you feel, but you have to be open to absorb your surroundings. Looking back at my younger self, I knew that that person was at least listening and watching before they was just comin off the top of their head with something. I was twenty-seven to thirty-one years old, so I had to absorb things from the older folks and then be able to drop something that was believable coming from me. It had to be honest.

QUESTION 5: In terms of freestyle rhyme ciphers, none of that ever gets documented anywhere. It just goes up in the air. I've seen MCs just close their eyes to visualize what they're going to say. Some people have described that as like a higher power speaking through that MC. Can freestyling be thought of as a practice that goes against commercializing the art form?

BRADLEY: I've been writing a piece, my latest one for the *New York Times*, and it's actually about visual arts. Something emerged from this work that resonates with what you've articulated about freestyle artists. The question is this: At any given moment, certain art is in the spotlight, and hip hop has been in the spotlight for a while—and a certain kind of hip hop, commercially available hip hop. But artists create in the absence of light as well. Artists create in the absence of recording and monetizing their work. Sometimes the most powerful art, as you said, enters the air and goes up to the heavens and lives in the moment of its conception and no longer. There's power in that kind of artistic expression. There's a power that I think has a spiritual component that's really profound and even in some ways achieves what recorded formats cannot. I am all in for having spaces for all of us creating for the sake of creation, for the sake of connecting in a communal context, for the sake of communing with nature, not always just for having a product at the end.

CHUCK D: The fact is that you can document it now, but also your cipher will document for your cipher's needs and purposes. Before, you couldn't document it as easily. You couldn't spread it as easily. I think it's in a good space, but it takes nurturing and care because it could slip into a bad space by not maintaining it or not making it diverse enough. The beautiful energy can actually propel it to good places.

QUESTION 6: We've heard Professor Bradley's analysis of hip hop poetics. A few sessions ago, we heard Professor Scot Brown mention how you were a rhyme innovator [see chapter 4], and he asked us to listen to "Bring the Noise" as an example of how you were doing "the triplet flow" before a lot of cats were doing it. Who were some MCs that impacted you?

CHUCK D: To me, my favorite MCs of all time are Run D.M.C. Their music, objective, visuals. They were able to entertain, where a lotta times, rhymers usually miss one or two elements. They had it all. Rakim changed the style of hip hop rhyming in 1986/87 with "Eric B Is President" and then "My Melody," where he was the first MC that didn't rhyme to the beat. The beat rhymed to him. He and KRS-One were poets. But as I've said before, Rakim is our Miles Davis. He was like Louis Armstrong to jazz phrasing. The beat followed him. When I did *Yo! Bum Rush the Show,* I was on another beat trying to catch up with the beat. But when I heard Rakim, he changed the phrasing of hip hop. Melle Mel's like Wilt Chamberlain. Number two was Kool Moe Dee, but he was way down at number two. Even he himself admitted it. When I first heard Melle Mel, I'm like, "How the . . . ?!" He doesn't get talked about, because he came out so early. And then Ice Cube, particularly "How the West Was Won." So, me and my homie Ice-T, we're in the category of kind of lookin at this talent and activity going on. LL Cool J. If you got thousands of people in a stadium, he got everybody eating out his hand in the concert. So there's some greats out there.

The nineties brought on a whole different level of accents, styles, and flows. In terms of the nineties, I liked Method Man and Redman for a lotta different reasons. I like both of their voices. I like their style. I like their flow. I like when they work together. I like the fact that Redman is quite simplistic, and he uses his words like blocks and comes up with good phrases. I like Method Man's menacing stanzas, you know what I'm saying? He has great metaphors. And I liked DMX's energy [RIP]. Back when Jay-Z did the Hard Knock Life Tour, I thought what Jay-Z brought to the table was rap's first lyrical rhyme circus or some shit like that, the P. T. Barnum of rhyme. He just brought a lot of cats that brought different characters down and damn near—I could kind of see them doing like lyrical gymnastics on trampolines, you know what I'm saying? Somersaults and shit. He brought out Beanie Sigel. Memphis Bleek did his thing. Amil was there. I listened to everything. I could go on, but we gotta thank Professor Adam Bradley for being with us tonight.

BRADLEY: It's so good to be with you and with this class and the energy that you all have built here. It's contagious. I'm gonna take it with me and just keep doing the work. Thank you so much for this.

CHUCK D: Everybody in this class knows that they're not just students; they're teachers as well. And then we become the students too. From my perspective, as somebody that listens, watches, and studies, I've been at the back of the classroom while y'all been in the front this whole time. Sam and Tabia and Dr. Alim, we all understand that we're students, too, watching y'all.

NOTES

1. See H. Samy Alim, "'Every syllable of mine is an umbilical cord through time': Toward an Analytical Schema of Hip Hop Poetics," in *Roc the Mic Right: The Language of Hip Hop Culture* (Routledge, 2006), 126–54.

2. "The Heart Part 5" was released with a video in May 2022 just weeks prior to this lecture, as the first single of Kendrick Lamar's *Mr. Morale & the Big Steppers*.

3. See Adam Bradley and Andrew DuBois, *The Anthology of Rap* (Yale University Press, 2013).

4. See Adam Bradley, *Book of Rhymes: The Poetics of Hip Hop* (Basic Civitas, 2009).

5. See H. Samy Alim, Awad Ibrahim, and Alastair Pennycook, eds., *Global Linguistic Flows: Hip Hop Cultures, Youth Identities, and the Politics of Language* (Routledge, 2009); and Marina Terkourafi, *The Languages of Global Hip-Hop* (Bloomsbury, 2010). See also Quentin Williams and Jaspal Singh, *Global Hiphopography* (Springer, 2023).

6. See Adam Bradley, "The Artists Dismantling the Barriers between Rap and Poetry," *New York Times*, March 4, 2021, https://www.nytimes.com/2021/03/04/t-magazine/rap-hiphop-poetry.html.

7. See Houston A. Baker, "A Many-Colored Coat of Dreams: The Poetry of Countee Cullen," in *Afro-American Poetics: Revisions of Harlem and the Black Aesthetic* (University of Wisconsin Press, 1988), 45–87; and Arnold Rampersad, "The Poetry of the Harlem Renaissance," in *The Columbia History of American Poetry*, ed. Jay Parini (Columbia University Press, 1993), 452–77.

8. See Henry Louis Gates Jr. and Kwame A. Appiah, eds., *Zora Neale Hurston: Critical Perspectives Past and Present* (Amistad, 1993); and Irma McClaurin, ed., *Black Feminist Anthropology: Theory, Politics, Praxis, and Poetics* (Rutgers University Press, 2001).

9. See Jay-Z, *Decoded* (Random House, 2010), with dream hampton.

10. See *The Smithsonian Anthology of Hip-Hop and Rap* (Smithsonian Folkways Recordings, 2021), a multimedia collection.

11. See Common with Adam Bradley, *One Day It'll All Make Sense* (Simon & Schuster, 2011).

12. The RAP Lab (Laboratory for Race and Popular Culture) is an interdisciplinary space for developing and exchanging ideas at the intersection of race and popular culture.

13. See Henry Louis Gates Jr., *The Signifying Monkey: A Theory of African-American Literary Criticism* (Oxford University Press, 1988).

14. See A. D. Carson, "Owning My Masters: The Rhetorics of Rhymes and Revolutions," PhD diss., Clemson University, 2017.

10 Show 'Em Whatcha Got

HIP HOP AND THE VISUAL ARTS

Chuck D and Joan Morgan

H. SAMY ALIM: Our last public event at the California African American Museum was held on March 11, 2020. We featured Rakim, Talib Kweli, and Chuck D himself on that evening. Now what happened the morning of March 12, 2020? The pandemic shut LA *down*. I can't tell you how happy we are to be back in this space again with Chuck D and to be here with all of you, as we keep on marching through. As faculty director of the UCLA Hip Hop Initiative, I'd like to acknowledge the tremendous work of Tabia Shawel, the assistant director of the Ralph J. Bunche Center for African American Studies at UCLA, and PhD student Samuel Lamontagne, who will soon be Dr. Samuel Lamontagne as he wraps up his dissertation. Without them, and without the support of Bunche Center director Kelly Lytle Hernandez and Bunche associate director Gaye Theresa Johnson and the support of the California Legislative Black Caucus, none of this would be possible. Of course, Kevin Abrantes, Lorrie Boula, Dominique, and everyone at Soul Kitchen Music, thank you all very much. We're eternally grateful.

It's time to welcome Professor Chuck D! Rapper, producer, graphic artist, author, and political activist, Chuck D rose to prominence through his groundbreaking, politically conscious hip hop recordings and performances. Chuck D assembled DJ Terminator X, Professor Griff, and Flavor

Flav, along with Hank Shocklee and Bill Stephney, to form one of the most prominent and powerful hip hop groups of all time, Public Enemy, who was inducted into the Rock & Roll Hall of Fame in 2013 and honored with a Grammy Lifetime Achievement Award. From *Yo! Bum Rush the Show* to *It Takes a Nation of Millions* to *Hold Us Back* to *Fear of a Black Planet*, Chuck D's booming voice urged us not to believe the hype and always fight the power. As the UCLA Hip Hop Initiative's inaugural artist-in-residence, he teaches undergraduate and graduate students about the history, evolution, and futures of hip hop culture, bustin up many long-held myths about hip hop along the way. Professor Chuck, as the students on campus affectionately refer to him, has not only been incredibly generous with his time, but he's also dropped knowledge and wisdom on us for *ten straight weeks*, giving us all an opportunity to learn at the feet of one of the major figures of the hip hop cultural movement. On behalf of all of your students, Chuck, at UCLA and all of us at the Hip Hop Initiative and the Ralph J. Bunche Center and the Department of Anthropology, a deep, heartfelt thank you. Please give it up for Chuck D! [*Applause.*]

Now I have the distinct pleasure of introducing my long time friend and colleague, Dr. Joan Morgan. Believe me when I tell you that we couldn't have found a better interlocutor for tonight's conversation. Dr. Joan Morgan is the program director of the Center for Black Visual Culture at New York University. She is an award-winning cultural critic, feminist author, Grammy-nominated songwriter, and pioneering hip hop journalist. Morgan coined the term "hip hop feminism" in 1999 when she published the groundbreaking book *When Chickenheads Come Home to Roost: A Hip-Hop Feminist Breaks It Down*, which is taught at universities globally.[1] I myself, as Joan knows, have taught the book repeatedly in all my hip hop courses. Regarded internationally as an expert on the topics of hip hop, race, and gender, Dr. Morgan has made numerous television, radio, and film appearances, among them HBO Max, Netflix, Lifetime, MTV, BET, VH1, CNN, WB Eyes, the Spin, and MSNBC. She has written for numerous publications including *Vibe, Essence,* and *British Vogue.*

Dr. Morgan has been a visiting scholar at the New School, Vanderbilt, and Duke University and a visiting assistant professor at the School of Cultural Analysis at NYU. She was a visiting lecturer at Stanford University's Institute for Diversity in the Arts, where she was awarded the prestigious Dr. St. Clair Drake Teaching Award. She is the first visiting scholar to ever receive it, and I'm smiling because I know how prestigious that award is and the incredible work you did with those students, Joan. In fact, earlier today, Joan and I had a chance to visit an amazing art exhibition by one of our mutual former students, Kiyan Williams, at the Hammer Museum.[2] The reverberations from Joan's time with us on campus are still being felt, and the fruit continues to be borne until this day. Not only does Joan continue to mentor her former students, she's a mentor for Unlock Her Potential and serves on the board of trustees for the National Young Arts Foundation. And you heard it here first, folks: she's currently working on a screenplay adaptation of her first book, which has been optioned for screen rights! I am happy to say that in 2024–25, the UCLA Hip Hop Initiative will celebrate the twenty-fifth anniversary of *Chickenheads* and hip hop feminism with Dr. Morgan as our artist-in-residence!

Along with Chuck D, Jeff Chang, Brian Cross, Davey D, dream hampton, Emile YX?, Medusa, and Ben Caldwell, Joan Morgan is a member of the UCLA Hip Hop Initiative's National Advisory Board. Please put your hands together for Dr. Joan Morgan. [*Applause.*]

CHUCK D: Thank you. Dr. Morgan, we seem to do this once every fifteen years, right?

JOAN MORGAN: Yes! I'm laughing because you have known me way before I was Dr. Morgan, so hearing you say it is like, "Oh, yeah. Okay." [*Laughter.*]

CHUCK D: It's a beautiful thing. I tell people that your status doesn't happen overnight. This class has been a great joy and pleasure. I have to say this to get it started right quick. To the student body of this class, raise your hands today in the audience, ANTHRO 159: Rap, Race, and Reality with Public Enemy's Chuck D. Thank you for *every moment*. We've shared a lot of beautiful moments during this ten week program, which concludes with the best for last. What we talked about in each one of those ten weeks, it will last beyond the ten weeks. Every second, every dynamic moment, will last a lifetime, to dispel all the myths, to be able to look at yourself and say, "I am the art, I am the culture," and to be able to take it forward. When people step to you in the middle of the barbershops, salon, bar, middle of a sports game, or whatever, and they tell you what hip hop is and what it ain't, you can maybe not get confrontational, but you can kind of look at them and roll your eyes and say, "Okay, look, I got the best learning," and you turn into a teacher yourself. We learned as much as we taught, and big thanks to Tabia Shawel, Samuel Lamontagne, and Dr. H. Samy Alim. Yo, he's a genius with an uppercase G, because what he envisioned in his mind he made happen and manifest to this point today. Reaching back to the last moment that we were here the day before the pandemic, like he said, when myself, Rakim, and Talib Kweli talked about something that he manifested into being a course at UCLA. It's always a collective effort. I hope many wonderful things come out of this collaboration. Give yourselves a round of applause. And we hope nothing happens tomorrow. [*Laughter.*]

Now, I told Dr. Morgan earlier today, "I got some difficult questions to ask you," but knowing me as the class does, these questions are not difficult for *you*. They're difficult for *me* to ask.

MORGAN: I thought I was the one to ask difficult questions, but okay.

CHUCK D: You know, as we say, we don't have lectures; we have conversations. And the conversations are cyclical rather than cynical. They go round and round, and she's from New York, so she knows how verses and bars go more than anybody. She's written bars and books. When you read *When Chickenheads Come Home to Roost*, you say, "Well, damn, I can retain this!" I've known this lady for a long time, but I could have sworn *Chickenheads* was out in '86, but really '99 was the year. I think it was the buildup, because you was always movin and shakin in all the right circles and putting the voice out there. Me and Harry Allen, we'd run into you, and we'd run into each other at universities around the country and be on panels.

MORGAN: I really want to start this by thanking everyone for having me here. To Samy Alim, as always, I thank you for your vision and for the expansiveness and generosity of the spirit with which you do this work. Thank you for always being so visionary, for never thinking about hip hop in a small way, for always believing that it could do big things. We actually met at Stanford a gazillion years ago at one of the very first hip hop conferences that Stanford ever did in 2006. I think that he's just always believed in the culture as being rich, impactful, and important. When someone around you believes in it in that way, they encourage you to keep seeing it that way too. What you do really does make incredible things possible and it changes people's lives. I think that's important to acknowledge.

To Chuck, I want to acknowledge something to you. I've been writing about hip hop for a long time, and when I started writing about it, I want to say that's maybe like '88, '89, there was not a lot of support. It's telling that your visual artwork of Ice Cube is on display here tonight because that's one of the first hip hop pieces I ever wrote for the *Village Voice*. I was saying a lot of things that were not popular at that time about hip hop, misogyny, and men's role in it, and women's role in it. Sometimes at the *Village Voice* they would just point me to my hate mail. That is no exaggeration. I was very young, maybe twenty-four or twenty-five years old. Chuck was one of the few male artists who always let me know, "Keep doing what you are doing. You are doing exactly the right thing."

To everyone here, I also want to publicly acknowledge that Chuck D is the best person to lead us through this journey of hip hop because it's rare when you find someone who has literally laid the cornerstone and foundation of the culture, guided us through its most embryonic stages, grounded us through its really difficult growth periods—through massive capitalist growth, through massive commercialism, through the really terrible bouts of misogyny, through regional shifts and changes. Chuck can tell you when hip hop was really just localized in New York, and then of course he has that great quote that it became the CNN of Black America. Hip hop has gone through so many growing pains, and he has been there every step of the way, never really receding, never becoming a passive voice, never letting us doubt his investment. In many ways, I think he's been that guiding father figure from the very beginning, even as a very young man. So I thank you for always encouraging me, for believing in me and my work, and for passing my work on to your daughters. You felt like that was important to do. You've just been a champion for me for all these decades and I cannot thank you enough for that.

CHUCK D: We had intent to do the right thing. We were doing art, we were doing music, but we needed you. Even if I gave you a sword to chop my head off, that's what had to happen for the balance of the music. In my first couple of records, I was very clear on what I felt. I also feel that the ability to make albums at a particular time allowed me to counter that with a balance. If it wasn't for a person like you putting it out into the world, like, "Okay, listen, we're here too. We got to all be accountable to this," we wouldn't have had that balance. This is at the tail end of the eighties, at the top of the nineties. The nineties was a period that was really a rough mixed bag of anything and everything coming out. What we were able to deal with in my prime time at the beginning of the nineties as opposed to the end of the nineties, led into your book, and you saw a lot of things that culminated at the end of your articles. Not only did we *need* you at the end of the eighties, but we needed you in the nineties too. But how did you feel at the *end* of the nineties?

MORGAN: And then I have a question for you. At the end of the nineties, I was pregnant with my son, who is now here and twenty-three years old. He was always a blessing, but I was so glad that he came at that time because it almost gave me permission to step out. The end of the nineties, for us particularly, it was the rise of so much. It was like hip hop had gone from being this small, cultural, intimate phenomenon where we all kind of knew each other to being a multibillion dollar industry. I don't know how many of you live in gentrified neighborhoods right now and you're feeling and experiencing the violence of gentrification. Imagine that kind of violence amplified into a culture that grew and shaped you and you knew something drastic and potentially really hazardous was about to happen. At the same time, you were powerless to completely stop it. Also, you needed in some ways for the music to become the dominant force that it eventually became.

On the fiftieth anniversary of hip hop, defining the culture is still something that those of us who have grown up in the culture really struggle with in many ways. How did you grow up with this thing that has raised you and defined you? We used to have a very convenient answer: "It's the four elements. It's rap, it's graffiti, it's dance, it's the DJing." But it's become so much more than that. It's time to reconsider what hip hop is. To me, though, hip hop is always home. Hip hop is the thing that made me. Hip hop is the thing that shapes me. Hip hop is also the thing that frustrates me the most, and it's also one of the things that has brought me the most joy.

In the nineties, hip hop made a lot of what I call devil's bargains at the crossroads, particularly for me as a woman. I wrote about this in *She Begat This: Twenty Years of the Miseducation of Lauryn Hill.*[3] All of a sudden it was like, here is the red velvet rope, and the women who helped build this culture, make this culture, enjoy this culture, we were the first ones that you tossed out. I never questioned if women have a role in hip hop. I don't understand how to *not* have a role in hip hop. I literally grew up on its teat. It milked and nursed me. All of a sudden we were being discussed as "the woman problem." I felt angry. I felt betrayed in many ways. We put a lot on Lauryn Hill's shoulders, as if we expected her to save the genre. There were musical things happening and some of the music was really great. Some of it really was not. It was just commercial, you know? I'm coming from a period where every single hip hop album that dropped in the late eighties, you wanted to own it because it was important. So it was a difficult time, and having my son in some ways gave me a way to step back.

In stepping back, that's how I could produce *Chickenheads*. I needed the time to really reflect and think about this shifting landscape and what I needed to do to navigate it and to work out my relationship with feminism. Because what I was constantly being told is that those two things can't coexist. "You can't love hip hop *and* be a feminist." I needed to reconcile that for myself first and then present my argument to the world.

One of the things I also want folks to know about Chuck is that writing about hip hop in the nineties could be dangerous, like physically dangerous. If people didn't like what you said, they would absolutely step to you *hard*. It wasn't an exchange of words. There are plenty of hip hop journalists who have caught pretty bad beat-downs by angry artists. Our dear friend Greg Tate, who has recently passed, one of the things I learned from Tate was that you can criticize something that you love in a paper and it'd be okay [see chapter 7]. One of the reasons that I knew it was okay, Chuck, was the way you dealt with it. You weren't trying to beat nobody down, you know what I mean? You were really interested. You didn't agree with all of what he said, for sure, but you were really genuinely present for the engagement. It taught me a model of how artists and critics, who both love a culture, could engage each other for the betterment of the culture. I think that's a really important quality and moment with you that people don't really know about enough.

CHUCK D: It was a time when, I think, my years helped me. I was a college graduate by 1984. We talked about hip hop every day and every night from 1980 to 1984. We thought we were scientists in it. We thought it was good boxing. It was good verbal sparring, as far as words and opinions and philosophies. I remember one time it was me, Robert Christgau, and Greg Tate at *The Voice* goin at it, challenging me on Frantz Fanon [see chapter 6].[4] I'm like, "I'm not fuckin reading Frantz Fanon today!" [*Laughter.*] It was good. It ended good. At the same time, you felt a little isolated because here I'm bringing these invisible battles at another level. Meanwhile, the next ten years coming in, who's going to speak up for that?

I've been explaining to the class that if I wanted to separate the eighties and the nineties, you had collectives, and you had groups, and you even had all women groups. They had their collectives and the men had groups. Very rarely did you have a soloist that would capture someone's attention long enough to be like, "Okay, but I'm going to get back to my group thing," whether it be Salt-N-Pepa or Finesse & Synquis or Wee Papa Girl Rappers from the UK, and Stetsasonic, or even a combination like Digable Planets at the edge of the nineties. It was a group thing. I make a lot of comparisons to the game of baseball where in the 1970s the game of baseball with Black people was still hot.

I remember in 1979, knowing that I'm going to vote for a president in 1980, and I voted for Angela Davis. I fell victim to the numbers, math, and the game of politics. I was like, "Wow, it was Ronald Wilson Reagan versus Jimmy Carter. Every vote that wasn't for Carter was gonna be a vote somewhere else, and Reagan's gonna get in." Then came twelve years, the reign of terror.

For some reason, I'm out there in Long Island, and there's an influx of super cocaine and guns. You couldn't find a gun in Roosevelt in 1975. You might find them in the Bronx in 1972, but you found the guns from former veterans, cats that kept their toolies in the closet or grandpas that didn't want their daughters met. You had guns, but you ain't have ammo. All of a sudden, I could get a gun from anywhere. That happened in the Bronx around '74, '75. It happened in Long Island, '78, '79. Then you got the whole 1980s. That was the beginning of the destruction of the Black neighborhood and collectivism. We weren't doing things collectively. We were doing things solo.

The last situation for this collectivity in our music was maybe we could do it like the Temptations did it. We could do it like the O'Jays,

Commodores, the groups in the seventies and the sixties, Motown and all that. In rap music and hip hop, we gonna Grandmaster Flash and Furious Five it. We're gonna Sequence it, or Sugarhill Gang it. We're going to still be a collective. That changed after the 1980s. "We'll isolate you to one person, and then we're going to start picking it apart." So we always talk about, "Yeah, it's a billion dollar industry in the year 2000," but rest assured, ain't no Black hand near the cash register. So we had arguments in the beginning, but we all kind of knew where it was headed too.

MORGAN: I have a question for the audience. How many of you knew that Chuck was a visual artist? People don't know that about you.

CHUCK D: But they don't know nothing about me. [*Laughter.*] I come from the era—and you're very familiar with this—the era that I'm coming from, born in 1960, it was sort of like, you ain't in grown folks business nor do you want to be in grown folks business. But really, more importantly, grown folks ain't trying to be in your business either. That's a different world since the year 2000 with gadgetry. Back in the day, it wasn't offensive to say, "No, that's none of your business." That is a clear statement; it's not offensive. "Yo, Chuck, what's up man? How you blah-blah-blah," "It's none of your business." Today when you say it and when you actually text it uppercase, then you got somebody waiting outside your virtual door. So I might have been whatever, but I would tell people they don't need to know this about me. Better yet, was I one of the producers of the Bomb Squad? Yeah, but you know me as Chuck D, the MC. I don't need to be that dude too.

But in Iso-ball, as they say in basketball, or in solo world, now everybody gotta be like, "Oh, I could do it all!" In the multitasking era, now they've all turned into, "Okay, my résumé is that I'm a jack of all trades, and I'm the master at the same time of everything." That isn't true when you talk about the assembly line of production and getting things done in regular life. Whatever happened to "What I can't do, you can do, and whatever you can't do, I could do, and together we got a team to make it really solid and strong." Especially when you had groups like Digable Planets and the Fugees. With the Fugees, you had Lauryn Hill, Pras, and Wyclef. The three of them covered the total ground of how we wanted to feel as a community, even when the community was being shattered up.

MORGAN: I want to talk to you a little bit about process, because there were things with the artwork that the audience isn't privy to. When I think of you as an MC, it is the voice. I can't ever forget the first time I heard it. I mean, Chuck's boom is *commanding*. It's like, "Stop every fucking thing that you're doing and listen to me right now."

CHUCK D: Y'all should have heard Lorenzo Ridenhour. When my father talked, he could yell over a mountain. As a kid, you could not go up to him and say that you didn't hear him calling you. You couldn't say no, because *everybody* heard him. So a lot of my voice is DNA. But just being loud ain't enough. Then you gotta do the work of what you're going to say with that volume. So I don't know, as far as talking about my art, it's unfair for me and what I've done in music as an MC to be connected with my visuals. Although, as we've talked about also in class, today people tend to listen with their eyes. We're in a visual age. Matter of fact, listening is increasingly becoming a quality of the past. People got to see in order to believe. We're in the era of sight, sound, story, and style. And sound might be all the way at the bottom.

I know sometimes when you teach a class and if you're up front talking, you think about how you can animate what you're saying so students can see your words. Maybe thirty years ago, one way to embellish your words was with volume, because everything everybody listened to was loud, whether it was good or wack. But we're in a time right now where volume ain't always the answer to everything. We gotta get to a point where we are listening, because listening today is what we used to call "the fine print." You want a new app on your phone and the first thing you want to do is scroll and press, "I accept."

Visually, I was always an expressive person. I come from the 1970s and 1980s. For example, when I was in art class, nude models was every minute. I would do a three-hour class with nude models, and then my boys would come up to the campus to throw down a party, and they'd look at my portfolio and want to come up to the class. I was like, "It's a different thing, dawg. It's different." "Yeah, can we hang up there?" "No, no, you cannot." But it was easier to explain what art was and wasn't, especially to those knuckleheads. Today it is a blur between what is art and what is not art. People are into the arts because they are taught to purchase the arts, but do they know the arts and where the arts come from? What role does art have right now? We're at a point where we might need it to be loud, or we might need it to expose some things, especially as we're heading into fascism.

MORGAN: I mean, they're good questions, but I think they've been the questions we've been asking in terms of the art world for a long time. Who has the right to really direct the art market is another one, right? Because so often those are the people who can afford to buy art, and in particular, *our* art. Deborah Roberts is one of my favorite artists.[5] Unless something drastic happens, there won't be a Deborah Roberts piece hanging in my home. So our connection to art, even as Black and Brown people, even if we love it, is different than the people who can purchase it.

I'm going to come back to this question, but I don't want to lose this thing on volume, because I think that you said something really important about how you make people listen. When I look at the quality of your visual artwork, there is a consistent thread that I've seen in the maybe thirty pieces of yours that I've looked at. If this was sonic, I would say it was somebody turning down the volume so that you all would have to lean in and listen, which is such an interesting choice for somebody who is considered having one of the most commanding voices in hip hop. Not just loud, but also no one flows like you. No one is supposed to be able to rap at the volume that you do and flow the way that you do. I used to just sit, listen to it, and be like, "What kind of voodoo science is this, really?" But then these visual pieces make you kind of lean in to hear what's being said, if they were sonic. They're softer pieces that make you ask different kinds of questions. These on display tonight are portraits, but you have other pieces that look like they're tour-scapes, or almost like internal thoughts of what the DJ is thinking while he's spinning. I just want you to talk about that a little bit.

CHUCK D: One word. And it's not what you think it is. Ayahuasca. Listen to me when I tell you all. Listen. That doesn't mean you'll go out there and look for DMT [dimethyltryptamine] on every street corner. My dad passed away in 2016. This is somebody I talked to every day for fifty-five years. After he passed, the silence was deafening. I was introducing myself into the arts and going back and forth. I had already toured 116 countries. When you tour as much as I tour, that is fantastic. You're playing stadiums. People are screaming. But it's your downtime that you have to maximize. I created my visual art a lot of times in hotels. I had to turn my hotel room into a studio. What led into that, coincidentally, it wasn't an escape as I got back into my art. But one time, I wanted to know where my dad's spirit was, and I was just toying with my art. Of course, I'm writing music, toying with my art, kind of doing things on the phone apps. At that point—and I'll be real brief with this—everyone's telling me, "Oh, yeah, his spirit is in a better place," like, all this stuff you've been hearing for half a century. Yo, really, I was hearing it, and all this is cool and all, but I needed to know somewhere where I can get an answer to this silence.

Then it was suggested to me by one of my bandmates, Tim Commerford of Rage Against the Machine. We have the Prophets of Rage group.[6] He told me about one time when he did DMT. He was so descriptive, but he was describing something that happened twenty years earlier. He said he only did it once, but he was so descriptive. And then my Pilates coach said that she's actually part of a community. This is not long after my dad passed. I said, "This could be like an answer for me that nothing else has given me." Matter of fact, my daughter was like, "Daddy, try weed first or something!" [*Laughter.*]

And my camp shaman, she was a Philadelphia coach from Peru, she had been trained by the best. She came and gave me a one-on-one session for four hours, and it was like a complete looking inside. She realized I had no trauma, no scar tissue inside. I felt it. It was funny as a muthafucka. The room started bending and all that. Then I was like, "Okay." And I heard somewhere, I mean for a split second, "Son, I love you." It was almost like my voice. I kind of sound like him. It goes right through the middle of my head! I knew I wasn't imagining shit. Matter of fact, halfway through the door in my office swung open and stayed there. I was like, "What the fuck?" Then Pat said, "Oh, yes, alright, that's not him." I was like, "Yeah, but when I come down off this journey, I'm gonna check this door out and see what's happening." Even to this day, I still stare at the door. Long story short, I felt I had the answer I was looking for.

One year later, in 2018, I had enough. I don't have to do it again, but I decided to do it with a community. It was about eight or nine people there. I said, "Okay, I kind of got the answers before, but I'm doing it again a year later in a tribute anniversary." So I said to my Pilates coach, it was at her house, "Give me a stack of paper and bring me down some pens." Now this is real shit, y'all. It doesn't mean it's going to work for everybody, because everybody responds in their own way. She gave me a stack of paper and a stack of pens. We had the ayahuasca administered. Ayahuasca is the psychedelic sacrament; DMT is the material from plants. It's illegal. It was administered at the top of the four hours. I did eighty-three illustrations in four hours! I just sat in one spot in the living room, and my hands were moving and drawing from the energy. Now, a sketching technique is you usually do the outline and you go in. That has been true my whole life. This was different. I was sketching the energy and it formed the outline for eighty-three illustrations. The thing about it, when I was doing it, I didn't have to look at the paper, and my head was clear as a bell, like we're talking right now. When I stopped, then the room started to bend. I was looking back to my hand, and it was just doing the illustrations. When you come down, of course, you rest, you take your enzyme, or whatever. My hands were doing this [moving on their own]. From that point on, I made eighteen thousand illustrations. *Eighteen thousand.*

All these illustrations are actually almost all dealing with how we see energy from the universe. Somebody might look at my illustrations, and I can't even release them publicly because they'll be like, "What the fuck?" They'll say, "They're dope though." [*Laughter.*] Then they'll end up saying, "Well, I don't think this comes from you." And I'm like, "Yeah, these are not Chuck D illustrations." I'll explain what I mean. You're seeing the style actually come out very kinetic. I have a kinetic style, and I learn how to actually do the inside working to the outside, with a little outside working into the inside. They're illustrations. They're not paintings, but they are also renditions. This is why I tell people, "When you talk about artists, art is short for artificial." It means it's a facsimile of life. You don't have to produce carbon copies. People think an artist is somebody who gives you photo realism. We know photo realists like Chuck Close and people like that, or whatever people want to post on Twitter or Instagram. But art training means to think about what you can do coming from you to interpret what you see, not only what you see, but what you hear, and most of all, what you feel. That's art interpretation without trying to be purist about it. A lot of times, when I talk to people who want to be artists and they want to have a photo, I say, "You have the photo, but look away from the photo." Look at the photo for two seconds, work away from it for twenty, and then you'll start to create art. Art is also not a thing where there is competition, because it comes from within yourself. It's not competing against anything.

But also, Joan, back to the original conversation about music, hip hop comes from a time where you had to discover and carve out your own identity. You didn't sound like nobody else, and if somebody sounded like you, they was biting your style. So they couldn't bite your style if your style was really unique. "Damn, I can't bite LL Cool J because that dude is just like . . ." It's about refining whatever you're good at manifesting into greatness so you can be only imitated but never duplicated. That's the biggest difference in the beginnings of hip hop and rap music, that they could not duplicate some of these individuals. They could not duplicate a group. Even if the group had individual members that could be duplicated, you could not duplicate them together when they were a unit. That was the strength of rap music and hip hop, being unduplicated by any other art form. Rock bands get it. Because when Paul McCartney and John Lennon and then Ringo Starr and George Harrison got together as the Beatles, and then they played together for like a year straight every day in Hamburg, Germany, when they come out of there, it's gonna be magic that you can't even explain.

MORGAN: Thank you, Chuck. I think Samy's giving us that look. It's time for Q&A.

ALIM: We got a lot of beautiful people in the house with us. Chuck, I gotta tell you publicly, when I first looked at this work, it is haunting. It makes you *feel* immediately. It draws you in. In fact, it captivated me and brought me closer to the object. It's very emotive. I don't expect to be able to be drawn in in that way. Everyone please come up here after this conversation and really take some time to view Chuck's beautiful artwork. We have Chuck's portraits of Prince, Ice Cube, and Nina Simone.

QUESTION 1: To Joan, what would you like hip hop scholars to focus on in the future?

MORGAN: I would like scholars at the UCLA Hip Hop Initiative to take a really expansive approach when considering the contributions of hip hop. There's obviously the music. There's obviously graffiti. There's obviously great dance culture, but there's so many things that aren't really that obvious. For example, so many of your screenwriters now, the shows that we're talking about with Black content on Netflix, those guys started as hip hop journalists, people who have gone on to make major moves beyond the hip hop context. Some have become major stylists or makeup artists. Hip hop was a birthplace for so many different kinds of careers because it became central to our lives. I would not be a writer today if I hadn't been a hip hop journalist first. So in this period where we're looking at a fifty-year anniversary, I think it's time to take what we academics call the *longue durée*, or the long view, of the many different tentacles this art form has had globally. I think this is a perfect opportunity to do that because the time is right, and I think the UCLA Hip Hop Initiative is the right place.

QUESTION 2: My name is Melloe Won. I host the classic hip hop radio show called White Label Radio. During the pandemic, I lost my day job at the Staples Center. During that time, I created and teach a hip hop history class, which is certified now. So I'm a hip hop history teacher. This is the first one in high school history in California. The crazy thing about it is I barely graduated from high school, and I don't have a college degree. Hip hop saved my life again. Chuck, we use your music in the social studies class. I been wanting to ask this question for like thirty years—What was your mindset in creating "Black Steel in the Hour of Chaos"? The first part of that song gives me chills every time, when you talk about the letter from the government.

CHUCK D: 1967. I'm six going on seven years old. South Ozone Park, Queens. At my grandmother's house, she and my grandfather won foster parents of the year in 1964. It was always like twelve or fourteen boys in the house. We call them our uncles. We played with them, of course. They're teenagers. One of the uncles was named Milton. He was a foster kid there. He just got out of high school in June of 1967. Sure enough, boom boom boom! Knock on the door. "Milton Jones?" says a guy in a military outfit, spiffy, as he ran out of the car passing out letters on the block. Milton goes to the door and takes the letter. The military dude goes round back to the car. He opens it up. Reads the letter. Stares at it, like, "What the fuck?" Drops it on the living room table, shell-shocked. Because I could read a little bit at six or seven, I saw the letter: "Milton Jones, you are hereby drafted in the United States Marine Corps. You're supposed to report to duty in North Carolina, en route to Southeast Asia," when your ass was all happy-go-lucky for the summer of 1967. "Summer of Love? Not your ass, you heading to Vietnam!" Sure enough, he had to go to Vietnam. Was he ready? Did he want to go to service? Hell, no! "You better go." Got two of the boys out of that house.

"I got a letter from the government the other day / I opened and read it, it said they were suckers / They wanted me for their army or whatever / Picture me, giving a damn, I said never." That's where that came from. Real stories. Now, he didn't get killed, but he came back in 1971 with a screwed up mentality, if you saw the movie *Dead Presidents*. He came back with a Purple Heart, shrapnel in the leg. Me and my brother used to play with our G. I. Joes with his Purple Heart. He didn't give a damn about that. Matter of fact, every single one of the boys from that household that went to Vietnam came back twisted. Two of them stayed up in the Bronx, had to go to methadone clinics to clear themselves of whatever the military had done to them in Vietnam. Vietnam was real.

It was the 1960s. You're talking about the assassination of one president. The assassination of Malcolm X in New York. Medgar Evers. Robert F. Kennedy. You're thinking, "I thought he's going to run for president? Oh, presidents get killed." Dr. Martin Luther King. I'm not reading about it; I'm eight years old. Yo! The whole city of New York shut down. Mom's dressed in black for two days. She went to work. When Public Enemy came about, we wasn't really doing much backtracking. We was giving you what we experienced in the sixties. The rest of the groups that was in the eighties kind of came from the seventies. We came from the sixties. Our age was our advantage, especially in terms of spittin. That's why Ice-T is the other counterpart. He's giving you dialogue from another period of time. He's always like time capsules. That's why he's kind of like my brother on the other side, the Westside.

QUESTION 3: You talked about how people used to really focus on creativity. Right now we have TikTok taking over everything and people are really biting songs, dances, no credit, no citations. What responsibilities do you see us having as consumers and as producers of art to be able to reframe hip hop towards creativity, towards the dopeness that we know it should be focused on?

CHUCK D: Well, speaking for everybody in the class, a lot of people had nine weeks with me so they could answer that question. We talk about that every week. This great man right here, Prince [Chuck D pointing to his portrait of Prince], told me in 1999, "Be on top of technology or it'll be on top of you." He said, "Master your gadgets, because if you don't, they will master you." I'm not of the generation that says, "Oh man, I never use a phone" or "Damn it, that's from the devil." No. But as you get older, you gotta figure out in your frame of life, is this a toy or is it a tool? If your six-year-old daughter or son, little brother or sister, got a phone, you know damn well most of the time it's a toy. If you're twenty-four years old and you got a phone, you better figure it out. It has to be less of a toy the older you get. Now, the problem that we have is that we have people forty and fifty years old and they use it more as a toy than a tool. I mean, no shade on you if you fifty-four years old taking selfies, but I'm just saying. [*Laughter.*]

You have to grapple with this and try to figure out how you own your *self* before the ownership of yourself is in technology and gadgetry, to the point that if you don't have yourself, you've got to get money to buy yourself back. This is the era that we're going into for the rest of the 2020s, into 2030. We have a lot of uncertainty in the world right now. One thing we can talk about is how we put some of the sharp boundaries in culture and then still let culture grow to be free. Once you get into complexities of culture and art, it takes a collective to be able to decipher the geniuses that are out there. So asking academics for answers cannot put you in a bad place. In terms of academia, you can call it what you want, but in this decade, you cannot afford to call it corny. It will be life-saving. Our community is right here on the edge of the University of Southern California campus. You can see, when we don't pay attention as a collective, then the chickens come home to *shoot*.

Finally, I want to say that we had the bomb class. I know other rappers have done classes all over the map, but this class manifested from Dr. H. Samy Alim's mind from the last time we sat on this stage together. It's top of the pile, because the best thinkers that society has to offer is stacked in that class and dropped science, dropped the bomb, brought the noise, and actually gave you knowledge for a lifetime. The rest of you all that wasn't there, I know you're like, "Damn, I wanted to take that!" But that brother right over there made it happen. As they say, it don't happen just because it need to happen; you gotta *make* it happen. So I go full salute, Dr. Alim, for making it happen. Tabia Shawel, Samuel Lamontagne, thank you. Thanks to all the film crew in the trenches that's gonna put this in the documentary film.[7]

I want to make a final point about this class. Across the US, superintendents have been throwing up their hands in the air like, "I give up." In Black towns, superintendents have been giving up since at least the early nineties. The schools don't know how to deal with kids in Black towns. Now, in white America—just to follow the simplistic American Black-white binary—they've been throwing their hands up since the year 2000, since Eminem. They're like, "I don't know what to do with these bad-ass white ass kids trying to be Black." So now it's an American issue, and they wanna fix it without spending money. That's the problem. They won't pay no Black people. But out of this class, there will be guidebooks. There will be books. There will be all kinds of curricula so teachers will have less of an argument with the administrations in their towns, thanks to the brilliance of the educators who came to this table. It's real simple and plain when it comes down to our community, being able to get the guidelines, follow it, and just being able to say, "Listen, this is good for us. This music, this culture, this is good for us."

NOTES

1. See Joan Morgan, *When Chickenheads Come Home to Roost: A Hip-Hop Feminist Breaks It Down* (Simon & Schuster, 1999).

2. See Joan Morgan, Brittney Cooper, Treva Lindsey, Kaila Adia Story, and Esther Armah, "The Pleasure Principle: Articulating a Post–Hip Hop Feminist Politics of Pleasure," in *Freedom Moves: Hip Hop Knowledges, Pedagogies, and Futures*, ed. H. Samy Alim, Jeff Chang, and Casey Philip Wong (University of California Press, 2023), 349–75. The chapter includes Morgan's interaction with Kiyan Williams, whose debut institutional solo exhibition, *Between Starshine and Clay*, was presented at the Hammer Museum in 2022. See https://www.kiyanwilliams.com/.

3. See Joan Morgan, *She Begat This: Twenty Years of The Miseducation of Lauryn Hill* (Simon & Schuster, 2018).

4. See Robert Christgau, *Is It Still Good to Ya? Fifty Years of Rock Criticism, 1967–2017* (Duke University Press, 2018).

5. CAAM exhibited Deborah Roberts's work "Deborah Roberts: I'm," March 19–August 22, 2022. Roberts is a mixed-media collage artist whose work addresses issues of beauty, race, gender, and identity for Black youth.

6. Prophets of Rage (founded in 2016) brought together members of Public Enemy, Rage Against the Machine, and Cypress Hill as a supergroup that emphasized activism and social justice in response to the rise of right-wing politics in the United States.

7. The documentary film about Chuck D's residency at UCLA is titled *In the Hour of Chaos: Hip Hop Art & Activism with Public Enemy's Chuck D*. The film was directed by H. Samy Alim, Tabia Shawel, and Samuel Lamontagne and produced by Aaref Rodriguez and the Bad Man's Son media production firm. It premiered at the Grammy Museum in downtown Los Angeles on August 24, 2024, and was followed by a dialogue with H. Samy Alim, Joan Morgan, and Bryonn Bain. On June 2, 2025, the film was screened at the Hammer Museum in Los Angeles, followed by a dialogue with H. Samy Alim, Joan Morgan, Jeff Chang, and Chuck D.

Bibliography

Abdurraqib, Hanif. *A Little Devil in America*. Random House, 2022.

Alexander, Michelle. *The New Jim Crow: Mass Incarceration in the Age of Colorblindness*. New Press, 2010.

Alim, H. Samy. *Roc the Mic Right: The Language of Hip Hop Culture*. Routledge, 2006.

———. "Translocal Style Communities: Hip Hop Youth as Cultural Theorists of Style, Language, and Globalization." *Pragmatics* 19, no. 1 (2009): 103–27. https://doi.org/10.1075/prag.19.1.06ali.

Alim, H. Samy, Jeff Chang, and Casey Philip Wong, eds. *Freedom Moves: Hip Hop Knowledges, Pedagogies, and Futures*. University of California Press, 2023.

Alim, H. Samy, Awad Ibrahim, and Alastair Pennycook, eds. *Global Linguistic Flows: Hip Hop Cultures, Youth Identities, and the Politics of Language*. Routledge, 2009.

Alim, H. Samy, and Geneva Smitherman. *Articulate While Black: Barack Obama, Language, and Race in the United States*. Oxford University Press, 2012.

Alim, H. Samy, Quentin Williams, Adam Haupt, and Emile Jansen. "'Kom Khoi San, Kry Trug Jou Land': Disrupting White Settler Colonial Logics of Language, Race, and Land with Afrikaaps." *Journal of Linguistic Anthropology* 31, no. 2 (2021): 194–217.

Allah, Mal'kiy 17. "Sonny 'Abubadika' Carson and the Hip-Hop Generation." *Amsterdam News*, June 6, 2024. https://amsterdamnews.com/news/2024/06/06/sonny-abubadika-carsonand-the-hip-hop-generation/.

Anderson, Maureen. "The White Reception of Jazz in America." *African American Review* 38, no. 1 (2004): 135–45.

Appert, Catherine. *In Hip Hop Time: Music, Memory, and Social Change in Urban Senegal.* Oxford University Press, 2012.

Armah, Esther. *Emotional Justice: A Roadmap for Racial Healing.* Berrett-Koehler, 2022.

Bailey, Giselle, Hannah Beachler, dream hampton, and Raeshem Nijhon, dirs. *Ladies First: A Story of Women in Hip Hop.* Netflix, 2023.

Bain, Bryonn. *Rebel Speaks: A Justice Movement Mixtape.* University of California Press, 2022.

Baker, Houston A. *Black Studies, Rap, and the Academy.* University of Chicago Press, 1993.

———. "A Many-Colored Coat of Dreams: The Poetry of Countee Cullen." In *Afro-American Poetics: Revisions of Harlem and the Black Aesthetic.* University of Wisconsin Press, 1988.

Belafonte, Harry, with Michael Shnayerson. *My Song: A Memoir of Art, Race, and Defiance.* Vintage, 2012.

Blackstock, Nelson. *Cointelpro: The FBI's Secret War on Political Freedom.* Pathfinder, 1988.

Bloom, Joshua, and Waldo E. Martin. *Black against Empire: The History and Politics of the Black Panther Party.* University of California Press, 2016.

Bocquet, José-Louis, and Philippe Pierre-Adolphe. *Rap ta France.* La Sirène, 1996.

Bolden, Tony. *Groove Theory: The Blues Foundation of Funk.* University of Mississippi Press, 2020.

Bosch, Tanja E. "Radio as an Instrument of Protest: The History of Bush Radio." *Journal of Radio Studies* 13, no. 2 (2006): 249–65. https://doi.org/10.1080/10955040701313420.

Bradley, Adam. "The Artists Dismantling the Barriers between Rap and Poetry." *New York Times*, March 4, 2021. https://www.nytimes.com/2021/03/04/t-magazine/rap-hip-hoppoetry.html.

———. *Book of Rhymes: The Poetics of Hip Hop.* Basic Civitas, 2009.

Bradley, Adam, and Andrew DuBois. *The Anthology of Rap.* Yale University Press, 2013.

Brown, Scot. "A Land of Funk: Dayton, Ohio." In *The Funk Era and Beyond: New Perspectives on Black Popular Culture*, edited by Tony Bolden. Springer, 2008.

———. "SOLAR: The History of the Sounds of Los Angeles Records." In *Black Los Angeles*, edited by Darnell Hunt and Ana-Cristina Ramon. New York University Press, 2010.

Bullie, Jacinda, Jacquanda Salter-Villegas, and Leyda "Lady Sol" Garcia. "'Protection from Police Who Hinder Respiratory Airways': Hip Hop Theatre and Activism with Kuumba Lynx in Chicago." In *Freedom Moves: Hip Hop*

Knowledges, Pedagogies, and Futures, edited by H. Samy Alim, Jeff Chang, and Casey Philip Wong. University of California Press, 2023.

Burnim, Mellonee V., and Portia Maultsby, eds. *African American Music: An Introduction*. 2nd ed. Routledge, 2015.

Burton, Susan. *Becoming Ms. Burton: From Prison to Recovery to Leading the Fight for Incarcerated Women*. New Press, 2017.

Carson, A. D. "Owning My Masters: The Rhetorics of Rhymes and Revolutions." PhD diss., Clemson University, 2017.

Carson, Clayborne. *Civil Rights Chronicle: The African-American Struggle for Freedom*. Publications International, 2003.

Chang, Jeff. *Can't Stop Won't Stop: A History of the Hip-Hop Generation*. St. Martin's, 2005.

———. *Water Mirror Echo: Bruce Lee and the Making of Asian America*. Mariner/HarperCollins, 2025.

Chang, Jeff, and David "Davey D" Cook. *Can't Stop Won't Stop: A History of the Hip-Hop Generation*. Young adult ed. St. Martin's, 2021.

Christgau, Robert. *Is It Still Good to Ya? Fifty Years of Rock Criticism, 1967–2017*. Duke University Press, 2018.

Clark-Herrera, Sonya, Measha Ferguson Smith, hodari blue fka Adorie Howard, Reagan Ross, and Casey Wong. "Ripples of Hope and Healing: Sustaining Community by Creating a Social Justice Arts Ecosystem." In *Freedom Moves: Hip Hop Knowledges, Pedagogies, and Futures*, edited by H. Samy Alim, Jeff Chang, and Casey Philip Wong. University of California Press, 2023.

Common, with Adam Bradley. *One Day It'll All Make Sense*. Simon & Schuster, 2011.

Cooper, Brittney, Susana M. Morris, and Robin M. Boylorn, eds. *The Crunk Feminist Collection*. The Feminist Press at CUNY, 2017.

Cullors, Patrice, and asha bandele. *When They Call You a Terrorist: A Black Lives Matter Memoir*. St. Martin's, 2018.

DAM, Omar Offendum, and Ramzi Salti. "'Al-shaab yurid isquat al-nitham!': Sustaining Revolution in Palestine and Syria through Hip Hop." In *Freedom Moves: Hip Hop Knowledges, Pedagogies, and Future*, edited by H. Samy Alim, Jeff Chang, and Casey Philip Wong. University of California Press, 2023.

Davis, Angela. *Freedom Is a Constant Struggle: Ferguson, Palestine, and the Foundations of a Movement*. Haymarket Books, 2016.

———. *The Meaning of Freedom: And Other Difficult Dialogues*. City Lights, 2012.

Day, Lynda R. *Making a Way to Freedom: A History of African Americans on Long Island*. Empire State, 1997.

Day, Wendy. "Warning: Hip Hop Artists Need to Know about Today's 360 Record Deals." *Davey D's Hip Hop Corner*, February 5, 2010. https://hiphopandpolitics.wordpress.com/tag/music-industry-politics-360-deals/.

Desmond, Matthew. *Evicted: Poverty and Profit in the American City*. Crown, 2016.

Dowsett, Sudiipta, Lucas Marie, Dianne Rodger, and Grant Saunders. *Representing Hip Hop Histories, Politics, and Practices in Australia*. Routledge, 2023.

Dyson, Michael Eric. "The Culture of Hip-Hop." In *That's the Joint: The Hip-Hop Studies Reader*, edited by Murray Forman and Mark Anthony Neal. Routledge, 2004.

El Zein, Rayya. "From 'Hip Hop Revolutionaries' to 'Terrorist-Thugs': 'Blackwashing' between the Arab Spring and the War on Terror." *Lateral: Journal of the Cultural Studies Association* 5, no. 1 (Spring 2016).

Evans, Freddi Williams. *Congo Square: African Roots in New Orleans*. University of Louisiana Press, 2011.

Fanon, Frantz. *Black Skin, White Masks*. Editions du Seuil, 1952.

———. *The Wretched of the Earth*. Francois Maspero, 1961.

Gardell, Mattias. *In the Name of Elijah Muhammad: Louis Farrakhan and the Nation of Islam*. Duke University Press, 1996.

Gates, Henry Louis, Jr. *The Signifying Monkey: A Theory of African-American Literary Criticism*. Oxford, 1988.

Gates, Henry Louis, Jr., and Kwame A. Appiah, eds. *Zora Neale Hurston: Critical Perspectives Past and Present*. Amistad, 1993.

George, Nelson. *Hip Hop America*. Viking, 1998.

Glissant, Édouard. *Poétique de la relation*. Gallimard, 1990.

Goodloe, Marcus. *King Maker: Applying Dr. Martin Luther King Jr.'s Leadership Lessons in Working with Athletes and Entertainers*. Dream Life Loud, 2015.

Gosa, Travis L., and Erik Nielson, eds. *The Hip Hop and Obama Reader*. Oxford University Press, 2015.

Grant, Colin. *Homecoming: Voices of the Windrush Generation*. Vintage, 2020.

Greenlee, Sam. *The Spook Who Sat by the Door*. Wayne State University Press, 1969.

Guinier, Lani, and Gerald Torres. *The Miner's Canary: Enlisting Race, Resisting Power, Transforming Democracy*. Harvard University Press, 2003.

Hammou, Karim. *Une histoire du rap en France*. La Découverte, 2012.

Haupt, Adam. "Black Thing: Hip-Hop Nationalism, 'Race' and Gender in Prophets of da City and Brasse Vannie Kaap." In *Coloured by History, Shaped by Place: New Perspectives on Coloured Identities in Cape Town*, edited by Z. Erasmus. Kwela Books, 2001.

Haupt, Adam, Quentin Williams, H. Samy Alim, and Emile Jansen, eds. *Neva Again: Hip Hop Arts, Activism, and Education in Post-Apartheid South Africa*. HSRC Press, 2019.

Hill, Marc Lamont, and Mumia Abu-Jamal. *The Classroom and the Cell: Conversations on Black Life in America*. Third World Press, 2011.

James, C. L. R. *Black Jacobins: Toussaint L'Ouverture and the San Domingo Revolution*. Secker & Warburg, 1938.

———. *A History of Negro Revolt*. Secker & Warburg, 1938.

Jasiri X. "1Hood: Hip Hop Art, Activism, and Media Creation in Pittsburgh." In *Freedom Moves: Hip Hop Knowledges, Pedagogies, and Futures*, edited by H. Samy Alim, Jeff Chang, and Casey Philip Wong. University of California Press, 2023.

Jay-Z, with dream hampton. *Decoded*. Random House, 2010.

Johnson, Gaye Theresa. *Spaces of Conflict, Sounds of Solidarity: Music, Race, and Spatial Entitlement in Los Angeles*. University of California Press, 2013.

Johnson, Gaye Theresa, and Alex Lubin, eds. *Futures of Black Radicalism*. Verso, 2017.

Kelley, Robin D. G. Foreword to *The Vinyl Ain't Final: Hip Hop and the Globalization of Black Popular Culture*. Pluto Press, 2006.

———. *Freedom Dreams: The Black Radical Imagination*. Beacon Press, 2002.

Kelley, Robin D. G. *Yo Mama's Disfunktional! Fighting the Culture Wars in Urban America*. Beacon Press, 1998.

Keyes, Cheryl L. "Empowering Self, Making Choices, Creating Spaces: Black Female Identity via Rap Music Performance." *Journal of American Folklore* 113, no. 449 (Summer 2000): 255–69.

———. *Rap Music and Street Consciousness*. University of Illinois Press, 2002.

———. "Verbal Art Performance in Rap Music: The Conversation of the 80's." *Folklore Forum* 17, no. 2 (Fall 1984): 143–52.

Khomami, Nadia. "#MeToo: How a Hashtag Became a Rallying Cry against Sexual Harassment." *The Guardian*, October 20, 2017. https://www.theguardian.com/world/2017/oct/20/women-worldwide-use-hashtag-metooagainst-sexual-harassment.

Kitwana, Bakari. *Why White Kids Love Hip Hop: Wankstas, Wiggers, and Wannabes, and the New Reality of Race in America*. Basic Civitas, 2005.

Kruse, Kevin M. *White Flight: The Making of Modern Conservatism*. Princeton University Press, 2005.

Kumar, Divya. "Florida Law Offering 'BOGO' Tuition for STEM Majors Raises Faculty Concerns." *Tampa Bay Times*, July 5, 2021. https://www.tampabay.com/news/education/2021/07/05/florida-law-offering-bogotuition-for-stem-majors-raises-faculty-concerns/.

La Llama Rap Colectivo and H. Samy Alim. "'Luchando Derechos' in Neoliberal Spain: HipHop Visions beyond Racism, Xenophobia, Islamaphobia, and the Gentrification of El Raval, Barcelona." In *Freedom Moves: Hip Hop Knowledges, Pedagogies, and Future*, edited by H. Samy Alim, Jeff Chang, and Casey Philip Wong. University of California Press, 2023.

Lamontagne, Samuel. "France through Race: Beyond Colorblindess." *Ufahamu* 42, no. 2 (2021): 99–VII.

Lorde, Audre. *Sister Outsider: Essays and Speeches by Audre Lorde*. Crossing Press, 1984.

Lornell, Kip, and Charles C. Stephenson Jr. *The Beat: Go-Go's Fusion of Funk and Hip Hop*. University of Michigan Press, 2001.

Madhubhuti, Haki, and Maulana Karenga, eds. *Million Man March/ Day of Absence: A Commemorative Anthology*. Third World Press, 1996.

Mandela, Nelson. *Long Walk to Freedom: The Autobiography of Nelson Mandela*. Back Bay Books, 1995.

Maxwell, Ian. *Phat Beats, Dope Rhymes: Hip Hop Down Under Comin' Upper*. Wesleyan University Press, 2003.

McClaurin, Irma. *Black Feminist Anthropology: Theory, Politics, Praxis, and Poetics*. Rutgers University Press, 2001.

Meehan, Kevin. *People Get Ready: African American and Caribbean Cultural Exchange*. University Press of Mississippi, 2009.

Mega, Emiliano Rodriguez. "Charles Is Jamaica's Head of State." *New York Times*, May 6, 2023. https://www.nytimes.com/2023/05/06/world/americas/jamaica-monarchyreferendum.html.

Meghelli, Samir. "'Fear of a Black Planet': The Transnational Racial Politics of Hip-Hop in France, 1990–1991." In *Hip-Hop en Français: An Exploration of Hip Hop Culture in the Francophone World*, edited by Alain-Philippe Duran. Rowman & Littlefield, 2020.

Mendelberg, Tali. *The Race Card: Campaign Strategy, Implicit Messages, and the Norm of Equality*. Princeton University Press, 2001.

Minestrelli, Chiara. *Australian Indigenous Hip Hop: The Politics of Culture, Identity, and Spirituality*. Routledge, 2016.

Miyakawa, Felicia. *Five Percenter Rap: God Hop's Music, Message, and Black Muslim Mission*. Indiana University Press, 2005.

Moore, Leroy, and Stephanie Keeney Park. "'When Can Black Disabled Folks Come Home?" In *Freedom Moves: Hip Hop Knowledges, Pedagogies, and Futures*, edited by H. Samy Alim, Jeff Chang, and Casey Philip Wong. University of California Press, 2023.

Morgan, Joan. *She Begat This: Twenty Years of The Miseducation of Lauryn Hill*. Simon & Schuster, 2018.

———. *When Chickenheads Come Home to Roost: A Hip-Hop Feminist Breaks It Down*. Simon & Schuster, 1999.

Morgan, Joan, Brittney Cooper, Treva Lindsay, Kaila Adia Story, and Esther Armah. "The Pleasure Principle: Articulating a Post–Hip Hop Feminist Politics of Pleasure." In *Freedom Moves: Hip Hop Knowledges, Pedagogies and Futures*, edited by H. Samy Alim, Jeff Chang, and Casey Philip Wong. University of California Press, 2023.

Morrison, Toni. *Beloved*. Knopf, 1987.

Negus, Keith. "The Business of Rap: Between the Street and the Executive Suite." In *That's the Joint! The Hip Hop Studies Reader*, edited by Murray Forman and Mark Anthony Neal. Routledge, 2004.

Osumare, Halifu. *The Africanist Aesthetic in Global Hip-Hop: Power Moves*. Palgrave, 2008.

Perry, Imani. *Prophets of the Hood: Politics and Poetics in Hip Hop*. Duke University Press, 2004.

Pough, Gwendolyn. *Check It While I Wreck It: Black Womanhood, Hip-Hop Culture and the Public Sphere*. Northeastern University Press, 2004.

Powell, Michael. "Separate and Unequal in Roosevelt, Long Island." *Washington Post*, April 20, 2002.

Rakim, Chuck D, and Talib Kweli. "Sweat the Technique: The Politics and Poetics of Hip Hop." In *Freedom Moves: Hip Hop Knowledges, Pedagogies, and Futures*, edited by H. Samy Alim, Jeff Chang, and Casey Philip Wong. University of California Press, 2023.

Rakim, with Bakari Kitwana. *Sweat the Technique: Revelations on Creativity from the Lyrical Genius*. Amistad, 2019.

Rampersad, Arnold. "The Poetry of the Harlem Renaissance." In *The Columbia History of American Poetry*, edited by Jay Parini. Columbia University Press, 1993.

Robinson, Cedric. *Black Marxism: The Making of a Black Radical Tradition*. University of North Carolina Press, 1983.

Rose, Tricia. *Black Noise: Rap Music and Black Culture in Contemporary America*. Wesleyan University Press, 1994.

Roy, Arundhati. *Azadi: Freedom. Fascism. Fiction*. Haymarket Books, 2020.

Rys, Dan. "A History of Hip Hop's Complicated Relationship with the Grammy's." *Billboard*, February 8, 2017. https://www.billboard.com/music/rb-hip-hop/history-hip-hopcomplicated-relationship-grammys-7684970/.

Sharpe, Christina. *Ordinary Notes*. Farrar, Straus and Giroux, 2023.

Simpson, Leanne. *As We Have Always Done: Indigenous Freedom through Radical Resistance*. University of Minnesota Press, 2017.

Smitherman, Geneva. *Black Talk: Words and Phrases from the Hood to the Amen Corner*. Houghton Mifflin, 2000.

———. "The Power of the Rap: The Black Idiom and the New Black Poetry." *Twentieth Century Literature* 18, no. 4 (October 1973): 259–74.

———. *Talkin and Testifyin: The Language of Black America*. Wayne State University Press, 1977.

Southern, Eileen. *The Music of Black Americans: A History*. 3rd ed. W. W. Norton, 1997.

Spady, James G. "Mapping and Re-membering Hip Hop History, Hiphopography, and African Diasporic History." *Western Journal of Black Studies* 37, no. 2 (2013): 127–37.

———. *Marcus Garvey: Jazz, Reggae, Hip Hop, and the African Diaspora.* Marcus Garvey Foundation, 2011.

Spady, James G., H. Samy Alim, and Charles G. Lee. *Street Conscious Rap.* Black History Museum, 1999.

Spady, James G., H. Samy Alim, and Samir Meghelli. *The Global Cipha: Hip Hop Culture and Consciousness.* Black History Museum, 2006.

Spady, James G., Stefan Dupres, and Charles G. Lee. *Twisted Tales in the Hip Hop Streets of Philly.* Black History Museum, 1995.

Spady, James G., and Joseph Eure. *Nation Conscious Rap: The Hip Hop Vision.* Black History Museum, 1991.

Strausz, Sté. *Fly Girls: Histoire(s) du hip-hop féminin en France.* Au diable vauvert, 2010.

Streeter, Kurt. "Kneeling, Fiercely Debated by the N.F.L, Resonates in Protests." *New York Times*, June 5, 2020. https://www.nytimes.com/2020/06/05/sports/football/georgefloyd-kaepernick-kneeling-nfl-protests.html.

Sugrue, Thomas. *The Origins of the Urban Crisis: Race and Inequality in Post-War Detroit.* Princeton University Press, 2014.

Tate, Greg. *Everything but the Burden: What White People Are Taking from Black Culture.* Crown, 2003.

———. *Flyboy in the Buttermilk: Essays on Contemporary America.* Simon & Schuster, 1992.

Terkourafi, Marina. *The Languages of Global Hip-Hop.* Bloomsbury, 2010.

Vincent, Ricky. *Funk: The Music, the People, and the Rhythm of the One.* St. Martin's, 1996.

Welsing, Frances Cress. "The Cress Theory of Color-Confrontation and Racism." *Black Scholar* 5, no. 8 (1974): 32–40.

———. *The Isis Papers: The Keys to the Colors.* C. W., 1991.

Williams, Nanon. *Still Surviving.* Breakout, 2003.

Williams, Quentin, and Jaspal Singh. *Global Hiphopography.* Springer, 2023.

Williams, Robert. *Ebonics: The True Language of Black Folks.* Institute of Black Studies, 1975.

Woods, Clyde. *Development Arrested: The Blues and Plantation Power in the Mississippi Delta.* Verso, 2017.

Index

Page numbers followed by n denote notes.

A$AP Rocky, 192–93n4
Abdurraqib, Hanif, 251
abolition movements, 220
Aboriginal people, 226
Above the Rim (movie), 72
Abrantes, Kevin, 278
academic funding sources, 41–42
academic partnership for cultural preservation, 242
Ackerman, Paul, 166
Adams, Eric, 73, 233
Adler, Bill, 30
AF3IRM (Association of Feminists Fighting Fascism, Imperialism, Refeudalization, and Marginalization), 248–49
African griot tradition, 12
Afrika Bambaataa, 66, 84, 107, 142
Afrocentricity, 98
Afro-Korean hip hop festival, 264
Afro-pop, 63
Aftermath, 145
"Ain't No Stopping Us Now," 79
Aktuel Force, 175
A-lan Holt, 20–21
Alim, H. Samy, 1–2; reexamining hip hop from artists' perspectives, 11–21; the politics and poetics, activism and aesthetics of hip hop, 33; 53; community organizing, 65–66; Black migration and funk, 128; women MCs in Cape Town, 138–39; gender politics within capitalist constraints, 154–56, 157; global hip hop, 183–84, 188, 190–91; Black radicalism and internationalism, 195–96; 294
All Hail the Queen, 156
Amansure, Bernadette, 139
amapiano, 63
"American Pie," 269
Amil, 144, 276
ancestral intelligence, 244
And You Don't Stop! (radio show), 4, 171
Angie B., 136
Anthology of Rap, 261
Anthrax, 127, 128, 268
"Anti-Nigger Machine," 86
Apple, 122
Arab world, hip hop in, 70
Ariefdien, Shaheen, 18, 187
Armstrong, Louis, 108, 109

Arnold, Larkin, 119
art: education for incarcerated people, 247–49; interpretation, 290; as medicine, 240–41
artists: artistic expression, power in, 274–75; authority, 37–38; desperation in, 149, 154; relationship to the community, 58–59, 63; women, 141–48
Atlantic, 119
Atomic Breakers, 176
The Autobiography of Mistachuck album, 57
Ava DuVernay (MC Eve), 161n7
ayahuasca, 289–90
Azor, Hurby "Luv Bug," 137–38

Bahamadia, 143–44
Bain, Bryonn, 214, 223; deconstructing bad faith arguments blaming hip hop culture, 228–29; on transforming consciousness, 240–41; vision for a radical reimagining of justice, 237–38
Bain, K, 253n14
Banner, David, 100, 104
Baraka, Amiri, 208–9, 211
Barge, Gene, 32, 115, 257
Bar-Kays, 107
Barnes, Dee, 147
Barnum, P. T., 276
Barrett, Amy Coney, 216
Bayview - Hunters Point, 16
Beanie Sigel, 276
Beat Poets, 211
"Before I Let Go," 125–26
Belafonte, Harry, 103, 104, 115, 200, 236
Bell, Thom, 38, 79
Benna, Zyed, 189
Benny the Butcher, 237
Berry, Chuck, 175, 176
BET, 159–60
Beverly, Frankie, 125
Bey, Yasiin (Mos Def), 235
Biggie, 90, 144
Big Hass, 242
"The Biker," 122, 123
Bing Crosby, 109
Bin Hassan, Umar, 43n4
Black Arts Movement (BAM), 43n2, 69, 208–11
"Black Cat," 115
Black childhood, protecting, 248–50
Black creativity for survival, 3, 12, 16
Black geography, 26–27, 50–51, 114, 164, 171. *See also* Black migration
The Black Image Corporation (exhibition), 75n11
Black Lives Matter (BLM), 103, 105n5
Blackman, Toni, 138, 152
Black migration, 28–30, 112, 128, 131, 164, 171, 173, 176, 184; cultural impact of, 28–30, 48–51, 53–54; migration patterns, 27–28. *See also* Black geography
Black music, social obligation in, 38–39
Black News Network, 207
Black Noise, 13, 18, 21
Black on Both Sides, 235
Black Panther (film), 85, 105n4
Black Panther Party, 84, 229, 244, 250
Black Panther (superhero), 85, 105n4, 175, 176
Black Power movement, 69
Black queer identities, 19, 20
Black Spade, 98
"Black Steel in the Hour of Chaos," 60, 226
Blackwatch, 98
Black women: activism, 216–17; overrepresentation of, 204; presence, systematic diminishment of, 197; professors, overrepresentation of, 204; and record labels, 212. *See also* women in hip hop
Blake, Jacob, 254n27
Blaq Pearl, 139
blockbusting, 22
Blondie, 138
Blues People (Baraka), 139
Bo$$, 147–48
Bomb Squad, 122
Bonham, John, 111
Bonnie N Clyde, 107
Boogaloo: The Greatest Story Never Told-Identity Theft (documentary), 62, 99, 106n13
Book of Rhymes: The Poetics of Hip Hop, 261, 262–63
Boseman, Chadwick, 105n4
Boula, Lorrie, 4, 278
"Boyfriend," 147
Bradley, Adam, 259, 260–61, 262–64, 265–68, 269, 270, 271, 273–74, 275
Brand Nubian, 24
Brantingham, P. Jeffrey, 45n25
B-Real, 217
"Bring the Noise," 116–17, 127, 275
Bring the Noise (cultural app), 4
"Brothers and sisters!," 129
"Brothers Gonna Work It Out," 86
Brown, Foxy, 138

Brown, James, 107, 109, 110, 257
Brown, Scot, Dr., 113–14, 115, 117, 119, 125–27, 128–30, 275
Bruno Mars, 125
"B Side Wins Again," 87
Buddy Bolden, 108
"Burn Hollywood Burn," 86
Burnside, Timothy Anne, 272
Burton, Susan, 232
Bush Radio, 187
BWP-Bytches with Problems, 147

CAAM, 295n5
"California Love," 129
Cameo, 126
Campbell, Luther, 51
"Candy," 126
Can't Stop Won't Stop: A History of the Hip-Hop Generation (Chang), 46–51, 57, 75
"Can y'all get funky?," 107
Capitol Records, 119
Cardi B, 141, 146, 147, 154
Cardo, 125
Carolina Dirty, 152–53
Carson, A. D., 273
Carson, Lumumba, 106n13
Carson, Sonny, 106n13
Caruso, Enrico, 108
Casablanca Records, 119
Cash, Johnny, 214
Cash Money Records, 52
Catch a Fire album, 54–55
CBS Records, 79
Chang, Jeff, 46–51
Cheba, Idris, 172
Chess, Leonard, 257
Chess, Marshall, 120
Chess, Phil, 257
Chess Records, 32, 44n20, 115, 119, 257
Chic, 113–14
Chicago Defender (Black newspaper), 56
Chicano rock, 61
Childish Gambino, 268
Chip Fu, 230
The Chronic, 88, 128
Chuck D, 1–8, 70, 89; childhood influence of hip hop culture, 22–23; collective feeling and cultural memory, 36–37; contrasting authentic Black liberation figures with manufactured entertainment, 84–88; as cultural steward, 282–83; deconstructing bad faith arguments blaming hip hop culture, 228–29; early years, 23–25; on evolution of recording technology, 31–34, 78–84; on grief, artistic transformation, and the nature of creative authenticity, 288–91; on hip hop's shift from collective to individual focus, 284–86; on maintaining artistic integrity in a hyper-connected world, 286–88; on mentorship through technology, 77–78; personal history as political foundation, 292–95; prison shows, 35–36; on radio shows, 25–27; warnings about the intersection of cultural manipulation, technological control, and political authoritarianism, 241–42. *See also* Public Enemy
Clark, Mark, 130
Clark-Herrera, Sonya, 65, 75n12
"Class Suicide: The Black Radical Tradition, Radical Scholarship, and the Neoliberal Turn," 200
Claudio, Thomas, 190
"Clean up the Ghetto," 39
Clear Channel Communications, 95, 106n12
Clinton, George, 110, 112–13, 129, 211
Clotilda (slave ship), 238, 253n19
Coachella music festival, 67, 68, 131–32
COINTELPRO program, 218
collective: artistic tradition, change in, 211–13; cultural expression, suppressing, 202–5; hip hop, 20–21, 77, 87, 90, 95, 97, 99, 138, 140, 153, 181, 196, 198, 207, 211, 235, 245, 263, 274, 281, 285–86; sessions with community members, 245–47; songwriting workshops, 235
Collins, Bootsy, 107, 110, 113, 125
Columbia Jazz Club, 114
Commerford, Tim, 289
Commodores, 286
community building, 241–42; and hip hop culture, 58, 63–64, 235–36, 241–42; and music, 65
Community Capacity Development (CCD), 253n14
community radio, 187
Congo Square, 46, 108
consciousness, 15, 16, 117, 139, 142, 156–57, 166, 173, 176–77, 179, 183, 241
contextualizing music, 181–82
"Contract on the World Love Jam," 86
Conway the Machine, 237
Coogler, Ryan, 105n4
Cook, Davey D, 88
Cooke, Sam, 111
Cooper, Brittney, 155

cooperative economics and wealth distribution, 95–97
Cornelius, Don, 125
corporate scholarship, 229–30
Cotillion Records, 119
Countee Cullen, 265–66
the Coup, 149
Crew Grrl Order, 144, 152, 223
"Crumble," 224
Cullors, Patrisse, 105n5
cultural aesthetic, 101
cultural appropriation, 99–102, 190, 197
cultural code-switching and musical exposure, 268–69
cultural criticism, 210; physical danger of, 284
cultural dialogues and solidarity, 173–74
cultural healing practices, 243
cultural movements and power structure, 70–71
culture commodification, 70
Cypress Hill, 217

D. Larue, 153
D. O. C., 122
Da Brat, 157
Daddy-O, 164
DAM, 190
Dâm-Funk, 125
D'Amour, Chagrin, 172
Dance, Bobby, 145
Dave, 104
Davey D, 52, 84, 86; on community building vs. institutional scare tactics, 88–89; on institutional knowledge vs. cultural erasure, 88; on mentorship and reciprocal responsibility, 89–91
Davis, Angela, 187, 220–21, 229
Davis, Miles, 114
"Day-O (Banana Boat Song)," 103
Deadly Venoms, 153
Dean, James, 71
"Dear Mama," 72
Debbie D, 140
December 12th movement, 106n13
Decoded, 266–67
Def Jam, 30, 147, 211
Desmond, 210
desperation in artists, 149, 154
Destroy Man, 175, 176
Digable Planets, 285, 286
Digital Underground, 71, 230
disco, 29, 79–80, 111–12
Disturbing tha Peace, 144
DJ Battlecat, 125
DJ Chabin, 175
DJ Cotton Candy, 149
DJ Jazzy Joyce, 149
DJ Kap, 90
DJ Quik, 125, 129
DJ Spinderella, 149
DMX's energy, 276
Dominique, 278
Donna Summer, 149
"Don't Believe the Hype," 5, 7, 34, 56, 87, 129
Dope Saint Jude, 139
Dorsey, Thomas, 109
Do the Right Thing (movie), 36, 86, 117, 230
Down with This, 175
Dr. Dre, 69, 122–23, 125, 128, 129, 145
Dr. Funkenstein, 113
"Dr. J," 23
dream hampton, 69, 251
Droop-E, 97
D-Shot, 96
DuBois, Andrew, 261, 263
dubplates, 29
Dunnavant, Justin, 238
Dupri, Jermaine, 143
Duteil, Sidney, 174–75
DuVernay, Ava, 143, 146, 156
Dyson, Michael Eric, 155

E-40: Charlie Hustle: The Blueprint of a Self-Made Millionaire (documentary), 90, 92, 96–97, 98
Earth, Wind & Fire, 123
Eavesdrop, 138–39
Eazy-E, 158, 215
"Ebonics," 193n5
Ebony (magazine), 55, 56
educational and cultural programs in prisons, 224–26, 247–50
educational reform through arts integration, 211
Egyptian Lover, 125
Eisenhower, Dwight D., 74n3
Eisenhower Interstate System, 48–49
El Chojin, 191
Eldritch, Andrew, 127
Elliott, Missy, 143, 214
Emile YX?, 66, 75n16
Eminem, 167, 202, 237, 265
Enjoy Records, 52
Envoyé spécial (TV show), 177

EPMD, 129, 232
"Eric B Is President," 275
Erving, Julius, 23
"Every Brother Ain't a Brother," 114
Everything but the Burden: What White People Are Taking from Black Culture (Tate), 197
Eve with DMX, 144

Fab 5 Freddy, 98
Fad, J. J., 122, 143, 152, 232, 265
Farrakhan, 218
Farrell, Perry, 201
Fatback Band, 32, 44n20, 113, 256, 257
"Fear Not of Man," 235
Fear of a Black Planet, 83–84, 86–88, 91, 95, 117
50 Cent, 238–39
Fight the Power: How Hip Hop Changed the World (documentary series), 4
Fight the Power: Rap, Race, and Reality, 3
"Fight the Power," 35–36, 42n1, 86, 87, 131, 187, 191–92, 260
Figures of Speech, 143
"Final Count of the Collision between Us and the Damned," 87
Finesse & Synquis, 285
"First Lady," 144
Flavor Flav, 122
flow as universal human expression, 259–60
Fly Girls (Strausz), 142, 143, 178
Foo Fighters, 201
Foxy Brown, 145, 146, 147, 160
France, right-wing politics and music, 185–86, 190
Frazier, Walt "Clyde," 78
"Freakshow on the Dancefloor," 107
Freedom Dreams (Kelley), 177–78
Freedom Moves: Hip Hop Knowledges, Pedagogies, and Futures, 20, 65, 191
Free Huey and Free Angela, 229
freestyle rhyme ciphers, 270, 274–76
freestyling, 223, 225
Fresh, Doug E., 137
Fresh Prince, 232
Fugees, 286
Funkadelic, 101, 113
"Funkbox Party," 52, 137
Funk Brothers, 111
funk music: artistic creation, technology, and cultural power, 131–33; artists by region, 110; bands, 107, 115; and Black Americans, 110–11; Black record music era, 113–15; corporate strategy of manufactured division, 118–24; current scenario, 125–26; demand for solo, 123; electro funk, 107; and hip hop, 115–18; lyrics, 109–10; original artists, 125; and rap, 123; recorded music, 108–10; rock, 111; 1960s, 110; 1970s, 111; 1980s, 112–13; as universal language transcending genre, 111–12
Funky 4 + 1, 138, 152
"Funk You Up," 136, 142, 265
Furious Fives, 46, 114
Futures of Black Radicalism and *Spaces of Conflict, Sounds of Solidarity* (Johnson), 195, 196, 220

"Galaxy," 24
Gamble, Kenny, 38
Gamble and Huff, 79
Gangsta Boo, 144, 145
Garcia, Alicia, 105n5
Garvey, Marcus, 173
Gary Byrd, 114
Gates, Henry Louis, Jr., 271–72
gay anthems, 127
generational fragmentation, 70–71
generational knowledge, 88
Ghostface Killah, 153
Giovanni, Nikki, 138, 152
"Girlfriend," 147
Giuliani, Rudy, 230
Gladys Knight, 152
Glissant, Édouard, 178
The Global Cipha: Hip Hop Culture and Consciousness (Meghelli, Spady, and Alim), 174
global hip hop culture: decentering American Hip-Hop supremacy, 163–66, 170; diasporic consciousness, 172–74; French Africans and hip hop, 172, 173–78; global cultural circulation and local adaptation, 165–71, 180–81; as hope for marginalized, 187–91; Palestinian context, 190–91; and political power, 183–86; visibility, inclusiveness, and representation, 181–82
Godessa, 139
"Go Green," 144
Goodloe, Marcus, 104
"Good Love 6-9-9-6-9," 115
"Good Times," 113–14
Gordy, Berry, 55
Gotsch, Kara, 252n4

graffiti, 26, 93–94
Graham, Larry, 110
Grandmaster Caz, 114
Grandmaster Flash, 46, 59, 97, 114
Greenlee, Sam, 224
Green Street Studios, 91
Griffey, Dick, 125
grimes, d. sabela, 245–46
Griner, Brittney, 192n3
Griselda Records, 237
Guinier, Lani, 225
Gunna, 202

Hammou, Karim, 172
Hampton, Fred, 130
Hank Shocklee, 122
Hard Knock Life Tour, 276
Harlem, cultural development in, 27–28
Harry, Debbie, 138
Hasél, Pablo, 201
"Have a Nice Day," 143
Hawkins, Taylor, 201
Hayes, Isaac, 115
Haywood, Leon, 129
Heal the Hood, 66, 75n16, 104
"The Heart Part 5," 277n2
Hendrix, Jimi, 108, 111
"Here Comes the Judge," 32, 44n20, 115–16, 256, 257
Heresy, 152
"Heritage," 265–66
Hernandez, Kelly Lytle, 278
Highland Bowl music festival, 130
Hill, Lauryn, 142, 152, 236, 261, 284, 286
hip hop: age and authenticity in, 267–68; anger into artistic expression, 274; as art form, 17, 232–33, 291; artistic responsibility, 58–60; artist's relationship to the community, 63–64; as Black cultural expression, 11, 13–14, 18; as branded commodity vs. living culture, 241–42; Caribbean influence, 49–50; changes that influence, 39–40; collective definition vs. individual interpretation, 198, 200–202; collective power vs. individual struggle, 95-97; collectives, 20–21, 77, 87, 90, 99, 138, 140, 153, 181, 196, 198, 207, 211, 235, 245, 263, 274, 281, 285–86; commercialization of, 67–68; and community building, 58–59, 63–64, 235–36, 241–42; corporate consolidation and market manipulation, 51–53; corporate scholarship, 229–30; creativity of, 87–88, 91, 97–98, 116; criminalization and stigmatization of, 93, 208; as critique systems of power, 245–46; cultural appropriation of, 99–102; as the cultural arm of capitalism, 102–3; cultural influences on, 228; deep literary and poetic roots, 256–58; development of, 11, 12–13, 38; education of the disenfranchised communities through, 234; as emotional outlets, 269; and erasure of White supremacist violence, 251–52; evolution from conscious resistance to commercially driven and dangerous, 232–34; evolution from youth voice to universal medium, 268–69; as extension of ancient creative traditions, 255–57; and feminism, false binary between, 283–84; as a form of cultural resistance, 197–99; form vs. content in hip hop analysis, 267; functioning as both artistic expression and social force, 234–37; generational disconnect and time ownership, 60–61; gentrification of, 69–70; as global revolutionary tool, 70–71; global solidarity through digital platforms, 243–44; hollow victory problem, 239; influence of migration on, 48–51, 53–54; intentionality, 97–99; intersection with participatory theater and prison education programs, 247–50; in Jamaica, 48; language, 49–50; learnings from, 94–95; in Los Angeles, 51; as means of expression, 227–28; in Memphis, 47–48; need for literary documentation of, 270, 274–75; in New Orleans, 47; in New York, 49; as personal healing and recognition, 19–21; phrasing of, 13; as political response and institutional control, 129–31; as practice and as community, 245–47; practitioner-scholar collaboration in hip hop studies, 272–74; radical work within, 213–17; radio shows, 26–27; recording industry, 78–83; as replacement therapy, 60; rhyming in, 115–16, 257, 265, 275–76; and scapegoating, 242–43; scholarships on, 13–14; shift from collective to individual focus, 284–86; solidarity in, 88–90; in St. Louis, Missouri, 48; and technology, 92–93, 243–45; theoretical foundations of hip hop, 12; things for scholars to focus on in the future, 291–92; and understanding geography, 50; vision for a radical reimagining of justice,

237–38; and youth organizations, 65–67. *See also* global hip hop culture
Hip Hop Alliance, 4
hip hop criticism, 19–20; early feminist, 281–82
"Hip Hop 4 da Ladies," 245–46
hip hop feminism, 19, 279. *See also* women in hip hop
hip hop movements: and grassroots movements, 101–2; and political activism, 102–4
hip-hop narratives, challenging regional, 128–30
hip hop poetics: and academic legitimization struggles, 261; and aesthetic value of imperfection in Black musical traditions, 266; as alternative forms of cultural contribution, 262–63; connecting classical and contemporary poetics through, 261–62; and hybridity of language, 263–64; proto-rap analysis, 257; shift from audio-centered to visual-centered hip hop, 260; study of, 260–61; transcription accuracy and authorial authority, 266–67
hip-hop radicalism: collective resistance necessity, 207–8; vs. martyr worship, 206–7
Hollywood and Vine, 150
"Homey Don't Play Dat," 107
Horton, Willie, 202
Howlin' Wolf, 59, 120
"How the West Was Won," 276
Huerta, Dolores, 245
Huff, Leon, 38
human development, 238
human justice, 238
human rights, 238
Humphrey, Hubert, 130
Hurston, Zora Neale, 138, 266
hyphy movement, 99

Ice Cube, 124, 138, 142, 276, 282
Ice-T, 70, 72, 212
ideological incorporation, 188
'I Feel Love,' 149
"I Know You Got Soul," 13
immigration, 28, 173, 174, 176, 189
"In Between the Sheets," 36
"Incident at 66.6 FM," 86
in-migration, 28, 47, 48
intentionality, 97–99
intergenerational engagement, 117
intersectionality, 236
In the Hour of Chaos: Hip Hop Art & Activism with Public Enemy's Chuck D (documentary film), 296n7
The Isis Papers: The Keys to the Colors, 84, 104n2
Isley Brothers, 36, 108
It Takes a Nation of Millions to Hold Us Back, 78, 83, 129, 131, 159, 215
iTunes, 122
"I Wanna Do Something Freaky to You," 129
"I Wanna Testify," 110

Jackson, Jesse, 129, 188, 194n29
Jackson, Michael, 119
Jackson, Millie, 143
Jamaica: hip hop culture in, 48; migration to Britain, 54
James, C. L. R., 173
James, Rick, 113, 124
Jam Master Jay, 232–33
Jara, Victor, 44n21
Ja Rule, 238
Jasiri X, 66, 75n14, 251
Jay Worthy, 125
Jay-Z, 90, 120, 144, 266–67, 276
jazz-rock, 175
Jazzy Jeff, 232
Jean, Wyclef, 152, 286
Jeff, Jazzy, 159, 215
Jenner, Kylie, 146
Jet (magazine), 55–56
Jhonygo, 175, 176
jitterbug, 100
Jobs, Steve, 122
"Johnny B. Goode," 176
Johnson, Bob, 159
Johnson, Gaye Theresa, 196–97, 198–206, 208, 209–10, 212–13, 214, 216–17, 218–20, 278
Johnson, John, 56
Johnson, Lyndon, 130
Jones, Oran "Juice," 211
Juice (film), 71
June, Larry, 125
June, Lyla, 20
Junior Mafia, 144
Jupiter, Maya, 224; collective sessions with community members, 245–46; early influences, 226–27; on transforming consciousness, 239–40

Kaepernick, Colin, 69, 76n19
Kaila Story, 155

Kapanen, Mikko, 164, 178–79, 180–82
Karloff, Boris, 91, 92
Kasem, Casey, 26
Kavanaugh, Brett, 216
KBLA, 53
Kelley, Robin D. G., 43n9, 77, 177–78; scholarship development, 21–22
Kennedy, Dom, 125
Keppard, Freddie, 121
Keyes, Cheryl L., Dr., 139–44, 145–51, 153–54, 156–57, 261
King, Martin Luther, Dr., 130, 205
King Maker: Applying Dr. Martin Luther King Jr.'s Leadership Lessons in Working with Athletes and Entertainers, 104
"The King of Jazz," 121
King Records, 107
King Tim I, 113
"King Tim III (Personality Jock)," 32, 44n20, 256, 257
knowledge: as fifth element of hip hop, 103, 139; generational, 88–89, 197, 246; production through music, 40–41, 177, 199, 271, 294; of self, 98, 104n2, 164, 165; transmission, 105n9
Kokane, 125
Kool Herc, 29–30, 49, 53–54, 97
Kool Moe Dee, 276
Krip-Hop movement, 19, 236
KRS-One, 4, 69, 98, 103, 268, 275
Kurtis Blow, 4
Kuumba Lynx, 66
Kweli, Talib, 12, 281

LA Coliseum, 129–30
Lady B, 26, 137
Lady of Rage, 143, 146
La Llama Rap Colectivo, 66, 191
Lamar, Kendrick, 103, 124, 125, 213–14, 236, 260, 277n2
Lamontagne, Samuel, 9, 125; French hip hop and racial politics of France, 172–78, 185–86, 189–90, 196; 245, 271, 278, 296n7
language, 49–50, 182, 184, 263–64. *See also* hip hop poetics
The Last Poets, 43n4, 115, 116, 211, 257
Lateef, Yusef, 114
LA uprisings, 70, 76n19
Le Debrief, 175
Lee, Spike, 86, 117
Lee, Stan, 85, 105n4
"Le Freak," 114
legislative theater, 247
Leon Sylvers III, 125
Let Me Take You There, 150
"Let's Talk about AIDS.," 143
"Let's Talk about Sex," 143, 158
Levy, Morris, 119, 120
Lighter Shade of Brown, 218
Lightnin' Rod, 115, 211
Lil Baby, 267
Lil' Kim, 138, 144, 145, 146, 147, 160
Lil Nas X, 127
Lindsay, Treva, 155
Lindy Hop (dance form), 100
Lionel D, 175
Lisa Lee of Soulsonic Force, 140
Little MC, 176
Live Nation, 68
LL Cool J, 30, 124, 276
Lollapalooza, 201
long box, 82
Long Island, 23, 25–28, 54, 84, 114, 115, 285
"Look what I've Done for Them," 16
Lorde, Audre, 241
Lord Jamar, 24
"Louder than a Bomb," 85–86
Lower 48, 46
L'Trimm, 143
Ludacris, 144
Luhaka, Théo, 190
Lynch, Monica, 157
Lynx, Kuumba, 75n13
Lyrik, E. J. von, 139

Mag3, 177
Magnificent Montague, 129
Makeba, Miriam, 115
"Make Em Say Uhh," 52
Malcolm X, 240; Grassroots Movement, 251
Ma Rainey, 141
Mariño, Susi Álvarez, 66
Marley, Bob, 54–55
Martin, Trayvon, 105n5
Masekela, Hugh, 114
Massenya, Juan, 177
Masterdon Committee, 52, 137
Master P, 52, 104, 137, 144
Mauer, Marc, 225, 252n4
Maze, 125
Mbekeni, Amkelwa, 164, 179–82, 187
MC, performance techniques, 29
McFadden & Whitehead, 79
MC Hammer, 94, 145

MC J. B., 122
McLean, Don, 269
MC Lyte, 4, 98, 135–36, 137, 143, 146, 268
MC Sha-Rock, 138, 152
MC Solaar, 186
MC Trouble, 142
Medusa, 146
"Meet the G that Killed Me," 86
Megan Thee Stallion, 138, 140–41, 146, 155
Meghelli, Samir, 174
Melle Mels, 114, 176, 276
Melloe Won, 292
Memphis Bleek, 276
mental health, 239–40
Mercedes Ladies, 140
Merman, Ethel, 79
"The Message," 176
Method Man, 276
Mexican people in West Coast music, 217
Mia X, 144, 145
Michie Mee, 140
"Microphone Fiends," 13
Midnight Star, 107
Miller, Mac, 202
Million Man March, 218
Million Youth March, 104
Minaj, Nicki, 138, 146, 147
The Miner's Canary (Guinier and Torres), 225
Mingus, Charles, 114
Miranda, Lin Manuel, 244
misappropriation, 167
Miseducation, 152
The Miseducation of Lauryn Hill, 261
Mistah F. A. B., 98
mixtape as scholarly method, 263
Mkosi, Andy, 139
Mongolian Bling, 180
Monie Love, 138, 152
Moniquea, 125
Moore, Leroy F., 19–20, 99, 236
"More Bounce to the Ounce," 126, 129
Morgan, Joan, Dr., 19, 155; about hip hop's transformation and the personal costs of cultural criticism, 283–84; early feminist hip hop criticism, 281–82; economic barriers to cultural connection, 288; hip hop feminism, 19; on hip hop scholars focus on the future, 291–92; introduction, 279–80
Morrison, Toni, 202
Mos Def, 20
Motown movement, 39, 49, 111
Motown Records, 42n1
Mr. Magic, 26
Mr. Morale & the Big Steppers, 277n2
Mtume, James, 119
Muddy Waters, 120, 141
Mugzy, 96
Mural Music and Arts Project (MMAP), 65–66, 75n12
musical collaborations, 61–62, 128, 181, 188, 281
musical innovation and communities, 107–10
"My Melody," 275
My Mic Sounds Nice, 146, 156
MyVerse, 152

National Museum of African American History and Culture (NMAAHC), 272
Nation of Islam, 92, 218
Naughty by Nature, 157
Navajo Indigenous people, 241
Ndegeocello, Meshell, 147
Nelly, 104
The New Jim Crow (Alexander), 225
Newton, Huey, 85
"Night of the Living Baseheads," 13
Nikki D, 138
"911 Is a Joke," 86, 91
Nipsey Hussle, 44n22, 73, 94, 99, 125, 214
Nixon, Richard, 130
Nobody Knows My Name, 156
No Limit Army, 52
No Limit Records, 144
Nonchalant, 142
Notorious B. I. G., 90
Nubian queens, 157
Nuriddin, Jalaluddin Mansur, 43n4
"Nuthin' but a 'G' Thang," 129

Oaktown, 145
Obama, Michelle, 144
Ohio Players, 115
O'Jays, 79, 285–86
One Day It'll All Make Sense, 270
1Hood Media, 66, 75n14
"One Nation under a Groove," 101
Operation Ghetto Storm, 251
Ordinary Notes (Sharpe), 177
Osuna, Steven, 200
Oyewole, Abiodun, 43n4

Page, Jimmy, 111
Pam the Funkstress, 149

Paper Route Empire record label, 44n23
"Paper Thin," 143
Paradise Gray, 98
Paris City Breakers, 175
Parks, Gordon, 210
Parks, Stephanie Keeney, 19
Parliament-Funkadelic, 119
Parr, Vanessa, 150
participatory theater, 247
Pebblee Poo, 137
Peebles, Melvin Van, 210
PEPR, 180, 181
Perry, Imani, 17; scholarship contributions, 11
P-Funk, 129
Pharaohe Monch, 258
Pharrell, 266
Philadelphia International Records, 38, 79, 111
Philips, 81
Pigmeat Markham, 32, 44n20, 115–16, 256, 257
"Pillow Talk," 119, 149
Pips, 152
"Planet Earth, Planet Rap" (PEPR) radio station, 171, 242
"Planet Rock," 107
Poc Fu, 230
Poetic Justice (film), 71
"Pollywanacraka," 86
Polygram, 81
Pop Smoke, 73, 126, 134n13, 213
Port Arthur, 252n7
"Power to the People," 86
Pras, 152, 286
Prince, 113, 121–22, 124, 133n9, 149
"Princess of the Posse," 142, 157
prisons: criminalization as social control, 230–32; hip hop in education programs, 224–26, 247–50
Professor D, 140
Professor Griff, 138
Professor X, 106n13
Profile Records, 52
Prophets of Da City (PoC), 18, 187
Prophets of Rage, 217, 289, 296n6
Prophets of the Hood, 11, 17
Public Enemy, 21–22, 66–67, 83, 85, 91–92, 122, 123, 128, 214, 215, 272, 279; centering voice of incarcerated people, 232–33; group influence, 21–22; Paris tour, 176; into the Rock and Roll Hall of Fame, 10; strategic timing and market positioning, 35. *See also* Chuck D
Pump It Up! (TV show), 147
Pumpkin, 52
punk shows, 218. *See also* funk music

Queen Kenya, 142
Queen Latifah, 98, 137, 142, 143, 151–52, 156
Queen Pen, 147, 157
Queensbridge, 234
Questlove, 36, 130
Quinn, San, 16

racial capitalism: systemic influence, 21; term, 43n9
racial violence, 237, 238
racism in Australia, 227
Raekwon, 153
Rage Against the Machine, 289
Raimist, Rachel, 156
Rakim, 12–13, 164, 275–76
Ramsey-Ray, Kikanza, 248, 250
Ram Squad, 145
rap, 218; ancestral connection to ancient lyric poetry, 258–59; artists and recording industry, 83, 95; community involvement in, 42; generational distinctions in early, 257–58; historical roots, 32; knowledge production through, 40–41; lyrics, 258–60; musical development and genres, 24–25; origin of the term, 258; as unduplicated art form, 291
Rap City, 159
RAP Lab (Laboratory for Race and Popular Culture), 271, 277n12
rap-metal, 128
Rap Music and Street Consciousness (Keyes), 139
"Rapper's Delight," 32, 44n20, 113, 114, 116, 119, 136, 165, 172, 175, 256, 257–58
Rapsody, 144, 265
RapStation, 4
Rapstation.com, 164
"Rapture," 138
R&B (Rhythm & Blues), 125, 136, 166–67, 218
Reagon, Bernice, 144
Rebels, 176
Rebel Speak: A Social Justice Mixtape (Bain), 229, 232
Recording Industry Association of America (RIAA), 121–22
recording technology, evolution of, 78–84

Redman, 276
Reeves, Dianne, 145
regionalism, 101
regional musical identity, 61–62
representation, 115, 149–50, 160, 182, 204, 217–18
"Revolutionary Generation," 87
Rice, Tamir, 249, 254n25
Richie Rich, 98
Rich Slave, 44n23
Rick, Slick, 137
RICO (racketeer influenced and corrupt organizations), 202
Ridenhour, Lorenzo, 287
Rifkind, Steve, 113
Riley, Teddy, 147
"Ring My Bell," 79
Riperton, Minnie, 32, 115, 257
Rittenhouse, Kyle, 251, 254n27
Roberts, Deborah, 295n5
Robeson, Paul, 200
Robinson, Cedric, 43n9, 196, 198, 220
Robinson, Jackie, 166
Robinson, Joe, 119, 120, 136
Robinson, Sylvia, 119, 120, 136, 149, 167
Rocafella, 144
Rodney King, 118
Roe v. Wade, 216–17
Roof, Dylann, 251, 254n26
Rose, Tricia, 13–14, 15–16, 21–22, 69
Rotary Connection, 115
Roy, Arundathi, 238
Rubber Band, 113
Rubin, Rick, 30
Ruff Ryders, 144, 145
rumba, 173
Run D.M.C., 27, 111, 237, 275
Ruthless Records, 143
RZA, 113

Sadler, Eric "Vietnam," 122
SAG-AFTRA, 4
Salloum, Jackie, 190
Salt-N-Pepa, 137, 142, 143, 158, 285
Sanchez, Sonia, 11, 138, 152, 208–9
Santana, 61, 62
Scott, Travis, 67–68, 75n17, 125, 155, 201
Scott-Heron, Gil, 116, 211
self-determination, 99
self-hate, 217
The Sentencing Project, 225, 252n4
Sequence, 136, 140, 142
Sermon, Erick, 215
sexuality, 140–41
Shady Records, 237
Shä-Key, 158
Shakur, Tupac, 14–15, 71–73, 181, 269
Shanté, Roxanne, 138, 143
Sharpe, Christina, 177
Shawel, Tabia, 9, 196, 271, 278, 296n7
Shawnna, 144
She Begat This: Twenty Years of the Miseducation of Lauryn Hill (Morgan), 283–84
SHE Movement Radio, 148
Sheri-Sher, 140
She Rockers, 138
"Shine & the Great Titanic," 272
Shmurda, Bobby, 126
Shocklee, Hank, 32
Shocklee, Keith, 122
"The Show," 137
Sigel, Beanie, 145
"The Signifying Monkey," 272
Silkk the Shocker, 52
Silk Tymes Leather, 143
Silverman, Tom, 157
Simone, Nina, 115, 157
Singleton, John, 71
Sirius XM Radio, 138
Sistas with Attitude, 144, 145, 147
Sisters of Mercy, 127–28
Sister Souljah, 3, 142
"Skin Tight," 115
Skyywalker, Luke, 51, 57
Slingshot Hip Hop, 190
Sly Stone, 211
Smiley, Tavis, 53
Smith, Bessie, 141
Smith, Parrish, 215
Smith, Will, 159, 215
Smitherman, Geneva, Dr., 163
The Smithsonian Anthology of Hip-Hop and Rap, 268
Snoop Dogg, 124, 128
SOLAR Records, 125
solidarity, 217–19
Son Houses, 141
Sony, 83
Sonya C, 144
Sony Walkman, 82–83
Soul Sonic Force, 107
Soul Train, 126
Soul Train Records, 125
SoundCloud, 121, 164
The Source hip hop magazine, 52

South Africa, hip hop artists in, 18, 69, 138, 169, 179–80, 187, 247
Spady, James G., 18, 157, 209
speed rapping, 265
Spice Girls, 153
Spike Lee, 36, 260
spirituality, 157
Spring Records, 32
"Stairway to Heaven," 111
Staples, Mavis, 124
Staton, Candi, 149
Stay Tuned, 176
stereotyping artists, 71–72, 155–56
Stetsasonic, 118, 164, 285
Stevie Wonder, 114
Sticky Fingaz, 155
Stone, Angie Brown, 136
Straight Outta Compton (movie), 70
Strausz, Sté, 178
street consciousness, 139
Street Conscious Rap, 155
Sugarhill Gang, 44n20, 114, 136, 256
Sugar Hill Records, 120, 167, 265
suicides, 239
Sulee B Wax, 176
Summer Jam 1995, 90
Summer of Soul, 36, 130, 134n14
Superbowl Halftime show, 69
"Superrappin," 46
"Supersonic," 143, 265
Sweet Honey in the Rock, 144, 152, 153
Sweet Tee, 142

Tafari, Natasha, 139
TAFE, 246
Tate, Greg, 197, 284
Taylor, Johnnie, 129
T Bone Burnett, 151
technology and music, 78–84, 131–33, 243–45, 294
Telecommunications Act, 106n12
Tempest, Kae, 138
Terminator X's album, 49
Terry, Clark, 145
"That's the Joint," 138
Theater Gates, 75n11
Theater of the Oppressed, 247
"This Is Not America," 37
Thomas, Rufus, 129
Thompson, Ahmir "Questlove," 134n14
3.5.7 (Oaktown 3.5.7), 145
Three 6 Mafia, 144
TLC, 142, 158
Tometi, Opal, 105n5
"Tone that Blackness down," 117
Too $hort, 92
Torres, Gerald, 225
Torres Strait Islander people, 226
"To the Beat Y'all," 137
toxic masculinity, 239
transformative creativity, 97–98
Traoré, Adama, 190
Traoré, Assa, 190
Traoré, Bouna, 189
Troutman, Roger, 129
True, Amy, 138
Tubman, Harriet, 220
Turner, Ted, 55, 207

UCLA Hip Hop Initiative (HHI), 1–3, 271, 278, 296n7
Uncle Jamm's Army, 125
Uncle Jam Wants You, 125
Universal Negro Improvement Association, 173
Unsung documentary, 38
U.T.F.O., 143

vagrancy laws, 231
Vertical Hold, 136
Viacom, 159–60
Vic Mensa, 236
Village Voice, 282
"Vincent (Starry, Starry Night)," 269
Vogue, 172
"Voice Notes," 181–82

"Walk This Way," 111
Wallace, George, 130
War, 24
"War at 33 1/3," 87
Ward, Anita, 79
Watts Prophets, 115, 116, 257
Watts Rebellion, 129, 130
Wattstax concert, 129
Wee Papa Girl Rappers, 138, 285
"Welcome to the Terrordome," 86
Welsing, Frances Cress, Dr., 84, 104n2
West, Kanye, 121
Westside Gunn, 237
Wexler, Jerry, 166
When Chickenheads Come Home to Roost: A Hip Hop Feminist Breaks It Down (Morgan), 19, 279, 284
White, Barry, 118
White, Maurice, 115

White Label Radio, 292
Whiteman, Paul, 121
white supremacy, 183–84
Whittaker, Yolanda, 142
"Who Stole the Soul?," 86
WILD 94.9FM, 95
Williams, Alexander, 271
Williams, Nanon, 224, 252n1
Williams, Robert, 193n5
Williams, Shameema, 139
Williamson, Lisa, 3, 142
Windrush generation, 54
women in hip hop, 179–80, 285; background of artists and influence, 156–57; categories of women artists, 141–48; creating platforms for their content, 148; cultural gatekeeping, 158–60; desperation, 149, 153–54; disproportionate representation, 150–52; experiences of, 139–41; expressing their sexuality, 141; gender, authenticity, and cultural gatekeeping, 157–58; gender and authenticity, 157–58; images and stereotypes, 155–56; influences, 142–43, 157; international rap groups, 138–39; looks of, 146–47; men as mentors for, 145; and rap music, 223, 265–66; and record industry, 144, 145–46; representation of, 149–50, 204; sexist capitalist order, 154–55; as soloists, 152–53. *See also* Black women
Wong, Casey Philip, 65
woo (dance form), 134n13
Woodfox, Albert, 230–31
"Wrath of My Madness," 157
Wu-Tang Clan, 113, 153, 181, 230

X Clan, 98, 106n13, 117
XL Middleton, 125

YG, 99, 125
Yo! Bum Rush the Show, 6, 21, 28, 77, 276
YOMA, 139
Yo! MTV Raps, 159, 232
Young, Earl, 79, 111
Young Dolph, 44n23
Young Hearts Run Free, 149
Young Jeezy, 100, 104
Young Stoner Life Records, 202
Young Thug, 202
Yo-Yo, 138, 142, 145

Zackey Force Funk, 125
Zeppelin, Led, 111
Zimmermans, George, 105n5, 251
Zulu Nation tradition, 67

Praise for Chuck D

"Chuck D is a stone-cold genius. And I say genius in every sense of the word, as an artist and MC, as a musical producer, as an intellectual, as a writer and as a public speaker and a radio personality. I know where his intellect is. I know where his heart is. And if you just told me that Chuck was going to be a visiting lecturer here at UCLA, it wouldn't matter what he taught, I'd say, 'That's great, that's fantastic. It's going to be really dynamic.' This course is an integration of the significance of the form of the culture by someone who was inside the music in conversation with a whole range of people who occupy a position both inside and outside the music. To me, the class was an opportunity for a breakthrough in hip hop studies and maybe a paradigm shift in hip hop studies. There was nothing like sitting there talking to Chuck D and looking out into the audience at a room packed full of people from all walks of life, on the edge of their seats, holding onto every word."

—Robin D. G. Kelley, author of *Freedom Dreams*

"Public Enemy was and is a culturally sustaining pedagogy that gave us the education we were supposed to be getting while we were being *miseducated* in public schools. Over much of the last three to four decades, Chuck D's music and activism have taught so many of us. This book is unique in that it captures Chuck D—or "Professor Chuck," as we affectionately referred to him on campus—at his professorial best, engaging UCLA's brightest students, leading hip hop studies scholars, and some of the nation's most insightful writers and thinkers on hip hop culture. Chuck D's brilliance is on full display as he lays out a blueprint for hip hop studies in the academy while he lectures, laughs, and learns alongside folks from UCLA and the broader community. The impact that he was able to have on us over just ten weeks was immeasurable. We want to continue that. All that energy. All that intellectual insight. All that motivation and that inspiration. We all have a collective sense of how historic Chuck D's residency and course were. This book and its accompanying documentary film are attempts to preserve and share it with the world."

—H. Samy Alim, author of *Roc the Mic Right*

"People are encouraged to look very narrowly at somebody like Chuck, who is so multilayered and multitalented and is a public intellectual in every sense. Not only does he know the genre of hip hop from its beginnings all the way till now; he is someone who knows rock. He knows all the things that blues contributes to hip hop. He knows why bluegrass and folk music are so important. But not only that, he's genuinely a curious public scholar. He's somebody who keeps up with everything that's going on, not just so that he can talk about it but because it informs who he is as a person and as an artist. There's a kind of encyclopedic knowledge that Chuck has that is not always seen by others. But nonetheless, if you're talking about someone who is an icon and who is committed to the craft, I think that there's almost nobody like him in hip hop who can span so many different ways of talking about hip hop to people who listen to hip hop but also can reach across genres and talk to people like he's a part of that genre as well. He has a very expansive sense of how hip hop fits into a context that's historical but also how other things fit into hip hop itself as a context. Nobody really has the knowledge like that or is as committed to the acquisition of that knowledge as Chuck."

—Gaye Theresa Johnson, author of *Spaces of Conflict, Sounds of Solidarity*

"Chuck D is the best person to lead us through this journey of hip hop because it's rare when you find someone who has literally laid the cornerstone and foundation of the culture, guided us through its most embryonic stages, grounded us through its really difficult growth periods—through massive capitalist growth, through massive commercialism, through the really terrible bouts of misogyny, through regional shifts and changes. Chuck can tell you when hip hop was really just localized in New York, and then of course he has that great quote that it became the CNN of Black America. Hip hop has gone through so many growing pains, and he has been there every step of the way, never really receding, never becoming a passive voice, never letting us doubt his investment. In many ways, I think he's been that guiding father figure from the very beginning, even as a very young man. I've been writing about hip hop for a long time, and when I started writing about it in '88, '89, there was not a lot of support. Chuck was one of the few male artists who always let me know, 'Keep doing what you are doing. You are doing exactly the right thing.'"

—Joan Morgan, author of *When Chickenheads Come Home to Roost*

"Chuck has always been the person, from our generation going back, who was able to articulate exactly what the importance of hip hop was for

Black youth and, by extension, other marginalized youth and all youth around the world. He doesn't just talk about the importance of culture; he teaches us that importance of making change. We've always followed him in that way from the moment that he stepped out with *Yo! Bum Rush the Show* all the way through to now. He's consistently been that person. He's got this exceptional mind and unmatched commitment. He comes along at exactly the moment where there are so many attacks on Black folks and on communities of color, from the postwar period into the civil rights period to the Black power period. He was able to step into the limelight—as difficult and dangerous as it was to do that—at that particular moment and say, 'Here's where we need to go.' For him to be here and to be able to articulate that now for another generation of folks is a gift."

—Jeff Chang, author of *Can't Stop Won't Stop*

"Chuck D is a continuation of the Paul Robesonist tradition of taking your art and weaponizing it and using it as a tool for the liberation of your people. Paul Robeson, Harry Belafonte, Nina Simone, all those artists, they come out of this tradition of speaking truth to power. Public Enemy, as an organization, was an enhancement of what earlier artist-activists were doing. There's an intentionality to the organization and to the music. They sampled James Brown, Malcolm X, Minister Farrakhan, and others, and then you had Chuck, who has this booming voice, being able to crystalize complex issues down to a rhyme form that you can understand. That's the brilliance of Chuck D and Public Enemy. Chuck is the tip of the spear of a larger organization that really captured the political and social longings of a people. It's because of Chuck that an entire generation of people were guided to move in a particular political and cultural direction."

—Davey D, coauthor of *Can't Stop Won't Stop* (Young Adult Edition)

"The early hip hop from people like Public Enemy, they were deeply entrenched in the culture and they were reaching back, *way* back, and showing us the beauty and the vitality, as well as the strength and the power, in our language and in our culture. Groups like Public Enemy had all been releasing these fabulous, powerful songs. Back in the 1970s, I called it 'the power of the rap.' You had so many new Black poets—Don L. Lee (Haki Madhubuti), William Thigpen, and so many others. It was out of this context that Chuck D, Public Enemy, and all the political Black hip hop artists emerged. Chuck emerged as a leader, and his impact is still being felt."

—Geneva Smitherman, author of *Talkin & Testifyin*

"Chuck D is the Malcolm X of hip hop. If there's anybody who inspired me as a teenager growing up in New York City, the way that Malcolm X was inspired by the Nation of Islam, by the Fruit of Islam, marching, doing the steps, it was Chuck and the S1Ws of Public Enemy. That was the inspiration, seeing Chuck, seeing his counterpart, Flavor Flav, cutting up and acting a fool, these brothers were that energy for me. It was so rebellious. It spoke truth to power. It challenged all these ideas about who people who look like us are. And it gave me the inspiration to do the same."

—Bryonn Bain, author of *Rebel Speak*

"Chuck D is the best tour guide you could have to hip hop because he's touched so much of the culture over his years. He's one of those rare artists that is just as relevant in this moment as he was in 1989. To have that kind of longevity is a testament both to his skill in artistry and to his dedication to the craft, to always evolving, to being in context."

—Adam Bradley, author of *Book of Rhymes*

"One of the things about Chuck D is, first of all, he's politically astute. When you think of Public Enemy and the messages, it's politically conscious rap. I would say at this time, Chuck has proved himself to be among the best to really articulate the power of hip hop, the seriousness of the culture. He's always very honest, because hip hop is about realness. He's telling you the truth. It's not about some of the negative elements that the industry tends to exhibit. Chuck D knows that and has committed himself to preserving the culture's legacy and importance."

—Cheryl L. Keyes, author of *Rap Music and Street Consciousness*

"Chuck D is the man to tell us about hip hop because he also was socialized *by* hip hop. Even before he becomes a recording artist, because of the kinds of things he was involved in as a deejay, as somebody who was really into the music and culture, he has the ability to narrate the history, even the pre–'Rapper's Delight' rap music he knows about. He's actually seen and been involved in so much for the culture both as an activist and an artist over the course of his lifespan."

—Scot Brown, author of *Tales from the Land of Funk*

"When you think about political consciousness and hip hop, most people think about Public Enemy and Chuck D. As he told us, the album *Fear of a Black Planet* was written like a dissertation. He is a scholar, so his teaching a class at the university level makes sense. In terms of his teaching, you have to remember that he's toured the world, performing in front of hundreds of thousands of people. So as a professor, he is an expert of keeping people engaged. He cracks jokes. He shares stories that nobody's heard before and keeps people entertained in a way that is more powerful than traditional academic approaches, which made this course a unique experience for everyone."

—Samuel Lamontagne, University of California, Riverside

"When considering an artist-in-residence who thinks of the history, the politics, the music and art form, and can bring all those elements together and create something extraordinary, I couldn't imagine anyone better to serve as our inaugural artist-in-residence. He's unmatched. I think Chuck D's residency changed my perspective of what universities can look like and what learning can look like. Chuck changed the dynamic in terms of who we usually see as professors. As an artist, Professor Chuck became the teacher, and all of us were his students. At the same time, he was always humble, always open to learning from this next generation of young people and to coming up with solutions to our social and political issues as a collective."

—Tabia Shawel, University of California, Los Angeles

Founded in 1893,
UNIVERSITY OF CALIFORNIA PRESS
publishes bold, progressive books and journals on topics in the arts, humanities, social sciences, and natural sciences—with a focus on social justice issues—that inspire thought and action among readers worldwide.

The UC PRESS FOUNDATION
raises funds to uphold the press's vital role as an independent, nonprofit publisher, and receives philanthropic support from a wide range of individuals and institutions—and from committed readers like you. To learn more, visit ucpress.edu/supportus.